Praise for

Help! There's a Toddler in the House!

'I really like this book – it's clearly written, humorous and ractical. We'll definitely use it in our outpatient clinics; the hapters provide a nice way for parents to think about behavior, hy it's occurring, and what to do about it."

– David P. Wacker, Ph.D.
Professor, Department of Pediatrics
Children's Hospital of Iowa
University of Iowa Hospitals and Clinics

"This is a really terrific, must have, book. The strategies are so easy to understand and implement. Dr. Reimers' common sense treatment approaches are invaluable tools for parents and a wonderful reference for professionals."

– Gina Richman, Ph.D.
Director, Child and Family Therapy Clinic
Kennedy Krieger Institute
Assistant Professor, Johns Hopkins University School of Medicine

Also from Boys Town Press

Common Sense Parenting® of Toddlers and Preschoolers
(Book and Audio Book)

Common Sense Parenting® (Book and Audio Book)

Good Night, Sweet Dreams, I Love You:
Now Get into Bed and Go to Sleep!

Raising Children without Losing Your Voice or Your Mind

Changing Children's Behavior by Changing the People, Places,
and Activities in Their Lives

Common Sense Parenting DVD Series:
- Building Relationships
- Teaching Self-Control
- Correcting Misbehavior
- Preventing Problem Behavior
- Teaching Kids to Make Good Decisions
- Helping Kids Succeed in School

Common Sense Parenting Learn-at-Home Kit

Competing with Character

No Room for Bullies

Who's Raising Your Child?

Parenting to Build Character in Your Teen

Adolescence and Other Temporary Mental Disorders (DVD)

There Are No Simple Rules for Dating My Daughter!

Dealing with Your Kids' 7 Biggest Troubles

Practical Tools for Foster Parents

Fathers, Come Home

For Young Children

The WORST Day of My Life EVER! My Story of Listening
and Following Instructions…or Not!

My Trip to the Zoo

Visiting My Grandmother

I Like Birthdays!

I Like Holidays!

Getting Along with Others

For a Boys Town Press catalog, call **1-800-282-6657**
or visit our Web site: **www.boystownpress.org**

HELP! There's a Toddler in the House!

HELP! There's a Toddler in the House!

Proven Strategies for Parents of 2- to 6-Year-Olds to Survive and Thrive through the Mischief, Mayhem, and Meltdowns

THOMAS M. REIMERS, Ph.D.

BOYS TOWN Press

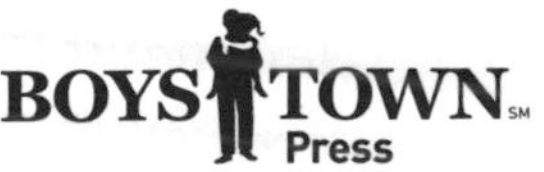

Boys Town, Nebraska

Help! There's a Toddler in the House!
Published by Boys Town Press
14100 Crawford St.
Boys Town, NE 68010

ISBN 978-1-934490-19-8

Boys Town Press is the publishing division of Boys Town, a national organization serving children and families.

Publisher's Cataloging-in-Publication Data

Reimers, Thomas M.

Help! there's a toddler in the house! : proven strategies for parents of 2- to 6-year-olds to survive and thrive through the mischief, mayhem, and meltdowns / Thomas M. Reimers. -- Boys Town, Neb. : Boys Town Press, c2011.

p. ; cm.

ISBN: 978-1-934490-19-8
Includes index.

1. Parenting. 2. Toddlers. 3. Preschool children. 4. Child rearing. 5. Parent and child. 6. Child development. I. Title.

HQ774.5 .R45 2011

649/.122--dc221103

10 9 8 7 6 5 4 3 2 1

Boys Town National Hotline
1-800-448-3000
A crisis, resource and referral number for kids and parents

This book is dedicated to…

Sarah and Laura, who helped me learn the art of parenting. Your toddler years are gone, but not forgotten. I couldn't be more proud of you.

My lovely wife, Kristi, who every day is a model of what a wife and parent should be. We have benefited as a family from your passion and commitment.

The thousands of families who have allowed me to take a few steps with them on their journey. It has been an honor and a privilege.

Acknowledgments

Thank you to my parents, Bob and Sylvia Reimers. Their steadfast love, encouragement, and pride have provided a foundation for both my strivings and accomplishments. Words are not adequate to express the gratitude and appreciation I have for my former mentors and advisors – Drs. Allen Branum, Michael Fatis, Nancy Fenrick, and David Wacker – who supported and believed in me. Thank you for showing me and so many others how "it's" done and providing the motivation to try and emulate, but certainly not replicate, the example you set.

I am very grateful to Dr. Pat Friman for giving me the opportunity to write this book and, more importantly, for the opportunity to work at the finest life-changing organization on the planet. Thanks to wordsmith maestro, Stan Graeve, who regularly demonstrated how to turn a sow's ear into a silk purse. Finally, thank you to my colleagues at Boys Town. On a daily basis, your dedication and commitment to excellence motivates and inspires me to challenge and better myself.

For more author information and parenting features, visit our Web page!

BoysTown.org/toddler

Table of Contents

chapter 1

Essential Ingredients for Effectively Parenting Your Toddler

"Before I got married I had six theories about bringing up children; now I have six children and no theories."

– John Wilmot, English Poet

I don't know about you, but no one handed my wife and me a manual when we walked out of the hospital with our children. Actually, that's a good thing. Because of the uniqueness of children, having a manual, even if one existed, wouldn't do much good. It also would remove a lot of the fun that comes with parenting. Did I say fun? Yes, I said fun. Now you may be rolling your eyes and saying to yourself, "Fun was the last thing I had on my mind when reaching for this book – more like frustration." Everyone seems to have an opinion about parenting. That may explain why so many bookshelves bend low from the weight of all that advice being put into paperback. Some of these "how to" parenting books emphasize the "art" of parenting while others emphasize the "science." Most make promises about revealing the truth about parenthood. In these pages, you will discover something new about all three – the art, science, and truth of parenting.

As a clinical psychologist for more than twenty years, I have had the pleasure and honor of working with thousands of parents, children, and families. Much of my advice and counsel has been rooted in science. Over time, however, I have found myself emphasizing the art of parenting. It's not very difficult to describe the facts and science of human behavior. The challenge is knowing how to use that knowledge in a positive and purposeful manner when it comes to your own family. It's a subjective endeavor because there is no such thing as parenting absolutes. At least not absolute truth. The uniqueness and challenges that come with each and every child, coupled with the often complicated and varied experiences that parents bring to their families, literally make it impossible to claim absolute truth. Yet, there are many time-tested principles and strategies that make family life more enjoyable for a vast majority of parents and children. I will do my best to describe those strategies in these pages.

My hope is that this book will provide you with practical techniques that will make parenting easier and help you appreciate the uniqueness and challenges that your child brings to your world. Your child is a work of art, and most great works of art, like Rome, were not built in a day. Parenting is a lifelong endeavor that is constantly shaped and changed by many seen and unforeseen events. The techniques involved in the science and art of parenting can be learned. When combined with parents' love and commitment to their children, the outcome is almost always positive.

Here are nine essential ingredients to serve as "food for thought" as it pertains to shaping, managing, and teaching behavior.

Parents Are Teachers

When our children are born, our first concern is their health and well-being. We want them to be healthy and grow and develop normally. Once we get past those concerns, we want them to behave. Eventually that cute bundle of joy will start crawling, climbing, walking, and talking. Our concerns go from their health to their behavior. We are forced to think about how we are going to discipline them. Unfortunately, many people see little difference between discipline and punishment. In part, that is because many parents were themselves raised by parents who believed in the "spare the rod, spoil the child" philosophy. Perhaps you remember a parent's occasional use of physical punishment more vividly than any affectionate pat on the back or hug. Therefore, it's important that you determine what discipline means to you and what approach you will take to teach your child all of the positive behaviors, social skills, and appropriate language he needs to be successful in life. It's important to adopt or develop a general philosophy of discipline, including what actions that involves. I use the word "discipline" throughout this book because it has a general meaning for most of us. By discipline, I'm referring to the behavior-changing strategies you use to teach and promote positive behaviors and to decrease negative behaviors.

When you think of the word "punishment," what does it mean to you? Punishment, by definition, means that a behavior stops or decreases following an action a parent takes in response to a child's behavior. In other words, your child does something you don't like so you do something your child doesn't like, and the behavior stops or decreases. Taking away a child's outside playtime because he pulled his sister's hair, for example, hopefully decreases how often he pulls her hair in the future. Sometimes, it's not so much what a parent does but what a child does to himself. Touching a hot stove stops him from touching the stove again, at least for a while. Getting bitten by a growling dog limits or stops him from petting growling dogs in the future, or he avoids all dogs for a period of time. Punishment decreases, eliminates, or suppresses behavior. Because of that, it plays an important role in each of our lives and also should play a role in your job as parent and disciplinarian. However, punishment should be a **part** of your discipline approach, not your entire approach. All children, even adults, need to receive some corrective actions in order to learn. All of the negative consequences that are applied to children's inappropriate behavior should get their attention, correct the misbehavior, and discourage children from doing it again. In essence, punishment has a role, but not in the way that most of us tend to think about punishment. It should certainly be the smallest part of your overall discipline approach. Parents who use punishment as their only method of discipline often raise children who are angry, aggressive, or experience unnecessary guilt about their behavior.

If discipline is not punishment, then what is it? Effective discipline involves teaching. Teaching includes verbal instructions, modeling, practice, correction, and praise. When it comes to your child's behavior, you are your child's teacher and disciplinarian. Discipline should involve a combination of teaching strategies that include the following:

Information and Instruction

Your children need to know what is expected of them before they can do it. They need you to clearly communicate your expectations in a variety of ways. Just as you were not handed a manual on how to take care of and manage your newborn when you left the hospital, no child is born with an internal instruction guide on how to behave.

Modeling and Training

Teaching involves telling, showing, and demonstrating how to do something and what it looks like. A large percentage of what children learn at this age comes from watching parents, siblings, and peers. As your child's teacher, you need to be good at modeling and demonstrating behavioral expectations. With your toddler or preschooler, this will involve a lot of effort in telling, showing, and demonstrating appropriate behaviors.

Carrots and Sticks

The carrots are the smiles, comments, and gestures you make to let your child know that you are pleased with her behavior. This might involve nothing more than a gentle touch or kind word. The important thing is that you don't take your child's good behavior for granted. Let her know that you are aware of what she did or said. Don't make the mistake of taking good behavior for granted because "that's what she is supposed to do." Frequent praise or positive attention increases the likelihood that you will see the appropriate behavior again and provides a nice contrast for your child when you correct her behavior. Discipline also involves letting your child know what she did wrong. Correction (the stick) can take different forms and vary depending on your child's age and the misbehavior. This might include a frown, a verbal reprimand, time-out, or removing a privilege.

Repetition and Practice

Your child likely won't "get it" the first, second, or third time you teach or correct a behavior. Be prepared to provide the same consequence over and over again to help your child get the message. Children do not learn as quickly as adults, and they need lots of practice and repetition. This can be tiring and exhausting at times, but it's a necessary part of shaping and changing behavior.

Effective discipline includes an array of teaching techniques that start with the most positive and least restrictive strategies and progresses to the point where your child's behavior is shaped and transformed to its most desirable.

Anger Is Not a Parenting Tool

Why do parents get angry at a child? Maybe it's because their son gave the cat a milk bath, or he sent twenty-five Hot Wheels zooming down the heating vent. Maybe their anger resulted from the thrown spaghetti that landed in the elderly lady's hair at the local diner. Or, it could be the masterpiece their little Picasso created on the freshly painted wall. The causes are endless. But the fundamental reason that parents become angry is the same – they care.

There is no one you love more, worry more about, spend more time thinking about, or spend more time with than your child. Because of the bond you have with your child, you're going to experience a range of emotions, including anger.

There is absolutely nothing objective about being a mom or dad. That is why discipline can be such a challenge. If parents could strip the emotion out of their behavior-management and discipline strategies, they would be much more effective. That's why most parents would likely be better at managing the behaviors of their friends' or neighbors' children than their own. Let's face it, when somebody else's child calls the guy at the checkout stand "fatso," you're glad the little one isn't one of yours, but you're not going to get emotionally upset. (You might even laugh.)

The frustration parents experience when they are angry or emotionally upset is at one end of the emotional spectrum. On the other end is all the joy and happiness that come from the wonderful moments and positive experiences children bring to a family. Of course, it's easy to be happy, smiling, and praising children when things are going well. The challenge is figuring out how to control anger and frustration when things do not go as planned.

No one cares about your child more than you do. Therefore, when it comes to helping your child develop positive behavior, you may need to spend time identifying what triggers your anger and frustration and how best to manage those feelings. Remember, when it comes to managing behavior, you are the teacher. Good teaching requires good communication. Think of the last time someone – coach, boss, or stranger – yelled at you or vice versa. Were the screams effective? Did you learn a lot? Did you respond by getting angry, or did you do something to stop the person from yelling and screaming? Anger is often the result of frustration. When it comes to children, your frustration can result from a wide range of events, some of which include specific misbehaviors. Other times it is the circumstances, not the children, that prove frustrating, especially when you lack the tools (self-control, behavior-management, and communication skills) to manage a situation. And even if you have the tools, they are much less useful if you're yelling and screaming.

The bottom line is that there are countless things that can upset the apple cart and make you frustrated. Here are a few suggestions to help you keep your emotions in check:

Be realistic.

Being realistic means focusing on your child's behavior at a given moment and helping her learn a new behavior or skill as best she can without always basing it on what other children her age are doing. Being realistic about your child's behavior and ability to behave as expected in certain situations will keep you from becoming overly frustrated by unreasonable expectations. Look at your child's behavior in the context of age, development, and the situation. The behavior of young children is like the weather, wait an hour or so, and it will change. Some children achieve certain skills and behaviors early, some later. However, in time, nearly all children achieve the skills and behaviors they need to be successful. No matter what the behavior or the situation, remember "This too shall pass."

Break the cycle.

Moms and dads are aware of certain behavior-changing techniques because they learned them from their parents or acquired them on their own. Sometimes parents don't want to repeat those techniques, such as corporal punishment or yelling, with their children. For example, some parents come from families that scream. They come from generations that communicated and interacted with each other by talking loudly at best and yelling at worst. When so much yelling and screaming goes on, it can become the norm. If this or other negative discipline habits have become the norm in your family, you have probably found that they are not only ineffective, they're exhausting. The good news is that as you develop more effective strategies to add to your collection of discipline tools, the need to always scream, spank, or give in will disappear.

Know what hot buttons trigger your anger.

A hot button may be a child's behavior that seems to occur over and over again and one which you have difficulty managing. (Your son always tells you "No," for example). It might be a behavior (say, whining) that occurs only in certain environments, such as a church or store. Perhaps the behavior is relatively minor to others, but for some reason embarrasses you. In any respect, it's important to be aware of the specific behaviors or situations that cause your frustration level to go up or cause you to get angry. Additionally, it's important to be aware of those physical and emotional cues that tell you you're becoming angry or frustrated. Those cues can vary but might include physical changes, such as a flushed face or increased heart rate. Or maybe you dwell on negative thoughts or engage in negative self-talk. It's also important to be aware of events that have absolutely nothing to do with your child. Perhaps you're having a bad day because a friend moved away, a spouse lost a job, or the family pet died. We all experience events on a regular basis that cause us to feel sad or frustrated. These events set the stage for more frustration and less patience when it comes to managing children's behavior. Being aware of them can help you avoid taking your feelings out on your child.

Use discipline techniques that are not emotionally upsetting to you.

Regardless of the techniques you use, it's important that you feel comfortable using them and believe they will produce the behavior change you want. If you find yourself becoming emotionally upset because of a strategy, technique, or consequence, stop using it and find another approach. When parents use strategies that are emotionally upsetting to them, they tend to use them inconsistently and mostly out of frustration. Techniques that are used inconsistently and out of frustration almost always lead to ineffective behavior management. Because you need to use these tools on a regular and consistent basis, you must be comfortable and confident enough to use them. Although they may be time consuming and exhausting, the discipline and teaching techniques themselves should not cause you emotional distress.

Have a plan.

Being aware of the triggers or hot buttons that push you over the edge is one thing, but having a strategy or plan in place to handle them is another. The situations and circumstances surrounding those triggers will likely determine what you can do to manage them. What you do will vary greatly depending on whether you are home alone with your child or at a public event. Having a plan can involve taking a brief break, going for a walk, taking some deep breaths, calling a friend, or reading. Strategies like this can help you manage your frustration and deal more effectively with your child's behavior.

Practice putting out small fires.

It's always easiest to put a fire out after the first spark or when the flame is low. Once the fire is raging, there is little you or anyone else can do. Thus, a good time to practice using anger-control strategies are when fairly minor and insignificant events occur. Behaviors that cause a mild irritation or annoyance offer a good opportunity to practice positive self-control strategies. Practicing ways to manage your frustration when you're fairly calm puts you in a good position to use those strategies when your frustration is high, and your anger is starting to build. Waiting to use those techniques until the fire is raging may be too late.

Have a back-up plan.

A back-up plan usually involves having some additional support. We all get to a point where everything we try generates little success, and we need some outside support. Having a friend or family member you can call, a neighbor who can watch your children, or someone who can stop by and lend a hand may be enough to get you through some rough patches. Make a list of individuals who will support you when you need it most.

Give yourself a break.

There will absolutely be times when you lose control, yell, and get angry beyond anything you thought possible. The tendency for many parents is to become frustrated with their child and themselves. As human beings, we are emotional and because we are emotional, we become angry. It happens to all of us. Take time to recognize that "Yes, I am human" and "I'm not perfect." Once you calm down, take time to look at the situation, think about what you could have done differently, and plan how you will do things differently next time. If necessary, apologize to your child or anyone else who felt your wrath. The frustration you feel toward your child and with yourself will lessen as your ability to manage behaviors improves.

Consistency Counts

Being consistent means being predictable. "No" means "No," and "Yes" means "Yes." Consistency implies that the rules are the same day in and day out and that following or disobeying those rules will always result in the same consequence – positive or negative.

Just as you come to expect certain levels of predictability and reliability from those you live, socialize, and work with, your children also learn how predictable and reliable you are in enforcing expectations and consequences for their behavior. That pattern of predictability, or consistency, sets the foundation for how effective you will be at managing behavior and family relationships. This is especially true if your children are difficult, strong willed, and persistent with their behavior.

Consistency is important because it helps your child's world become more predictable. Increased predictability gives your child a greater sense of security. Predictability can apply to everything from daily schedules and bedtime routines to your child knowing that picking up toys when asked will result in a smile or hug. Being consistent when it comes to behavior management allows children to make informed decisions about their behavior and lets them know that you are in charge. When you establish clear boundaries and predictably apply positive and negative consequences, your children will feel more secure. Just as your children might find it confusing if their teacher gives them different answers to the same questions, they can get confused if you respond differently or not at all to the same behavior (throwing a toy block at the cat results in time-out on one occasion and no consequence on another, for example). Your children will learn best, and behave better, if they hear or receive the same response to the same behavior from you over and over. On the other hand, if your responses differ or are non-existent (doing nothing), it will take much longer for your children to learn what it is you're trying to teach (if they learn at all).

What happens if you're not consistent? First of all, it's important to clarify what consistent means. Nobody is consistent one hundred percent of the time. When I refer to consistency, I'm suggesting you be as predictable as you can and follow through to the best of your ability. I realize there are all kinds of circumstances that get in the way of being consistent. Many of those you can control. Later, I will discuss how you can improve your consistency.

What happens when there is a lack of consistency? First, it takes much longer for children to learn when the "message" is inconsistent. For example, say seventy percent of the time a teacher tells students that one plus one equals two. The rest of the time, the teacher provides a different answer. So, thirty percent of the time students are told a different (wrong) answer. Is seventy percent consistency good enough? If you want to learn math or change behavior, the answer is no. Of course, no parent (or teacher for that matter) can be consistent **all** the time. However, if you have difficulty being predictable and consistent, don't be surprised if your child does not respond to your discipline efforts and does not change his behaviors as quickly as you would like.

For certain behaviors, inconsistency makes things worse. For example, if your toddler's whining has a big payoff (getting more attention or getting something he wants), it may be worth it to him to continue whining even if the payoff only occurs a small part of the time. Let's say that eighty percent of the time you consistently apply a negative consequence when your son whines. You may end up teaching him to whine louder and more frequently because twenty percent of the time you give him what he wants or at least offer additional attention. For him, the twenty percent payoff is worth it. For many children, especially those who don't persistently misbehave or whine, being consistent eighty percent of the time may be sufficient to stop a misbehavior and/or teach new positive behaviors. But for strong-willed children and those looking forward to the payoff, inconsistency encourages more of the misbehavior.

Inconsistency can influence a child's behavior much the same way "payoff schedules" in a casino influence the behaviors of gamblers. It's the random wins that cause gamblers to keep gambling. When parents are inconsistent with discipline, their children don't win all the time, but they do win once in a while. And it's those inconsistent responses to misbehaviors that cause the misbehaviors to continue or get worse, especially if an important payoff sometimes follows. Most children don't have to receive a payoff all of the time or even most of the time. Rather, receiving a payoff occasionally may cause them to continue their behavior indefinitely. They forget all the times they lost (whining resulted in time-out, for example) but remember the occasional times they won (whining resulted in a candy bar at the check-out). The occasional win keeps them coming back. If you want the frequency and severity of your child's behavior to worsen, give in occasionally and randomly. If the payoff to your child is worth it, the behavior will continue.

The impact of consistency also is related to the "value" of a behavior. Think about how important a particular behavior is to your child. What is the potential benefit to her for engaging in that behavior? If your child throws a tantrum to avoid a particular task, and she despises that task more than anything in the world, consistency in your response will be crucial. For example, if your daughter hates picking up toys, she is much more likely to persist with a tantrum or some other inappropriate behavior to avoid picking them up. Not having to pick up the toys, even once, may be worth nine or ten consecutive tantrums. This may be true even if it means the tantrum results in time-out or the loss of a preferred activity, such as playing outside or watching television. In other words, she would rather sit in time-out or lose outside playtime than pick up toys. (As I will discuss later, your daughter will soon learn that she will need to pick up those toys once the time-out is over, making the tantrum less useful to her.)

Thus, if your child is engaging in a particular negative behavior because he really wants something or really wants to avoid something, consistently responding to him becomes especially important. This also reinforces the importance of picking your battles. Focusing on too many behaviors increases the likelihood that you won't be as predictable or consistent as you should be to all of them.

If a behavior has been a problem for years and you have been inconsistent in managing it, you simply cannot expect the behavior to change in several days, weeks, or maybe even months. In fact, if you have struggled with a particular behavior for years, it means the behavior is challenging to change and previous strategies to correct the behavior did not "work." This also means your child likely received a lot of payoff for the behavior, which serves some particular purpose for him. Behaviors that take years to evolve and develop are going to take a considerable amount of time to change. This does not mean that the behavior cannot change. You simply have to prepare yourself for resistance and a fair amount of personal frustration as your child challenges your consistency.

Your child has learned to use certain behaviors to get his way. As you try to change that behavior, and your child's behavior no longer provides the benefit to him that it once did, you may see the behavior increase. This is what psychologists call an "extinction burst." For example, if you stop responding in some way to your child for engaging in a behavior that had been useful to him, such as screaming to get more food, he will likely scream louder and longer until he realizes that screaming doesn't get him more food – it gets him quality time alone in a corner. Your child is simply using a tool (screaming) that has worked for him in the past. When the screaming does not get him what he wants, he will likely scream more frequently and with more gusto. He's thinking, "It will work eventually, right?" If it does, count on him screaming even louder the next time. However, if you continue to ignore or apply a negative consequence for the screaming, the screaming may continue off and on but each episode will get shorter and less intense. If you hang in there, and teach him that screaming doesn't "work" anymore, it will eventually stop. Praising him for an alternative behavior (quietly asking "More please," for example), along with a brief time-out each time he screams, can speed up the behavioral change.

When trying to understand the importance of consistent discipline in response to your child's behavior, think of examples where consistency shapes your behavior. Take driving a car, for example. From time to time, you may exceed the speed limit. On some occasions, you might go over the speed limit by only a few miles per hour. Other times you may exceed it excessively. Sometimes you speed on purpose and other times it's accidental. The number of times you get caught and ticketed for speeding is probably considerably less than the number of times you actually drove too fast. If you received a ticket every time you broke the speed limit, you would rarely speed. Imagine if a satellite monitored your speedometer, and you received a speeding ticket in the mail each time you exceeded the speed limit. At some point, it would become so costly to speed that it would no longer be worth it. Whether you would continue to speed would depend on how costly the ticket is to you. Another variable that might affect your willingness to break the speed limit is how important it is to get where you're going. If you have an emergency or need to be somewhere at all cost, the financial expense of speeding is likely unimportant. If, on the other hand, you have had several speeding tickets in the last several months, and you will have your license revoked if you speed again, you are much less likely to speed. Unfortunately, the learning history for most of us involves breaking the speed limit with no adverse consequences. Thus, we continue to speed until we get caught. At that point, most of us slow down, even if only temporarily. Over time, you forget about the ticket and start speeding again. But if the speeding tickets were always forthcoming, the number of times you broke the speed limit would be few and far between. These same principles hold true when it comes to your child's behavior. If you want to improve his "driving habits," you must praise him for his good driving and consistently "ticket" him when he breaks the rules.

Practice, Practice, Practice

Most adults are one- or two-trial learners. They are able to learn from a particular experience, whether it was positive or negative, and determine whether or not they want to do that behavior again. When test-driving a new car, trying a new restaurant, listening to music, or visiting a friend, our experiences often determine whether we ultimately purchase the car, return to the restaurant, or spend more time with our friend. We don't usually need to do it over and over again to make a decision. As adults, we're able to learn more quickly because we have more experience and have made more mistakes. We can look into the future and determine whether a choice we make or behavior we engage in will produce the results we want.

Children do not have the advantages we have when it comes to learning. Their behavior and the choices they make are often based on immediate needs. The future is five minutes from now, not five days or five weeks from now. Because of their learning history, development, and need for immediate gratification, children need to get the message (the consequence) over and over and over. This is not what most parents want to hear. Every parent would like to have that one magical consequence that instantly and indefinitely changes a behavior. I hate to tell you this, but that consequence doesn't exist. Rather, it's repetition, and lots of it, that will help create lasting behavioral changes. Consistently and repeatedly providing meaningful consequences to your child is time consuming and somewhat exhausting, but necessary.

You have likely had one or more experiences in your life that affected your behavior for a long time. Maybe you burned yourself while cooking, had a car accident, or earned a bonus at work. Each of those single experiences changed how you cooked, drove, or worked. Unfortunately, you cannot provide as significant or meaningful an experience to your child each time you apply a positive or negative consequence. There are simply no parenting techniques and consequences that can have the same impact as cutting yourself with a knife, sliding off the road, or cashing a bonus check. Because those types of "impact" consequences don't exist, you're left using the most appropriate and meaningful consequences that you can – over and over again. It's repetition, consistent repetition, that will change your child's behavior, not the size or impact of the consequence. Besides, would you really want your child to experience the negative and potentially harmful consequences that go along with an "impact" consequence? Of course not. To the contrary, to help your child avoid certain dangers, you spend a lot of time (and a lot of repetition) teaching your child lessons such as how to keep his hands away from a hot stove so he won't get burned or how to respond to your command of "Stop" well before he gets near a busy street. And because your voice, your behaviors, and the consequences you use will never be as powerful as some natural consequences (burning a hand after touching a hot stove), you need to be repetitive. Not only do you need to do it over and over, you need to do it consistently so that your child can learn from the consequence. Providing a consequence, no matter how meaningful, in an inconsistent way only delays how long it takes for your child to benefit from what you're trying to teach.

One benefit of repetition is that your child learns a new skill or behavior much faster. The distance from the start line to the finish line becomes much shorter. The old adage "Practice makes perfect" certainly applies here. Think about certain skills you learned throughout your life, such as riding a bike, driving a car, tying your shoes, shooting a basket, writing, reading, or typing. Learning skills like these require frequent practice. It's likely you didn't learn to ride a bike the first time you got on one. In fact, you probably learned more quickly if you got back on after you fell off. If, on the other hand, you put the bike away after you fell off and only got back on once every few months, it probably took a much longer time (if ever) to learn to ride a bike. The same is true for the behaviors you're trying to teach your children. No matter how consistently you apply a meaningful consequence, if it's applied infrequently, it will take much longer for your child to make a connection and/or have enough feedback to adequately learn what is necessary. For example, showing your child once or twice how to tie his shoes properly is not going to be sufficient. Demonstrating and providing feedback to him thirty or forty times will probably do the trick.

Repetition also is important when teaching children to be safe. When it comes to behaviors that affect your child's safety, you obviously don't want to wait until your child puts himself in a risky or harmful situation. This is where the use of repetition is helpful. For example, if you're trying to teach your child to remain a certain distance from the street, why wait until he is standing on the curb before saying "Stop!"? It makes more sense to practice walking with your child and teach him what to do when he nears a street. This gives you multiple opportunities to praise him for following your limits or to firmly reprimand him if he disobeys or gets too close to the street.

Creating opportunities for your child to test the limits, and doing so repetitively, will help him learn quickly and safely.

You also can create "training" or practice opportunities where you safely place your child in situations that worry you or are potentially dangerous, such as when your child climbs kitchen drawers to get on top of the counter, sticks objects in outlets, or gets too rough with animals. If you wait until such situations happen naturally, you put your child at risk. Let's face it, would you rather wait until your child puts a butter knife into an electrical outlet before teaching her how dangerous that is? Or, would you rather spend time (and practice) safely teaching her that going near outlets earns her negative consequences (reprimands or time-out) and staying away from outlets earns her positive consequences (attention or praise)? Spending time with your child and providing consistent and repetitive consequences or outcomes allows you to teach important "do" and "don't" behaviors in a safe and controlled manner. This approach also works for other aggressive or harmful behaviors as well as everyday activities, such as brushing teeth or taking baths. Carving out time to teach your child what to do or what to avoid will not only benefit your child, it will give you some peace of mind.

Immediacy (Sooner Is Always Better than Later)

Providing immediate actions and consequences to your children is important if you intend to teach them new skills and behaviors. Most things (objects, relationships, or jobs) we value are due, in part, to the commitment, time, and effort we put into them. Your ability to value things that take time to acquire and your ability to delay gratification for long periods of time develop as you get older. Your toddler does not have that ability – AT ALL! Delayed gratification to a toddler is one or two seconds, not one or two days or weeks. In fact, for some toddlers, "instantly" is a very long time. Because of their inability to delay gratification, the opportunity for frustration certainly increases.

Consistency and repetition are essential ingredients in effectively parenting toddlers and preschoolers. A third ingredient that is equally important is immediacy. Immediacy is how quickly you provide a positive or negative response (a hug, a smile, a frown, or a time-out) after your child's behavior. Immediacy is important for all toddlers and preschoolers, but it's especially true the younger your child is. Providing an immediate response also is important when you're trying to teach or shape a new behavior or skill.

Immediacy is an essential ingredient when it comes to your discipline efforts. There probably is no stopwatch that can accurately measure the length of time between the word "No" leaving your lips and your toddler's atomic reaction. The idea of waiting hasn't landed anywhere near your child's brain at this point. The immediate anguish your child shows when you say "No" to the doughnut he wants and the instant joy he expresses when you say "Yes" to another bedtime story, is just one indication of your child's concept of time. As children age, they gradually get better at delaying gratification. Hopefully, by the time they enter school, they have the patience and understanding that allows them to wait in line, take turns, or finish tasks before starting something new.

Young children's limited concept of time also causes them to view their world in "generalities." In other words, events get blurred and anything that happened in the past was yesterday and anything that happens in the future is tomorrow. Because of this, responding as immediately as possible to your child's behavior helps to pair the behavior with the outcome. That is, your child learns that certain behaviors result in smiles, hugs, and praise, while other behaviors result in frowns, reprimands, and time-outs. If there is too much distance between your child's behavior and your response, the behavior will not be learned or it will take much longer than you want for it to be learned. And because of your child's poor concept of time, providing a delayed response to her behavior is sometimes no different, or possibly worse, than little or no response at all. For example, giving your toddler an afternoon treat because she made her bed early in the morning has little meaning. She will enjoy the treat, but may not make the connection between the two. It's more effective to reward her for making the bed as soon as it's made. Likewise, forbidding your four-year-old to play with neighborhood friends on Friday because he used "bad" language on Thursday will probably have little effect on his language or behavior. Responding to a behavior when it happens is essential.

Making every effort to provide immediate and consistent consequences on a repetitive basis should be your focus, especially early in your child's life. Consistency and repetition without immediacy will reduce the impact you have on your child's behavior and will lengthen the learning curve. Remember, consistency refers to how predictably you provide the same consequence or type of consequence to your child for a specific behavior. Increased consistency gives your child an opportunity to make a decision as to whether he wants to continue or discontinue a behavior, knowing that a particular response will reliably follow that behavior. A lack of consistency creates some confusion and raises a question in your child's mind. (Will this happen or not?) As a result, behavior change occurs much more slowly. Repetition is connected to opportunity. The more opportunities your child has to learn, especially when combined with a consistent response, the more quickly he learns. Finally, adding immediacy to consistency and repetition puts icing on the cake. Consistency and repetition are important, but less effective without immediacy. For example, you might consistently respond to your child by praising her for a particular behavior. However, if the time between her behavior and your praise varies considerably, the impact of your praise will be less effective. So even though you're providing a consistent response, your child is not given the advantage of connecting her behavior with your praise. You will be most effective if you're not only providing consistent praise, but are doing it immediately and as often as possible. Thus, consistency, repetition, and immediacy can be some of your most important parenting "tools" – if you use them.

The Power of Praise

I have no idea if the expression, "It takes more muscles to frown than to smile," is true. I've heard it many times and just assumed it was. Regardless, research shows that even people who are forced to smile report feeling happier than those who don't smile. And I think most of us would agree that it's more enjoyable being around someone who is smiling than one who is frowning or scowling. Wouldn't you rather approach someone who is laughing than someone who is grumbling? Similarly, do you enjoy receiving praise from your family, friends, and coworkers? Or, would you prefer they keep those comments to themselves and simply point out when you've made mistakes or done something wrong? Most of us know from experience that we enjoy getting positive feedback, feel better when we're smiling, and prefer being around happy, pleasant people. Research backs this up, too. It's well documented that relationships are much stronger when there are at least three times as many positive interactions as there are negative ones. In other words, parents who provide three positive interactions for every negative interaction are much more likely to see more positive behavior in, and have a better relationship with, their children. Praise also increases the likelihood that children will seek out parents' positive attention. These positive interactions can come in all forms, including smiles, hugs, kisses, and praise statements.

Look at the following math problems. What do you notice?

5+2 = 7   1+3 = 4   4+4 = 8   3+2 = 9   4+3 = 7

Did you notice that four out of five are correct, or that one answer is wrong? We sometimes have a tendency to focus on what is wrong rather than what is right. Likewise, there is a tendency for parents to take their children's positive behaviors for granted. Perhaps you've heard a parent say, "I shouldn't have to tell my child every time he does something right, he's supposed to do it anyway." I would agree that perhaps we don't need to praise our children for their "nice breathing" or other routine events of the day. However, it takes so little effort to simply acknowledge children's positive behaviors and accomplishments that taking them for granted and saying or doing nothing makes little sense. With just a little effort, positive behaviors can be promoted and reinforced. This is especially important for young children. They are, by nature, sponges for attention. They also are in their formative years, a time when you're trying to shape and teach new skills and discourage negative and inappropriate behaviors. Therefore, it's important to consistently and frequently attend to and focus on positive behaviors, including those you might take for granted. In general, you want to practice "catching your child being good." By doing this, you will encourage him to engage in behaviors you want to see more of while discouraging him from learning or engaging in negative behaviors. This is especially effective when you offer praise and positive attention for appropriate behaviors and deliver negative consequences to discourage or correct inappropriate behaviors.

When it comes to praise, it has to be meaningful and immediate. There needs to be a logical connection between your positive attention and your child's behavior. He needs to see the connection between what you're saying or doing and his behavior. It's also important to provide praise or an acknowledgment immediately. If you wait hours or days to acknowledge something he did, he'll likely give you a blank stare. Your toddler's memory is simply not long enough to recall what he did in the past to deserve your positive attention, even though he likes it. In addition, praising him for the sake of praising or not connecting the praise to something he did or said will do little to change his behavior. Of course, there is nothing wrong with giving your child a hug and telling him you love him just because you do. It's required! Still, when the goal is to praise and acknowledge positive behaviors to encourage your child to repeat those behaviors, you need to do the best you can to connect your praise with your child's actions.

The alternative to providing very little praise or acknowledgment is to respond negatively each time your child makes a mistake, engages in some inappropriate behavior, or behaves inappropriately. To only respond to your daughter when she does something "wrong" will create a highly negative relationship because all of your interactions focus on correcting behaviors and pointing out mistakes. Although addressing negative actions and words are a necessary part of managing a child's behavior, it should be a smaller part in relation to the positive interactions you have with each other. If you find yourself spending more time correcting than praising, it's time to look for ways to turn that around and change the pattern.

United You Stand, Divided You Fall

It's important for parents to maintain a united front when establishing rules and applying consequences. It's easy to understand why you should maintain a united front but very difficult to do. Many parents come into their partnership with different ideas about what parenting should look like, what rules should be established, and what forms of discipline should be applied. When two people are working together to raise children, there is almost always some natural disagreement. Children are the first to figure this out. They are like lawyers combing through a contract looking for a loophole or seeking out the slightest weakness in the prosecution's case. Once they find it, they leap on the opportunity. Remember, all children, but especially toddlers and preschoolers, are looking for opportunities to do more of what they like and less of what they dislike. They also have very little control over their world. They are told where to go, when to wake up, what to wear, and what to eat. If they can use their language or their behavior to create more control and make life more enjoyable for themselves, why shouldn't they? Well, there are plenty of reasons why they shouldn't. One obvious reason is that young children know what they **want**, but they don't know what they **need**. Also, children who can work one parent against the other tend to weaken parental authority. If you want to establish a more united and consistent front when managing your child's behavior, make sure you do the following:

Communicate.

Increased communication between parents will solve many of the problems that cause children to work parents against each other. Communication can take on many forms. Let's say your child won't accurately communicate to your spouse what demands you made, what limits you set, or what consequences you applied. You then have to make sure your instructions are communicated in some way to the other parent. (That being said, it's important for children, as they get older, to be given the responsibility of communicating accurately to Mom what they were told by Dad and vice versa.) This requires follow through and follow up by both parents. For example, if you told your child that she cannot go in the backyard to play, make sure you also communicate this to your partner. And don't forget to verify by checking the backyard in case your child "forgot."

You also need to communicate and discuss with each other the behaviors you want to teach or discourage, including how those behaviors are defined and what appropriate consequences can be applied when the behaviors happen. For example, if you're teaching listening skills, it's important to discuss and define what listening looks like, what each of you expects from your son or daughter, and how you're going to respond (positively and negatively) based on your child's compliance. This will help establish consistency, whether you're home together or apart. It also will reduce your child's confusion and frustration. Failure to communicate basic expectations can create situations where one of you gives little if any consequences for a particular behavior while the other gives severe consequences for the same behavior. This will inevitably cause more behavior problems because of your inconsistency and poor communication.

Another important area to focus on is your overall parenting philosophy. This is something most parents rarely do. Instead, they tend to focus on the specific behaviors happening during a day or week. Discussions about an overall parenting philosophy or style never get on the agenda. Spending time talking about what your expectations are for your child's behavior, which behaviors are most important to you, and the types of positive and negative consequences you're comfortable applying should be discussed on a fairly regular basis. The values and morals you hope to promote in your child throughout her life will likely influence your overall parenting approach. The nature and content of this discussion will change as time progresses, your child matures, and the behaviors and issues you focus on change. Maintaining regular and consistent communication about the behavioral and emotional issues facing your child, as well as your parenting philosophy, will help avoid unnecessary squabbles.

Keep disagreements about parenting private.

There will be many times when you will disagree about certain behaviors or the type and severity of the consequences. As difficult as it is, the most important thing you can do in those situations is to provide support to the other parent, even if you disagree. It's little help to you, your partner, or your child to openly disagree about the consequences given or the behaviors targeted. Instead, spend time away from your child discussing your concerns and how to manage behavior problems. Try to find some agreement about appropriate behavior and consequences. This will avoid giving your child the impression that there is disagreement about how to manage a particular behavior and, hopefully, increase the consistency between you and your partner the next time a similar behavior occurs.

Follow the "'No' from one is 'No' from all" motto.

Since the days of the cave dwellers, children have learned quickly to go to parent number two after hearing "No" from parent number one. This will probably never stop. However, this does not mean you must accept this "fact." When parents frequently communicate with each other about limits or when one has said either "Yes" or "No," it gives the other parent an opportunity to reinforce the limits that were set. It's equally important to reinforce your child for accepting "No" and accepting limits. At the same time, it's also important to make it clear to your child that once he is told "No" by one parent, going to the other parent will not give him a different answer. It will, however, earn him additional consequences for not accepting "No" and ignoring a parent's authority. By establishing this expectation early and following through with it all the time, your child will learn to accept authority and "No" answers. You also reduce the energy and time your child spends trying to manipulate you.

Have family meetings.

Having a weekly meeting with the entire family can be helpful for a lot of different reasons. A family meeting gives everyone an opportunity to discuss the week's events, review the progress and success of individual family members, talk about plans for the upcoming week, and discuss the rules, chores, and behavioral expectations for each child. These meetings should be kept very positive, focusing on progress and success. They also should be opportunities to remind everyone about any chores that need to be done or to discuss behaviors between siblings that need more attention. Having both parents reinforce and support each other on the behavioral expectations for each family member also helps establish a united front. Preschool and school-aged children probably benefit most from these meetings, but having brief meetings when your child is a toddler can help establish the routine.

Be united even if apart.

Consistency is especially important for children whose parents are separated or divorced. A common source of frustration for many parents is when discipline efforts and behavioral expectations change or are different from one parent or home to the other. Children often get confused when the rules are different between Mom's house and Dad's. Other problems can arise when one parent has less contact with a child. Instead of establishing behavioral limits and maintaining good discipline practices, the parent may relax the rules out of guilt.

Unfortunately, divorced parents sometimes also add their relationship problems, such as finances, visitation issues, and personal grudges, to the mix. Communication may never have been a strong point during the relationship and probably won't improve much under these circumstances. Regrettably, it's during times of separation, when children have changing or multiple home environments, that they critically need consistent behavioral boundaries and discipline practices. It provides them with a much-needed sense of security.

Regardless of the reasons for a separation, the bottom line is that children will learn more quickly and change their behaviors more immediately if all caretakers use the same rules and discipline efforts. The more the rules change and the more inconsistent the discipline efforts are, the more likely it is for children to become confused and exhibit inappropriate behavior. Children also will try to work one parent or caretaker against another or make a parent feel guilty about the separation. Anything you can do to establish greater consistency in your children's lives, the better off everyone will be.

Think before you speak.

Emotional parenting almost always fails to produce positive outcomes. Take time to think about how you are going to respond to your child, including what you will say and what consequences you will give. This will help you respond in a way that is consistent with what you and your spouse agreed on and will help you avoid making a comment or applying a consequence that is based on emotion rather than logic and common sense.

A Balancing Act

Setting limits for your child's behavior is an important part of parenting. The limits you set and the consequences associated with those limits will naturally change as your child matures and the behavior changes. Trying to determine what limits to set, which behaviors to set limits for, and how to respond when those limits are tested can be challenging. In general, limits should always be set in situations or for behaviors that can affect your child's safety or well-being. Beyond that, the limits you establish should be directly related to what skills, language, and behaviors you're trying to teach and develop. The limits you establish at mealtime, bedtime, playtime, and family time should mirror the behaviors you expect to see from your child.

Your child's age can provide some general measurement about what you can expect from him behaviorally in different situations and settings. However, the limits or boundaries you set should be based more on your child's current and past behavior than his age. As your child learns from the consequences he receives for following or breaking behavioral limits and expectations, you should gradually allow him to have more independence. If you keep the limits too tight by reacting before your child has an opportunity to succeed or fail, you deny him any learning opportunity. He will become more dependent on you to intervene when he needs help, or he will become more defiant because of a lack of independence. Likewise, if you allow your child too much independence before he's ready, there is greater opportunity for many "mistakes" and negative consequences. Little learning will happen, and the interactions you have with your child will too often be negative. For example, let's say you're trying to teach your son to dress himself. If you constantly intervene each time he has difficulty putting on a sock or buttoning a shirt, he'll never learn. He'll wait for you to help him. On the other hand, if you never intervene, his frustration will likely get the best of him. (He may end up attending kindergarten in his birthday suit!) Finding a balance between allowing your child to try it on his own, knowing that you will offer guidance and assistance when necessary, will promote learning across all behaviors.

Striking a balance between having limits and allowing your child greater independence is tricky. Ideally, you will increase independence when your child demonstrates she can be successful within the limits you set. Gradually allowing her to have more responsibility and more independence will help her learn new behaviors. She also will develop a greater sense of security and confidence in her ability to be successful.

Again, your decision on what limits to set, and the amount of independence you allow your child, should be based on your child's current behaviors and skills, not just age. There are many teenagers and adults who enjoy plenty of independence even though their behaviors suggest they need more limits. Likewise, there are many five-year-olds who demonstrate levels of behavior and responsibility that exceed those of their older siblings and peers. Also, if you avoid having specific expectations for your child based on age, you won't get so frustrated when he does not meet your expectations. This is not to suggest you shouldn't have any age-based expectations. Many developmental milestones are based on age, such as walking and talking. However, children's skill levels vary considerably. Some progress quickly, others slowly but surely. It's better to focus on your child's individual ability and performance rather than assume she should be able to perform a behavior or skill simply because she has reached a particular age.

Rome Wasn't Built in a Day

Wouldn't it be nice if you could potty train your child in a day, have him dress himself by eighteen months, and perhaps play Beethoven's Fifth by age three? Forget that. Wouldn't it be even better

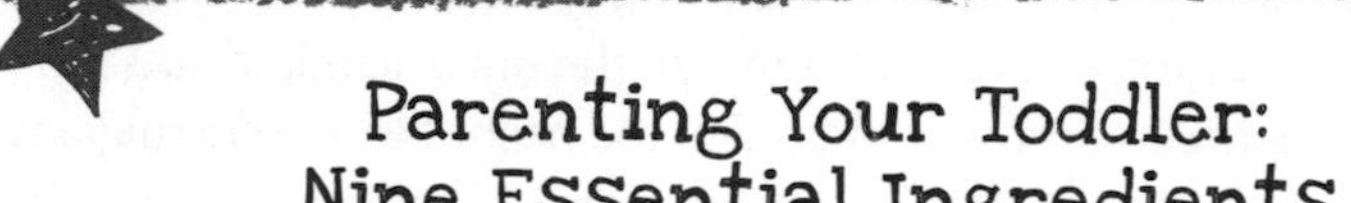

Parenting Your Toddler: Nine Essential Ingredients

1. As a parent, you also are a teacher. Remember: Teach don't preach.
2. Anger is not a parenting tool. Keep your cool.
3. Be consistent with your praise and correction. That's key.
4. Provide many opportunities for your child to learn new behaviors.
5. Respond as quickly as possible to your child's positive and negative behaviors.
6. Don't take good behavior for granted. Catch your child being good and offer praise.
7. Find a balance for the expectations you have for your child.
8. As parents, whether together or apart, stand united.
9. Be patient. Behavior changes slowly, but it does change!

if you could take him shopping without having him throw a tantrum? How about sleep through the night? Or make a car trip across town without pulling a sibling's hair? There are certain times, especially when you're dealing with a negative behavior, that time can't go fast enough. Then there are the enjoyable moments and behaviors that go by too quickly. Those ten-minute tantrums seem like ten years, while the thirty-minute school plays seem like thirty seconds.

Parents are often very impatient when it comes to how quickly their child learns a new behavior or skill at home, but less so in other settings. For example, if your child is in preschool or kindergarten, you probably are excited about all of the things she's learning. You patiently observe as she learns colors, numbers, and letters, and you smile with pride when she sings a song she learned for the school concert. By year's end, she may know most of her letters and numbers or be able to recite two or three short songs from memory. Of course, she benefits from having one instructor who consistently teaches her numbers, letters and songs, day in and day out. The fact that this occurs over nine months is completely fine with you. By contrast, when your child can't poop in the toilet after four weeks of training or doesn't stop hitting a sibling after a series of time-outs, you get impatient and frustrated. Unlike in school, however, your child may have multiple "teachers" (grandparents, friends, babysitters, and siblings, for example) who use different potty training and discipline methods. The key to relieving your frustration is to appreciate that learning takes time, whether it's the ABC's, the 123's, or going number two in the potty chair.

There is no accurate way to predict how long it will take to change your child's misbehaviors or to teach new skills. In fact, focusing on how long it takes will only be frustrating. As a rule of thumb, to change a negative behavior you should plan on at least one or two weeks for every month your child exhibited the misbehavior. So, if you have been dealing with a particular negative behavior for a year, plan on a minimum of twelve weeks before you see meaningful behavioral change. That is assuming, of course, you work consistently and diligently to correct it. There are a number of other variables that also will affect behavior change, including how frequently the behavior happens, your child's level of determination and will, and the payoff or reward your child gets from the behavior. Always keep in mind, however, no matter how difficult a day your child may be having or how long the behavior has gone on, the behavior will eventually change. One or two behaviors do not define your child. After all, you yourself eventually slept through the night, learned to use the toilet, learned to eat with utensils, and (hopefully) stopped having tantrums. It will happen for your child, too. The important thing is that you develop a plan, apply it, modify it as needed, and consistently move ahead until the behavior changes.

Your child's behavior is a work in progress that will have many ups and downs. Even on the roughest days, much can be learned and enjoyed. Enjoy the process, use each day to learn from your mistakes, and take satisfaction in the successes.

A Practical Example of the Benefits of Immediacy

Let's say you want to teach your child to interact appropriately with the new family dog, Cassie B. You obviously want your child to play and interact with Cassie in a way that is safe and enjoyable for her and the dog. There are several ways for your daughter to learn how to properly care for and interact with Cassie. One way is natural interaction. She will learn, over time, that certain actions and behaviors make the dog growl, bite, or run away and other behaviors that make the dog play and be affectionate. Using naturally occurring interactions as a teaching approach, however, puts both your child and the dog at risk. Another approach you can take involves explaining all the appropriate and inappropriate ways she should interact with the dog. Again, because of her age and limited ability to process verbal information (actions mean more than words at this age), you will not be able to educate her quickly or in the manner that you desire. So, if those two approaches are not the most effective options, what is? The one that involves immediacy, modeling, repetition, and consistency.

As you model and demonstrate how to interact with Cassie B, it's important to immediately respond whenever your child engages in appropriate behavior, such as gently petting and playing with the dog. Immediacy becomes even more important, however, if you catch her acting inappropriately, such as grabbing a handful of fur or throwing objects at Cassie. Waiting to respond to such inappropriate behavior may have a potentially negative or harmful outcome.

When you closely monitor your child's interactions with a pet or any animal, immediately pairing your praise, smiles, and compliments with her appropriate actions provides a valuable lesson. Likewise, offering a quick verbal reprimand or redirecting her when she gets too aggressive helps your child see the connection between her behavior and your response. Thus, it's the consistent and immediate responses, along with providing repetitive opportunities to interact with the family pet, that help your child learn which behaviors are appropriate. This approach greatly increases the likelihood that she will continue to repeat behaviors and actions that lead to positive interactions with Cassie. As you continue to see your child interact appropriately with Cassie, and your confidence grows in your daughter's ability to independently and successfully interact with the animal, you can reduce your supervision. The need for immediate, repetitive, and consistent responses also can gradually fade. However, anytime you teach and shape new behaviors, providing immediate feedback is very important.

chapter 2

Getting Your Child to Listen without Shouting or Begging

Lila Jones was frantically wiping off the kitchen table and sweeping up breakfast crumbs as her four-year-old son Tyson played in the family room. It was a hectic morning, and Lila was running late.

"Tyson, it's time to pick up your toys. We need to leave for Grandma's house," Lila shouted from the kitchen as she put the breakfast plates in the dishwasher. Tyson was playing with his pet cat, Tiger, and ignoring the instruction. A few minutes passed and Lila repeated her request. Still Tyson played on.

More time passed before Lila said, "Tyson, would you be a good boy, please, and pick up your toys? We need to get to Grandma's house."

Tyson ignored her again. Lila finished cleaning and walked into the family room. "Tyson, come on. Let's pick up the toys now," she urged.

"No, Mommy!" he cried emphatically.

"Don't 'No, Mommy' me Tyson. I said it's time to pick up your toys. NOW!" snapped Lila. Tyson looked up, screamed "No," and ran from the room. Annoyed, Lila gathered up all of Tyson's toys, tossed them in the toy box, found Tyson hiding in his room, and carried him to the car.

Problem solved? If this scenario played out in your home, would you…

A. Require your child to pick up the toys even if it causes you to be late?

B. Put your child in time-out and then make him pick up the toys?

C. Dial 1-800-Super Nanny?

D. Ask your child to pick up the toys after you return home from Grandma's?

E. Try something else?

Any of these may seem reasonable to you, including simply forgetting the episode ever happened. However, when your child refuses to follow instructions or totally ignores you, there is a problem. He or she is not listening, and no amount of pleading, begging, scolding or screaming will make your child a better listener. The decisions you make before your child decides if he is going to listen may make the biggest difference when it comes to helping him be a good listener. When parents have difficulty getting a child to follow directions, they often wonder whether there is something wrong with the child's hearing. Numerous children have visited the audiologist before coming in to see me. Hearing involves the ear and brain receiving, interpreting, and processing sound into useful information. Listening involves taking that information and using it in a meaningful way, as in following directions. Nearly all toddlers have perfect hearing, but they don't have perfect listening. In this chapter, I will outline strategies that will help you teach your toddler how to listen.

Control the Message: Act like a Traffic Light

Being a good listener, or following directions, is not a natural, in-born trait for any of us. Children are taught to be good listeners, but they also learn how "not to listen." When parents complain about a child who ignores their wishes or disregards their rules, they like to couch the problem in terms such as, "He never follows my instructions," or "She is so stubborn, she won't do what I ask." But what they're really saying is, "My child doesn't listen!"

Following directions is important for a variety of reasons. Children need good listening skills to complete daily chores, get dressed, do homework, and clean up. It helps them to become toilet trained and develop friendships. These skills also are critical in a variety of situations that could affect their safety. When children don't listen, they don't follow the wishes, requests, or directions of their parents and other adults. This can put their health and well-being at risk – grabbing the sharp end of a knife, running into the middle of a street, or touching a hot burner. One way to deal with and change these types of misbehaviors is to improve children's listening skills. All children can learn how to be better listeners, especially if they have a great teacher – a parent like you!

You communicate messages to your child all the time. Like a traffic light, you send signals that you want your child to obey. Real traffic lights work predictably, going from green to yellow to red. Imagine, however, if a traffic light changed color randomly. No one would know when to speed up, slow down, stop, or go. Obviously, no parent wants to be as confusing as a malfunctioning traffic light. You want to be consistent. The more predictable your communication signals are, the more predictable your child's behavior will be.

To communicate consistently, consider the three colors of a traffic light as three steps or stages you follow when telling your child to do something. In the first stage (green light), your child is carefree and goes about her business. In the second stage (yellow light), you interrupt your child's activity by making some type of request (quiet down, stop, or clean up). It's here that signals can get lost or confused. If your child ignores you or refuses to follow your request, what do you do? Repeat yourself? Talk louder? Give up? Ideally, you move to the third stage (red light). You give your child a choice or ultimatum, such as this: "Please turn off the TV now, or TV privileges will be gone for the rest of the day."

Your child now has the choice of listening to you and receiving your praise, or ignoring you and losing TV privileges. By giving your child a choice, you encourage her to think about what to do next, knowing that a consequence (good or bad) will follow whatever choice is made. (The consequence acts as a motivator to encourage better choices and behaviors.)

We could spend all kinds of time discussing complicated theories as to what affects a young child's compliance. And although there are a number of factors that affect compliance, it often boils down to one fundamental reason: It doesn't feel good! When it comes to day-to-day activities, young children like to focus on one thing – themselves. They cherish anything that is fun and enjoyable. If given a choice between picking up toys or playing in the backyard, they run outside. If given a choice between sitting on Dad's lap and watching the latest Disney movie or brushing their teeth and going to bed, the toothpaste stays in the tube. Young children operate from a very concrete and self-absorbed perspective. Their wants and needs come first (or so they think). When left to their own whims, they can never eat enough candy, watch enough television, drink enough juice, or have enough playtime. That's why they need a traffic cop, and like it or not, that's you.

You have the unenviable task of putting an end to the "fun." Whenever your child is told to stop doing something enjoyable, or worse, told to do something he or she considers "no fun," you see and hear resistance. Crying, whining, complaining, arguing, and ignoring are some of the more popular ways the six-and-under crowd communicates displeasure. They have learned that such behaviors may just help them get what they want. Their relentless pleas of "Just ONE more" and "No, I don't want to," or their overly dramatic and embarrassing tantrums (at home or in public), have a way of softening the resolve of even the most determined parents – parents for whom "No" always means "No" and "Yes" always means "Yes." You might have to use your imagination to picture this kind of parent, because such a parent doesn't exist. If you've never given in to a child's whining, pleading, or complaining, then you've never been a parent. And therein lies the challenge.

In general, no one likes to have limits set, but we all have them. No one likes to be told "No," but it's a part of life. As a parent, it would make life so much easier if you could always say "Yes." But that's not possible and wouldn't be good even if it were. Your job is to figure out when to hold firm and when to be flexible, when to allow "one more time" and when to demand "a last time." Unfortunately, this is when communication signals often get crossed or stop working. Some parents, for example, get stuck on the yellow light. They make lots of requests but allow their children to do as they please. They never talk about choices and consequences. Other parents threaten to use consequences but never deliver. These empty promises teach children that it's okay to ignore a request or not listen because there is no consequence for not doing what was asked. Then there are parents who whiz right on by the yellow signal. They leap frog from green to red, immediately punishing their children without so much as a warning or giving them the opportunity to change their behavior on their own. This swift justice may prompt temporary behavior changes, but at what cost? Most likely, the children are responding out of momentary fear while growing resentful of their parents' unfair and harsh punishment. In the end, children are not learning how to be better listeners based on the choices they made. Rather, they are behaving out of fear.

In your home, what kind of messages do you send to your child? Do you follow the predictable pattern of a traffic light, or are you all over the road? Do you get stuck on yellow? Do you live on red? Do you just go with the flow? The good news is that there are a number of things you can do to help your child become an excellent listener.

Communication: It's All in the Delivery

How you communicate with your child has a significant impact on the behaviors you see or don't see. The following strategies will steer you toward better communication so your child learns to be a better listener:

Give an "eye" for an "aye."

A common form of communication involves yelling something across a room to a child who then responds with complete silence or an "Okay" that sounds completely insincere ("I heard you but I have no plans to do it."). It's important that your child hears what you're saying, but it's even more critical that she understands you. To aid understanding, make eye contact when you give your child an instruction or make a request. This nonverbal cue communicates seriousness, helps focus attention on what you're saying, and decreases the chances that your child will ignore you or refuse to do what you ask. You also will make it clear that the request is important because you took the time to tell her directly.

In the digital age, we have the capability of communicating with others and making requests without ever seeing each other. We talk on the telephone, send text messages and emails, and post our thoughts on social networking websites. We probably communicate and make more requests long distance than we do in person. In fact, the interactions you have with your child probably involve little eye contact – talking while driving in the car or chatting while she plays in the park. By taking the time to make eye contact, you can grab your child's attention. Trying to have the same impact from a distance puts you at a disadvantage. Getting a three-year-old to put his shoes on when you are face to face is difficult enough, expecting him to do the same thing when you're three rooms away is, at best, unlikely.

Children learn quickly that there is no urgency to follow an instruction if their parents are preoccupied. Any demands or instructions children hear do not have the same level of importance compared to the ones Mom and Dad make face to face. If you really want your child to listen and follow your instructions, you have to take the time to get down on your child's level, make eye contact, and be direct. Is this time consuming? Sometimes. Is it necessary? Absolutely. Making eye contact when giving an instruction is a surefire way to focus your child's attention and show him that it's time to listen. Once your child responds more quickly to verbal requests and follows instructions more predictably and routinely, you won't always have to establish eye contact or kneel down to eye level. However, until compliance becomes fairly predictable, maintaining good eye contact is critical. Having eye contact with your child when making a request will hopefully reinforce "in sight, in mind" rather than "out of sight, out of mind."

A KISS says it best.

Avoid making complicated demands, providing lengthy explanations, or giving detailed descriptions of what needs to be done. Simply and succinctly state your instruction or request. Droning on and on about what you want your little one to do, or how or why he should do it, accomplishes nothing. Your child's attention span is too short and vocabulary too limited for any long-winded commentary. Here's an example of saying too much about putting on a coat: "It's raining, and you have a cold. I want you to put on your jacket and find your umbrella before we leave the house. I don't want you to get all wet when we walk from the parking lot to the library."

You can say the same thing with a KISS (**K**eep **I**t **S**hort, **S**imple): "Please put your coat on now." Instructions that are short and simple are easy for your child to understand, remember, and follow.

Vague is never in vogue.

"Don't get in trouble." "Be good." "Be careful." "Look out!" These generic phrases are heard every day. Whether said to adults or children, there is usually some specific purpose in mind. If you're driving with a friend and another car abruptly cuts you off, you might shout, "Watch out!" If your toddler found a way to climb on to the kitchen counter, you might say the same thing. However, when it comes to young children, they typically do not have enough experience to know that climbing on to the counter could be dangerous. Saying "Watch out!" is a warning to get down from the counter. Whether your child realizes that is what you mean is another story.

You will frustrate yourself and your child if you make vague, general demands. At this age, making generic requests, such as "Be good, "Look out," "Don't get in trouble," or "It's time to clean up," are too ambiguous and leave too much to interpretation. These phrases may mean something to you, but your child won't know what you are asking. As we get older, we're able to take specific examples and experiences and associate them with general concepts, such as good, bad, dangerous, risky, or fun. However, at your child's age, words must be more concrete than conceptual. What does "be good" mean? When you say "Clean up," what do you want your child to actually do? What exactly is your child supposed to "look out" for? You want to be specific without being wordy. Too many details, like too many generalities, distort the message. So, if saying "Be good" means "Keep your hands and feet to yourself" or "Clean up" means "Pick up all the toys from your bedroom floor and put them on the shelf," then say that.

One is enough.

"Bryce, will you hang up your coat, put your shoes on the step, and feed the dog?" "Jasmine, please move your coloring book off of the table, put away your crayons, and wash your hands."

The ability to multi-task is an admirable skill, and one you want your children to develop – someday. However, when giving instructions to children younger than six, a single instruction is best. Let's face it, it's difficult enough to get a toddler to comply with one demand, why add more to it? Most young children don't have the memory needed to handle more than one request or demand. If you string together multiple tasks in one request, you will likely find yourself in a frustrating predicament. Putting multiple tasks in one request increases the likelihood that your child will have greater difficulty completing all the tasks, let alone remembering exactly what you said. Any frustration you feel over your child's failure to complete each of the tasks should be directed inward, not at your child. You asked too much, too soon. Too much information is simply overwhelming. Keep it simple and straightforward by sticking with a single request. When your child is older (kindergarten and beyond), handling multiple tasks and absorbing more information should become easier, and you can add a second or third request to reflect his new skill level. But until your child learns to handle a single request, one is enough.

Act, don't yak.

Perhaps the most important thing you can do to help your child listen and do what you ask is to follow up with any demand you make by providing consequences. Acknowledge the effort your child puts forth to complete a task, and praise him when the task is done. Don't take it for granted. Provide a smile, hug, or an encouraging word. Show your appreciation. Likewise, if your child fails to follow through on a request, remove a privilege. If you tell your child there will be consequences, follow through. By consistently following up your words with actions, you teach three important lessons:

Lesson One: Your child learns that she has choices to make, and there are positive and negative consequences associated with those choices. Past consequences can help shape future decisions.

Lesson Two: You reinforce your role as the authority figure.

Lesson Three: Your child learns that your words are followed by actions. On thc flip side, if you make promises you don't keep, you undermine your authority and make it easier for your child to ignore you. Words not followed by your actions equals your child's inaction.

Seize the moment.

The attention span of most young children is often equal to their height: short. If children could simply learn just by listening to what we tell them, parenting would be much easier. Alas, we have no such luck. Anytime your child listens to you and follows your instructions, offer immediate praise ("Awesome job!" or "Nice work!") or positive attention (smile, hug, or gentle touch). If he doesn't listen and ignores your instructions, a negative consequence – a frown, guided listening (explained later), or loss of a privilege, for example – should be immediate, too. Because children have a poor concept of time, the longer you wait to react to their behavior, the less effective your response or reinforcement will be. Your words should follow their actions. For example, your five-year-old picks up his toys without prompting. Waiting five or ten minutes before acknowledging or praising his actions reduces the effectiveness of your praise. Although he is happy to receive it, your son might not know what action earned him your positive attention. Negative consequences work the same way. If your daughter runs from the family room leaving a trail of crayons through the house, respond immediately. If you delay providing a consequence (for whatever reason), she may not realize what behavior earned her the negative consequence or wonder why she wasn't told to stop when she did it. Waiting too long to provide feedback denies you the best moment for reinforcing your child's positive behaviors or correcting the negative ones.

Say "you do" (not "we do").

If your intention is to assist your child with accomplishing a task, then saying things such as "**Let's** pick up the toys," "**We** need to clean up," or "It's time for **us** to finish coloring" are perfectly clear requests. However, assistance isn't usually the goal when requests like this are made. Parents often make these types of requests to soften them or to be "nice." The result is usually a confused child waiting for a parent to help. Since helping your child is probably not your intention, don't imply that you will. Your child, with good reason, will expect help from you when you say "we" or "let us." When that help never comes, either the task goes unfinished or the child throws a tsunami of a tantrum. Leave out "we," "us," "let's," "our" and any other similar words from a request when you expect your child to work on his own. Instead, statements such as "Pick up your toys, please," "You need to put away your art supplies," or "It's time for you to finish coloring," will send a more direct message with less confusion.

Say "do" not just "don't."

Asking your child to do something is usually more instructive than saying don't do something. Blurting out phrases, such as "Don't hit," "Don't shout," "Don't bite," or "Don't kick," comes easily and naturally. Telling your child what behaviors you do want to see takes more effort and thought, but has benefits. By telling your child what to do, you're setting him up for success instead of always reacting to negative behaviors when they occur. Also, as your child matures, he can rehearse the positive statements in his head as a reminder of what he should do as opposed to rehearsing a laundry list of negative behaviors he's supposed to avoid. Other examples include "Use your quiet voice" instead of "Don't scream," "Keep your hands and feet to yourself" instead of "Don't hit," and "Roll the truck on the floor" instead of "Don't throw toys."

Ask no questions, please.

When your spouse says, "Can you pick up a gallon of milk on your way home from work?" or your boss asks, "Could you have that report ready by the end of the week?" you know those aren't really questions. They are demands or expectations posed as questions to give the impression that one has a choice. In reality, we know the spouse expects milk at the end of the day, and the boss expects the report on Friday. Saying "No" is not an option. Unfortunately, when you use questions to tell children what to do, they don't read between the lines. They assume they have a choice, and often they choose what is in their best interest. If you expect your child to hang up her coat, don't ask, "Can you put away your coat?" If your son needs to put his bike in the garage, don't ask, "Would you like to put your bike in the garage?" If you need your twins to get ready for bed, don't ask, "Can you two please put your PJs on?" The obvious answer to these questions, especially when a child is in the middle of a fun activity or isn't ready to put the bike away or go to bed, is "No." When you need something done, use declarative statements: "Please put your bike in the garage" or "Put your coat away, please." There should be no question about your expectations.

Don't multi-ask while multi-tasking.

"Why do I have to tell my child so many times to do something?" is one of the more frequently asked questions and complaints I hear from parents. My response, "Why do you ask so many times?" Repeatedly asking the same thing again and again, usually in an increasingly loud voice, only gives you strained vocal chords. If no consequence comes from not listening the first time, second time, third time, or fourth time, why should your child expect a consequence after you loudly repeat yourself a fifth time? Instances like this can cause anger and frustration because your child is not doing what you ask, or you think your child is deliberately being disrespectful or defiant. In some cases, that may be true. Eventually, the battle ends when your child picks up the coat because she wants to stop that horrible loud noise (your yelling), is fearful, or eventually gets around to picking up the coat. The battle also can end when you, exhausted by the whole experience, hang the coat up yourself or decide to let it go and leave it where it is. Yelling or repeating your request over and over only encourages your child to tune you out because she knows there will likely be no consequence. In addition, if you make a request when you're trying to do a half dozen other things, the likelihood that you won't follow through and your child will ignore you only increases. If it's important that your child do what you say, then stop what you're doing and let your child know that you mean business. Once she learns that a positive or negative consequence will follow her actions after the first request, she will tune in quicker and more often. The bonus: Once your child learns that actions follow words, there is no need to raise your voice. Consider the traffic light again. It doesn't get brighter when we ignore it. Rather, it always goes predictably from green to yellow to red. You can create the same predictable routine when giving instructions to your child.

Stay calm.

You will be a much better and more effective teacher to your children if you're able to manage your emotions. If you make a request and your child fails to follow through, respond in a firm, direct, and calm voice. Your first instinct may be to raise your voice in order to get your child's attention and motivate action. This may make you feel like you're doing something constructive, but it doesn't really accomplish much. Your child will likely do or say anything to get you to quiet down, but learning how to calm you down may be the only lesson learned. Yelling and other exaggerated behaviors just add unnecessary tension and stress. If you want to communicate effectively, maintain a firm, direct, and neutral voice so that the focus is on the content of what you are saying rather than the emotion.

Catch 'em being good.

As a parent, which of these behaviors are you most likely to respond to: Your daughter helps her brother stand up after he falls, or she pushes him to the ground? Your son throws toys all over the family room, or he picks them up and puts them away? There are more than a few parents who will immediately jump on any misbehavior or act of defiance from their children but then say and do nothing when their children actually do what they are told or act appropriately. Their focus always seems to be on the negative. These parents will say that children don't need to be rewarded for doing what "should be done." According to their logic, rewards are earned for the big things (whatever "big" is) not the little things (such as listening, complying, or any other social skill). As a parent, don't let yourself become complacent or take for granted the good things your child does. Listening and following instructions are not character traits that children are born with. They are behaviors that must be taught and reinforced.

Imagine if your boss only paid attention to you when something went wrong. Everything you did right was ignored but every flaw or misstep was highlighted or exaggerated? You would not be motivated to improve, and you would not enjoy your job. The same is true for children. If their positive behaviors are met with silence and their mistakes are met with immediate criticism, what message are you sending? An affectionate embrace or a few kind words to reinforce positive behaviors can be just as powerful and motivating as delivering a negative consequence after a misbehavior. In addition, consistently providing positive attention when your children are listening and corrective action when they are not listening provides a nice contrast when either type of behavior occurs.

Knowing how to communicate more effectively with your toddler so you're not sending mixed or confusing messages is half the battle. You may actually start to see some behavior changes simply by changing the way you provide instructions. But if you want to see lasting behavioral changes, you have to do more than know how to talk. You can't just talk the talk. You have to walk the walk and that means "teaching."

Teaching Is More than Talking

It was a quiet morning as Keshaun played with blocks while his mom paid a few bills. When mom finished her paperwork, she walked into the family room to tell Keshaun it was time to get ready for his doctor's appointment. She knelt beside him, made good eye contact, and said, "Keshaun, it's time to stop playing. Please take your blocks and put them in the plastic bin."

"No!" Keshaun screamed as he grabbed a fistful of blocks and scooted away.

If you were Keshaun's mom, how would you respond?

A. Place Keshaun in time-out.

B. Offer to help Keshaun pick up the blocks.

C. Tell Keshaun that he won't be able to play in the park this afternoon if his blocks are not picked up.

D. Donate the blocks to charity.

If you chose "A," you run the risk that Keshaun would rather sit in time-out than pick up his blocks. With option "B," helping Keshaun now can send a mixed, confusing message. Also, what will Keshaun expect the next time Mom asks him to pick up the blocks? Option "C" only makes sense if you had immediate plans to go to the park. Because Keshaun has a limited concept of time, removing the option of playing in the park that afternoon is too far away to have any meaningful impact on his behavior at that moment. Finally, with option "D," giving the blocks away may create a case of "out of sight, out of mind." Keshaun may be perfectly happy playing with other toys. It also punishes any other children in the family who enjoy playing with the blocks. Each option is reasonable, yet has potential risk. So, what should you do?

Many parents find themselves repeating a request over and over until they lose their patience and begin pleading or lecturing. Anytime you use more words than actions, you're going to lose. When it comes to fairly simple tasks that need to be done in a timely manner, using a technique called "guided listening" can be very effective. This is a great way to help your child complete a fairly simple task in a timely manner. Guided listening allows parents to immediately respond to a child's refusal or defiance without repeating the request over and over and without a lot of frustration (on the part of the parent, that is). Using guided listening allows two important things to happen:

- The task gets completed fairly quickly.
- Your child learns that you will back up your words with actions.

When using guided listening, you may need to follow as many as four steps or as few as two:

Step One: Make a brief and specific request or demand. The request should be simple enough that it can be completed in about thirty seconds. Simple tasks can include hanging up a coat in the closet, putting puzzle pieces back in their box, or placing cups on the dinner table.

Step Two: Give your child up to ten seconds to comply with your request. If he does what you ask, praise him for listening and following your instructions.

Step Three: If your child does not listen or follow your first verbal request within ten seconds, repeat the request **one time** and gesture to your child what needs to be done (point at the coat and then the closet or gesture at the puzzle pieces on the floor, for example). By combining words (the request) with gestures, you make sure your child understands what needs to be done. Again, give your child ten seconds to comply with your request. If he complies with the request, offer praise ("Great job!") or give a thumbs up, smile, or hug.

Step Four: If your child continues to ignore you or be defiant, provide gentle physical guidance to complete the task. This includes gently placing your hands on your child's shoulders or back and guiding him toward the task. It also could involve placing your hand over his to "help" him place an object in a box or hang up a coat.

Here is an example of using physical guidance when your child ignores your request to pick up a toy off the floor and put it in a toy box:

- Walk with your child to where the toy is on the floor (place your hand on her shoulder or back or walk side by side).
- Physically guide or prompt your child to pick up the toy.
- If your child refuses to pick up the toy, gently place your hand over hers and "help" her pick up the toy.
- Walk with her to the box and help open the lid.
- Point to the box and work together to put the toy in the box.
- Help your child close the toy box lid.

Physical guidance should **never** be done in an aggressive or hostile manner, which could easily happen when you're frustrated or rushed for time. Don't shout or shove. Don't grab hold of your child too firmly. (Guided compliance is not about "manhandling" your child.) Avoid lecturing your child as you guide her through the task. At the same time, you should **not** praise her or provide positive reinforcement (extra playtime or a snack) for finishing the task. Such reinforcement could encourage your child to ignore future requests until you "help" with a task that she should do on her own. Rewards, including verbal praise and privileges, are appropriate when your child complies with requests **without** your help.

If your child is like most children, she won't enjoy being guided through a task. Sometimes, you may see or hear some mild resistance, such as pulling an arm away or talking back ("Don't! I can do it myself."). In these situations, continue to gently guide your child until the task is completed. If your child is more aggressive or confrontational (screaming, hitting, kicking, biting, and/or pinching), firmly say, "No hitting" or "No biting," and use time-out (see Chapter 10). After time-out, repeat the request. If your child continues to refuse, resume the guided listening procedure. Guided listening only continues as long as you're able to provide gentle guidance. Use time-out anytime your child engages in aggressive or destructive behavior. It's important that you repeat this process until your child finishes the requested task.

Don't be alarmed if you hear angry words coming from your little one, such as "Don't touch me," "You can't make me," or "You're not the boss of me!" As much as possible, ignore the language and focus on the task at hand. If you respond or react to your child's comments, it takes attention away from the task and reduces the effectiveness of whatever point you want to make. Focusing on your child's language, and not the task, also increases the likelihood that you will hear more colorful language in the future.

Tips for Success in Using Guided Listening

One way to increase your odds of being successful and comfortable using guided listening is to practice with your child multiple times a day. For starters, have your child complete a variety of simple tasks that can be done in fifteen to thirty seconds. Some tasks might be enjoyable or easy, and your child will do them willingly. When that happens, be generous with your praise. Other requests will probably be ignored, giving you a chance to practice and guide your child's listening. When you begin to practice guided listening (at least during the first few days), try to make one request every hour. Before making a request, be sure you have the time to follow through and are not occupied with other activities or obligations that will delay or interrupt practice time.

Sometimes, guided listening will not be practical or workable. Time-consuming tasks are generally not suited to this technique. For example, if the toy box looks like it exploded in the playroom because stuffed animals, games, dolls, and blocks are strewn around the room, it's not a good idea to use guided listening for the task of cleaning up the room. Such a request is too large and time-consuming, and it would be impractical if you had to provide physical guidance to pick up each item. Instead, a more specific task, such as asking your son to pick up all of the red blocks and put them in a container, would be manageable and appropriate. After the red blocks are picked up, you can practice again by picking up only the stuffed animals. Such requests are less daunting and time intensive than asking a child to clean an entire room. Similarly, asking your child to pick up his clothes and put them in the hamper is a task that lends itself to using guided listening, much more so than asking him to clean his entire bedroom.

Whenever you use guided listening, or any other teaching technique with your child, remember to couple the technique with effective verbal and nonverbal communication:

- Make and maintain eye contact (an eye for an aye).
- Be direct and specific (no questions, please).
- Keep the request simple (a KISS says it best).
- Stay calm.

Using Grandma's Rule

Another strategy you can use to motivate your child to listen more and refuse less is the Premack Principle, popularly known as Grandma's Rule. This rule works best in situations where it's not critical that a task be completed immediately. Your parents probably used this with you when you were a child. Grandma's Rule says that BEFORE a child is allowed to do something fun, a less-than-enjoyable task must be done first. For example, when Ty comes home from school he likes to play on the computer. But before he is allowed to log on, he must take the family's golden retriever on a walk. If the dog isn't walked, computer time is denied.

There are many activities or responsibilities that children do not start or finish as consistently and reliably as we would like. Picking up toys, putting away clothes, and washing hands are just a few. There also are many other activities that we can count on them to do, almost to the point of being predictable. These activities vary from one child to the next, but popular and predictable behaviors include playing outdoors, watching TV, getting on the computer, playing videos, eating special snacks, and doing arts and crafts. If you know there are certain activities your child likes to do and there are other activities that need to be done but don't happen regularly, doesn't it make sense to use one to motivate the other? Besides, how many of us get to play before we work? Are you allowed to take a vacation anytime you want with a promise to your boss that you will do your work later? With Grandma's Rule, you simply require that the work or task gets done before the fun. That is the easy part. The difficult part is making sure that you follow through with this rule once you have established it, as this easy-to-relate-to scenario illustrates:

Sarah was playing with play dough in the kitchen. To keep from making a mess, she laid old newspapers on the floor and on top of the table. While she was making a bowl out of blue play dough, the doorbell rang. It was her friend Cecelia, inviting Sarah to play at her house.

"Dad," Sarah said excitedly as she raced back to the kitchen "Cecelia wants me to come play at her house. Can I? Please Dad!"

"Sure, but you need to clean up this mess in the kitchen first," ordered Dad.

"But Dad, Cecelia can only play for a half hour. Can I clean up after I'm done playing? I promise I'll clean up," Sarah begged.

"Okay, but make sure you clean this up as soon as you get back," said Dad.

"Oh thank you!" Sarah screamed as she raced out the door.

When Sarah returned home from Cecelia's, she immediately went to the family room, turned on the TV to watch her favorite show, and plopped down on the couch. Hearing her come home, Dad went to the family room and reminded Sarah that she had a job to do.

"Sarah, you need to clean up your mess in the kitchen, remember? You promised."

"I know, but I have to see this show. It's a new one."

"No, Sarah. I'm sorry, but you have to clean up. That was our agreement," said Dad.

"Will you help me? It's a really big mess," Sarah asked.

"No. You made the mess, and you need to clean it up," replied Dad.

"Okay, but after my show."

"Now Sarah!" was Dad's stern reply.

Sarah continued to protest and plead with her dad to let her watch the television show. Dad grabbed the remote and turned off the TV. Sarah then grabbed the remote back and threw it against the couch. She yelled, "You're mean, and I'm not cleaning up the kitchen!"

Dad sent Sarah to her room for time-out. Sarah slammed her bedroom door, and everyone in the house heard her stomping her feet and tossing objects around the room. Meanwhile, a friend of the family was due shortly for a visit. Dad couldn't leave the kitchen in such a mess and since Sarah was in meltdown mode, he had to clean it up himself. He would deal with Sarah later.

If you were passing judgment on how Dad managed Sarah, would you say…

A. Passes with flying colors.

B. A strong performance, but could use some fine-tuning.

C. Fair effort.

D. Needs some work.

E. Back to the drawing board.

Stories like this play themselves out in every home. In this case, Dad made one fairly significant mistake: He allowed Sarah to play (going to Cecelia's house) before she finished her work (cleaning up the kitchen). Once Sarah got what she wanted, there was no motivation for her to clean up the kitchen. What would have happened if Dad had made Sarah clean up the table before she went out to play? Sarah might have grumbled and whined, but most likely she would have cleaned up the table fairly quickly, especially with her friend waiting outside. As we know, kids are pretty good at saying or doing just about anything they can to get what they want. Why not tell Dad you will clean up later if it means you can play right away? Wouldn't you like to get paid first, before doing any work, instead of doing the job and then getting paid? But that's not how life works, and it does not or should not work that way for your children.

To avoid situations like the one just described from playing out in your household, here are four steps you should follow when using Grandma's Rule:

Step One: Identify a behavior you want your child to improve on or a task you want your child to complete more reliably and regularly. This might include hanging up clothes, putting away toys, or emptying the trash.

Step Two: Identify an activity your child enjoys or regularly engages in without any prompting from you. You should have little difficulty coming up with an activity that your child enjoys and probably does on a daily basis. It's also important the activity be one that your child plans to do in the very near future or engages in regularly. Otherwise, there is little motivation for your child to complete the task.

Step Three: In language your child will understand, explain to him what specific task needs to be completed (picking up toys) BEFORE he can do a favorite activity (ride his bike). Do NOT give in and let your child do his preferred activity first, no matter how many promises are made that the task will get done later.

Step Four: Praise your child for completing the task, and let him do whatever activity was promised. Stay mindful of the rule and monitor your child so he continues to do what is asked of him before doing his own thing.

You may be wondering what to do when your child fails to complete a task. You can't wait forever, and in some cases, your child may be deliberately trying to wait you out. Your child may be thinking that if he holds out long enough, you may eventually give in and let him do what he wants. Better still, maybe you will do the task for him. Instead of entering into this cat-and-mouse game, you have a better option.

Give your child a reasonable but set time limit to complete a task. (Keep in mind that at this young age, children have a very poor concept of time. It's helpful to use some event as a reference point, such as breakfast, lunch, or dinner.) Let's say you told your daughter she needs to have her toys picked up before she goes outside to play.

Success with Guided Listening

Fed up with daughter Mercedes' constant refusals to pay attention and follow her requests, Mom decided guided listening might be better than repeated pleading. So, when Mom asked her daughter to put away her pajamas, Mercedes ignored the request and expected the usual routine where Mom asks multiple times before finally giving in and doing it herself. But this day was different. Mom looked at Mercedes, asked her to put her PJ's away, and – to Mercedes' surprise – didn't leave the room. Mercedes' mom pointed to the pajamas, repeated her request for Mercedes to put them away, and then pointed to the closet. Mercedes looked at her mom with a smirk on her face. After several seconds of silence, Mom gently placed one hand on Mercedes' shoulder, the other on her back, and guided her toward the pajamas. Mercedes, feeling self-conscious and confused, said, "Don't. I'll do it."

"Mercedes, you didn't listen when I asked you the first time, so I guess I need to help you," replied Mom.

Mercedes jerked her shoulder, trying to get away from Mom. She continued to be resistant as her mother gently guided her through the task. Mercedes quickly learned that if she followed her mother's directions right away, she could avoid Mom's "help." After about a week of using guided listening, Mom noticed that Mercedes responded to requests sooner. Mom also was pleased that her daughter was starting tasks without having to be asked four or five times.

Mercedes didn't always complete a task with a smile on her face, but she was listening. Mom still hears an occasional "No," but that usually is followed by a reluctant-sounding "Okay" when Mom reminds her that she can either do the task on her own or have Mom "help" her.

However, she decides she's not going to pick up her toys – ever – because she doesn't care if she ever goes outside. In fact, she is looking forward to spending more time with you in the house. This is not the reaction you were looking for. At this point it's time to set limits. Tell her she has until lunchtime to have the toys picked up. If the toys are not picked up, you will pick them up and put them away. Here comes the real motivator: Explain to her that if you need to pick up the toys, she will not be allowed to go outside for the rest of the afternoon, and she will lose access to all electronics for the remainder of the afternoon. (The length of time you use to deny privileges can vary, but it should be relatively short – hours or the rest of the day – not days, and certainly not weeks.)

Your child may look at you with a "who cares" expression, and you may think it's not working. But remember, the important thing is that you established a rule, stuck to the rule, and applied consequences accordingly. Following through and doing what you said you would do will, over time, go a long way in establishing your position of authority. Also, if history is any guide, your child will likely only test your limits a few times before figuring out that picking up the toys is a small price to pay in exchange for access to fun activities.

Being Selective with Your Praise

For most of us, it's easier to focus on negative behaviors than positive ones. We tend not to gossip about what people do well. In our lives, we're quick to notice the annoying habits of spouses, co-workers, and whoever happens to be driving in front of us. The same, unfortunately, is true when it comes to our children. The bad always seems to get our attention while the good is taken for granted.

Children love attention, and your toddler is no different. He will take as much as he can get. Just as a sports fan can't watch enough football or baseball, or a bookworm can't read enough books, some children can't get enough attention. Your child's need for attention is actually a good thing and can help you become even more effective as a parent. In fact, you should make an effort to positively interact with your child three times as often as you provide a negative comment or consequence. Many parents tell me they are more likely to have three negative interactions for every positive interaction with their child. That ratio needs to be reversed.

The three-to-one ratio is not some random number pulled out of a hat. Research has well documented that this ratio (or higher) of positive-to-negative interactions significantly improves relationships between parents and children and also between spouses. When the ratio is too low or negative (more negative interactions than positive), the relationship between child and parent, or between spouses, becomes more strained and problems are more likely to occur. When one thinks about this, it seems to make sense. Think of a family member, friend, or co-worker who constantly complains or whines about something or someone. We all know someone like this. When you see him or take his calls, you wonder what he's going to complain about today. You probably don't listen very carefully or attentively, and the complaints probably go in one ear and out the other. On the other hand, think of a family member or colleague who rarely has a negative thing to say and, for the most part, is upbeat and positive. If she comes to you with a complaint or negative comment, you probably pay close attention and look for a way to offer support. In short, you respond differently to the constant complainer than you do to miss happy-go-lucky. Your history has shaped your behavior and the degree to which you respond to that person's requests.

Now think about the types of interactions you have with your child. If you're frequently negative (always correcting, complaining, and criticizing), should you be surprised when your child tunes you out? She thinks she's heard it before, and it's the same old tune. So when you do have important feedback to give, she pays little attention. But if you can turn that around, so you have three positive interactions for every negative one, your child will be less likely to ignore you. Will she occasionally tune you out? Maybe. But the contrast between the more frequent positive and the less frequent negative interactions will stand out, making it much more likely she will listen. It also will make your child appreciate and enjoy the next positive interaction with you.

If the goal is to have three positive interactions for every negative one, how do you get there? Use selective praise. This technique is an easy way to influence your toddler's behavior while increasing your positive-to-negative interactions. With selective praise, you shower attention on the good by following these steps:

> **Step One:** Choose a behavior you would like to increase in your child (completing a task without whining, using good table manners, covering the mouth when coughing or sneezing, or using a quiet voice).

Step Two: Use forms of attention or praise that are meaningful to your child. This might include smiling, nodding, gentle touching, giving a thumbs up, hugging, or using verbal praise when your child is engaged in the positive behavior you want to see. If you're having a hard time finding an opportunity to praise a specific positive behavior (because it hasn't happened yet), you can offer positive attention when the negative behavior is absent. For example, when your child stops crying and is calm, or when he sits quietly instead of stomping his feet.

Step Three: When offering verbal praise, be specific. Make sure you associate your praise with the specific behavior you want to reinforce. For example, rather than saying "Nice job of listening," say "Nice job of putting the blocks in the container." This will help your child understand what behavior earned your positive attention.

Step Four: When mild forms of negative, attention-seeking behaviors happen, find ways to ignore them. You might turn away from your child or walk away. When you're in a situation where you cannot physically walk away or leave, try turning your head or closing your eyes.

Step Five: Continue to selectively praise the behavior you're addressing, while ignoring other neutral or negative behaviors, until your child begins to seek attention using a more appropriate behavior.

Step Six (if necessary): If your child engages in a fairly significant negative behavior at any time, especially one that you cannot ignore or that would be wrong to ignore (biting, using profanity, hurting a sibling, or destroying property), use a consequence, such as time-out or loss of a privilege.

Here is how selective praise might look and sound:

Devin was having a bad morning. It was time to head to preschool, and his parents told him to get dressed and eat breakfast. He whined while getting dressed. He didn't like his shirt. At breakfast, he whined about the food. His cereal was too soggy. When his father told him to get in the van, he whined about having to sit in back. Each time Devin whined, his parents reacted in different ways. Sometimes they tried to fix things for him, other times they ignored him. Occasionally they became frustrated and yelled at him to "STOP!" Nothing seemed to work. Devin's parents decided they needed to have a plan that focused more on the positive. They chose to use selective praise to acknowledge Devin's appropriate language and behavior during mealtime (Step One). They agreed they would praise Devin for his appropriate words and behaviors and ignore his whining. Before lunch, they put their plan into action. Devin's dad asked him to wash his hands before eating. Devin said, "Okay, Dad" and promptly washed his hands. Dad offered quick praise, "Devin, nice job of washing your hands. I like it when you listen the first time I ask."

Devin's parents continued to smile, and they praised Devin when he helped set the table (Steps Two and Three). When Mom asked Devin to pass the bowl of peas, he complained, "Why do I have to do it? Dad's closer." Mom ignored him and repeated her request

The Saturday Box

Getting children to pick up their toys is a problem every parent experiences. Guided listening and Grandma's Rule are preferable techniques to promote all types of demands, including picking up toys. However, sometimes an additional consequence is needed. If putting toys away properly is an issue in your home, try using a "Saturday Box." The Saturday Box technique works like this:

Specifically ask your child to pick up the toys that need to be put away, and give him a set time to do it. If the toys are not put away in the time you specified, put the toys in the Saturday Box. (Helpful hint: Use a clear container so your child can still see the toys but not have access to them. This serves as a reminder of what he's missing and helps avoid the "out of sight, out of mind" phenomenon that can happen with children who have lots of toys to choose from.) Toys in the Saturday Box cannot be removed or played with until Saturday, regardless if they were put in the box on a Friday or a Sunday.

(Step Four). Devin grabbed the bowl and then complained how heavy it was to lift. His mother ignored his whining (Step Four), took the bowl of peas from him, served herself, and set the bowl down. She then started a conversation with her husband. Devin looked at his mother somewhat surprised, as if he expected a reprimand from her because he complained or, at the very least, a thank you for handing her the peas. He received neither. Throughout the meal Devin's parents used praise, smiles, and warm eye contact to reinforce his appropriate table manners and polite language. They turned away from him or ignored him when he complained, whined, or was negative (Step Five). If Devin didn't know better, he would have thought they were doing this intentionally!

Mom and Dad noticed that Devin's whining and negative language seemed to increase during the first few meals they tried selective praise. However, as time went on, meals became much more enjoyable, and Devin's table manners and behavior improved significantly. Devin's parents also discovered they could use selective praise to shape other annoying behaviors, including his habit of arguing when playing board games and interrupting them when they watch movies.

When using selective praise, be sincere in your interactions and use a variety of verbal statements ("Nice job asking!") and nonverbal gestures (smile) to communicate your appreciation. When your child falls back into negative habits, such as whining, ignore the behavior or tell your child you can't understand him when he uses that voice. If his whining persists, send him away with the admonition that he needs to come back later and ask again using his normal voice. Try to keep your interaction as brief as possible. Too much attention given to negative behaviors may inadvertently encourage more of those behaviors, especially with a child who craves any form of attention. Your child needs to learn that he will get **nothing** from you as long as his whining continues. If he returns and uses a pleasant or natural voice, acknowledge the appropriate tone and then answer his question or give him what he asks. Repeat this strategy until the whining disappears. If possible, try to get other adults (grandparents, aunts and uncles, teachers, caretakers) and siblings to use the same approach. If the whining receives some "payoff" from others, it will take longer to extinguish.

Taking a Time-out

Another technique you can use to improve your child's listening skills is time-out (see Chapter 10 for a more complete discussion of time-out). When possible, however, you should first start with one of the techniques previously described (selective praise, guided listening, or Grandma's Rule) and modify the way you communicate with your child. A potential problem with time-out is that it may not always be a negative consequence. For example, if you have a job or task to complete but consider it unpleasant (cleaning out the garage, washing windows, or filling out tax forms), you will probably look for any excuse to do something else, including sitting quietly by yourself! It's the same for your child. There may be times when he would rather sit alone than complete a particular task. Thus, if he refuses to do a particular task and you send him to time-out, you might unintentionally reward his noncompliant behavior. That being said, there are certainly times when time-out should be used as a consequence for noncompliant behavior or in response to misbehaviors associated with noncompliance. If your child becomes aggressive (hits, kicks, or bites), destructive (throws or breaks things), or is openly defiant (says "NO!" and runs away), use time-out. There also are certain behaviors or situations where the other techniques are either not useful or are not effective. In those cases, the use of time-out can be helpful. Instead of time-out being your first and only response to a child's failure to follow an instruction or listen to a request, approach the situation more methodically. Here is an example:

1. **Make a direct demand:** "Cheyenne, please put your shoes in your room."
2. **Offer praise for compliance:** "Thank you, Cheyenne."
3. If Cheyenne does not comply with your request, **use guided listening or Grandma's Rule**. If those techniques cannot be used or are unsuccessful, or if your child is openly defiant ("No, and you can't make me!"), then use time-out as a consequence.
4. **Tell your child the specific behavior she did not do, and then put her in time-out:** "Cheyenne, I'm

sorry you didn't put your shoes in your room like I asked you. Time-out."

5. **Place Cheyenne in time-out.**
6. **Repeat your request after time-out is over.** If Cheyenne completes the task, offer quick praise ("Thank you!"). If she refuses to do what you asked, return her to time-out. Continue this process until the task is completed.

Again, time-out has a place in managing noncompliant behavior, but it's one of several options that can be used to bring about a change in behavior. Sometimes, time-out might go on far longer than you would like, especially with a stubborn and strong-willed child who has nothing but time on her hands. However, if you can continue with time-out, followed by repeating your request until the task is done, it can be quite effective in motivating behavioral change.

What a Chore

Laura's mom grumbled to herself as she made her daughter's bed – again. Laura will start kindergarten soon, and her mom is worried about her lack of responsibility. During the past year, Mom gave Laura a number of simple chores to do. Sometimes the chores got done. Sometimes not. The inconsistency drove Mom crazy. Out of frustration, she tried offering Laura an allowance as motivation. It didn't help. A chore chart with colorful stickers stuck on the refrigerator was the next trick. That didn't help much either. How is Laura ever going to survive in school, her Mom wondered. If she can't complete chores, what about homework? Is Laura going to be this irresponsible as an adult?

Many parents often wonder at what age their children should be able to do chores and do them consistently. Such questions often come up around the time children head to preschool and kindergarten, where expectations and responsibilities increase. But just because children are old enough to start school doesn't necessarily mean they are mature enough to complete their chores or do them correctly. While it's true most kindergarten-aged children are able to do one or two simple tasks on a regular basis, it's their developmental skills that usually determine their success. Ideally, "shaping" children's behavior and encouraging responsibility begins at an early age. Teaching children to be good listeners and follow instructions when they are two and three will set them up to be more responsible and independent when they are four and five. To help your child enjoy more success when it comes to finishing tasks and doing chores, avoid some of these common missteps:

You overestimate your child's skill level.

This may seem obvious, but it's important to make sure your child is physically and developmentally capable of completing any chore you assign. Is he tall enough to place silverware on the table? Does she have the motor skills needed to pick up small toys? Does he know how to measure the right amount of food for the fish tank? Don't assume your child has the skills or knowledge necessary to complete a particular task simply based on age. When you're unsure or when a task is new, model and teach the task a few times before asking or expecting the job to get done independently and correctly.

You overestimate your child's attention span.

How long will your child be able to focus on any given task? Attention spans vary, regardless of one's age. Your child's willingness to watch a television show, sit in front of a computer screen, or play videos is not an accurate measure of attention span. Most children can pay attention to highly stimulating images for long periods of time. The question you have to consider is how long can your child sustain her attention when performing tasks she considers boring or no fun? To get a sense of your child's natural attention span, watch her do everyday or routine tasks. If she's easily distracted and the chores go unfinished, then lengthy and complicated tasks will have to wait. Instead, start with simple, shorter tasks. This will help build her confidence and independence while keeping you from getting frustrated or disappointed because you had unrealistic expectations.

You overestimate your child's reading ability.

There is obviously no point in writing down the chores your child needs to complete if he cannot read. Very few two- to six-year-olds are able to read, or read well enough, to understand a written request or chore chart. However, children at this age should be able to understand symbols and pictures that depict chores. If you have access to a digital camera, take pictures of your child performing a chore as well as a favorite or preferred activity. Take a snapshot as your toddler performs each step of a task, and then show those images to your child and provide more specific instructions when necessary. If using a camera is not an option, try cutting pictures out of magazines that depict a chore or show someone doing a similar task. Paste the magazine picture or your digital photo on the chore chart to help your child understand what task needs to be done and when. The photo of the preferred activity (placed next to the picture of the task) will provide a reminder of the reward that awaits when the chore is complete.

In addition to being mindful of exaggerated expectations, there are a number of proactive and practical steps you can take to encourage your child to stay focused and finish daily and weekly chores. One includes developing a chore chart you can use daily and eventually weekly.

The Chore Chart

Start with one chore. If your child is four to six years old, she is probably capable of completing more chores than this. However, you want to set your child up for success so start small. Pick a chore that your child understands and can physically complete. Begin by taking the time to perform the chore for your child while she watches. You may need to do the chore two or three times so she learns and remembers how to do the task. Then ask your child to help you do the task, but allow her to take the lead. Offer praise and helpful support as you work together. Keep any criticisms to a minimum. After you do the chore together, ask her to do it by herself while you watch. Praise her effort and offer suggestions when she struggles, but let her finish the task on her own.

Because you're starting with just one chore, you can use a simple daily chore chart. It should include a description or picture of the chore, the time of day it needs to be done, and a positive consequence or reward that will come once the chore is completed. Again, you may have to use pictures or images to represent the chore if your child is unable to read words. For example, you might use a picture of your child making his bed. To the right of this picture, have an arrow point-

ing to an image of him doing a fun activity (the positive consequence or reward for making his bed), such as playing outside.

To maximize the usefulness of a chore chart, you should focus on having your child master a single chore (which may take up to a month) before adding any additional tasks. When your child successfully completes a chore for that length of time and gets into a routine, add a second chore. However, avoid adding too many tasks (more than three) on any given day, and keep the tasks simple enough that your toddler can complete them within a matter of minutes. Again, you can use pictures or symbols to illustrate the chore and when it needs to be done. For example, you might design a chore chart that depicts one chore that needs to be completed in the morning and one in the evening. On the top half of the chart, put an image of the sun (indicating morning) with an arrow pointing from the sun to a picture of a chore or morning task (your child making his bed). Have a second arrow pointing from the chore to a fun activity or reward (picture of a favorite snack). On the bottom half of the chart, put an image of the moon (indicating nighttime) with an arrow pointing to a task (brushing teeth) that needs to be done in the evening. Have a second arrow pointing from the task to a reward, such as a picture of you reading bedtime stories.

When your child successfully demonstrates that she can routinely complete two or three basic daily chores, you can introduce a weekly chore chart (best suited for children who are school aged). This chart should highlight tasks that do not need to be done daily but rather once a week or only on weekends (organizing the toy room or emptying the bathroom wastebasket, for example). Again, structure the weekly chore chart like the daily chart, using pictures and arrows. As your child matures and learns to read better, you can transition from pictures and symbols to words.

Some children benefit from seeing their progress. It makes them feel better about themselves and keeps them motivated. Affixing stickers or other trinkets to the chore chart when tasks are completed correctly is a form of praise and can help reinforce your child's efforts. The more stickers your child sees on the chart, the more visual reminders he has of his successes. Stickers are an easy and creative way to publicly recognize and reinforce your child, especially if he likes seeing the stickers. However, not all children value stickers. If your child happens to be one of them, then forego the stickers. Also, be aware that children can lose interest in stickers, sometimes after only a few days or weeks. If your child loses interest, discontinue the stickers. But don't stop reinforcing the expectation that the chores must be completed before any positive consequence or reward is earned. Once these chores become a habit, the chore chart can and should be faded out. Its purpose is simply to turn chores into routines and is not meant to be used indefinitely.

The Chore Reward Jar

A chore reward jar is another motivational technique that can give you more flexibility in rewarding and reinforcing your child's efforts to finish tasks. Ideally, the jar works best with school-aged children (five- and six-year-olds) who are capable of delaying gratification for longer periods of time. Creating a reward jar is fairly easy and quite effective at making children pay closer attention to their chores. To create a chore jar for your child, follow these three steps:

1. Talk to your child about the types of rewards (small, medium, and large) she would like to earn for completing chores and tasks. Examples of rewards you

might use include a special snack (small), renting a video (medium), and having a friend stay overnight (large).

2. Select a glass or clear plastic jar and stick several pieces of masking tape to the jar at different points from top to bottom. On each piece of tape, write the name or paste a picture of a reward that you discussed with your child. The rewards should go from smallest to largest in ascending order (small rewards close to the base; medium rewards in the middle; large rewards near the top).
3. After your child successfully completes a chore, place a marble, poker chip, cotton ball, or other token in the jar. When she completes enough chores that the tokens inside reach the height where you wrote the name or pasted the picture of a reward on the outside of the jar, give her that reward. Do this until the jar is completely filled and the highest reward is earned. When the jar is full of tokens, you can start over again using the same rewards or choose new ones.

Just as your child can lose interest in the stickers you put on the chore chart, he also can lose interest in a reward jar. This typically happens when it takes too long to reach a reward. If it takes longer than one week for your child to earn a reward, consider using a smaller jar, larger tokens, or moving the reward lines closer together.

Additional Chore Considerations

Perfection is not the goal.

It's unlikely your child will complete a chore **perfectly** the first time, or possibly ever. That's okay. The goal should be having the task completed to the best of his ability, whatever that may be. What you want to see from your child is effort and perseverance. When you see that, praise him. When you don't see much of an effort, or your child gives up, provide more instruction, offer encouragement, or use a more meaningful consequence.

Misery loves company.

Children are less likely to complain and whine about doing chores if they can do them with others. Certain chores are easily performed by several people. Many hands make light work! If your toddler has older siblings, have everyone participate in the chore. For example, have your children clean their rooms and pick up toys at the same time or have them work together to set the table or clear the dishes. When everyone has a job to do, no one can use the excuse of being treated unfairly as a reason for not doing the work. Be sure to clarify what specific job or task each child has to do so you avoid conflicts.

Consistency is key.

If you don't expect your child to complete a chore when it should be done, whether it's a daily or weekly task, then your child will assume the chore is not important to you. The chore may not be all that meaningful, but your child doesn't need to know that. The purpose of assigning chores is to instill responsibility, develop a work ethic, and foster a sense of accomplishment. To avoid sending contradictory messages, stick to the chore schedule and make sure your child finishes tasks on time. Eventually, the chores should become routine so that you only need to offer a quick verbal reminder to your child. Always remember that the assigned chores are your child's responsibility, not yours. Make sure your child understands there are consequences (good or bad) for finishing and not finishing chores.

Final Thoughts

I have covered a lot of ground in this chapter, as the concepts and behavioral issues associated with listening and compliance are so intertwined. When it comes to helping your child be a good listener and follow instructions, the keys are communication and consistency. How you communicate to your child will affect how well he listens and, ultimately, follows your directions. The more consistent, or predictable, your communication signals are, the more predictable your child's behavior. You need to be as predictable and consistent as a traffic light.

When you communicate a request or an instruction, remember to engage your child. Make eye contact and avoid distractions. Keep your instructions short and specific. Use concrete words your child understands. Tell him what to do, not just what he can't do. Keep it simple by giving one instruction at a time. When your child does what you ask or you catch him being good, praise his behavior. Use positive and negative consequences to reinforce and motivate behavioral change. Use guided listening, Grandma's Rule, selective praise, and time-out to shape your child's behavior. Most importantly, be a teacher and role model. Be willing to use and demonstrate the same skills and behaviors you want to see from your child.

What Every Parent Needs to Know About "No"

Have you ever said "No" to your child? Of course you have. There is not a parent alive who hasn't said the word "No". The use of "No" certainly has its place, but only if it's used effectively. The problem is, "No" is just a word. Likewise, a tornado siren is just a sound, and a traffic signal is just a light, that is, until they are paired or associated with something that is meaningful to us. We take action when we see flashing lights on a police car, see a traffic light turn red, or hear a tornado siren because we know that they are associated with important, meaningful events. If your child is going to respond to you when you say "No," then he needs to know that there will be some meaningful action associated with it. If you're going to use the word "No," and I highly recommend that you do, then you might as well make it as effective as possible. Saying "No" is important for a lot of different reasons, some of which include managing minor behaviors, but others involve your child's safety (reaching for a dangerous item, going near a busy street). Here are a few things to consider when helping your child learn the meaning of "No."

"No" is not a suggestion.

When you say "No," it means "Stop." Providing immediate consequences, consistently and frequently, will help your child learn this.

Volume is not the solution.

If you say "No" and your child ignores you, repeating it multiple times and then saying it as loud as you possibly can is not going to help your child understand the meaning of "No." It will just result in her putting her hands over her ears or becoming very good at tuning you out - even when you're yelling at 5,000 decibels. Just as a stoplight does not get brighter when it turns red, there is no need to make your "No" louder. Remember – act, don't yak.

Action is the key.

After you have issued one "No" – that's right, one "no" – your child needs to receive feedback from you. That is, if he stopped and complied with you saying "No" then praise him for doing so. Don't take it for granted that your child has some inborn ability to respond to "No"; he doesn't. On the other hand, if your child ignores you after you have issued one "No," respond in the most appropriate manner necessary to help your child understand that "No" is not a suggestion, it is a demand. On some occasions, it may be that you simply need to physically redirect your child to another activity. In other situations you may need to physically prevent your child from doing something that is dangerous, or, if she is engaging in some inappropriate behavior, a timeout may be required. Saying "No" multiple times, with no meaningful consequence, dilutes the value of "no," by teaching your child that it's a demand that can be ignored. This, in turn, reduces your authority as a parent, and increases the likelihood that your child will learn to ignore future requests. On the other hand, providing immediate and meaningful consequences after you have issued a "No", will help your children value and find meaning in your command, and will serve as a future cue that they need to pay attention when they hear "No."

"No" is a part of life for all of us, especially when it comes to raising children. "No" can either be your friend or foe. Say it once and follow it with praise or action and it will be your friend. Say it over and over, perhaps at a high decibel, with little or no meaningful action on your part, and it will be your foe.

chapter 3

Don't Have a Fit: It's Just a Tantrum

To celebrate Justin's fourth birthday, his mom, Portia, ordered cupcakes from a local store to take to Justin's preschool. As she drove to the store, Portia reminded her son of the rules, "Remember, stay by my side and keep your hands to yourself."

Portia picked up the cupcakes at the bakery counter and headed to the checkout lane with Justin by her side. As they walked, Justin caught a glimpse of the toy aisle. He bolted toward the toys and immediately grabbed a red truck. Mom followed shortly and took the toy from his hands, placed it back on the shelf, and said, "No. It's time to go to preschool."

Justin dropped to the floor and screamed at the top of his lungs. When Mom reached to pull him up, he thrashed around and kicked at her. When Portia finally got him upright, he let his legs go limp and flopped to the floor. By this time, other shoppers, including the cashier, were watching. Embarrassed, Portia picked her son off the floor, put him in the grocery cart, and swiftly moved to the checkout line. Justin continued to scream and cry at ear-shattering decibels. Because it was early morning, the store only had one cashier on duty and, of course, three customers were already in line. As Portia waited, what thought was most likely running through her mind?

A. "Everyone please stop looking at me."
B. "I should just forget these stupid cupcakes and get out of here."
C. "I came here to get cupcakes, and I'm not leaving until I've paid for them."
D. "I should just let him have the truck so he will be quiet."
E. "I don't care if it's his birthday. We're going out to the car and having time-out."
F. Most of the above.

If you have been in this situation in the past, these thoughts are probably familiar to you. Tantrums are difficult to manage at home, let alone in public. Regardless, it's important to learn how to manage them wherever they occur. In this chapter, I will discuss some of the causes for tantrums and, more importantly, what to do about them.

What Causes Tantrums?

If you have ever been confused or frustrated trying to program an electronic gadget or gizmo, then you probably know how your toddler feels on a daily basis. For toddlers, there are many circumstances, situations, and emotions that lead to frustration and eventually to tantrums. Some parents actually refer to their toddlers' tantrums as "Old Faithful" because they occur so regularly. Tantrums are an inevitable part of toddler life.

Tantrums can involve behaviors that range from whimpering, whining, crying, and screaming to hitting, kicking, stomping, pounding, and holding one's breath. These meltdowns can happen most anywhere – in the home, at the mall, in a church, or in the car. Let's face it, there is no such thing as a "good" place to have a tantrum, unless you are three or four years old. Tantrums occur for a variety of reasons and usually at the most inopportune times. Often, they erupt out of feelings of frustration, but tantrums also can be caused by a lack of communication skills, a desire to avoid certain tasks, or a desire to gain access to something, such as a toy or a parent's attention. Let's take a closer look at some of the causes that lead to toddler tantrums:

Frustration

Frustration has many flavors. Young children, especially toddlers, are developing very rapidly. As they develop a greater sense of independence and an ability to control their environments, they usually want to take on more than they can handle. However, their emotions, along with their communication, intellectual, and social skills, are all developing rapidly but not at the same pace. Their language and communication skills are typically not developing fast enough to match their curiosity and all that comes with it. Because toddlers typically understand more than they can express, their inability to communicate their wants and needs becomes a frustrating experience. Also, their still-developing gross and fine motor skills lead to more frustration when trying to open containers, play with toys, or operate electronics. Fatigue also influences a toddler's frustration level. Because toddlers and young children have such a limited range of coping strategies (or tools) available to them, they tend to vent their frustration with the biggest tool in their box – the tantrum.

Poor Communication

Most two-year-olds have a vocabulary of around two hundred to three hundred words. By the time they are three, their vocabulary expands to around a thousand words and continues to expand significantly as they age. In addition to a limited vocabulary, most toddlers have difficulty clearly articulating what they want to say. Most parents can understand about fifty percent of what their toddler says. Those who do not live with the child understand even less. When your child has difficulty telling you what he or she wants because of a limited vocabulary, poor articulation, or both, the stage is set for a tantrum.

Most adults are able to communicate with one another fairly effectively. However, you probably can think of situations where you were not able to clearly communicate your ideas, and people did not understand what you were trying to say. Perhaps you have experienced this while talking to a customer service representative over the phone or when visiting a foreign country. Fortunately, most of us can reason our way through these situations and understand that these frustrating experiences are few and far between. For most toddlers, however, poor communication is a daily – often multiple times per day – experience. Fortunately, as language skills improve, tantrums tend to decrease. Those head-spinning, Godzilla-like meltdowns will come to an end at some point, sooner or later.

Limited Skill Sets

If you have ever struggled with an "easy to assemble" product, a well-sealed package, or a remote control to your DVD player, you have some sense of the frustration toddlers experience when trying to work with something beyond their skill level. You often see this when toddlers play with toys that are complex or too difficult for them to manipulate. In your home, you probably have toys appropriate for children of all ages. Children receive toys as gifts from relatives and friends or have access to toys that belong to older siblings. Because of their natural curiosity, toddlers are certainly going to attempt to play with these toys, which may be too difficult to or too sophisticated for them to operate. This, along with their limited skills, makes playing with these toys a challenge. This can lead to frustration and a potential tantrum. By no means, however, is this limited to toys.

Toddlers are naturally curious about what is behind closed doors, in dresser drawers, on shelves, and under beds. As they explore their world, they will find themselves in situations they shouldn't be in, including attempting to manipulate objects not designed for them. Emptying tubes of toothpaste and seeing how far a roll of toilet paper will stretch throughout the house are just the start. Being aware of the toys that are inappropriate for your toddler and making a note of problem spots around the house can help reduce the number of potential tantrums.

Mismatched Playmates (Birds of a Feather Play Together)

Most toddlers engage in "parallel play," which means they play cooperatively with others side by side. As they grow older, however, they do more interactive play, meaning they learn to share, take turns, and engage with others. It's important to know whether your child has social and play skills that are comparable to those of other children at daycare, in the neighborhood, or at home. Children who are paired with playmates who have play skills that are considerably higher or considerably lower may be at risk for increased frustration. For example, Todd has more advanced play skills than Mitch. Todd expects Mitch to share and take turns while playing, but Mitch has not developed those skills. So when Todd takes a prized toy away from him because it's "his turn," Mitch throws a tantrum.

As the old saying goes "birds of a feather flock together" certainly applies to children and their socialization. The more you can match children based on their play and social skills, the less opportunity there will be for mismatches and, hopefully, fewer tantrums.

Emotional and Physical Health

Most of us are aware that we tend to be much less patient and more easily frustrated when we are tired, sick, or hungry. Hopefully, for you, this is the exception and not the rule. With young children, fatigue, hunger, and periodic illness are more the rule than the exception. Having adequate sleep is especially important for toddlers. There is a reason that most children under the age of five take a nap. (Maybe we all could use one.) Just as any parent can tell you, when a child becomes overly tired, the probability for tantrums and irritability increases dramatically. This also is true when they are hungry or not feeling well. Being aware of these high-risk circumstances can make managing your child's behavior somewhat easier because you can reduce the demands you place on children when they are fatigued, hungry, or ill.

Unwanted Requests

In the world of most toddlers and preschoolers, any activity (It's time to go to the store!) or demand (It's time to pick up your toys!) that interrupts their fun is likely to be met with resistance. If that resistance (tantrum) allows a child to continue her fun and avoid the interruption, one can assume she will pull that tool (the tantrum) out of her bag of tricks (responses) in the future.

Children quickly learn that their tantrums can, at times, allow them to avoid certain activities. This is especially true for preschoolers. As children get older and start to better associate how their behavior has certain outcomes, they are more likely to take advantage of it. Most children do not intentionally plan on having a tantrum as a means of avoiding some task. Rather, they have simply associated their tantrums with avoiding certain tasks and activities they don't enjoy.

Children vary in terms of their willingness to complete requests in which they are asked to "do" something versus when they are asked not to do something ("don't"). Making note of whether or not your child seems more likely to tantrum with a "do" or "don't" request may provide valuable insight as you look for triggers that set off tantrums.

Need for Attention

As we get older, our options for gaining the attention of others become fairly broad. For some, it can involve wearing a new outfit. For others, it might mean a new sports car or maybe a new hairstyle. We can lose weight, volunteer our time to a charity, and improve our attitude, too. The options for young children, however, are limited. That's why tantrums prove to be popular.

Many children have learned to associate their tantrums with either positive or negative attention from parents. Moms and dads respond to their children's tantrums in a variety of ways, such as picking them up, yelling at them, feeding them, rocking them, or trying to distract them. If your child learns to associate your response with something pleasurable, it can motivate him to have or prolong a tantrum in the hopes it will result in something enjoyable. But how do you know if your child is having a tantrum simply for attention or because he wants something? You can find out by walking away when he has one. If he follows you, it's highly likely he hopes to gain something positive from his behavior. Maybe he wants something to eat, to play a game, or to go outside and play. The bottom line is that he wants something and is trying to convince you to give it to him. Besides, what could be more convincing to you than a tantrum? It's the outcome (Did I get what I wanted or not?) that is associated with the tantrum that determines how long and how intensely it continues, now and in the future.

These are some of the most common variables or causes that lead to tantrums. Understanding them can help you become more aware of both the internal (physical and emotional) and external (communicating, getting attention, and avoiding activities or demands) factors that contribute to your child's behavior. Within each of those causes, there are likely to be specific triggers that increase the likelihood of tantrums.

Disabling the Triggers

All of us experience triggers that lead to frustration. For example, driving in heavy traffic may make you frustrated. That does not mean you will be frustrated every time you hit the road. However, specific triggers, such as someone cutting you off or weaving in and out of lanes, can increase the chances you will become frustrated in heavy traffic situations. Understanding the triggers for your child's tantrums can help you identify the specific triggers that increase the odds your child will have a tantrum. For example, you might know your child is much more likely to get upset when she is asked to do something when she's hungry or tired than when she is well fed and rested. Or, you might know that asking your child to stop playing with a favorite toy will almost always cause a tantrum. Combining what you know about the triggers and causes of your child's tantrums allows you to, at times, avoid or prevent some of those tantrums. At other times, it will help prepare you to manage the tantrum effectively, knowing that a tantrum is likely coming, especially in situations where it may be unavoidable. For example, you may know that one cause of your child's tantrums is fatigue. The trigger might be asking him to pick up toys. A tantrum is much more likely to occur if he feels more fatigued than rested. Thus, you have learned not to ask your child to pick up toys before naptime or bedtime.

One strategy that parents find helpful is to keep a record or journal of "tantrum times." This is fairly simple to do (see page 74) and allows you to learn a little bit more about the circumstances surrounding tantrums. In your journal, you can list the triggers and/or causes that are associated with your child's tantrums. Examples might include being tired, feeling hungry, feeling ill, hearing a "do" request ("Please put your socks on."), hearing a "don't" request ("Don't turn on the television."), or wanting attention. You also can describe your response to the tantrum and how your child reacted to you. Over time, you will be able to identify the causes and triggers that were most commonly associated with

Tantrum Journal

Date & Time	Trigger/Cause (Circle all that apply)	Describe Trigger	Child's behavior	My Response	Outcome
7:35 PM Monday Aug. 4	"Do" Request "Don't" Request Attention Ill Tired Hungry Other__________	*Bedtime.* *Jade was tired. I asked her to brush her teeth.*	*She cried, ran from the bathroom, and pounded fists and feet on floor.*	*I placed her in time-out.*	*Jade finished time-out and brushed her teeth.*
3 PM Thursday Aug. 7	"Do" Request "Don't" Request Attention Ill Tired Hungry Other__________	*I took the toy from Jade after she repeatedly banged it on table.*	*Jade followed me around the house screaming and crying.*	*I ignored her.*	*She eventually stopped and started playing with another toy.* *I then praised her for playing nicely.*

your child's tantrums. You also will be able to review how you reacted to your child's tantrum and how your child responded to your actions. Keeping this type of information for a brief period of time can increase your awareness, improve your ability to predict your child's tantrums, and ultimately manage them more effectively.

An Ounce of Prevention to Cure a Pound of Tantrum

Caeley definitely needs a nap. Her toys are all over the floor. The rule for Caeley is that all toys need to be picked up when she is done playing with them. Her mother is fighting off a head cold that she's had for a week. Caeley's mom prides herself on consistently enforcing the rules she has for her daughter. She looks at the toys on the floor and knows Caeley needs her nap. She debates whether to make Caeley pick up the toys now or after the nap. If you were in her situation, what would you do?

A. Put Caeley down for her nap.

B. Take a nap yourself after putting Caeley down.

C. Have Caeley pick up the toys after her nap.

D. Have Caeley pick the toys up now, before her nap, to reinforce the importance of following rules.

Any of the above are appropriate choices. However, "A," "B," and "C" probably make the most sense. By putting Caeley down for her nap, Mom understands how fatigue affects her daughter's behavior. Asking her to pick up toys when she is tired only increases the chances for a tantrum. It also reduces the probability that the toys will get picked up at all. Taking a nap while Caeley sleeps makes sense, too. Because Mom doesn't feel well, she is less likely to follow through on the demands or instructions she gives Caeley. Finally, having Caeley pick up her toys after the nap is the best of all worlds. She can have her nap, and Mom can get rest and still follow through with the rules. Although "D" is acceptable, it doesn't make as much sense in this situation because it most likely will cause a meltdown. Then, Mom will have more trouble getting Caeley down for her nap. Given how Mom is feeling, it increases the odds of her losing her cool and Caeley, too. In this case, an exception to the rule makes sense.

When managing tantrums, just as much time should be spent finding ways to prevent them as trying to manage them. There are many simple modifications you can make either to your daily routine or how you intervene with your child that can help both of you get through the day peacefully (relatively speaking).

The following techniques are designed to help you prevent or, at the very least, reduce the opportunities your child has to tantrum:

Know your child's triggers.

Being aware of the situations or times that put your child at higher risk for having tantrums can help you avoid many of them. Knowing that your child is most likely to tantrum before naptime, bedtime, or when you're on the phone can help you prepare for those situations. Maybe your experience shows that running errands with your toddler at the beginning of the day is better than at the end of the day. Or, your toddler is more likely to have a tantrum on long outings (more than two hours) than shorter ones. In addition, it's important to know your limits. Asking your child to follow an instruction or play a game when you are not in a position to participate emotionally or physically will only increase the likelihood that one or both of you will lose your cool.

Intervene early.

If your child gives you some initial warning signs that he is becoming frustrated or is about to throw a tantrum, step in and distract or redirect him. This can reduce the chances of a tantrum. You have probably learned which distractions work best, whether it's making a funny face, pointing at something going on outside, or reminding him of a favorite toy. As your child becomes more verbal and is able to communicate more effectively, reminding him to "use his words" and communicate his frustrations can certainly be helpful. In general, providing a distraction when you see smoke will often help you prevent a fire.

Catch them being good.

There is a tendency for parents to take positive behavior for granted. By providing a reasonable amount of attention to your child when she plays cooperatively, masters a difficult toy, or completes a task, you can motivate her to continue to do more of the same to get your approval. Also, it helps remove the need to throw a tantrum for attention (if she seeks attention through tantrums). Providing frequent praise and positive attention for accomplishments (finishing a puzzle, for example), activities (coloring quietly), and appropriate behavior (playing cooperatively with a sibling) also provides a nice contrast when negative consequences need to be applied.

Occasionally hand over the controls.

Giving your child control when appropriate and whenever possible can be very helpful. This is especially true when children get older and closer to school age. For good reason, young children have very little control over their lives. Parents typically tell them when to get up, what to wear, and when to eat, among other things. Giving control to children in certain situations allows them to have a sense of greater independence, and many children simply find having a choice in certain matters to be reinforcing. For example, you might ask your child, "Do you want to read books before your bath or after your bath?" The point isn't that you are asking him if he wants to read books or wants to take a bath. To the contrary, the fact that your child is going to take a bath is implied in the statement. The question is whether he wants to read books before or after the bath. There are a variety of other situations where you can provide similar types of control. Other examples include, "Would you like apple juice or orange juice with your breakfast?"; "Do you want to take your nap with your nightlight on or off?"; or "Do you want to pick up your toys by yourself or would you like me to help you?" Providing a choice in these types of situations as opposed to telling your child "You're having orange juice for breakfast" or "We'll read books after your bath," can lead to cooperation instead of chaos.

Use the "out of sight, out of mind" principle.

There are certain items or things in your home that are off limits to your child. It might be a particular food, toy, or kitchen utensil. You know if your child sees one of these items, she is going to want it, and putting it away or telling her "No" will lead to a tantrum. For items that are off limits, it's sometimes helpful to keep them out of sight and away from your child. It will simplify your life (and your toddler's), and you will have one less tantrum to manage. Controlling your child's access to these out-of-reach, off-limit items can prevent tantrums in a number of situations. Take, for example, toys that are too complicated or inappropriate for your child's particular age. A challenge many parents have is that children of different ages play with different types of toys, even if the toys are not age appropriate. Possible solutions include having different colored toy boxes for each child's toys or keeping each child's toys contained in a certain bedroom or area of the house. There will inevitably be times when an "off-limits" toy or item gets in your child's possession. However, doing your best to limit access to these "tantrum causing" items will certainly be worth your time.

One caveat to note: There are situations where you want your child to explore off-limit areas or items. For example, when your child is approaching an electrical outlet with a toy or attempting to crawl on a glass table, he will benefit from having you set limits ("No!"), followed by redirection and either praise for compliance or time-out for noncompliance. Ideally, you want your child to do this often enough until he gets the message that an area of the house, certain toys, or household items are off limits and not worth the bother. This is a safety issue, and you want your child to learn it well enough that he will avoid the area or object even when you're not there. This is different than removing an item that has no safety implications and is simply a trigger for an unnecessary tantrum.

Know when to say "No."

Many parents find that the first word that comes out of their mouths regardless of the situation with their toddler is "No." Asking yourself why the answer should be "No" before you actually say it can sometimes prevent many meltdowns. Pick your battles so that when you do say "No," your children know that you're prepared to back it up. This will help reinforce the fact that "No" doesn't mean "Maybe," and that a tantrum won't change your mind. Often, parents say "No" out of their own convenience, which is certainly understandable. However, the next time you say "No" to your child when she asks if she can pull the pots and pans out of the bottom drawer or get out the play dough, take a few seconds to ask yourself, "Why am I saying 'No'?" If you really don't care if she plays with the pans or the play dough, why say "No"? Unless you have a reason for saying "No," asking "Why not?" may result in fewer tantrums and more enjoyment for you and your child.

Communicate both verbally and nonverbally.

As mentioned previously, one primary cause of toddler tantrums is their developing language and communications skills. Toddlers' command and use of language varies widely. As their creative, inquisitive, and developing minds move at light speed, their language skills do not always keep pace. This disconnect, and the frustration that goes with it, leads to many tantrums. However, as toddlers evolve into preschoolers and as their language skills improve, the frequency and intensity of tantrums tends to decrease. From a preventive standpoint, think "action" plus "words." Teaching and modeling the words your child is learning, as well as using actions and other nonverbal ways to help your child communicate better, will help promote language skills and reduce the frequency of tantrums. This can involve repeating a word while pointing to the object (cup) or teaching a word that goes with a particular emotion (mad). This helps your child associate requests or words with particular tasks. Pointing to the toys and toy chest while asking your child to pick up the toys and put them in the chest provides verbal and nonverbal communication that will help your child understand your request better. This can be effective for preschoolers as well as toddlers, but it's a more effective strategy for children whose language skills are just emerging.

Provide a heads-up.

Some children do very well adapting to changes in their routine while others have a complete volcanic meltdown. If your child has difficulty switching gears, whether it's stopping a play activity to get dressed or turning off the television to run errands with you, providing as much warning ahead of time can be helpful. This might involve giving your child a warning that an activity needs to stop (saying, for example, "Time to start putting your crayons away. We will be going to Grandma's soon."), or reminding her that it's about time to get into the car. Also, being aware of where your child happens to be in a particular activity can go a long way toward eliminating tantrums. For example, if your child is coloring a picture and is nearly done, there is no point in asking her to stop at that moment when waiting a few seconds or even a couple of minutes will allow her to finish, making the transition easier. Similarly, if your child is a few minutes away from wrapping up a television show, waiting for the show to end or letting her know that you will leave once it's finished makes more sense than grabbing the remote and abruptly turning off the TV without warning.

Know* your *limits.

Just as it's important to know whether or not your child is fatigued, hungry, or ill, you need to be aware of your own mental and physical health. Parents who are rundown, hungry, or ill are much more likely to lose self-control. Losing your temper and yelling, especially about routine day-to-day events, not only affects you and your child emotionally, it also increases the odds you will join your child's tantrum. Being more self-aware may help you change your daily schedule or pick your battles more carefully when you're not feeling one hundred percent.

Keep your cool.

Although tantrums are a normal part of the toddler years, they can be frustrating and exhausting. Since you have already been through this phase in your own life, there is no reason to revert back to your childhood. In other words, maintain your cool to the best of your ability when your child throws a fit. This will help you and your child manage the situation more effectively. I understand this is much easier said than done – for everyone. However, losing control, yelling, screaming, and essentially having your own tantrum will do nothing to help manage your child's behavior. Developing ways to calm yourself, whether through deep-breathing exercises or distraction techniques (counting to ten or walking away), will help prepare you for the inevitable. Remaining calm also allows the focus to remain on your child's behavior, not yours.

Connecting Solutions to the Source

Sometimes prevention is not enough. The techniques I just described can help reduce the frequency of tantrums but are unlikely to eliminate all of them. Unfortunately, the cure for tantrums has yet to be discovered. When prevention is not possible, looking a little closer at what may be causing the tantrum can help direct you toward strategies or interventions that are more effective. This section highlights three of the more common causes of tantrums (frustration, attention, and avoidance), and helpful strategies you can use in those situations.

Frustration

We all experience frustration from time to time. I don't expect that to change anytime soon. However, all frustrations are not created equal. Just as certain situations cause us more frustration than others, the same is certainly true for toddlers and preschoolers. Thus, different types of frustration require different types of responses. For example, the frustration you experience in heavy traffic is different from the frustration you experience when you can't operate software on your computer. In the case of traffic, there is not much that can be done. You need to figure out how to manage your frustration on your own. In fact, having others in the car with you, or near you, probably makes matters worse. In the case of the computer program, you probably need someone to teach you how to run the program to reduce your frustration. Once you develop better skills, your frustration level will likely lower. Likewise, the kind of frustration we experience when we have difficulty communicating with someone, whether a spouse or coworker, is different than the frustration we experience when we struggle to open something or have too many groceries in our arms. In one case, finding more effective ways to communicate helps lower frustration. In the other, having some support or help is enough to manage the frustration.

Have you ever had an itch that you couldn't quite reach? Pretty frustrating, right? You can use the acronym ITCH to remember the various interventions available to you when your children are frustrated. ITCH stands for…

I - Ignore

T - Teach

C - Communicate

H - Help

Ignore.

For the majority of tantrums caused by frustration, especially with toddlers, ignoring is usually the best approach to take. These are situations where silence truly may be golden. A young child will often experience frustration for a variety of reasons and in situations where there is little you can do. There also are situations where nei-

Whining

Imagine a finely manicured hand with clear polish on the nails. Now imagine those nails running slowly down a chalkboard. Hear it? That's the same sound most parents hear when their children start to whine. Whining often accompanies or precedes tantrums, but not always. Children whine for all kinds of reasons, usually because they are upset about something or because whining in the past has gotten them something they wanted. They also are more likely to whine if they are sick or fatigued. Regardless, it's annoying and unnecessary, which your toddler has yet to learn. The good news is that you can manage it fairly easily and effectively. Here are a few tips:

- **Point out to your child when he is whining.** Sometimes your child may not be aware he's whining.
- **NEVER give your child what he wants when he whines.** This will only cause him to whine more.
- **The best way to respond to your child when he whines is to tell him you don't understand him.** You might say, for example, "I can't understand a word you're saying. You'll need to talk to me in a big boy [big girl] voice."
- **Silence is golden.** Ignoring the whining until you hear a tone of voice that is acceptable will send a message to your child that whining has little payoff.
- **Don't model whining.** Adults are just as capable of whining as toddlers. Do yourself and your toddler a favor by using appropriate behavior and language when you're frustrated.
- **Reward appropriate language.** When your toddler uses an appropriate tone of voice, especially when asking for something or voicing a complaint, acknowledge and praise him. You might say, for example, "Thank you for talking so clearly. It helps me understand what you want." This is especially true if the appropriate voice was used first. Either way, it's important your child understands that talking in an age-appropriate voice is recognized by you and has benefits.
- **Distract.** Sometimes a simple distraction is enough to get your child off the whining platform.
- **Time-out.** A good old-fashioned time-out is sometimes necessary when the whining persists and all other efforts have not done the trick.

ther you nor your child may know what caused the tantrum. You simply need to let his emotions run their course. Just as there is not much a passenger in your car can do to help you manage your frustration with traffic, there are times when there is little you can, or should, do when your child is having a fit. Trying to talk to your child or help him usually just makes the tantrum intensify. Allowing him time to unwind and then redirecting him to a different activity or offering some assistance is usually the best course to follow. Ignoring can involve anything from reading the paper to talking to another family member to simply pretending that the child flopping around like a gaffed fish in front of you is invisible. Going to another room and shutting the door behind you is another option. And if you're worried that going to another room will prevent you from keeping an eye on your child, trust me, you will know exactly where he is and what he is doing. Just listen!

Teach.

Tantrums triggered by frustrating toys or activities create an opportunity for you to teach. Whether it's a toddler trying to figure out how to operate a robotic toy or a preschooler learning how to ride a bike, frustration is going to be part of the experience. Most parents have watched their children become frustrated trying to write their name, put a block in a board, or color within the lines. In some cases, it's simply a matter of practice and persistence. Repetition is always a plus. However, as a parent, you can make sure your children have the skills necessary to do the task. If your child lacks the motor skills to tie his shoes, for example, put that activity on hold until he has the basic skills he needs to be successful. Also, it's important to provide plenty of modeling or demonstration. As your child makes progress, the teaching and encouragement should continue. If your child is frustrated because he doesn't have the knowledge or information he needs, explaining and demonstrating the task for him can be a learning experience for both of you. The payoff for you is that it's usually very rewarding. Most parents don't soon forget the look on their children's faces when they finally figure out how to tie their shoes or stay on a bike for more than a few seconds.

Communicate.

Toddlers' brains and bodies are developing and expanding at an astronomical rate. Their curiosity and interest in a variety of things far exceeds their ability to understand them and certainly exceeds their ability to communicate about them. Also, even if a child is able to form the words he needs to communicate to a parent, his ability to articulate his thoughts and the parent's ability to understand what he's saying often leaves much to be desired. This certainly is going to lead to frustration on the part of the child and the parent. In these situations, you can help by either repeating words for your child or demonstrating the words. For example, you can point to a food item on the table that your child is trying to say, or you can allow her to take you by the hand and show you what she is saying. In situations where others (relatives, caretakers, neighbors, or teachers) can't understand what your child is saying, you should bridge the communication gap. You, better than anyone outside the family, is in the best position to know what your child is saying. You can help grandparents and friends understand what your little one is saying by repeating phrases and words for them or by encouraging your child to show or demonstrate what she wants. Helping your child combine words with non-verbal actions (saying "Open" while pointing to the toy chest, for example) is one way to encourage better communication. Doing the same for your child's preschool teachers, coaches, and other caretakers will be helpful to them. Identifying different ways for your child to improve her communication will certainly help reduce frustration. The good news is that communication skills and verbal skills improve pretty quickly and dramatically for most children.

Help.

How often do you feel like there is not enough time to get everything done, including caring for your children, preparing meals, and paying bills? Some days you probably wish you had a nanny, cook, and butler. Young children sometimes experience similar types of frustration but for different reasons. It may be because they can't quite reach far enough to adequately make their beds, or they can't reach a cereal box on the shelf that is too high. In these situations, ignoring them certainly would not be appropriate. These children don't need to be taught anything – they know how to make the bed or prepare a bowl of cereal. Their communication also is fine. They simply need help. The problem, however, is not every child wants help. Most, in fact, want to do it themselves! The ideal time to help your child in these situations is at the very first sign of frustration. When your daughter is struggling, step in and ask, "Can I help you?" Hopefully she will say or nod "Yes" and realize that her frustration will disappear with some simple help. In many cases, however, a child says, "No, I can do it myself." By all means let her try. (There are benefits for a child who gets frustrated but then solves a challenge independently.) If your child's frustration increases, again offer to provide some assistance. If she continues to resist and her behavior eventually dissolves into a tantrum, ignore the behavior and walk away. For one thing, you don't want to reinforce the tantrum. You offered several times to help, and your child chose not to accept it. Secondly, stepping in and helping at that moment simply serves to reinforce her strong will and refusal to accept help. Once your child calms down completely, briefly review the situation with her. Say something such as, "I'm sorry it was so frustrating for you to make your bed. You didn't want my help when I asked earlier. Would you like me to help you now?" If your child says "No," leave it at that. However, remind her that you are available to help whenever she needs assistance. If she does accept your help, provide what little assistance is needed and reinforce the effort she put forth.

Frustration is simply a part of life for all of us. It's especially true for young children and their daily routines. From a parenting standpoint, identifying the sources of your child's frustration, if possible, can help you develop the best approach to helping him work through a normal part of development.

Attention

Toddlers and preschoolers learn to associate their behavior with all kinds of attention, both good and bad. In their world, sometimes any attention is better than none. So just because you are giving them a stern look, raising your voice, or providing a brief lecture, don't assume it will discourage tantrums. Some children engage in a number of behaviors, including tantrums, simply to gain some form of attention. If your child has learned that a tantrum will quickly gain your attention, regardless if it's positive or negative, you will need to vary how you interact with your child in those situations.

An important thing to do, especially if you feel your child has tantrums to gain some attention, is to look at how you "attend" or respond to your child in general. For example, out of every ten interactions you have with him, what percentage is positive and what percentage is negative? As a general rule, you should have three positive interactions for every negative one. This increases the likelihood that you are taking the time to attend to your child's positive behaviors and not taking the behaviors for granted. If you feel as though the majority of your interactions are negative, work on "catching your child being good" and look for opportunities to praise and positively interact with him. This by itself will decrease the need for your child to tantrum to gain your attention and also makes the negative reprimands and corrections more meaningful. Also, make sure your attention is meaningful. In other words, your child needs to associate your attention and praise with something that he has specifically said or done. One way to make your attention meaningful is to avoid generalizations. Meaningful praise is specific and genuine. For example, praising your child by saying, "Thank you for putting away your art supplies. That's very helpful" is much more meaningful than saying, "Thanks for being such a big boy."

So how do you know if your child throws tantrums to gain attention? One way is to look at how you respond to your child when she has a meltdown. If your tendency is to comfort and support her, she will naturally associate the tantrum with positive attention. However, even if your interactions are negative during tantrums, the tantrum could still be motivated by a desire for attention. Fortunately, most toddlers and preschoolers make it fairly easy for you to know if they are trying to gain your attention. Children who tantrum to gain attention typically look at parents to see what their reaction will be, reach their hands out asking for a hug or to be held, or follow parents as they walk away. While you may want to pick up your child or engage in a conversation during these times, doing so may only add fuel to the fire.

There are several steps you can take to effectively manage tantrums that are done for attention. First, children often don't think about what else they can do when they're emotionally upset. Redirect your child to some activity that he enjoys or is calming. If he responds to the redirection and calms himself, you can provide the attention your child wants. Second, the easiest and most appropriate thing to do is ignore the tantrum and walk away. If other adults or children are present, ask them to walk away, too. This will allow your child to work through the tantrum on his own and expend some emotion. Unfortunately for most attention-motivated tantrums, this is not the end. Third, if your child reaches his arms out for you, asks for hugs, or wants a kiss, tell him you will hold him once he calms down (for at least a few minutes). This also applies to others who may be present. You're not being cold and careless by doing this. The main thing here is that your child learns that the tantrum will not result in additional attention. You also don't want to unintentionally reinforce the tantrum. Your child will quickly learn that once he has adequately calmed down, he will have some of your attention. Once he has calmed down for a few minutes, provide some appropriate attention. Focus on some activity ("I like the tall tower you're building," for example) that he has chosen to engage in after the tantrum. The goal is for your child to associate his calm demeanor with your attention as opposed to associating it with the tantrum.

If your child does not calm down after the third step, and/or the tantrum intensifies, provide him with a quiet place to calm down. This is different than a time-out. You're not punishing your child for the tantrum. Rather, you are simply giving your child a quiet place to calm down without your support or the support of others. This will give your child an opportunity to develop self-calming skills and also eliminates the possibility of him using a tantrum to gain attention from you or others.

If the tantrum escalates to the point where your child becomes aggressive or destructive, then a time-out is appropriate. At this point, your child should be told that he is in time-out because of his aggressive or destructive behavior. When the time-out is completed and your child continues to tantrum, redirect him again to a quiet place to calm down. Through this process, your child learns several things:

- Calming down on his own results in increased attention from a caretaker.
- He can calm down on his own without assistance from others.
- If he hits, kicks, or break things, he'll go into time-out.

Overall, the point of these interactions is to help your child develop better self-calming skills and learn that whining, screaming, and crying will not gain him increased attention from you. Once he learns this, his need to have a tantrum for attention should hopefully decrease, especially if you provide your child with attention for other, more positive, behaviors.

Avoidance

Tantrums often occur when children are asked to complete a particular "do" or "don't" request. These are requests that either prevent them from doing something they enjoy or direct them to do something they don't enjoy. Whether you're making a "do" (start) or "don't" (stop) request or saying "No" to your child, you are establishing limits and creating expectations that your child does not like or wants to avoid. Welcome to parenthood.

Here are some suggestions to help you manage your child's tantrums when he doesn't want to start or stop a particular task.

When He Won't "Start:" As you watch your daughter simultaneously flop on the floor and howl like a hound dog, wouldn't it be nice to convince her that the energy she is expending far exceeds any she would have spent by simply completing the requested task? For toddlers and preschoolers, it's not always about the time spent doing a task, it's about the interruption to their world. You can pretty much predict that, at least with certain "do" requests, your child will tantrum before any effort is put forth to complete the task. You also can probably predict which tasks are most likely to cause a tantrum. The main point here, as has been made several times, is that once a request is made, it needs to be completed. A tantrum can't get in the way of the task's completion. And the last thing you want your child to learn is that the tantrum allowed her to avoid the task.

You have several options available to you when it comes to managing tantrums that occur during "do" requests. The simplest is to give your child some time to blow off steam and then repeat the request. If your child miraculously complies, certainly praise and reinforce the behavior. If not (and you can pretty much count on it), one option is to simply repeat the request while guiding your child through the task (see guided listening in Chapter 2). Once the task is completed, do not praise your child. (Offer praise only if she completes the task without your guidance.) Simply walk away. This will teach your child that the task was completed, albeit with your "help," and her tantrum did not get her out of doing the task.

Sometimes a task is not one that can be guided. You also may be uncomfortable guiding your child through the task because of his physical size or other factors which make that difficult. If that is the case, your child should be placed in time-out until he calms down. When he's calm, return him to the task. The back-and-forth process between the time-out and doing the task should continue until the task is finished. This can sometimes be fairly exhausting. For a preschool-aged child, you can tell him the task needs to be completed by a certain time (before dinner, for example), and if it's not, he will lose additional privileges.

When He Won't "Stop:" An old expression suggests that it's best to leave a party while it's still fun. Toddlers have never and will never believe this. Asking a toddler to stop doing something fun is like asking a fish not to swim. Doing so, however, often results in a tantrum. Just as it's important for your child to do what you ask, it's equally important for him to learn to stop a particular behavior. In many situations it's about safety. Learning to respond to "Don't touch the stove," "Don't go near the street," or "Stop" is as much about safety and well-being as anything else. Fortunately, you have many opportunities each day to reinforce the importance of following "don't" requests. Here are some strategies that can help you:

Pick your battles.

Is this a behavior that really needs to stop? Sometimes parents tell their children to stop something or not do something, but really have no good reason for it. Knowing why you're telling your child to stop or to refrain from a behavior will give you some conviction to follow through with the demand.

Try redirection first.

Sometimes it's easier to redirect your child to another behavior that is more acceptable or more appropriate. For example, "Come to Mom" may be more effective than "Don't go near the street." Children often respond more effectively to "do" requests than "don't" requests. Giving them something to do (help Daddy build a block tower) that competes with the behavior you're concerned about (throwing blocks at the wall) may be the most effective strategy in many situations. Once you tell your child to stop a behavior or refrain from something, the main consideration is that it does in fact stop – and fairly quickly. If your child does stop the behavior, praise his compliance and redirect him to some other activity. Otherwise, the behavior is likely to return. If the behavior does not stop, physically guiding your child to another activity or implementing a brief time-out can be effective.

Use time-out.

When a time-out ends, return or direct your child to some activity or toy. Reinforce his engagement in the activity and provide meaningful attention. If the behavior persists, repeat the time-out and then continue to redirect your child back to another activity, possibly in another location.

Don't Let a Tantrum Turn "No" to "Yes"

One word that gets the adrenaline surging and heart pounding in every toddler is "No." It can send most toddlers and many preschoolers into a head-spinning, body-flopping, ear-piercing orbit. For them, "No" simply means it's time to pump up the volume, and it's game on! This results in some of the more frustrating experiences for parents and certainly tests everyone's parenting skills. Most children at this age operate under the premise "If it feels good give me more of it, and if it doesn't, I want nothing to do with it." Toddlers are focused on those things they can do, eat, or watch as immediately as possible. Delaying gratification is not a skill that has been well developed at this age. Also, basic reasoning skills are almost nonexistent. The excessive amount of time parents spend trying to explain and reason with their children simply goes in one ear and out the other.

None of us like to be told "No." We all seem to believe that if we are simply given everything we ask for and the answer is always "Yes," then life would be much easier. Although that may be debatable, the reality for all children is that this is not going to happen. The fact is, saying "Yes" all the time and giving children everything they want could be one of the worst things for them. Setting clear limits is much more beneficial.

An important but hard to remember idea when your child is throwing a tantrum is that this is a teaching opportunity. The key thing to understand is that you don't want your child to learn that a tantrum will make you change your mind from "No" to "Yes." Your child only has so many tools available to her. If a tantrum changes your behavior or results in a positive outcome for her, she will keep using it to get what she wants. You want to teach your child that tantrums are not an effective tool, and she needs to use something else. Hopefully your child has learned to use other, more positive, behaviors (making requests using an "inside" voice or saying "Okay," for example) that don't involve screaming, yelling, and flopping on the floor.

Toddlers and preschoolers learn quickly that the word "No" means something fun is about to stop or something they want is not going to happen. Because they have a limited number of tools and all the time in the world, they really have no reason to accept "No" answers, at least initially. Unfortunately, most toddlers also learn that if their tantrums are long and hard enough, they may be able to wear their parents down to the point that "No" turns into "Yes."

Hearing "No" after asking for a toy, food, or an activity is simply an invitation for a child to ask a thousand more times. There's an old expression, "One 'Yes' is worth a thousand 'No's.'" In other words, telling your child "No" over and over again until her pleading exhausts you and causes you to say "Yes" only reinforces her persistence. Children who cry, whine, and plead for something even after being told "No" are no different than gamblers sitting at a roulette table losing time after time after time. Sometimes, like gamblers, children's persistence pays off and their number comes in (when they hear "Yes"). They quickly forget about all the times they were told "No," and they revel in their victory. How many times have you heard people talk about how much money they won playing the slots or blackjack? What you often don't hear is how much money they spent before hitting the jackpot. They, too, have learned that if they hang in long enough, they may get lucky. For toddlers, persistence is like hitting the jackpot, especially if their tantrums, whining, and crying eventually lead you to change the verdict from "No" to "Yes." Your job is to make sure your toddler never wins or hits the jackpot. "No" has to mean "No." Of course, this is much easier said than done.

Here are some strategies you can use to help your little gambler learn to place his bets on something other than throwing a tantrum when he hears the word "No:"

Make sure "No" is the answer you want to give.

Parents tend to allow the word "No" to leave their lips without thinking about it. If your child is making a request or asking for something, the best thing you can do before saying anything is to ask yourself, "Why not?" Being selective about when you say "No" allows your child, over time, to become more willing to accept it. If the answer is always or usually "No," your child has nothing to lose by appealing (throwing a tantrum) your decision.

Give a brief reason.

It's okay to provide a brief rationale as to why you said "No." However, keep it brief and avoid long explanations. Discussing your decision or providing a lengthy explanation will just add fuel to the fire and give your child the impression that the decision is up for discussion.

If the tantrum continues, ignore it and walk away.

If your child follows you, establish limits, namely that he needs to entertain himself in some appropriate way. Following you around the house is not one of them. If your child continues to follow you repeating his request, set more limits. Tell him that if he keeps asking despite being told "No," there will be additional consequences. This might involve time-out or the loss of privileges. You need to find some meaningful way to impress upon your child that the conversation is over. Your answer is final and his continued whining and pleading will result in additional consequences.

Praise compliance.

Of course, if your child accepts "No," and eventually he will, make sure to praise and reinforce the behavior. Show your pleasure that he accepted your answer.

Tantrums come in all shapes, sizes, and flavors. There is much to gain by looking at the circumstances in which tantrums occur, the causes and triggers for them, as well as the strategies that have succeeded and/or failed in the past. Doing so will greatly increase your ability to manage tantrums in the future. Some patience and persistence on your part will help you better manage your child's meltdowns, and you will become more effective as a parent and teacher.

Taking the Fun Out of Smearing, Smashing, Crushing, and Pouring

Toddlers find creative ways to make a mess out of almost everything. Whether it's coloring a masterpiece on their bedroom walls, plastering windows with handfuls of spaghetti, or dropping a sibling's favorite toy into the toilet, there is almost no end to the messes that can be made. Sometimes these "destructive" behaviors occur out of frustration. Other times they occur out of curiosity or for entertainment. Regardless of the cause, if they find some delight in the chaos they create, it's important for you to find ways to remove the "fun."

If your child has crushed a toy, smeared peanut butter on the carpet, or urinated on a bathroom wall, your first response should be a firm "No," followed by a time-out. These types of destructive and/or disruptive behaviors require an immediate response that associates the child's behavior with some negative consequence. However, just using time-out may not be sufficient because when time-out ends, the mess remains. Therefore, you should make your child responsible for helping clean the mess. Doing so is a logical, natural consequence associated with his destructive behavior. In other words, he made the mess so it's important he help clean it up. A technique called "overcorrection" can be an effective way to send your child the message that he's responsible for his actions, and he will need to correct his mess. There are basically three simple steps for using this technique:

1. **Any destructive behavior, regardless of the cause, should result in a firm verbal reprimand ("No!"), followed by a time-out.**

2. **When time-out is over, return your child to the "scene of the crime" and direct him to clean up the mess.** His age and motor skills will determine the degree to which you may need to help. For example, if your three-year-old daughter dumps a bowl of ravioli on the floor, it probably makes the most sense for you to clean up the majority of the mess, leaving just enough for her to do on her own, such as wiping the floor with a wet cloth and drying the floor. If it's your six-year-old who made the mess, he may be capable of cleaning everything up from start to finish. Your child may not do as thorough a job as you, but that's not the point. The important thing is that he's involved in cleaning the mess he made. Other than broken glass or other

messes that have safety concerns, there is really no limit to what your child can clean up. There is no reason why he can't clean up the food he threw or spit out, the walls or furniture he colored on, the floor or walls he peed on, the bathroom where he dumped all the shampoo, or the pillowcase where he hid the chocolate chip cookies.

3. Once the initial mess is cleaned up, identify some other "mess" that needs to be cleaned. If your child colored on a wall, for example, have him clean other scuffmarks on walls in the house. If he stomped a half-pound bag of potato chips into his bedroom carpet, have him clean another floor in the house. The basic message here is that your child is not only cleaning up the mess he made, he's also helping to overcorrect, or improve, the environment beyond his mess. The bottom line is that your child is being held responsible for his actions. Hopefully, it will give him pause the next time he thinks about dying the dog's hair purple or seeing how many bubbles a quart of shampoo can make in the bathtub.

chapter 4

Let's Get This Potty Started

As Charlie ran through the kitchen wearing nothing but a diaper, his mother wondered if it was time to start potty training. When his sister was two and a half, the age Charlie is now, she was fully trained. Mom noticed that Charlie exhibits many of the signs that his older sister did when she was successfully potty trained. He can stay dry for hours at a time and wake up dry from naps. His diaper also is dry after a night's sleep. His bowel movements are more regular, too, happening around the same time each day. Charlie seems to know when he has to go to the bathroom. He does a little "dance" before urinating in his diaper. Charlie even tells his mom when his diaper is soiled or wet, and he seems to show more interest in staying dry. As a result, Mom is using more appropriate "potty talk," such as wet, dry, pee, poop, dirty, and potty, and Charlie is showing more interest in potty training. He asks curious questions of family members who go to and from the bathroom. In addition, Charlie is becoming more independent by dressing himself. He's also eager to please, which may help the whole training process. What do you think? Is Charlie ready for potty training?

A. Yes

B. No

C. Maybe

Charlie certainly appears to have most of the skills he needs to be successful. Although parents tend to start thinking about potty training when a child reaches a certain age, there are actually several behavioral skills and signs that can indicate a child is ready. This chapter takes a closer look at those characteristics.

Toilet training should be a positive and rewarding experience for you and your child. That is often the case, but not always. Many parents feel pressure to toilet train their child by a certain age, often before the child is ready. Some parents feel pressure from others. The grandparents don't understand why their grandson isn't toilet trained yet while their next-door neighbor's sister's best friend's hairdresser supposedly toilet trained her daughter at nine months. Despite all these pressures, it's important to relax and pay attention to your child's behaviors, habits, and skills to determine readiness. When your child is "ready," the process will likely flow smoothly!

Is Your Child Ready?

What does "ready" mean? There are several factors to consider when determining readiness for toilet training. They include your child's:

Age

You probably should not start toilet training until at least the age of two. There are some children who are able to train earlier, but trying to train a child before she is ready may backfire and cause the process to take much longer than it should. Most children become successfully toilet trained between two and three. Girls tend to be successfully trained earlier than boys, and older children tend to be trained faster. Waiting until both you and your child are ready may actually make the process go smoother and faster.

Physical Readiness

There are several physical signs you can look for to determine if your child is ready for potty training. For example, does he have adequate bladder control? Can he go several hours at a time without urinating? Does he wake up dry (from a nap or in the morning)? Also, is he aware of having to "go"? Can he tell you or demonstrate through facial expressions (You know the one!) that he has to go? Is your child showing a preference for underwear instead of diapers?

Motor Skills

Your child should have good motor skills. She should have no difficulty walking from room to room. If you have steps, she should be able to climb them safely and easily. She should be able to pull elastic waist pants up and down. She also needs to be able to get to the bathroom on her own without help. You also should look for signs that your child is imitating you going to the bathroom.

Language Skills

It's important that your child has good language skills, meaning he can understand your questions and express his wants and needs. He needs to understand and express words such as wet, dry, and potty. Other important language skills include being able to tell you if he soiled himself ("I pooped," for example) or wet his diaper, or can tell you when he has to go to the bathroom.

Behavioral and Emotional Readiness

Your child needs to be able to follow one-step requests, such as "Sit down" or "Follow me." She also needs the ability to sit quietly (with or without an activity) for two to five minutes. It's also important that your child be cooperative when following these requests, including sitting on the toilet and removing clothes. If your child resists these simple requests or tantrums frequently when you go through the toilet-training steps, you may want to hold off. It may be necessary to first work on developing better instructional control or compliance with simple requests. It's also possible your child simply needs some time and emotional maturity before moving ahead with toilet training. Other behavioral and emotional signs to look at include your child's sense of social appropriateness. Does she become frustrated if she is wet or soiled? Children who are anxious to please their parents usually train more quickly.

It's Potty Time!

When you feel your child has the necessary skills and understanding for potty training, start the process. Here are some steps to follow so your child's daily productions find their way to the sewer instead of the landfill.

Show and tell.

You probably don't make a habit of inviting friends and family over to watch you urinate or have a bowel movement. While I'm not suggesting you start, it's important for your toddler to observe you using the toilet and for you to answer the questions your child has. Make sure you use simple words that are meaningful to your child so he can use similar words when it's time for him to go. Telling your child that mommy is going pee-pee or daddy is going poop is obviously better than saying, "Your parental unit is passing fecal matter into the commode, soon to be followed by an expulsion into the municipal sewage system so that it can be properly sanitized." Use basic, simple-to-understand words that make sense to you and your child.

Purchase a throne for your prince or princess.

Your child may need a potty chair to practice on before moving up to the big time. Make sure you purchase a sturdy potty chair that allows your child to place her feet firmly on the floor. It's also important to set the potty chair out well before you start the training process. This will create some natural curiosity, allowing you to discuss with your child what the potty chair is for. You should reinforce the idea that it's her special potty chair, and it's not for Mom or Dad. Feel free to let her decorate the throne or give it a name. Also, she should be allowed practice time to sit on it.

Using a potty chair instead of a toilet removes some of the natural fear a child has about falling in. I'm not sure who spends more time worrying about falling in the toilet, parents or young children, but using a potty chair removes that concern. (By the way, I've yet to hear about a child or parent falling into the toilet. But there is always a first.) If you use a regular toilet, you may need to purchase a step stool so your child can place her feet on it. When children sit on a toilet with their feet dangling, their abdominal and sphincter muscles tense up, making it difficult to relax and have a bowel movement or urinate. The next time you sit on a ledge with your feet dangling, imagine trying to relax enough to do number one or two.

Make time to rehearse.

People rehearse things like weddings that they presume they will only do once, so doesn't it make sense to rehearse an activity that will be done multiple times a day for as long as you live? Let your child practice sitting on the toilet so he becomes comfortable with it. Also, have your child practice removing his pants and underwear in the bathroom or wherever the potty chair is placed. You should also practice in different locations around the house because your child won't always be near the bathroom when it's time to go. Plan for situations where your child is in another part of the house or in the backyard. Practice walking (or trotting) to the bathroom, removing clothes, and sitting on the toilet. With boys, it's best to start the training process by having them sit down to urinate. Most fathers cringe when they hear this. Relax Dad. You can save yourself time and some cleaning supplies by having your son sit to urinate until he has the routine down fairly reliably. Once he gets it, the future firefighter can then work on aiming the stream at its intended target.

Wear appropriate attire.

Parents are often confused about what their children should wear during the training process. Questions I often hear include, "Should I allow my child to roam wild and naked through the house?" and "Should my child wear underwear, diapers, or training pants?" Training diapers have recently shown up on store shelves. They have some absorbency but allow a child to feel wet and some discomfort. This is simply an expensive way to get you to avoid the good old-fashioned approach of sending the Pampers packing. The best approach is to eliminate or remove access to diapers, pull-ups, or any similar product. Hide them away so only you can reach or see them. At night, however, you will want to continue using pull-ups as a safeguard against bedtime accidents. Young children often don't like having pull-ups or diapers removed. Let's face it, they've been wearing one for years and old habits die hard. They also are way too convenient. What toddler doesn't enjoy wearing his Port-a-Potty all day so he can play, run, climb, and explore without taking a break? Trying to train your child while he has access to diapers and pull-ups will only lengthen the process considerably and possibly defeat your efforts. So what should your child wear? Underwear is your best bet. You can even make an event out of it by letting him pick out specially designed underwear (with action figures or cartoon characters, for example) that he will want to keep clean and dry. Also, it's okay to have your child wear plastic training pants. It helps on the cleaning bill and lets your child adequately experience the agony of defeat.

Prime the pump.

You want your child to have lots of opportunities to practice. If your child is not drinking much or just drinking a typical amount, you may have only a few opportunities during the day to have him pee successfully. This also increases the likelihood that he will sit on the toilet and produce nothing, causing frustration or disappointment. That's why extra fluids are helpful. Allow your child to drink extra water or have more of a favorite beverage. Understand, however, that making your child into a miniature Hoover Dam may lead to a few more "spills." But it significantly increases the chances that he will achieve success when you put him on the toilet or, by some divine intervention, he actually heads there on his own. Either way, having multiple opportunities to reinforce your child's success certainly increases the speed and likelihood of success.

Have a parade.

This is not the kind of parade where you get to sit and watch. It involves you parading your child back and forth to the potty chair. There are several things to consider, including when and how often you should take your child to the potty chair. The most obvious times are when your child "assumes the position." For example, when you see that all-too-familiar stance that signals the beginning of a bombing raid (bowel movement) or that look of discomfort that suggests your child's bladder is about to explode like a water balloon. Those are good times to march your child to the potty chair as quickly as possible. Even catching your child midway through the process may give you an opportunity to reinforce partial success. Hopefully, you will recognize changes in your child's expressions or body language (having a red face or holding his bottom, for example) that indicate the need to urinate or have a bowel movement. Rather than asking your child if he needs to go, simply take him to the bathroom and have him practice sitting on the potty chair. This will eventually and ultimately lead him to go in the toilet. You can then bring out the balloons, candy, and confetti, which are important for any parade, to acknowledge the success. Other important times to take your child to the bathroom include ten to twenty minutes after meals. Children (and adults for that matter) are most likely to feel the urge to have a bowel movement after meals. Taking your child to the potty chair ten or twenty minutes after eating gives him a greater opportunity to have a successful experience. Also during the training phase, you can create more opportunities for success by taking your child to the potty chair every hour or so. If he is wetting himself in between trips to the bathroom, make the visits more frequent. However, if he has already demonstrated that he can remain dry for two or three hours, the visits can be less frequent.

Use positive practice.

Let's face it, your life was much easier when your child had a wearable toilet. Many children are understandably reluctant to sit on a stool. This is especially common during training because they are so focused on "success," they have difficulty relaxing. It may help your child if you sit with her while she is on the potty chair or toilet. Reading a favorite story, listening to music, or engaging in an activity may help her relax. At the same time, spending more time on the potty chair can increase the chances your child will be successful.

Reward success.

Your little one will probably be more excited about his success than you will – really! And although you don't need to provide a diploma following every "graduation," offering some type of reward will motivate your child to make deposits in the potty rather than in his pants. This is an important component to the entire training process. The nature and variety of rewards for successful toilet training are only limited by your creativity. The most common and best form of reinforcement is praise. Your smiles, hugs, and nice comments will go a long way toward reinforcing your child's success. Since this is an activity that is new to your child, you want to make it "party time at potty time" when he successfully voids in the toilet. The types of rewards and reinforcement that parents typically use include offering verbal praise, calling family members or friends to tell them of their child's success, giving a high-five or fist bump, offering a small piece of candy from a special dispenser, unwrapping small toys or trinkets, and playing a special game or reading a book that was reserved only for successful toilet training. Feel free to use any form of praise or reward you think will be meaningful and motivating to your child, without going overboard (buying expensive toys or games, for example). You want your praise and attention to be in line with the behavior you're trying to promote. That does not mean you should be excessive with your attention. As your child becomes more and more successful, start thinking about how you can fade out the reward (offering it less frequently) until you only provide verbal praise. When training is successfully completed, no special praise or attention will be necessary.

Prepare for accidents.

Successful learning involves making mistakes. During the training process, there will be accidents. Remember, you are teaching a new skill – one your child has yet to acquire. As the "teacher," it's important to be positive and encouraging even when you're frustrated. When accidents happen, help your child get cleaned up as quickly as possible and maintain a neutral or even positive demeanor. Having a neutral, matter-of-fact demeanor after repeated accidents can be difficult. Parents often say they get frustrated, raise their voice, or even yell. I understand the frustration. However, your child may be less motivated to sit on the toilet or be involved in the entire process if there is a chance you will breathe fire down her neck if she is not perfect. If you react neutrally when your child has accidents, but then smile, praise, or do a little dance when she is successful, the contrast will not be lost on her. Again, think of your own life experiences. Would you rather have a boss who only screams and hollers regardless of what you do or one who offers encouragement, attention, and the occasional raise?

Practice after accidents.

When you have cleaned your child up, have him practice (in a positive way) what to do the next time he feels the need to go pee or poop. Simply have him go to the bathroom, remove his clothes, sit on the toilet, and practice as though he were going "for real." This positive practice reminds your child of what he needs to do when he feels the urge to urinate or have a bowel movement and reinforces the skills needed to be successful.

Check for dry pants.

During the training process, your trainee will have an occasional accident. This may cause her to get upset, or she may not care. In either respect, check your child periodically (every thirty to sixty minutes) to see if she has wet or soiled herself. If she is clean, praise her. It's also helpful if you remind her to go immediately to the bathroom or to tell you when she first feels the urge to pee or poop. If she is dirty or wet, have her assist with the cleanup and practice the toileting routine.

Take a break.

Remember, you don't **always** have to finish what you start. That's not often true in most situations, but it is for toilet training. If you start the training process and realize your child isn't ready, even though you thought he was, stop. It's better to take a break for a month or two and then try again rather than push ahead to finish the job. Proceeding with toilet training when a child isn't ready can create a negative association between the toilet or potty chair and a child's willingness to urinate or have a bowel movement in the toilet. It could also cause a child to hold his urine or feces, causing potential medical problems and possibly pain or discomfort when he does number one or number two. Children who experience discomfort, especially with bowel movements, often hold their stools. This can lead to more painful bowel movements and further retention. If the pain occurs while sitting on the toilet, the negative association can often delay potty training by months and sometimes years. Also, none of us, especially children, are motivated to learn a new skill or engage in any activity if it's painful or emotionally upsetting.

Another sign your child may not be ready to be toilet trained is if he hides when he urinates or has bowel movements. Children often hide when they are concerned their parents will be angry or upset with them for not going in the toilet, or they have developed some type of negative association with the toilet or potty chair. Remember, children who train later train faster. Keeping the process positive and enjoyable for everyone will lead to success and positive memories.

What Could Possibly Go Wrong?

As a parent, you obviously focus on all the positives of toilet training – no more changing dirty diapers, no more buying diapers, no more carrying around diaper bags, and no more spending time running to the potty chair or toilet. These and many more reasons explain the interest in helping a child gain independence through potty training. Now, let's look at it from your child's perspective. You're asking him to replace a soft, warm, and absorbent Port-a-Potty (which allows him to urinate and defecate anywhere at any time) with less cozy underwear that is absorbent, but not in a good way. With the Port-a-Potty gone, you're asking him to sit on a cold "chair" with a hole in it. This funny looking chair has water in it and seems only slightly smaller than the backyard swimming pool. The funny looking chair is probably a little too high, so Mom or Dad has to pick him up and sit him on the chair. All this and your child doesn't know how to swim yet. As your child holds on to the toilet seat for dear life, you smile at him and say, "Relax! What could possibly go wrong?"

Remember, toilet training is a learning process and you are the teacher. An important part of learning is making mistakes. With toilet training there will be lots of mistakes. But you want mistakes to happen. They allow your child to experience the hassles of dealing with them, and they give you a chance to teach to situations so your child learns how to avoid similar experiences in the future. Sometimes, children do not become toilet trained as quickly as parents would like. Here are some of the obstacles that can slow the process down:

A Failure to Communicate

For your child to be successful, he needs to be able to tell you that he has to go potty. At the very least, he has to be able to gesture or demonstrate his need to use the bathroom. He also needs to be able to understand basic words and simple instructions. If your child lacks these skills, wait until he can follow your instructions and knows the words associated with using the potty. You can work on these communication skills daily until you're confident your child has acquired them.

Too Many Cooks in the Kitchen

If all of the generals have different battle plans, your little private isn't going to have a clue which one to follow. So, if your child is like many others and is cared for in a number of settings, including daycare, preschool, and your home, having one potty-training program will be important. If all of your child's caregivers use different toilet-training techniques, it will create confusion for your child and delay the entire process. Once you select a toilet-training routine, make sure all of your child's caretakers have a copy and follow it.

Harsh Reactions to Accidents

Of course you will be disappointed if your child has an accident. Get ready; there will be a lot of them. Showing your displeasure or using punishment, however, will only increase the odds of more accidents. If you are too critical, your child may hide in a corner to urinate or defecate, hide her underwear so you can't see accidents, or worse, hold her stool to try and avoid having a bowel movement completely. She might think, "If I don't have a bowel movement, how can I have an accident?" Sometimes parents unintentionally show their displeasure or reprimand their child for having accidents but then seem surprised when their child hides underwear or disappears to do number one or number two. There is a connection there, and the connection is you. Your response and the way you manage your child's accidents during the training process will go a long way toward improving your child's chances for success.

Too Much Pressure

Your child should be doing the pushing and straining. If you're pushing your child too hard to have success by taking him to the toilet too frequently, requiring him to stay on the toilet too long, or focusing too much on the training, your behavior won't be lost on him. It will likely lead to increased stress, making it difficult for him to relax. This could potentially lead to other problems, including constipation or being overly self-critical when accidents happen.

Pain

It only takes one painful bowel movement to disrupt the entire process. When your entire life history is all of three years, a large painful bowel movement is a momentous event. Just as the look on my wife's face as she gave birth to our daughters was not one of peace and tranquility, your child's reaction to passing a small redwood will not be one of serenity. There is a reason we remember both positive and negative events early in our childhood. It's because they happened for the first time, and they were really a big deal at the time. As we get older, we have many more of these experiences and they become less significant as time passes. Nobody enjoys pain, but children in particular really hate it. When is the last time your child asked you to go to the doctor to have an injection? The bottom line is, if your child has a large painful bowel movement, he very well may engage in all kinds of creative acrobatics to avoid sitting on the toilet again. You can help prevent this, in part, by being proactive. Make sure your child eats as many fresh fruits and vegetables as possible, increase his fluid intake (especially water), and monitor his stools throughout the training process. Always feel free to consult your pediatrician if there are constipation issues, especially after monitoring your child's diet. If your child does have a painful bowel movement, causing him to avoid sitting on the stool, make dietary changes and talk to your pediatrician so you can soften the stools as quickly as possible. As your child has more regular, soft stools, the pain and discomfort associated with a difficult bowel movement will slowly disappear.

A Rush to Flush

There is no such thing as three-minute toilet training. If you don't have time for training, then you should probably wait. Trying to train your child when you're extremely busy or trying to accomplish too many things in a short amount of time won't work. Initially, you may need to block off a weekend or a few days so you can give your child plenty of attention.

Significant Life Changes

If you or your family are about to experience some fairly significant changes, it's important to put off toilet training. Moving to a new home, expecting the birth of a child, or starting daycare are events that can be too disruptive. However, once the change occurs and you settle into a routine, you and your child will be in a better position to focus on the "big change."

A Lack of Awareness

Not paying attention to your child's physical signs can delay the training process. In nature, some animals engage in a mating dance. Well, your child engages in a waiting dance when it's time to go potty. Although many dances are similar, your child probably has his own unique moves. Maybe it's the "dance-in-place" trot, the "grab-my-privates" pirouette, or the "I've-seen-a-ghost" waltz. If you're not aware of changes in your child's language, facial expressions, or body movements, you may not know when he needs to get to the bathroom fast. Being more aware of these signs, especially during the training process, will help you get him to the toilet or potty chair quickly. This will help reduce the number of accidents and build your child's confidence.

Physical Problems

There are a number of physical and medical factors that can interfere with a child's toilet training. If you have any questions at all about whether a medical condition may be affecting your child's toileting skills or success, call your pediatrician. There are a number of common physical complications that can get in the way of potty training. If your child complains about pain or burning sensations when urinating, strains to urinate, or the urine is discolored, for example, it may indicate a urinary infection. Any form of diarrhea also is likely to cause accidents. If your child's stool pattern changes dramatically, it's important to check with your doctor. Certain antibiotics and food additives can cause stools to be loose, too. Sorbitol, for example, is a sugar alcohol used in many juices, such as pear and apple. Drinking excessive amounts of these juices can cause loose stools. Also, there are a number of causes of constipation. Some are dietary and some are medical. Holding your stool also can lead to constipation. Chronic constipation can put pressure on the bladder and cause daytime and nighttime accidents. Again, contact a physician if your child exhibits any physical signs that trouble you or seem out of the ordinary.

Dealing with Regression

It's not over till it's over. You will eventually reach a point where your child is in underwear, the diapers have completely disappeared from the house, and your child is reliably using the toilet. You might start to think, "Thank goodness, that's over!" Unfortunately, it may not be.

Most children will regress or have a few accidents along the way. This is a normal part of the training process, and there's no need to be concerned. Most importantly, avoid getting angry or punishing your child because you assume, wrongly, he did it on purpose. Most children will have a few accidents because they waited too long, were preoccupied, or ignored the physical cues their body sent them. If you believe your child isn't getting to the toilet in time because she is preoccupied with playing or ignoring physical cues, schedule a few extra toilet-sitting times. You also should have her take an active role in cleaning herself up and do some positive practice. (I'll get back to positive practice shortly.)

It's not uncommon for children to regress in their toileting skills if there is some major change that disrupts their lives. This could be anything from the birth of a sibling or death of a loved one to moving to a new home or starting a new school. Keep in mind, however, that your child has the skills and has already had success with toilet-training. A few general reminders and some increased structure and encouragement are usually all it takes to keep your child moving in the right direction.

Regardless of why accidents occur, you need to take action to keep your child on a positive path. Even though you may feel like sending him to toilet-training boot camp, there are simple steps you can take to help him practice his toileting skills. There are a couple of facts you probably know when you think about the entire training experience. One fact is that you and your child are happy and excited when he pees or poops in the toilet. The other fact is that you and your child are not happy when he has accidents. Therein lies the answer to the question of how best to respond to accidents.

Your child has the skills to know when he needs to go, where he needs to go (the bathroom), how to remove his clothes, and how to sit on the toilet. He also has the skills to assist you with cleaning up and changing. There is no reason why you should do it all. So, if your child has an accident, calmly (let's practice calmly) have your child help you remove the wet or soiled clothing, clean and wipe appropriately, put the soiled clothes in the appropriate place, and put on clean clothes. This is important for two reasons. First, your child is capable of doing it and needs to learn to take responsibility for the accident. Remember, it's no big deal (or at least act like it's not). Second, making the cleanup routine too convenient does nothing to motivate your child to pay attention to the physical cues. This is especially true if he's swinging like a monkey in the backyard or immersed in a computer game. Taking time away from play activities to change and clean himself should provide the lesson that it's much more costly to wait than to go. If you do this matter-of-factly and calmly, you keep the focus on correcting the situation rather than on you, the fire-breathing dragon who is yelling and screaming about another accident. Remember, this is about teaching a skill and expectations. Maintaining calm allows the focus to remain on your child's behavior.

The next step is to have your child practice the positive steps that comprise toilet training. This involves having him go from the point of the accident to the potty chair or toilet, removing his clothing, and sitting on the toilet for a minute or so. Repeat this multiple times as a means of reinforcing the steps of the skill.

Wetting at Night

Parents often have questions about children who wet the bed. The medical term for this is nocturnal enuresis. This is very common. Approximately one in seven girls and one in five boys at age six wet the bed at night. In some cases, there is a medical explanation for nighttime wetting. More often than not, it's a developmental issue that resolves itself over time. Many children who wet at night are described by their parents as heavy sleepers. When parents attempt to wake their children in the middle of the night to go to the bathroom, it's often difficult if not impossible. Doing so often results in less sleep for parents and little success at ending the bedwetting. Parents also try to limit the amount of fluids their children ingest after dinner or in the evening. This, too, will not stop the wetting. It just decreases the volume of urine that is produced.

Bedwetting is more of a social concern for parents and children than anything else. It's a frustrating problem for children and can cause embarrassment. So what's a parent to do? The short answer – not much. Certainly consult with your pediatrician if you have questions and want to rule out any medical condition. The second most important thing you can do is be supportive. Why is that the second most important? Because your first priority is to make sure you don't engage in any type of punishment. Don't yell, scream, or do anything that conveys or demonstrates displeasure or disappointment. It's extremely rare for a child to intentionally wet the bed. What would be the motivation? After all, do you pour a glass of warm water on your bed before you crawl in at night? If you do, please call me.

Some parents have had some success using special rewards (putting a quarter in a jar every night their child stays dry and then letting her spend the quarters when the jar is full or allowing their child access to a special breakfast food if he is dry in the morning, for example). This is successful about fifteen to twenty percent of the time and is certainly worth a try. However, even an approach like this may place too much focus on staying dry. This can set a child up for disappointment. It tends to be more successful for children who are older and have more extended periods of dry nights. Patience, rather than persistence, will be more successful when it comes to managing nighttime wetting. Note: If you have an older child who continues to wet at night, ask your pediatrician if he would benefit from using a wet alarm, a device used to help treat nighttime wetting. (Wet alarms are not typically used with toddlers.)

Reward, Rinse, and Repeat

If your child reaches school age (five or six) and continues to struggle with toilet training or he experiences success but begins having accidents years later, the following approach can provide a general framework to retrain your child and hopefully recapture that earlier success. This approach applies to children who have problems during the daytime with peeing, pooping, or both. (Please note: If your child was successfully potty trained and then starts to have urine or soiling accidents two or three years later, check with your pediatrician to rule out any possible medical conditions that are causing the problem).

Here are six steps to follow:

1. **Use positive practice.** Start by reminding your child of the physical cues she feels when it's time to urinate or have a bowel movement. Walk her through each of the training steps. Let her show you where she needs to go, what clothes to remove, and how to sit. Have her explain to you how she feels when she knows she has to go.

2. **Resume scheduled sit times on the toilet after meals and once in between meals if needed.** Be sure to prompt your child to use the toilet if you see her "doing the dance."

3. **Set up rewards for sitting and having a bowel movement (or urinating, if that is what you are focusing on).** You can award a sticker or a small candy for sitting, and you can provide special rewards for bowel movements. For example, you can wrap (use aluminum foil) small gifts, such as candy pieces, inexpensive trinkets, or little games, and have your child unwrap an item each time she goes number two in the toilet. These are short-term rewards for success, and they can be used during the initial training process. For older children, include longer-term rewards, such as playing at a favorite park on the weekend, or inviting a friend to go to a movie. You also can use a reward jar to track progress and motivate your child to continue using the toilet. (For examples of reward jars, see pages 62-63 in the Listening Chapter or pages 138-139 in the Mealtime Chapter.) Older children are usually motivated by a combination of short-term and long-term rewards. Another possibility for a short-term reward is to have your child gain access to a special toy or activity that is only available when she's successful. Allow her to have access to the toy or activity for thirty minutes or an hour, but then take it away until the next successful bowel movement.

4. **When accidents occur, remember your reaction is to be chill not shrill.** Have your child correct the situation by removing the soiled clothes, placing them in the appropriate place, washing and cleaning himself, and putting on clean clothes. Maintain calm as best you can. If your child isn't bothered about cleaning up, add another component. Have him sit and soak in the bathtub for five or so minutes to avoid "getting a rash." Don't provide toys or bubble bath. This can add to the "hassle factor" of having accidents. The soaking and cleaning up reinforces the idea that your child has to take responsibility for the accident and keep clean. After the cleanup, again have your child practice the steps for using the potty or toilet
5. **If your child is hiding underwear, try numbering them.** There should be negative consequences for hiding underwear.
6. **Keep a chart.** Keeping a record of the number of accidents, number of successful bowel movements, the consistency and size of the stool, and the amount of any medication taken can be very helpful when monitoring your child's success. It's also helpful to have a record if a pediatrician or psychologist is working with you. By monitoring the consistency of the stool, you can help regulate any stool softener your child may be taking or provide helpful information to the pediatrician if a softener is prescribed. In fact, if you have tried to fix the problem but continue to have little success, you may want to talk to your pediatrician about getting outside help.

Toilet training can and should be a positive experience for you and your child. Following the steps and strategies outlined in this chapter can make achieving success easier and, perhaps most importantly, help everyone enjoy the transition from Pampers to the potty.

Tips to Make Toilet Training a Success

- Toilet training is about learning, not discipline. Your job is that of a teacher, not a disciplinarian.
- Keep it positive. Praise. Praise. Praise.
- Yelling, screaming, and punishing will not make your child learn faster. In fact, it will probably delay the process.
- Make sure your child has the motor skills needed to get his or her clothes on and off easily.
- Training during the spring and summer is often more effective because children are more comfortable walking around the house with little or no clothing.
- Limit sitting on the toilet to around five minutes. If your child has produced nothing at that point, try again later.
- If more than one adult is involved with the training process, make sure everyone uses the same approach. Different strategies or methods will only lead to confusion.
- Never force your child to sit on the potty chair. Do not have your child remain in soiled or wet clothing. Changing clothes as soon as possible will remind him how much more comfortable it is to be dry, hopefully motivating him to use the toilet.
- Teach your toddler to wash hands after using the potty.
- Encourage older children to use the potty chair or toilet on their own, including when you see them straining or behaving in a way that suggests they need to go. Younger children will need more frequent prompting. Never ask your child if she needs to use the toilet, tell her instead. You will have better results if you say, "It's time to use the potty" instead of asking, "Do you need to go potty?"
- Provide more fluids when training how to go pee.
- Have older children (four and up) assist with cleanup. This can involve placing wet diapers in the trash, wiping themselves, or changing clothes. If you make the cleanup process too convenient, you won't encourage them to use the toilet at every available opportunity.
- Designate a spot where wet/soiled underwear can be placed.
- Before and during potty training, take your child to the bathroom with you. Moms and sisters can set the example for girls, and dads and brothers can set the example for boys.
- Teach appropriate toilet talk, such as pee, poop, and wet.

- Change diapers or wet clothes in the bathroom to associate that process with the location. Spend time with your child in the bathroom reading or listening to music to help him relax and remain on the potty or toilet long enough to do number one or number two.

- Celebrate throwing out the last diaper together. Follow that with going out to buy new underwear.

chapter 5

Mealtime: The Necessary Ingredients for a Happy and Healthy Eater

It was Sunday morning, and three-year-old Jessica was playing quietly in the backyard. Her parents were busy in the kitchen preparing lunch for a family get-together. The roast was cooking in the oven, and Jessica's father was frying potatoes in a skillet. Jessica's grandmother was bringing her world-famous sweet potatoes, and Uncle Jim was bringing a smoked turkey. As they looked over the menu, Jessica's Mom asked her husband, "What should we make for Jessica?" He rolled his eyes and said, "We shouldn't have to make anything for her. There's no reason why she can't eat some of the wonderful food that is being prepared." Mom agreed and said, "Yeah, you're right."

Jessica was a fussy eater. When she was a year old, she pushed away food that didn't smell or taste right, and she gagged on certain textures. She only drank milk if it was chocolate-flavored. Jessica's selective eating worried her parents. They were concerned she wouldn't get enough to eat. Her mother eventually fed Jessica anything she would eat. Her parents assumed it was just a phase she would outgrow. They continued to offer Jessica a wide variety of fruits, vegetables, and other foods but Jessica cried, pouted, closed her mouth, and pushed the food away. They even offered "special prizes," yelled, used time-out, and required her to sit at the table until she ate. But none of it worked. Jessica always held out until she was given one of her favorite foods. Jessica's routine became eating small amounts of her favorite foods at mealtime, snacking or "grazing" throughout the day on foods she found in the pantry, and drinking juices and other liquids she grabbed from the refrigerator.

When the family gathered for the Sunday meal, Grandma made a plate for Jessica that included sweet potatoes and Uncle Jim's turkey. Grandma also added fruits and vegetables to the plate and gave it to Jessica. Within seconds Jessica announced, "I'm not hungry." Grandma then placed a small bite of sweet potatoes on a fork and offered it to her. Jessica pushed the food away and pouted. It was a typical mealtime for Jessica. The episode elicited some sage advice from family members. Their comments included:

A. "Let her go hungry. She'll eat eventually."

B. "If you quit giving in to her, she'll eventually eat other foods."

C. "She eats too much junk food."

D. "She needs to eat a bite of what the rest of the family's eating before she can have her favorite foods."

If you were to offer advice to Jessica's parents, what would you suggest? All of the comments from family are reasonable and could possibly help improve Jessica's eating habits. Jessica is a fairly typical "picky eater." Many picky eaters do not enjoy food or mealtime the same way others do. This leads toddlers to refuse or avoid certain foods, often around the time when they are being introduced to solid foods. Other picky eaters have a perfectly normal experience consuming solid foods but develop negative eating habits for different reasons. If these habits are not addressed quickly, they become somewhat challenging to change. This is due, in part, to the frequency with which toddlers eat. Since most toddlers eat four or five times per day, their picky or fussy habits have four or five opportunities to be "fed" or indulged. It's not uncommon for children to maintain these eating habits for years before parents become frustrated and decide to change them. The good news is they can be changed.

The Basic Ingredients

Toddlers' diets are about as predictable as the weather. Sometimes they eat a lot, other times not so much. Sometimes, it seems they give more to the family dog than to themselves. When it comes to nutrition, the most important thing is for your toddler to grow and gain weight at an appropriate rate that meets your pediatrician's approval. Given how rapidly toddlers grow and develop, they clearly need the energy that comes from nutritious meals and snacks. Although there are certain rules of thumb you can use as guidelines (a serving size should be approximately one tablespoon for each year of age, for example), the bottom line is that your toddler will let you know when she is full or famished. You've probably learned by now just how much food to put on your child's plate, knowing that sometimes she will not finish it and other times she will ask for more. However, you should not expect your toddler to eat the same amount of food at each meal like most adults. A toddler's food intake is much less predictable. So, if your child is growing appropriately and consuming a fairly wide range of food items, you shouldn't be too concerned about how much she eats at any given meal.

As a parent, you probably worry less about how much your child eats and more about what she eats. Our on-the-go, drive-through society can make it too easy to eat foods that are high on convenience and taste but low on nutrition and variety.

Introducing a wide range of foods at an early age is important, even though your child probably won't like everything that is offered right from the beginning. It's not uncommon for young children to try a food item ten or fifteen times before deciding they want to include it in their diet. Exposing your child to a wide range of foods, with the expectation that he will reject certain foods and be cautious about others, should be the norm. Be patient, but persistent, when introducing different foods from each of the food groups. It's helpful if you prepare and present them in a variety of different ways. The thing you want to avoid is giving up on introducing a range of foods and allowing your toddler to eat only what he likes. Although it's certainly acceptable for a toddler to get most of his calories from a limited number of food choices, it's important that new foods be introduced on a regular basis to help expand his diet over time.

Mealtime is probably not a situation where you want to work on etiquette with your toddler (see Miss(ed) Manners on page 129). A toddler at mealtime is somewhat like a bull in a china shop. You can pretty much count on a major mess. Mealtime and manners are not a very good mix for young children. That doesn't mean you should completely avoid working on manners or let your child imitate Jackson Pollack on the kitchen walls. It just means you need to have realistic expectations. Most toddlers have limited attention spans, poor fine motor skills, and less-than-refined palates, so don't expect a fine dining experience anytime soon.

Mealtime Schedule

Paying attention to your child's mealtime schedule is one of the most important things you can do to promote a well-balanced diet. Most toddlers need to eat three regular meals and two snacks per day. By age two or three, they are capable of going two and a half to three hours between meals without eating. For some reason, however, many parents have turned their homes into twenty-four hour buffets where their toddlers can help themselves to snack foods in the kitchen pantry and juice boxes in the refrigerator. On top of that, rather than sitting down at a kitchen table to eat, the little grazers munch and sip on their snacks throughout the house. Parents then seem shocked when their children are not hungry at mealtime and push away less appetizing foods to instead munch on chicken nuggets before running off to play. And who can blame the kids. If there is no set mealtime schedule, there is no real motivation to eat at any given meal. Rather, why not just belly-up to the buffet and then run and play?

If you stick to a schedule that allows your child to eat three meals and one or two snacks a day (keeping meals and snacks separated by two and a half to three hours), you will eliminate many of the behavioral and selective eating patterns that most children experience. (If your child is thirsty between meals, offer a drink of water instead of juice boxes.)

Mealtime Routine

Once upon a time, in a galaxy far, far away, families used to eat nearly every meal together. What was once the rule is now the exception. In households where both parents work and kids are signed up for everything from soccer to underwater basket weaving, families find themselves eating on the go. And even when everyone is home together, rarely do they find time to sit down and eat together. I hope you can find the time, or make the time, to eat at least several meals together each week as a family. Even that, I realize, may be a tall order.

Whenever possible, make an effort to eat all meals at the dinner table. That means no walking around the house with a juice box or eating in front of the TV. It also means your children can't grab food off their plates and run to another room to play. (Keep in mind that walking or running while eating is a major choking hazard for children.) As shocking as it may sound, I'm suggesting you and your children eat your meal from start to finish at a kitchen or dining table. One reason why I advocate eating all meals at a dinner table is because of what psychologists call "stimulus control." That's just a fancy way of saying that we learn certain habits and ways of doing things if we perform a particular behavior in the same place or location. For example, in the chapter on sleep, I emphasize how important it is for children not to use their beds as trampolines, lounges to watch TV, or as all-star wrestling rings. By using the bed only or primarily for sleep, the bed becomes associated with just that – sleep. If it has too many other purposes or uses, the association between bed and sleep gets lost. The same thing is true with eating. If your children are allowed to eat whenever and wherever they want, they lose the opportunity to learn certain behaviors, manners, and customs associated with mealtime. They also lose the opportunity to socialize with family or friends during meals at the dinner table. In general, you want the dinner table to become associated with certain specific behaviors, which include not only eating food but behaving and socializing in an appropriate way. Just as you've established a morning or bedtime routine for your children, mealtime also should have its own customs and routines. Having mealtimes in one location will go far toward helping you establish that.

Make the Most of Mealtimes

Establishing appropriate limits and expectations at mealtime will help reduce or eliminate many of the behavior problems parents commonly experience. Here are some suggestions to help you set reasonable expectations for your toddler and, more importantly, make mealtime as pleasant as possible.

Keep the meal short.

For toddlers, sitting still is considered some form of medieval torture. You're more likely to win the lottery than have your toddler sit peacefully at the dinner table while everyone finishes their meal. Toddlers like to be moving, even when they're doing something that is important to them. It's reasonable, however, to expect your child to remain seated at the table for a specific amount of time. A good rule of thumb is four minutes for every year of age. So, your three-year-old should be expected to sit at the dinner table for a minimum of twelve minutes. Why set a minimum amount? One reason is because many toddlers learn that they can eat a few bites of food, tell Mom or Dad they're "full," and then run off to play. Of course, fifteen minutes later they're back complaining of hunger. If your toddler knows that he needs to remain at the table for a certain amount of time and is not allowed to leave, hopefully he will be more motivated to eat. You may want to use a trusty timer (in the beginning) to help your child understand how long he needs to remain at the table. Some children may need much longer to eat and may in fact be at the table for twenty to thirty minutes. That's fine. Setting a minimum time helps prevent problems for those children who are more interested in playing and grazing than eating a meal.

Eat with your toddler.

There's a tendency to feed children separately and for adults to eat after their children have finished. Although there may be times when this needs to be done out of necessity, you should sit down and eat with your toddler whenever possible. This gives you an opportunity to model appropriate behaviors for your child, praise and acknowledge her appropriate behaviors and manners, and make mealtime a more positive experience for everyone.

Remove distractions.

As you are well aware by now, it doesn't take much to distract your toddler. Her attention span is probably measured in fractions of a second as opposed to minutes. Your child may beg you to put in a

VeggieTales movie or turn on the Disney Channel when it's time to eat. Although that may entertain her and give you an opportunity to do other things while she eats, it may turn into a habit you wish you had never started. Having a TV on, or even allowing other children to play while your toddler eats, will do little to keep your child focused on the meal. In fact, it will almost certainly eliminate any opportunity now, or in the future, to have a conversation during mealtime. In general, it's best to turn off all electronics and remove toys from the table during mealtime. If your child wants to watch a television program or engage in some other electronic entertainment, she can do so after eating.

Use the power of praise.

Mealtimes are a terrific opportunity for your toddler to get all kinds of attention, both good and bad. Take the opportunity to provide your toddler with the positive praise he craves by pointing out how nicely he sits, how well he uses his spoon or fork, and how nicely he chews with his mouth closed. You also can focus on the characteristics of his food by asking him to comment on the different colors, shapes, and tastes of the food.

Shape the behavior you want to see.

It's important to set reasonable expectations for behavior at mealtime. This is especially true the younger your child is. Expecting your child to sit firmly on her chair, with perfect posture, may happen when she enters West Point. It's not going to happen now. Whether your toddler sits in a booster seat or a regular chair, you'll likely see her squirming, adjusting, and getting up and down. This may be annoying, or at least distracting, to you. However, as long as your toddler spends most of her time in the chair, continues to eat, and follows the rules you've established, let it go. As time goes on, your child will have a greater capacity and ability to sit calmly throughout the meal. For now, you should redirect your child to sit, praise her when she does, and expect a lot of squirming in the process. The same types of expectations should be established for using utensils correctly, chewing food appropriately, and other table manners. Because the fine motor skills of most toddlers are still developing, a spoon will be much easier to use than a fork and using a knife will be difficult. You can help your toddler by loading food on a spoon or cutting the food until she learns to use a knife. Also, toddlers love to pick up things with their hands, so let them do it. Having finger foods available will make mealtime easier. There's no rush to have your child eat every bite of food using only utensils. Let your child practice with utensils but also allow her to use her fingers or a spoon. That's the path of least resistance that will help eliminate some mealtime battles. At the same time, it gives your toddler time to develop proper eating skills.

Don't allow negative behaviors.

What toddler doesn't enjoy seeing how high he can spit a pea in the air, especially if it winds up in his sister's milk? It's also a lot more fun to see if Fido can catch a glob of macaroni and cheese in his mouth instead of putting it in one's own. And even though squishing spaghetti through their fingers may seem more fun than using play dough, such antics need to be corrected. If your toddler throws or spits food, you can manage it in the following way:

1. Begin by firmly saying, "No throwing food." If your child resumes eating properly, praise him.
2. If he continues to throw or spit food, turn him around in his chair (away from the table) for two minutes and instruct other family members to ignore him. If turning him around in his chair is not an option, remove his plate for two minutes. Repeat to your child, "No throwing food." After two minutes, turn him back around and redirect him to eat. Again, praise proper eating.
3. If your child spits or throws food again, remove him from the table and place him in time-out. After time-out, return him to the table for one last opportunity to eat. If he eats and behaves appropriately, praise his behavior. Any negative behavior from that point forward should put an end to mealtime.
4. If mealtime is ended because of spitting or throwing food, it is important that your child clean up the mess he made. (See pages 93-94 in Chapter 3 for steps you should take with your child.)

Keep toys off the table.

Children love to play with their toys. However, toys have no place at the dinner table and are a major distraction. It's important for your child to learn that mealtime is for eating, not playing. Remind your child that once he is done eating, he will be allowed to play.

Limit portion size.

Toddlers become overwhelmed when they have too much food or too many foods on their plate. For two- and three-year-olds, start with one or two food items at a time. Although toddlers vary in how much food they can consume, a general rule of thumb is that portion sizes should be approximately one tablespoon for every year of age. If your toddler consumes each portion of the two foods on the plate, you can add other foods. If not, offer your toddler additional, smaller portions until she gives you an indication that she is full or has lost interest in the meal. Also, consider having at least one food item that you know your toddler likes to eat, one item that she likely will eat, and one that is relatively new. Introducing new foods on a regular basis is important.

Keep trying.

Don't be discouraged if your child does not automatically like the "new" foods you introduce. We all have food preferences. Some of us like salty food, others sweet, and some spicy. Toddlers are no different. Some toddlers can't get enough fruit, while others avoid it like the plague (or perhaps broccoli). Relax. Your toddler will eventually learn to eat a wide range of foods from every food group. Having a well-balanced, nutritious diet doesn't require eating every food. It's likely you will need to introduce a new food to your toddler somewhere between ten to twenty times before he will readily accept it. This is especially true for those foods that your toddler has questions about. Research has shown the same thing to be true for animals living in the wild. They will often taste a new or foreign food as many as twenty times before deciding if they want to accept it into their diet. Allow your child to taste or simply lick a new food before expecting him to chew and swallow it. If you have the expectation that your child needs to chew and swallow a specific amount of a new food, you may be disappointed. Instead, allow your child to taste it multiple times and let him decide if he wants to slowly but surely include the food in his diet. My experience has been that following this process results in children accepting a wide range of new foods into their diets and parents avoiding needless battles.

Be a good role model.

If you expect your children to try new foods or use certain manners during mealtime, you should be their shining example. Healthy eating habits aren't restricted to children. There are plenty of adults who are unwilling to try new foods or who are very vocal about their displeasure with the way certain foods look, taste, or smell. Adults are not beyond belching so loud that they wake the neighbors or "passing" food like an NFL quarterback. Don't expect your child to try Brussels sprouts if you squirm and scrunch your face at the very sight of them. Your child's eyes will focus on you with laser precision when you take a bite of the very food you're pleading with her to try. Her ears also can perk up when you least expect it. If you and a spouse are eating "alone" or with friends, making negative comments about food may be heard by an unexpected audience. In either case, be mindful of the importance of modeling and demonstrating the behaviors and habits you want your children to acquire. Focus on the positive aspects of food no matter how much you may dislike some particular fruit, vegetable, or protein.

Get creative.

When possible, get creative with how you present snacks and meals. This can involve cutting or carving various fruits and vegetables into different shapes and figures or using cookie forms to create unique shapes. Finding creative ways to present food may make it more interesting to your children. You might even come up with some creative names for each of the food items.

Encourage a healthy appetite.

Have you ever noticed how much more appetizing food looks when you're really hungry? Even foods you typically wouldn't eat look good. You've also probably noticed that if you grocery shop on an empty stomach, you end up with more items in your cart than usual. Hunger has the same effect on your toddler as it does on you. A toddler is much more likely to eat the food you offer and try new foods if she has a healthy appetite. By sticking to a routine of three meals and two snacks, separated by two and a half to three hours, you'll give your toddler a better opportunity to broaden her diet and have enough energy until the next meal or snack. One caveat, however: It's not necessary to be rigid about the schedule. If you're close to a particular snack time or meal and your child is obviously hungry, feed her. You can then adjust the next meal or snack time accordingly. Just be careful you don't allow the schedule to "drift," meaning you start offering snacks randomly, and the schedule evolves into a grazing pattern.

Leave grazing to cattle.

If snack foods and juices are readily available to your toddler, it shouldn't be too surprising that he will not eat much when it's time for a scheduled meal or snack. Children who graze on snacks, juices, and other foods throughout the day are more selective and fussy at mealtime and consume less nutritious food. When it's time for them to eat, they tend to select only those foods that have the most appeal. These tend to be foods that are sweet or very tasty in some other way (salty, for example). They tend to avoid or refuse bland or more nutritious foods. This is not unlike what many adults experience during the holidays. Remember when you were at a family gathering and there were all kinds of hors d'oeuvres and snacks available? By the time the main course was served, your hunger was well satisfied by the goodies you nibbled on. You probably just ate what appealed to you and less of it. If you want your child to be interested in a variety of foods and consume a reasonable and healthy amount, don't allow grazing between meals.

Offer new foods at the start of each meal.

Have your child try a new food at the start of each meal when she is hungriest. Place a very small bite of a new food on your child's plate and ask her to try it. She doesn't need to eat a large quantity. You simply want her to sample or taste the food. Do not react strongly if she does not like the food. It's okay for her not to like it. If you force her to eat the food or a certain amount of it, it will make her much less likely to try it in the future. If she knows she can taste the food and turn her nose up at it, she will be more likely to try something new again in the future. Odds are if she tries it enough, she might actually like it.

Avoid the clean plate club.

The amount of food your child eats at any given meal, or on any given day, will vary dramatically. Children tend to eat more when their bodies are going through growth spurts and eat less when they are not. Their appetites also are affected by fatigue, illness, and a variety of other factors. If you've established a regular mealtime routine and discourage grazing, your child will take in the calories he needs. Requiring your child to "clean his plate" sends the wrong message and gives your child an opportunity to battle over control. Instead, place small but reasonable quantities of food on the plate. If he is still hungry, he can ask for more. If he doesn't eat all the food, at least there is less waste than if you had filled his plate full.

Close the café.

If your child refuses to eat the food you serve, **do not** replace it with another meal or food item. Doing so will only teach your child that you are now a short-order cook, and the café is always open. You can be sure that she will look for just about any reason to avoid the food you serve in the future and whine and complain until you make a peanut butter sandwich or cheese pizza. At each meal, if possible, make sure you include at least one food item that your child enjoys eating. If your child refuses to eat the food you serve, it's unlikely she will become malnourished or teeter on the brink of starvation before the next meal or snack is served. Additionally, if she doesn't eat a particular meal, don't provide her with a snack immediately afterwards. Some parents worry their children will not get enough to eat. However, offering them a snack after refusing a meal is no different than making them something else after they have refused to eat what you prepared.

Maintain balance between liquids and solids.

Some children enjoy drinking relatively large quantities of liquids, such as milk or juice. I've actually seen some children drink up to a gallon of milk a day. That type of milk consumption is obviously an exception. However, there are some children who would gladly drink two cups of milk at the beginning of a meal. While there's nothing wrong with milk (most children need three, four-ounce servings per day), the amount of milk they drink at the start of a meal should be monitored so they don't become so full they avoid eating. You may want to offer two to four ounces of milk with the meal and, if they request more, provide it during the meal.

Snack time does not need to be junk food time.

Consider offering the same quality of food at snack time as you do at mealtime. For some reason, parents tend to offer less nutritious food (crackers, chips, and sugary drinks, for example) as snacks. While there's nothing wrong with these items, there is value in offering more nutritious foods, such as apple wedges and carrots. Also, if you have food left over from a previous meal, and it's food your child enjoys, there's no harm in turning it into a snack.

Let your child make some choices.

If you're undecided about which foods within a particular food group you want to offer your children, ask them. However, do not ask open-ended questions, such as "Would you like some fruit with your meal?" Rather, provide limited choices, such as "Would you like apples or oranges with your meal?" or "Would you like macaroni and cheese or peanut butter sandwiches?" If they don't want either choice, then you can make the selection for them.

Don't be a clean freak.

Toddlers are messy. This is never more apparent than during mealtime. Your child will likely get food all over her hands, face, clothes, and body. Unless she is throwing food or playing with it inappropriately, let her make a mess even if that means she has more spaghetti sauce on her face than in her stomach. If you constantly wipe her face and clean her as she goes, you can disrupt the meal and her interest in eating. By waiting to clean up until after the meal, your toddler's eating skills will improve much more quickly than you might imagine.

Involve your child in mealtime preparation.

Going to the grocery store may not be one of your favorite things to do with your toddler or preschooler. One way to make the shopping experience more enjoyable is to have your child help you with the shopping. Allowing him to hand you certain food items or select foods that are part of his diet can make the shopping experience more enjoyable and help him be more engaged during mealtime. In addition, have your child help you prepare the meal. This might involve pouring ingredients into a mixing bowl, helping you stir food, or any number of age-appropriate prep work. Helping you shop and prepare the meal, even in a small way, may make your child more interested in the final product.

Assign mealtime tasks.

Two- and three-year-old children can do simple tasks at mealtime. In fact, it's a good time for them to do things, such as setting unbreakable plates and cups on the table or putting easy-to-hold condiments (plastic ketchup bottles) on the table. They also can help clear the table, as long as you select items for them to remove. Establishing this expectation will help your child take responsibility for assisting with daily tasks or chores.

Beware of "food jags."

Even though one of your goals may be to have your child eat a wide range of foods, many toddlers (eighteen months to three years) develop "food jags." Food jags are when young children like to eat the same food over and over again. This is fairly common for most toddlers and usually disappears in a matter of weeks. That doesn't mean you need to appease your toddler and offer her macaroni and cheese at every meal for three weeks. However, don't be too concerned if she frequently requests the same food. There's no sense in having a major battle over insisting she eat something different every meal. This phase will come and go fairly quickly.

Use popular condiments to introduce new foods.

Is ranch dressing the new ketchup? I'm starting to wonder, considering how so many young children love it as a dip and a sauce. Condiments, such as ranch dressing, can be used to introduce vegetables and other foods into your child's diet. There's certainly nothing wrong with allowing your child to dip a vegetable, or any other food for that matter, into salad dressing, ketchup, cheese whiz, or salsa. I've seen toddlers enjoy eating everything from pickles (including drinking pickle juice) to taco sauce. Using tasty ingredients, from melted cheese to half-and-half, can enhance the flavor of the foods you want your child to try. Once your child's diet becomes fairly predictable and well balanced, you can limit how much you modify foods using condiments.

Miss(ed) Manners

Parents often have questions about when to start teaching their children manners. The bottom line is that you can't start early enough when it comes to teaching manners of all shapes and sizes. However, you have to be realistic with what you expect them to learn and how quickly they will learn it. Manners, like many behaviors, are learned by watching and practicing. Most toddlers will repeat "Thank you" or "Please" because they have heard it and been prompted to say it hundreds of times. Eventually they figure out that doing so actually has some value.

When it comes to mealtime, toddlers and manners are a bit of an oxymoron. (They don't fit well together.) However, I think it's wise to decide which mealtime manners and routines are important to you and your family and start to have your toddler practice them, even though he won't understand why (but that's not a consideration for most toddler behaviors). If manners, such as waiting to eat until everyone has been seated, asking permission to leave the table when done, saying "Please" and "Thank you," and placing a napkin on one's lap, are important to you and will be part of your family's routine, start practicing now. Have realistic expectations for your toddler and expect to provide many reminders. Make sure you praise his "good manners" when you see them, especially if you did not prompt him. After he has practiced his "manners" hundreds of times, it will start to become a habit. At some point, much later, he will see the value of doing so. Just be patient and don't make this a central part of your mealtime experience. Let's face it, you have enough to "chew" on.

Pay attention to everyone's eating habits and mealtime behavior.

Since your little one cannot get enough of your attention, demonstrate how he can get more of it from you by giving attention to others. That is, provide praise and positive attention to other family members who demonstrate positive mealtime behavior, including their willingness to eat fruits and vegetables. This will peak your toddler's interest, and he just might try to mimic their behaviors in hopes of getting similar attention from you. Take advantage of your child's curiosity and eagerness to please by acknowledging the positive behaviors of others – the same behaviors you want to see from your toddler. When your child imitates those behaviors, lather him with praise.

The Picky Eater: Made, Not Born

Parents seem to focus as much, if not more, attention on their child's eating habits and mealtime behaviors than other behaviors. Perhaps this is because mealtime is so important in most cultures. We spend a tremendous amount of time thinking and talking about food well before it's even prepared. For some, the meal is almost anti-climactic given the amount of time spent considering and preparing the food versus actually consuming it. Just look at the number of television channels devoted to cooking or the many magazines that come out every month with a focus on food. In addition to nutritional concerns, it's the focus on food, mealtime, and the social activities surrounding them that may cause parents to get upset when a child won't eat a meal or acts out at the dinner table. After all, when Junior rejects the family's secret recipe and purple ribbon-winning meatloaf, he has basically insulted every cook in the family dating back to the Mayflower. And what would proper Uncle Ted say if he saw green beans being catapulted from "Fort Jeffrey" to the living room? Perhaps it's not so surprising that parents become concerned when a child becomes a selective or picky eater. This, of course, also leads to a number of challenging behaviors as the child attempts to, through any means possible, avoid certain foods.

Let's take a closer look at why children develop selective eating habits, how you can prevent or limit picky eating, and what specific strategies you can use to turn a picky eater into a pie-eating champion.

Where does picky eating come from? Most picky eaters are made, not born. Eating is a learned behavior. None of us have an innate ability to enjoy chewing and swallowing all the food that comes our way. Additionally, there are a number of physical, social, emotional, and behavioral factors that can quickly disrupt what most of us find to be an enjoyable process. Just as children can learn to become picky eaters, they also can learn to become better eaters.

All toddlers and preschoolers are, by their nature, somewhat selective and picky about their eating habits. This is part of a normal learning process that allows them to figure out what foods smell and taste like and how quickly they want a food item to come into their diet. Don't expect your toddler to readily eat anything in front of her. There's a "normal range" of curiosity and taste testing that is part of learning about foods and expanding one's diet. Thus, it's important for you to be somewhat flexible. As previously mentioned, there are a number of steps you can take to keep normal selectivity from turning into a persistent problem. Here are several factors that can affect how selective a child can be regarding food choices and diet:

Grazing

If I handed you a large chocolate shake and asked you to sip it throughout the afternoon, how hungry would you be at dinner? This is no different than your child snacking on crackers, eating from the pantry, or sipping on juice boxes during the day. Why would you think your child would be interested in eating dinner when he has been taking the edge off his appetite all day? On top of that, there's no real reason for him to eat anything but the tastiest of foods when he knows he can go back to the buffet after the meal is over. Children who graze between scheduled meals and snacks have no motivation to expand their diets. In fact, their only motivation is to eat foods that seem most interesting to them. The best way to turn a child into a selective and finicky eater is to allow him to eat and drink whatever he wants whenever he wants. If that is not your goal (and I assume it's not), stick to providing three meals and two snacks at intervals of two and a half to three hours.

The Menu

Imagine if you walked into a department store to buy a pair of shoes and the salesperson grabbed the first pair she saw, handed them to you with no other options, and then escorted you to the cashier. You would likely protest and ask to see a manager. Having a variety of different shoe styles, colors, and sizes is something we expect. We may "want" a particular style or color, but we don't necessarily "need" it. The fact is, our feet don't care what color or style the shoes happen to be. Just about any shoe can provide the protection and support a foot needs. Food is different. Our bodies and brains don't do very well eating only a few food items. Your child may "want" to eat only a few things, but his body "needs" a wide range of nourishment to get the calories, vitamins, and minerals necessary to grow and be healthy. So, if your child thinks she can refuse any meal you prepare, sending you back and forth to the kitchen until the "right" food comes out, know that she will gladly treat mealtime like a trip to the mall. She will send you back and forth until she gets what she wants. When she gets accustomed to eating only what she knows and likes, she's not likely to try much of anything else.

While it's certainly appropriate to provide choices to your child at mealtime, having at least one item she likes eating is certainly helpful. However, you need to make those decisions and choices *at the start of the meal*. Allowing your child to reject the food you prepare and replacing it with something she wants will only teach her that you've become a short-order cook. The take-home message will be that she can refuse any food at any meal because something more to her liking will replace it.

Some parents worry their child will not get enough to eat and if he misses a meal, it will somehow cause him to shrivel up and blow away. This is nonsense. Your child's nutritional status is much more likely to be compromised if you act like a short-order cook than it is if he has to wait for the next meal because he refused the current one. If your child refuses an opportunity to eat, the next meal will look that much better.

Temperament

Some children are simply strong willed and oppositional by nature. You say black, and they say white. If your child's attitude is that of a determined corporate CEO, you may need to spend a few minutes at mealtime and throughout the day working on better compliance and instructional control. Other chapters in this book, especially the one on listening, address some of the behavior management issues you will encounter when a child is being difficult or oppositional. The point to remember is that if you see oppositional behavior outside of mealtime, you will need to focus on teaching and promoting compliance before you can adequately manage mealtime behaviors.

Texture and Taste Sensitivity

A small minority of children react very negatively to certain tastes or textures of foods. This is a sensory issue that is not usually learned. Some children are extremely hypersensitive to specific tastes, causing them to react negatively to those tastes. Other children are able to consume liquids or even pureed foods but gag and choke on higher textured foods. These children require specialized intervention from occupational therapists, speech pathologists, and psychologists who are trained to manage these behaviors. There also are children whose hypersensitivity to textures and tastes is less severe and does not require specialized intervention but can set the stage for food selectivity. If you are concerned your child may be hypersensitive to specific tastes and textures that go beyond what would typically be observed in a toddler or young child, consult with your pediatrician. Further assessment and intervention may be warranted.

Expanding a Picky Eater's Diet

Sometimes, making adjustments to mealtime schedules, routines, and other mealtime practices is not enough to change the habits of picky eaters. More specific or targeted strategies are needed to gradually expand their diets. The key words here are "gradually expand." If your child has had months or years of selective eating, you're not going to change his eating habits in days or weeks. Remember, he has had four or five opportunities every day to refuse foods he didn't want in order to get his favorites. He won't give up that luxury easily. Therefore, the key is finding ways to gradually introduce different tastes and types of foods so that after weeks or months of sampling, his aversion to trying new foods subsides. In addition, the positive experience he has trying new foods will hopefully motivate him to add those foods to his diet or at least try other foods.

Here are some strategies to help you take your fussy eater from "Whoa!" to "Go!"

Consult an expert.

If you're concerned about your child being a picky eater, and if this has been a concern for years, the first thing you might want to do is consult with a nutritionist. If you have any concerns that

Five Rules for Creating Healthy Eaters

1. Meals and snacks are scheduled. Constant nibbling or sipping is the exception, not the rule.

2. There are a variety of food options available for snacks and meals so children have an opportunity to try new foods without being forced. (They also see Mom and Dad eating a variety of foods, too.)

3. Whatever you want children to eat more of, make it available. Whatever you don't want children to eat, keep it out of the house.

4. Adults determine what is served but children get to eat as much or as little as they like.

5. Meals are consumed with others, at the table, without TV or other distractions.

your child is not receiving enough calories, or if her nutritional status is being compromised because of selective eating, it's important for you to understand exactly what your child needs from a nutritional standpoint. Consulting with your pediatrician and a clinical dietician who specializes in children can provide you with valuable information. It's important for you to know whether your child is receiving enough calories, protein, minerals, vitamins, fats, and carbohydrates on a daily basis. If your child is deficient in the calories she needs, or is missing some critical minerals or vitamins, a nutritionist can help you identify foods to increase her caloric intake and address other nutritional deficiencies.

Use Grandma's Rule.

Grandma's Rule originally referred to the idea that children need to do their homework or chores before being allowed to play or do something fun. You can set up a similar rule when it comes to introducing new foods. The idea here is to require your child to taste or try a new food before having access to a preferred activity or item (going outside, watching a video, or playing on the computer, for example).

For this to be successful, you need to identify a particular activity or toy that is important to your child. To start, practice the rule outside of mealtime. Explain to your child that he will have access to an item or activity whenever he tries a new food during a scheduled snack time. Ease into the routine by picking a food item that you think he will be willing to try. In the beginning, allow him to lick or take a tiny bite rather than consume the whole thing. If he's compliant, let him enjoy a reward for five or ten minutes. Go back and forth until he learns the concept (tasting new foods equals access to something fun). Once he understands, then start using the strategy during meals. The goal is for your child to meet the relatively low requirement of tasting a new food, knowing that he will have brief access to the activity or toy at the end of the meal. If he refuses to try the new food, the meal should go on as usual. However, don't allow him access to the specified reward until the next mealtime rolls around. Hopefully this creates some motivation for your child to try new food without disrupting regular mealtime – if he elects not to try. If this is successful, you may want to vary the reward. It's important your child doesn't have access to the activity or toy at any other time during the day. Also, you should slowly increase the requirements for earning access to the reward, such as having to take larger bites or eat larger portions. It's important to do this gradually because the primary purpose is to increase your child's exposure to new foods.

Modify favorite foods.

One way to help your child expand her diet is to modify the foods she currently eats. Many selective eaters have convinced themselves that they must have a certain brand (Rice Krispies instead of Crispy Rice cereal) or flavor (strawberry milk rather than white) of food. I know children who will only eat cheese pizza if it comes from a particular chain restaurant. If it's made at home or by the local pizzeria, they refuse to eat it. Likewise, I've seen toddlers refuse to eat applesauce or yogurt if it's not served in the right colored bowl. There are explanations for this that I don't have the time or space to discuss here. However, the important thing is to help your child learn that she can and will enjoy foods that may seem vastly different to her but are basically the same. So, if your child likes yogurt, periodically offer a different brand or flavor. Do this with any of the preferred foods she enjoys. It will be important to start with a small taste or quantity of the "new" food so your child can see that trying something "different" isn't too different and can taste quite good. You also can combine a preferred food item with a new version (two different brands of applesauce, for example). Once you make progress helping your child accept slight variations to the foods she currently eats, you can slowly introduce totally new foods. This, like the other strategies, is a slow and time-consuming process. However, it can help you expand a child's diet.

Change the texture or temperature of food.

Consistent with the strategy of modifying favorite foods, some children are selective about the texture or temperature of their food. For these children, slowly modifying how the food feels, or its temperature, can be beneficial (soft versus hard, mushy versus crunchy, or smooth versus lumpy). For example, you might start by serving smooth and creamy mashed potatoes and then gradually transition or modify the dish so eventually you serve chunky mashed potatoes. It usually takes children weeks, often months, to move from one texture to another so be patient. Your child's acceptance of, and confidence in, consuming a particular texture can be your guide for when to move on to a new texture. If your child is sensitive to temperature, preferring foods that are cold or hot, use a similar strategy. For example, you might transition from warm macaroni and cheese to cold macaroni and cheese and eventually back to warm. Start with a temperature your child accepts and gradually warm or cool the food until you reach an optimal temperature. Fading will help your child learn to adjust to different textures and temperatures.

Hide it. Dip it. Modify it.

Take advantage of the wide range of condiments, dips, cheeses, and other ingredients that can alter (hopefully temporarily) the appearance or taste of foods. There's no reason your child needs to be introduced to a particular food in its purest form. By "dressing up" food, you can help your child become more accepting of foods that are "different." For example, you might start by introducing ranch dressing. Have your child dip his finger in the dressing and then taste it. He may need to do this multiple times before he will accept it. Once he discovers he likes ranch dressing (yes, that's possible), he can use it as a dip when he tries new vegetables. Other condiments and dips can be used in a similar fashion.

Step 1: Praise. Step 2: Praise. Step 3: Repeat steps 1 and 2.

It's important to reinforce and praise any effort your child makes to taste new or different foods. You probably look at your child's selectivity as verging on "ridiculous." I assure you, she doesn't see it that way. By encouraging and praising every effort she makes, with no specific expectations about how much she eats, you make it easier for her to continue to try. If you punish your child for not trying new foods or not eating particular foods, it does little to encourage her to make the effort in the future. Losing your patience, raising your voice, or becoming angry will do absolutely nothing to encourage your child to try new foods. It will only encourage her to spend as little time as possible at the dinner table.

Clean out the junk.

Some parents find it difficult to limit access to snack foods and other items that their picky eaters highly desire, and they do little to encourage them to try new and more nutritious foods. It may be necessary to completely eliminate or remove "unneeded" snack foods to reduce temptation (for you and your child). Once the tempting snacks and goodies are gone, don't replace them. Other family members may view this as a hardship, but their arguments won't hold up in court. Besides, it's only temporary. There are worse things than giving up some junk food for a while, at least that's what I've heard!

Use a reward system.

Sometimes a formal reward system can provide the additional structure and motivation children need to try new foods. With a reward system, your child earns a tangible reward for tasting or eating new foods. It also offers him more choices about what foods to try and helps "stack the deck" by motivating him to taste or try foods he otherwise would not.

Here are the steps of one potential reward system you may want to use:

There are two stages to creating this reward system. The first stage is designing the system, and the second stage is introducing the new foods.

Stage One: Creating a "Reward Jar"

1. Use a reward jar that your child can fill with tokens every time he tries new foods. Baby food jars or small clear containers work well. Initially, start with a small jar that will fill up quickly. This will allow your child to be frequently rewarded for his initial tasting and trying. You can increase the size of the jar once your child understands the idea and is motivated to try more foods. For tokens, you can use cotton balls, marbles, buttons, or other household items that can easily fit into the jar.
2. On a sheet of paper, draw a picture of a smiling face, frowning face, and neutral (expressionless) face. (Better still, have your child draw the faces.) When your child tries a new food (either by licking or tasting a small bite), have him rate the food by pointing at the face that represents his feelings. A smiling face means he likes the food. A frowning face means he doesn't like it, and a neutral face means he's unsure. (Be aware that you may have to define or explain the meaning of each face to your child.)
3. Every time your child tries a new food, he will earn a token based on how he rates it. When he points to a smiling face, he can put three tokens in the reward jar. When he points to a neutral face, he can put two tokens in the jar, and a frowning face means one token can go into the jar. (Any foods he rates as neutral or happy should be reintroduced each time you do this activity. This will discourage him from rating foods he doesn't like with a smiling face just so he can have more tokens. If he knows the foods he rates high will be offered to him again, he's more likely to use those ratings only for foods he truly likes.)
4. When the jar is full of tokens, your child earns a reward. The rewards you use are only limited by

your creativity. Whatever it is, it should be something he enjoys (having you read him a story, playing a game, or going to a playground, for example). You also can wrap small gifts in newspaper or tin foil and let him pick one from a basket. This visual display can help pique his interest in the prizes and stay motivated. Use your imagination to make the experience fun. However, your child should only have access to these rewards when he earns them for trying new foods. They should not be available to him at other times of the day. If he has access to these rewards, or anything similar during the day, it will reduce his motivation to try new foods.

5. When your child understands the concept of the activity and has earned a reward or two, you can increase the size of the reward jar. This means the number of food items he has to try before earning a reward also increases. For older children, you can eventually use a jar similar to the "Chore Reward Jar" described on pages 62-63 in the Listening Chapter.

Stage Two: Introducing New Foods

1. Find an ice cube tray or other divided tray that has at least four compartments or sections.
2. Identify four foods you want your child to try, and place an extremely small amount in each of the four sections (one food item per section). When you first introduce this activity, use four foods your child has consumed in the past. This will make it easier for him to sample the foods, earn rewards, and see the connection between trying foods and earning rewards. When he samples a food, ask him to rate it by pointing to one of the three faces. He will earn the number of tokens associated with that rating. After he samples a food, let him place the tokens in the jar.

3. After a few times of using foods your child is familiar with, introduce altered versions of those foods. You can alter them by changing how you prepare, cook, or season them. Do this a few times and then introduce entirely new foods. Initially, the new foods should be similar in taste or texture and not too drastically different from the foods your child has tried in the past. For example, you can replace a pear (one of his preferred foods) with a banana (a new food). Or, you can use deli turkey meat (new food) instead of deli bologna (a preferred food). Continue to gradually modify the foods as your child becomes more comfortable eating them before you introduce completely new and different foods.
4. Reintroduce the foods over and over again until your child has tried each food item at least ten to fifteen times. Continue to use foods rated as "neutral" and "liked" and add a new food to replace those rated as "disliked." You may want to start with six to ten food items and rotate them an adequate number of times in order to determine if he enjoys the food.
5. Keep track of the foods your child tries and how he rates them. That way you will know which foods to keep in the rotation and which to remove.
6. When you first start doing this activity, schedule it around snack time. This gives you two opportunities each day to introduce different and new foods.
7. When your child is more comfortable and cooperative doing this exercise at snack time, you can try it during regular mealtimes, too.

The reward system, and other similar techniques, is a way to gradually introduce children to new and different foods. When combined with the strategies described in this chapter, you can help your child gradually expand his diet and improve his nutrition while relieving your own worries about his relationship with food. Remember, however, this process will likely take months and sometimes years. But the end result will be worth it: a healthier, balanced diet.

If you feel your child's nutritional status and/or behavioral resistance to food is significant or leading to malnutrition, there are feeding specialists throughout the country who can provide more intensive assessments and interventions.

chapter 6

Punching, Pinching, Poking, Pulling, and Pushing

Nadia's father received a phone call from her daycare. Nadia was biting other children and occasionally pushing them, too. Although these misbehaviors happened at daycare, there also were instances in the neighborhood of Nadia pulling kids' hair. Nadia's parents first noticed her aggressiveness toward other children when she was about two. They consistently told her "No," and kept a close eye on her. They knew that children her age tended to be aggressive at times, but they expected her to grow out of it. She didn't. The hitting, biting, and pushing seemed to get worse as she got older. Nadia's parents were now receiving a lot of advice from family, friends, and daycare staff. Below is some of the advice Nadia's mom and dad heard. Which, if any, do you agree with?

A. When she bites, bite her back.

B. Anytime she's aggressive toward another child or adult, she should get a spanking.

C. Limit her access to other children until she outgrows the behavior.

D. Redirect Nadia at the first sign of any frustration or anger, before she becomes aggressive.

E. Put Nadia in time-out immediately after any aggressive behavior.

F. Encourage and praise Nadia's use of words rather than aggressive actions when she is frustrated or angry.

The first two suggestions (A and B), although popular, are not effective and may actually cause Nadia's aggression to get worse. Becoming physically aggressive toward children in response to their aggressiveness sends the wrong message. Research even suggests it may actually increase their negative behaviors. The third suggestion (C) is not practical. The last three pieces of advice, however, provide reasonable ways to respond to Nadia's aggressive behavior. In this chapter, I will identify what can cause children to become aggressive and the most effective ways to manage it.

What Is Aggression?

The word "aggression" seems to make behaviors, such as pushing, pulling, and pinching, sound much worse than they are. For young children, aggression essentially means they are not keeping their hands and feet (and sometimes mouths!) to themselves. They pull, pinch, push, kick, bite, and twist just about any body part available. There are two things to remember with these kinds of behaviors. First, the majority of these behaviors are fairly common, especially in toddlers. Aggressive behaviors become less frequent as children get older. By the time they are school aged, such behaviors are relatively infrequent. So, you should not be terribly concerned if your toddler is occasionally aggressive. It's more concerning if the behavior continues or becomes more frequent as your toddler approaches preschool and beyond. Also, boys tend to be more aggressive than girls. Secondly, it's important to remember that the aggressive behaviors of toddlers and preschoolers are different than the aggressive behaviors of adolescents and adults. When adolescents and adults are aggressive, they often intend to cause harm. That is not typically true for toddlers and preschoolers whose aggression is usually related to frustration, fatigue, lack of communication skills, and so forth. So, a two-year-old who is biting his peers at daycare is unlikely to become the next village bully.

Where Does Aggression Come From?

For most children, aggressive behaviors come from a variety of sources. In some instances, it's easy to determine a specific cause of the aggression. Oftentimes, however, there are a number of influences that affect the frequency and intensity of the aggression. Here are some of the factors that can influence your child's aggressive behavior:

Payoff in the Environment

Sometimes toddlers and preschoolers figure out that there is some payoff for being aggressive. This often happens with children who are physically larger or more persistent than their peers. They learn that taking a toy allows them to keep it or that pushing another child down lets them be first in line at the swing set. If this type of payoff happens often enough and/or there are no immediate negative consequences for the behavior, some children will use their aggressive behavior to their advantage. Also, some children learn that it's easier to give up a toy or a place in line than deal with an aggressive peer, thus motivating the aggressor to continue. Other children enjoy the attention (positive or negative) they immediately get from their aggressive actions. Regardless of what the payoff is for being aggressive, it's important you intervene as early as possible when this type of behavior happens. You need to take whatever action you can to remove any payoff to your child for being aggressive.

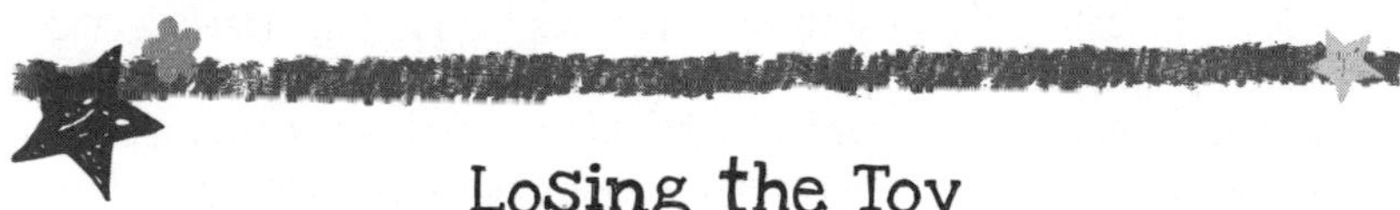

Losing the Toy

Brandon smiled from ear to ear as he pulled a toy truck out of his brother's hands. Not only did he get to play with the truck, he also got to hear his brother howl like a wolf. Brandon's joy was short lived, however. His mother responded by making him return the truck, sit in time-out for five minutes, and lose access to his favorite toy for the remainder of the day.

Aggressive Role Models (Monkey See, Monkey Do)

Our society is full of all kinds of examples of aggressive and, at times, violent behavior. If one flips through the television channels at almost any given time, they will observe All-Star wrestlers throwing each other out of the ring, Larry T. Lobster pounding SpongeBob into the sand with a bar bell, and a shoot-out on some city street. Modern media in all its forms provide countless other examples. I still remember a friend's four-year-old daughter running from the basement of our home screaming and crying while watching *Snow White*. I thought, what could go wrong watching *Snow White*? Then I remembered how the movie begins with the huntsman, who worked for the queen, chasing Snow White with a knife intending to cut out her heart. Even in classic PG entertainment, our children have plenty of opportunities to see aggressive and violent behavior in a variety of contexts.

You might be thinking, "Yeah, but it's only TV, and that's make believe." Keep in mind, nearly all children between the ages of two and six have significant difficulty distinguishing between reality and fantasy. Most children in this age group believe in Santa Claus, the Tooth Fairy, and Thomas the Tank Engine. The vast majority of children this age also believe what they see on TV, whether it's a cartoon, a video game, or professional wrestling. (That's right, it's not real.)

Changing the Rule

Caitlyn was expected to pick up all of the toys on the floor of her room each night before she went to bed. That was the rule! Her pleading and whining for help fell on deaf ears. The pleading and whining soon turned into full blown tantrums, with Caitlyn hurling toys faster than an All-Star pitcher. When her parents intervened, she began hitting and kicking. Time-outs and other consequences didn't seem to help. Her parents decided they and Caitlyn were too tired to focus on picking up toys before bedtime, so they changed the rule. The toys on Caitlyn's floor needed to be picked up each morning before she ate breakfast. Doing this in the morning, when Caitlyn was refreshed and hungry for breakfast, eliminated nearly all of the meltdowns and drama.

It's important for you to monitor the content of the media your child has access to, and it's especially important if your child is becoming increasingly aggressive. For example, if you see your five-year-old standing on the back of the couch with a stuffed animal over her head yelling, "I'm going to pound you back to the Stone Age," take a look at the programs she has access to in your home and elsewhere. You might be surprised at what you see and hear.

The above references the effects of media violence. A direct, and more meaningful, modeling influence occurs "live." Your child may be exposed to other children (and adults) who are aggressive toward each other at home, in daycare, or in the neighborhood. If so, watch to see if your child imitates their behaviors or make note if you observe an increase in aggressive behavior. Children who are frequently exposed to various forms of aggression not only imitate that behavior, but their aggression starts to become part of the "norm." This often leads to an increase in aggressive behavior in a variety of situations and environments.

Unwanted Tasks

Some children become aggressive when asked to complete an unwanted task, such as getting dressed, taking a bath, or picking up toys. This also can happen when a task requires them to stop doing something they enjoy and follow a demand, such as turning off the TV or putting on their coat. Sometimes parents have to guide their children through tasks, and their children respond by pushing, yelling, hitting, or running away. The children hope their aggressive behaviors will be rewarded – they will get out of doing a task or chore and continue to do what they enjoy. If the behavior has the intended result for the child (he doesn't have to put the coat on or turn off the TV), the aggressive behavior is rewarded. You can guess what will happen the next time an undesirable request is made and some physical assistance by a caretaker is required.

Hunger, Sickness, and Fatigue

Most of us are aware of how frustrated and impatient we can get when we're tired, hungry, or ill. This is especially true for toddlers. It's no surprise to see a child melt down when his stomach's growling, he's exhausted, or he feels sick. These meltdowns are sometimes

Biting

Although all forms of aggression have been grouped together, biting tends to get the attention of parents, daycare providers, and teachers more quickly than other aggressive behaviors. Perhaps it's because biting sometimes draws blood, or perhaps it's because it seems more deliberate or dangerous. Regardless, here are a few facts about biting and some strategies for taking the bite out of Little Count Dracula.

A few facts:

- About ten percent of children under age four have bitten another child at least once.
- Biting can be dangerous. The jaw is much more powerful than most other muscle groups.
- Biting occurs for several reasons, including undeveloped verbal skills, frustration, teething, attention, and feeling threatened.

What to do:

- Intervene early when you see frustration and use redirection.
- When a child bites or attempts to bite, provide a sharp "NO!"
- Remove the child from the situation and apply a brief time-out.
- Comfort the harmed child.
- Modify play activities/schedules, when possible, if biting seems to involve a specific child or during a certain activity or time of day.
- Monitor the "biter" closely during play activities.
- Reward the child for playing appropriately, using words versus actions, and asking for help.

Following the above steps will usually leave its mark on any biter. However, if biting persists and there is concern about the safety or health of other children, consider putting a safe but unpleasant liquid (vinegar or some other edible product) on the lips of the biter. This, when combined with a sharp "No!" and time-out, will clearly indicate that biting is not acceptable. Placing a small quantity of vinegar on a washcloth and applying it to the lips of the biter will associate the negative taste with the biting. This is one more reminder that biting is not allowed. You should always check with your pediatrician before doing this. Also, this option should be used only when all other efforts have failed, the biting is increasing, and the safety of others is a concern.

accompanied by aggressive behavior. For example, you have probably learned to make sure your child is well fed before a long car trip or to avoid certain tasks at the end of a busy day to reduce the risk of a tantrum. Being aware of how fatigue or illness affects your child's behavior will hopefully help you reduce opportunities for aggressive behavior to occur.

Communication Problems

Have you ever had an experience where you had difficulty communicating with someone? Maybe it was your spouse, a salesperson, or a cab driver in a foreign country. Do you remember how frustrated you were? Whether you raised your voice or reacted in some other inappropriate way, you probably had difficulty remaining calm and thinking about all of the options available to you. When adults are unable to communicate effectively, they often lose their composure, usually verbally but sometimes physically. When toddlers are unable to communicate effectively (which is often), they also lose their composure, both verbally and physically. The stomping, yelling, throwing, and hitting that you see from your toddler or preschooler is not some new dance he learned on Nickelodeon. These behaviors may be connected to his inability to express himself or communicate effectively. When children's thinking skills have moved ahead of their ability to communicate those thoughts and ideas, frustration builds. As they learn new and different things every day and their cognitive skills expand, their speech and language skills do not always keep up. This leads to frustration in a variety of situations, which then leads to hitting, kicking, biting, and pushing. The good news, however, is by the time children reach preschool and kindergarten, their thinking and speech skills are usually working at the same speed, and their level of aggressive behavior decreases.

Activity Level

Toddlers are, by their nature, very active and on-the-go. They are quick to grab, hug, run, jump, and reach. Their boundless energy shows up from sunrise to sunset. Because of this, someone or something will occasionally be banged, bumped, or bruised a little too roughly. It's not uncommon for someone to be knocked to the ground as a child rushes to be first in line, or for the girl next door to feel her stomach in her throat when a friend hugs her a little too tightly. There are countless examples of situations where a child's impulsive and exuberant behavior resulted in some type of aggressive response. Thus, when trying to understand the source of your child's aggressive behavior, take into account the behaviors that may be due to your child "acting without thinking." That isn't an excuse for the behavior but it's an explanation and an opportunity for you to work on helping your child learn to "wait," "stand in line," "keep hands and feet to self," "shake hands, not hug," and other skills.

Corporal Punishment

José's parents are increasingly frustrated because Josè kicks his sister anytime she annoys him. Spanking is their primary discipline technique for inappropriate behavior, such as kicking. After all, if spanking was good enough for Josè's dad when he was growing up, it's good enough for Josè. Even though they spank Josè every time he kicks his sister, it doesn't seem to help. In fact, Josè only seems to get angrier. Josè's father ends up spanking harder. It still has no effect, except now Josè tends to avoid his dad and hides after he fights with his sister. Josè's dad spanks less often because of its limited effectiveness and because he's concerned that his son avoids him. He's frustrated because if spanking doesn't work, what will?

When parents use corporal punishment as their primary method of discipline, they increase the likelihood their children will become aggressive. This is supported by volumes of research on the use of physical punishment. Additionally, if parents use corporal punishment when angry, they risk unintentionally causing harm due to excessive force. Also, many young children will model their parents' corporal punishment on siblings (spanking a sister for misbehaving, for example). Another disadvantage of using corporal punishment is that many parents don't feel confident about using it. They either use it just for severe behaviors or they use it inconsistently. Anytime you're unsure about using a particular discipline technique, the likelihood of using it consistently goes down along with its effectiveness. Finally, there is clearly a mixed message if you say, "Don't hit" and follow that with a spanking. From a cost-benefit standpoint, there are too many effective alternatives available to parents to justify using corporal punishment in response to a child's aggressive behavior.

Entertainment

Remember the little boy in school who pulled the pigtails of the girl sitting in front of him? Maybe that was you! Some children are just simply curious about what will happen if they pull someone's hair or push them. Depending on the reaction of the victim, they may find this to be fairly entertaining. Some children learn fairly quickly they can get a variety of unique reactions from others by pinching, biting, pushing, and kicking. They enjoy the squeals, shrieks, and cries that follow when they pinch, push, or hit a sibling or peer. Let's face it, they don't make toys like that! If your child is getting some type of entertainment value out of being aggressive, you need to close down the "show" and perhaps provide him with his own unique "box seat," sometimes known as time-out. Pay attention to your child to see if, in fact, his behaviors are intentional. The smirk on his face or the "Who me?" look may be your first clue.

Turning Lions into Lambs

You may not have the intention of turning your little lion into a lamb, but you can certainly take some of the growl and bite out of the lion. The following techniques can help you address aggressive behaviors before and when they occur. They also can help your child cope with frustration and learn self-control skills.

Watch. Listen. Learn.

When your children become aggressive, you probably respond immediately to put out the fire. This is certainly appropriate. At the same time, however, you can learn a tremendous amount by watching children in situations where they become frustrated or angry. Taking time to watch their interactions with others or while they are struggling with a particular toy or task can tell you a lot. You also can learn a significant amount by noting the circumstances, such as the time of day (when the aggression occurred), location, who's involved, the context (at playtime or in preschool, for example), health status (tired, hungry or sick), the "triggers" (Who, how or what started it?), and the outcome (any benefits). Chances are, you will see some type of pattern or common elements. Identifying a pattern allows you to more accurately predict when the behavior might occur and what might serve as a trigger for the behavior. You can use this information to teach your child better self-control skills in those situations. At the very least, it can help you intervene before the aggressive behavior occurs. It also may give you some guidance about what activities are most likely to cause frustration and where you need to be more watchful and attentive. Some parents like to use charts to document where and when aggressive behaviors happen. Feel free to document your child's behavior in a way that is helpful and easy for you. Review the example on the next page.

Once you have observed the circumstances surrounding your child's aggressive behavior, try to determine if there is a specific trigger for the behavior. A trigger is something that gets the behavior started. For example, does saying the word "No" consistently lead to hitting? Maybe the trigger is fatigue or a particular play activity. Perhaps it's when your child is told that she needs to stop an activity, take a bath, and get ready for bed. Knowing the specific triggers that tend to reliably predict your child's aggressive behavior allows you to promptly intervene or look for alternative ways to manage a situation to reduce the aggression.

After observing the circumstances surrounding your child's aggressive behavior and looking for triggers or causes of the behavior, you will be in a much better position to develop solutions. For example, if your child is overly tired or hungry, the solution is simple. If he is having difficulty communicating, and that seems to be the trigger, work on nonverbal ways for him to communicate. He also may need encouragement to use his words in those situations. Regardless, taking time to observe all of the circumstances surrounding your child's aggressive behavior will allow you to better manage the aggression. Here are other strategies you can use when your child is aggressive:

Intervene early.

Probably the best time to manage your child's aggression is **before** it happens. That's right, before it happens. It's obvious to you when your child has pushed, shoved, or bitten another child. What is less obvious are all of the events and warning signs that happen before such behaviors. Sometimes the hitting and kicking happen instantly and without warning. However, in many situations, the aggression is the last link in a chain. The chain is a series of events that start fairly small and get bigger until the explosion occurs. A chain

Aggression Chart

Date & Time	What was the trigger? (Who or what started it?)	Was your child ill, hungry, or tired?	What was the behavior (hitting, kicking, or biting, for example)?	Where did it happen?	Who was involved?	What was the consequence?
4 PM Tuesday	*Charlie tried to pull the truck away from Jeremy.*	*Both children probably hungry.*	*Jeremy hit Charlie with truck.*	*Bedroom*	*Jeremy, Charlie*	*Both boys sent to time-out. Neither boy could play with truck until after dinner.*

might look something like this: Your five-year-old is playing with a toy when a sibling reaches for it. The five-year-old says, "Don't," and the sibling walks away. Soon the sibling returns for the toy, and the five-year-old responds with a louder "Don't" and a gesture (makes a fist). The sibling leaves but returns again and attempts to grab the toy. He's met with a punch to the arm. You, of course, can't help but notice the punch (and the screaming that follows).

In this scenario, when is the best time to intervene? You guessed it, at the beginning of the chain. Had you intervened when you heard the first, or even the second and louder "Don't," the outcome may have been different. A simple warning to both children may have allowed them to consider their options (Do I continue to go after my brother's toy? What do I do if he keeps coming back?) and avoid physical contact. Both children played a part and had other choices available to them. There are a variety of situations that unfold like this. If you're able to pay attention to the beginning links in the chain, you can reduce the number of aggressive events and, more importantly, help your children develop effective problem-solving skills.

If there are specific triggers that consistently cause your child to become aggressive, and despite your best efforts to manage it, the negative behavior continues, you may have to limit your child's access to that situation as best you can. Although difficult, you may need to temporarily limit his access to a particular playmate, toy, activity, or whatever trigger is identified. Doing so may be the most effective thing you can do until he develops additional self-control skills and/

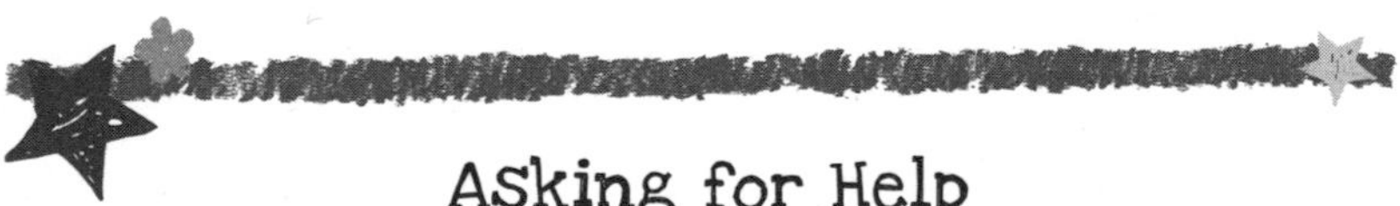

Asking for Help

Nathan was having difficulty opening a box of cereal. His mom heard him huffing, puffing, and pounding on the box. She went to him and asked, "Nathan, do you need help?" He nodded. Mom responded, "Nathan, say 'Help, please.'" Nathan repeated the words, and then Mom opened the cereal box. Although he continued to get frustrated on occasion, he soon started saying "Help, please" more frequently, and the puffing and pounding disappeared.

or enough time passes to allow for some period of maturity. If avoidance of a particular trigger is not possible or reasonable, continue to use the previously described strategies to provide the most effective intervention possible.

Use words rather than actions.

In Chapter 2, I emphasized the importance of parents using actions not words. When it comes to helping children manage their aggressive behaviors, they need to learn the opposite. That is, you need to encourage your child to use words not actions. Because of toddlers' developing language skills, they are much more likely to become frustrated because of their inability to communicate effectively. This is especially true if their language skills are just emerging. There are a number of ways you can help your child improve his communication skills. One way is to pair your child's emotional state with the word that describes it. If she feels sad, for example, say, "You're sad," and then encourage her to repeat the word. Do the same with other emotions, such as anger and happiness. Children need to understand the label that goes with their emotions before they can express them to others.

Along with teaching and pairing emotions with words, it's also important to teach children words that will have some value when they interact with others. Teaching and reinforcing the use of "Yes," "No," Help," "Please," and other similar words, in the appropriate context, is beneficial. For example, if Keisha is frustrated trying to operate a toy and doesn't know how to say "Help," she is likely to persist until her frustration becomes all consuming. On the other hand, if another child tries to take a toy away from her, Keisha saying "No" will hopefully be more effective than responding with a karate chop to the neck. (Assuming, of course, the other child understands what "No" means.) These issues are more relevant for toddlers. As children approach preschool age, their language is more advanced. Thus, an understanding of basic words and phrases is more commonplace. Also, you can teach older children more sophisticated language and expect more from them. I suggest you not only identify the emotion your child is experiencing, but also remind her to "use your words."

In a short amount of time, you can accomplish a number of things once you help your child communicate when she's frustrated. For example, if she is mad because she can't button a doll's dress, ask "Do you need help?" When your child nods her head, repeat "Help" and then prompt her to say the word. You might even prompt a "Please." When your daughter says "Help, please," you can button the dress for her. You might be thinking it would be a whole lot easier to just button it for her without the prompting. Of course it would. But when you take the time to pair words with an action, you teach your child a lot. As you repeat this over and over again, your child will quickly learn that she simply needs to come to you with "Help, please" to get assistance. She has learned a much easier way to accomplish a difficult task, which will eventually reduce her frustration. To allow her to struggle for an indefinite period or to do the task for her slows down the entire learning process. This is not to suggest you need to help in every situation. There are some tasks children need help with and others they need to learn on their own. However, if the situation involves a trigger that predictably makes her get angry, and eventually aggressive, intervening and prompting her to use words can defuse the situation. With a toddler, keep the language simple (no more than two or three words), have him repeat the word(s), and then provide a helpful action. Again, as your child gets older, the language you use can be more sophisticated, and your expectations for him to use words rather than actions should also increase.

Provide healthy outlets.

You're probably pretty clear about what and whom your child is not allowed to hit, kick, or push. But does your child know what, when, and where it's appropriate to blow off steam by kicking, hitting, or throwing? Having physical activities that allow your child to release some of his boundless energy is a good idea. Redirecting your child to an outside activity or to a corner of the house where he can throw, jump, or kick toys designed for such activity can provide an appropriate physical release.

Limit verbal reprimands.

Parents often wonder whether saying "No" is enough when their toddler hits or kicks. The use of a strong verbal reprimand, such as "No hitting," is an appropriate response, by itself, when a behavior first occurs. When it happens again, adding another consequence, such as time-out, is needed. For most children, hearing a verbal reprimand does not decrease a behavior. In fact, it can provide an opportunity for children to act more aggressively. The reason why is because children get very skilled at tuning out reprimands, especially if that is a parent's only response. They quickly can become immune to warnings and threats, especially if a consequence does not follow the warnings. When it comes to aggressive behavior, providing a verbal reprimand is a way of directly telling your children that the behaviors are unacceptable. Once they have a good understanding of this, which should happen fairly quickly, verbal reprimands should be accompanied by the use of time-out, the loss of a privilege, or some other negative consequence.

Use redirection.

This is a basic strategy that all parents should use with young children in a variety of situations and certainly applies to children who become easily frustrated and/or aggressive. Redirection simply involves prompting your child, either verbally ("Look at the puppy outside the window.") or physically (a tap on the shoulder and pointing to a different toy), at the **first** sign of frustration. You "redirect" your child from a problematic activity or situation to one that is not. Redirection should be used when there is a high probability for aggression. You want to give your child plenty of opportunities to manage frustration on her own, but only in those situations where you feel she can learn from doing so. If you've done your homework by observing your child's aggressive behavior and identifying what "triggers" her frustration and aggression, you can use redirection as a first-line defense to reduce the possibility of aggressive behavior. You also show her that other alternatives are available.

Redirection can take many forms. For example, let's say your three-year-old is upset because a friend is playing with her favorite toy and won't share. Rather than try to convince the friend to share the toy or ignore what appears to be a minor situation, simply point out another toy or two to your child. Or, you might engage your daughter in an activity that takes the focus away from her favorite toy. If she follows your redirection, provide some meaningful attention, such as praise ("You're playing so well."), a smile, or hug.

Follow through on demands.

If your child is being aggressive because he does not want to complete a task or is trying to avoid some activity, it's important that you don't give in and let him avoid doing or completing the task. You don't want to teach your child that his aggression works. As a result, you may have to physically guide him through the task regardless of his aggressiveness. Or, you may need to place him in time-out and then return to the task after time-out ends.

For younger and smaller children, it's sometimes easier to physically guide them through a task (putting on pajamas, for example) than it is to go back and forth between putting them in time-out and finishing the task. If the aggressive behavior occurs because you ended a fun activity (turned off the electronic game), it's important that you keep the game off, regardless of your child's behavior. Your child's aggressive behavior should result in a time-out. In addition, your child should not have access to the game for an extended period of time, especially if the behavior occurred early in the day and he has additional opportunities to play with it. If the behavior occurred at the end of the day, limiting access to the game the next day will be less effective because too much time has elapsed. The bottom line is that your child must learn that his aggression will not help him either get out of completing a task or allow him to continue doing a fun activity.

Use time-out.

For an in-depth discussion about time-out, see Chapter 10. I won't elaborate on its use here other than to say time-out may be your most effective response to aggressive behavior. Aggressive behavior requires an immediate response and one that will associate the negative behavior with a meaningful consequence for your child. Time-out provides the most effective way to communicate to your child that biting, shoving, or pinching is unacceptable. In other words, "If you're going to do the crime, you have to do the time." Time-out is a good technique to use regardless of the cause of the aggression. As your child matures, you will have additional options. For now, time-out should be used routinely when your toddler or preschooler is aggressive.

There is an additional consideration when managing aggressive behavior. Sometimes parents use time-out only when the aggression involves physical contact – when a child actually kicks, punches, pushes, or bites someone. I would suggest that even if a gesture is made (a swing and a miss!), you use time-out. Providing a negative consequence for gesturing an aggressive act sends a clear message that the behavior is unacceptable. By doing this, you intervene at the beginning of the "aggressive chain" of behaviors, which is the best time to manage the behavior. And even if the aggressive behavior is relatively minor, it's important for your child to receive the appropriate message. In fact, I would argue this is probably the best time to provide a consequence, such as time-out or loss of privilege. Intervening early can reduce the likelihood that a situation will become more severe.

Praise good choices.

While it's important to respond appropriately to your child when he's aggressive, it's even more important to offer praise and acknowledgment when he exercises self-control. If you see your child walk away from a sibling who is teasing him, play with a different toy instead of fighting over the one he wants, or ask you to help with a difficult task, don't take it for granted. Rather, praise him for the choice he made using very specific language. Whether he made the

Stopping the Teasing

Krystal liked to tease her five-year-old brother Desmond. She loved how he would scowl, yell, hit, and kick because it provided her with hours of entertainment. As a bonus, she enjoyed watching Desmond sit in time-out for his behavior. She always made sure Desmond saw her having fun while he sat alone. Desmond's behavior frustrated their dad. In addition to giving negative consequences to Desmond for hitting his sister, Dad spent a lot of time explaining to him what his other options are when he's teased. One day when Krystal was bored, she started her teasing routine. This time, however, Desmond didn't attack back. He grumbled a bit, but then turned and went to another room to play with the family dog. Desmond's father was watching and immediately told Desmond how proud he was for the good choice he made. He acknowledged how frustrating it can be to be teased and how hard it is to ignore it. Dad gave Desmond a hug and repeated how proud he was of him. This, along with Krystal earning a negative consequence, went a long way toward motivating Desmond to make similar choices in the future.

choice naturally or after some thought, your child should understand the importance of making the appropriate choice. Your acceptance and awareness of positive behaviors will go a long way toward encouraging him to make similar choices in the future.

Give comfort.

When I say give comfort, I'm referring to the child who is hurt not the one who was aggressive. Providing empathy and comfort to a child who has been hurt, while letting the aggressive child know that "Hitting hurts," accomplishes two things. It sends the message that hitting is wrong, and it provides positive attention and support to the child who was harmed. The harmed child gets the attention and support she needs, and the aggressive child sees that positive attention is given to the victim not the aggressor.

Be a positive role model.

Young children learn a tremendous amount from watching. This of course involves watching what you do in a variety of situations. You may consider this is a good thing, or it may make you a little nervous. In any case, you can take advantage of the opportu-

The Comfort Box

Angry or frustrated children are like bulls standing in front of a red cape. They have their mind on one thing. They are not thinking about what else they can do, or how they can control their frustration. Rather, they are thinking about the thing or person that made them angry. Putting together several activities and toys that provide comfort to your children can give them a calming option when they feel angry or frustrated. The comfort box is simply a collection of books, toys, stuffed animals, or other items that provide comfort and enjoyment. Keeping these items in one place, such as a plastic tote, allows for quick and easy access. It also provides your children with reliable activities they can turn to on their own or when prompted by you. I would suggest keeping these items in a specific location (a child's bedroom or hall closet) so everyone knows where to find them.

nity to model or demonstrate for your child ways to act appropriately when angry. You can do this by creating these situations or, better still, when you actually find yourself frustrated. The important thing is that you describe what you're thinking and feeling out loud for the benefit of your child. For example, you might be tacking a nail in the wall and hit your thumb. You could choose to swear like a sailor, and throw the hammer through the window. Or, you could use the situation to teach your child how to react calmly. You might say aloud, for example, "Ouch. I hit my finger with the hammer. It hurts and that makes Mommy angry. I'm going to put the hammer down and sit quietly until I feel better." You then might go sit in a comfortable chair for a few minutes before saying, "I feel better now. I think I'll try to hang the picture again." Any situation in which you're frustrated, or could potentially become frustrated, can serve as an opportunity to model a variety of self-control skills. Situations where you can model self-control skills can involve anything from trying to open a jar lid to accepting defeat after losing a card game to getting bumped into by someone.

The point here is that you likely experience naturally occurring frustration each and every day. We all do. Take advantage of these situations to show your child how you can react calmly and effectively. At the same time, when you overreact or react inappropriately, use the opportunity to teach a lesson. Explain to your child how you became angry and made a bad choice (explaining what that was), and then describe or demonstrate how you can correct the situation or do it differently next time. Also, it's important to show your child how you successfully managed a frustrating situation, including the steps you took to make "good choices."

Another option that fits with the idea of modeling is role-play. You can role-play various situations with your child, although it works better if your child is school aged as opposed to a young toddler. With role-play, you want to recreate situations that are problematic for your child and practice how to handle them better. Let's say, for example, your son frequently becomes aggressive because a neighborhood kid always teases him. You can recreate the situation and have your son practice different ways of responding to the teasing (walking away, ignoring, or telling the child to stop, for example). Some children enjoy role-playing with stuffed animals or dolls. This takes the focus off of them and allows them to participate more openly and cooperatively. So you might role-play first with your child using dolls or stuffed animals and then role-play with just you and your child. You can start by having your child describe or demonstrate an inappropriate or aggressive behavior (hitting) and then briefly discuss why it's unacceptable ("We don't hit. Hitting hurts.") From there, talk about more appropriate choices he has and practice those choices with him. This gives you a chance to praise his positive behaviors and allows him to rehearse a variety of different responses in a controlled situation. Some children are willing to role-play and others are not. If your child is willing to do this with you, you should take advantage of the opportunity and practice and rehearse multiple times.

Try to create as much emotion and realism as possible in the role-play scenario, including the emotions your child may experience in that moment. Identify and label the emotions to help him understand what he's feeling and provide appropriate choices or options for him to take when he feels angry or frustrated. Use the practice as a chance to prompt him to make better choices and to praise him for making better decisions. Positive practice can be very effective for school-aged children who are having challenges in certain situations or with certain individuals. Again, if you're able to spend time observing your children and learning about the circumstances and triggers that make them aggressive, you can create role-play situations that address those triggers.

You also might consider orchestrating situations between yourself and other family members that replicate high-risk situations your child may experience. For example, you could have your spouse take away a book you're reading and then verbalize your frustrations aloud. "Kelly, you took the book from me without asking. That makes me angry." (Remember to use language your child might use.) "Give it back please." Then have your spouse, or whoever took the book, give it back to you appropriately. You are limited only by your creativity. You want to model situations that are similar to or exactly like your child's experiences. There's no reason why you and other family members can't replicate play situations or other circumstances that are problematic for your child. Through role-play, you can demonstrate effective ways to manage frustration in those situations.

chapter 7

"Disturbance in Aisle Three!" Managing Your Child's Behavior in Public

Mrs. Chen was double-checking her to-do list before she and her four-year-old daughter Amy left for the store. The last item on the list was "Get Amy ready to go shopping." It was Mom's reminder to make sure she did the following before leaving for the store: feed Amy, discuss appropriate shopping behavior, and figure out how long Amy will tolerate shopping.

Amy ate her breakfast, so that was checked off the list. Mom then told Amy, "It's time to get ready to go shopping. Remember the rules: Stay by my side and no touching unless Mom says." She also reminded Amy that this was a looking trip for Amy, not a buying trip. Amy said "Okay," and Mom grabbed her purse to go.

When they arrived at the store and walked through the door, Mom gave Amy another reminder, "Remember, stay by my side and no touching." Amy nodded in agreement. There were five items on the shopping list, and Mom knew it would take about ten minutes to get everything. Ten minutes tended to be the amount of time that worked well for Amy. Past shopping trips that lasted longer ended in disaster. Mom learned to keep shopping trips with her daughter short. If she knew it would take a while, she made other arrangements for Amy.

As they walked through the store, Mom praised Amy for staying by her side and keeping her hands to herself. When they neared an item from the shopping list, Mom pointed to it and asked her daughter to put it in the cart. Then she praised Amy for being helpful. When they walked to the checkout line, Amy asked her mother if she could have some candy. Mom replied, "No Amy. Remember, this is a looking trip for you not a buying trip." Amy frowned and said, "Please." Mom held firm and responded, "No, Amy. We're just looking. No buying today." Then she prompted Amy to help her take items out of the cart, which Amy did. As they exited the store, Mom again praised Amy for doing such a wonderful job of staying by her side and not touching items. She bent down and gave Amy a hug as they walked to the car.

What positive actions did Mrs. Chen demonstrate during her shopping trip with Amy?

A. She made sure Amy's physical needs were met.

B. She made sure the length of time needed for shopping was reasonable for Amy.

C. She reviewed the behavioral expectations and rules with Amy.

D. She frequently praised and reinforced Amy for following the rules.

E. She gave Amy appropriate tasks to do while shopping.

Clearly, Mrs. Chen made a number of good choices and did a nice job of shaping Amy's cooperative behavior. You may be looking at the above example and thinking, "What fantasy world do these two live in?" Maybe your child has a ways to go before she can shop like Amy. However, when parents teach skills and set realistic expectations, all children can learn to demonstrate similar behavior.

Our behaviors tend to change depending on where we are. If you think about how you behave at home, at a football game, at church, and at work, you probably can describe different types of behavior in each of those settings. It takes little time for us to learn that the behavioral expectations at work differ from those at home which, in turn, differ from those at a ballgame. Children also learn that the expectations for their behavior vary in different locations as well. Unfortunately, it takes time for children to learn this. One of the challenges, especially for toddlers, is that their behavior doesn't change much from one location to another. It becomes the parents' responsibility to shape and teach them why the rules are somewhat different when they are in a museum, for example, versus their living room. By the time children reach school age, many have learned which behaviors are acceptable in different environments. The challenge most parents face is how to teach those behaviors and shape them as quickly as possible while avoiding complete frustration and embarrassment in the process.

Not only are parents aware that their own behaviors change in different settings, their children also realize it. Kids know they can expect a harsher or more lenient response depending on the situation. Children, at a very early age, learn they can get by with more behaviors in a restaurant or at Grandpa's house than they can in their own home. How many times have you seen a toddler munching on a bag full of chips or cereal during a church service? How many times has Grandma overridden your veto when your child asked for one more cookie? Children know there are certain rules they need to follow at home, but when they go out and about, they can test the limits and maybe get by with more. The longer this goes on, the stronger the behavior and pattern become. It shouldn't be too surprising then that children will react fairly strongly when parents eventually try to change their behavior outside of home. Also, because parents are often concerned about what others will think (about their behavior and their children's), they can be inconsistent with the consequences and strategies they know they should be using. This puts children at quite an advantage. For parents to regain the advantage, they need to be thoughtful, deliberate, and strategic.

Planning Ahead

When it comes to "teaching" appropriate public behavior, there is no better opportunity than when your child is out in public. Unfortunately, many parents avoid going out with their children because their behaviors away from home are so challenging. This limits the opportunities children have to learn appropriate social behavior in different environments. Instead of avoiding social situations, seek them out. But do it on your terms and in short time spans. By controlling when you go out and for how long, you can set your child up for success. Here are some general tips on how to plan ahead so your child can be more successful:

Ask yourself if the environment is a good match.

Before taking your child into any public setting, make sure he has the skills needed to be successful in that situation. I once had a mother complain that she could not get her daughter to sit still through church services. Her child would get halfway through the service and then get restless and leave her seat. It turns out this particular church service was more than two hours long. I was amazed her child made it even halfway through. It's important to have reasonable expectations about how long your child can remain in a particular setting and whether she has the behavioral skills to be successful. For example, if your son has difficulty staying at the dinner table for five or ten minutes, expecting him to sit in a restaurant for an hour is unreasonable. If he has not yet learned to whisper or use an "inside" voice, then spending extended time in a library or museum is questionable. The bottom line is this: Make sure your child can demonstrate a behavior at home before you expect him to do it in public.

Make sure all basic needs are met.

It doesn't matter how many hours you spend teaching your child how to behave or how much you plan ahead for an outing, if your child is hungry, tired, or thirsty, all that preparation means very little. Make sure your child's basic needs are met before you leave and have a plan in place to deal with those needs when you're out.

Stick to the plan.

Regardless of where you go, if there is a specific purpose to your outing, make sure you stick to it. If you make a list of the things that need to be done, it will help you be organized and allow your child to have some sense of what your plans are. For example, if you tell your four-year-old that you need to pick up three things at the market, she can count the items as you pick them up. Doing this will give her confidence that you will stick to the plan in the future. The more often you specifically tell your child what the plan is and stick to it, the more likely she is to know what to expect in the future. On the other hand, if you tell her you're going to the store to pick up three items and then wander around to do more shopping, which may take much longer than she can tolerate, your child will show her unhappiness and may be more resistant in the future. It doesn't matter if the plan involves going to the store to buy a few items or spending a day wandering around the zoo. What's important is that your actions match your words.

Review the rules.

Each environment has its own set of rules. If you're in a church or library, one main rule is probably to whisper or be quiet. If you're in a museum or expensive gift shop, having children keep their hands and feet to themselves is often critical. Depending on which environment you head to, make sure the behaviors and expectations are clear. Also, make sure the number of "rules" is limited so your child can remember them. There is no point in giving your daughter five rules if she can only remember two. It's also a good idea to keep the rules more general or broad (keep hands and feet to yourself, for example) so they cover a number of different behaviors.

Practice, practice, and practice some more.

Perhaps the most important thing you can do before heading to any public location, especially if you have specific expectations for your child, is to practice those expectations at home. You set yourself and your child up for failure if you assume he's going to change his behavior in public when he has never demonstrated the behavior at home. If you go to a place where your child's touching could end up costing you a pretty penny, practicing and role-playing at home makes perfect sense. You can, for example, teach your child how to keep his hands and feet to himself by playing a game. Pretend each item in your home belongs in a store and your rule is, "Keep hands and feet to yourself, and stay by Mommy's or Daddy's side." As you walk through the house, reinforce and praise your child for keeping his hands and feet to himself and by staying at your side. As soon as he reaches for something, offer a reminder ("Remember, stay by me."), followed by a reprimand ("No touching!"), and then a consequence (mini time-out) to make and reinforce your point. Practicing this multiple times until you're confident he can demonstrate the same behavior in public will help avoid a number of problems.

Similar types of practices and role-plays can be used at home for almost any situation imaginable. Whether it's using a quiet voice or sitting at the table, your child can practice the behaviors and activities at home. If he's not successful at home, despite your efforts, that suggests going to certain public places and expecting certain behaviors may be a challenge. You may need to wait until your child is older or the behavior improves. Or, you may need to have a back-up plan if your child struggles in certain situations.

Be a good role model.

For parenting in general, and certainly when in public, the old adage "Do as I say, not as I do" won't cut it. This is true for children of all ages, but especially for young children who learn a tremendous amount from watching others. There is probably no greater influence on children's behavior than parental behavior. You want your children to learn skills, such as taking turns, waiting in line, using a quiet voice, and using table manners. Demonstrating those skills in front of your children at every opportunity will go a long way toward helping them see that you believe the skills are important and you also practice them. It also helps to point out to children specifically what you're doing. They are not going to immediately pick up on the fact that you said thank you to the store clerk or patiently waited in line. Pointing these behaviors out to children when you do them helps children pay closer attention and, hopefully, learn the skills more quickly. For example, when standing in a line, explain to your child that everyone needs to wait his or her turn. Point out how the line gets shorter as you wait, and praise your child for waiting patiently with you. This is preferable to stepping out of the line to see what is taking so long and complaining about how slow the line is moving. It's easy to forget how off-the-cuff comments and gestures can send the opposite message of what you are trying to teach your children.

Pre-teach and re-teach.

Even if you spend time rehearsing and practicing behavioral expectations at home, children's memories tend to be fairly short. In addition, they often become excitable before going into any public place, especially if it's new or somewhere they don't go to very often.

Spending time pre-teaching skills and expectations to your children before they get to a destination is important. This includes reviewing rules on the way to your destination and again when you arrive. Even though it may seem like overkill, once you set foot inside a restaurant, library, store, or wherever, stop inside the door and again go over the rules with your children. This can give you some assurance and make it clear to your children that following rules is important. Also, it will hopefully help them be more aware of the rules when you need to provide a reminder or consequence for not following them.

Entertain your child.

If you plan on being somewhere for a length of time that goes well beyond your child's attention span, it's certainly appropriate to bring a few quiet play items along, such as electronic games (on mute), coloring books, dolls, or small toys. Bringing along some items to entertain your child will hopefully lengthen her attention span long enough to finish your task.

At first, keep it short.

If you're going to a new venue or public event, the best way to increase the probability for success is to keep the first visit or two very short. This will increase the likelihood your child will be able to follow the rules. It also gives you an opportunity to praise your child's efforts. For example, going to the store for a few items instead of shopping for an entire week's worth of groceries, spending thirty minutes at the museum instead of an entire morning, and attending a few exhibits at the zoo instead of seeing every one are excellent ways to keep the focus on your child's behavior rather than the activity itself. Understandably, this can be quite inconvenient for some parents. However, for children whose behaviors are especially challenging outside the home, gradually developing and managing their positive behaviors has to be the first step if longer outings are going to be possible. Time spent helping to shape these positive behaviors will be time well spent once children learn to be more successful as the length and number of outings increases.

Offer incentives.

You know why you're going to a public place, but does your child? Running errands or attending a meeting at school may be important to you but probably not to your toddler. Expecting her to "go along for the ride" and be cooperative may be a reasonable expectation, but it may not always happen. On occasion, provide your child with some positive outcome or benefit for going with you and, most importantly, for following your rules and expectations. This doesn't mean you need to reward her every single time she is cooperative in public. However, at least initially, reinforce your child's successful behavior in some small way that is meaningful to her. This might include allowing her to watch a favorite video when you return home, letting her have a treat at the end of a shopping trip, or just spending some individual time with her.

For a toddler, rewards need to be more frequent and somewhat more immediate in order to shape behavior. All children differ regarding their need for reinforcers or rewards as well as their ability to delay gratification. A preschooler, for example, can understand that he will have an opportunity to play a special game with Dad if he has the patience to wait for church to end. A toddler, however, is challenged by time and may need something more frequent (a shoulder hug or pat on the back during church, for example). In any respect, you're not "bribing" your child to be good, you're rewarding him for being cooperative. You're providing him an incentive to follow your rules and expectations in situations he may not enjoy. Once you have shaped your child's behavior and he demonstrates good behavior on a regular basis, rewards can be reduced and eventually eliminated. Of course, if you're somewhere you and your child both enjoy, using rewards isn't necessary.

Stay calm and collected.

Parents often have difficulty being consistent and remaining unemotional when their children act out in public. It's understandable to be concerned or embarrassed about what others might think. In public, it's much more difficult to use the same strategies with the same level of consistency compared to home. There is no time-out chair at the grocery store. However, try to remain calm and follow the plan you made prior to going out. This requires sticking to "no means no" and ignoring reactions from others. The bottom line is that ninety-nine percent of parents have been in your position or will be. Continue to remind yourself that this is a teaching opportunity and the time and effort you put forth will pay off eventually. Un-

Quiet, Please!

Silence or keeping very quiet is often necessary or required in some of the environments (libraries, churches, synagogues, museums, and movie theaters) where you frequently take your children. Whether or not the kids can stay mum is another question. The reality is, however, all children, including toddlers, need to learn "quiet" behaviors.

The best approach to teaching "quiet" behaviors in these settings is to mirror what you do when teaching your child about shopping or dining out. First, review your behavioral expectations. You can even create a practice environment in your home. You can pretend your home is a museum, for example. It's not too difficult to pretend the furnishings in your home represent ancient or rare artifacts. As you teach your child the rules (keep hands and feet to yourself, walk softly, and use a quiet voice), lower your voice to a whisper. Praise and reinforce your child for demonstrating quiet behavior and using an "inside" voice. Any problems your child has following the rules at the "museum" should earn her the same sequence of consequences described earlier (a reminder, a reprimand, and eventually removal – meaning a mini time-out or leaving the "museum"). Be sure to frequently praise and acknowledge your child's success when she stays quiet.

As with shopping and dining, it will be important to spend some time going to a library, church, or museum for brief periods of time before spending extended time in those locations. Again, pre-teach rules and expectations before going into the building and reinforce or praise any positive behaviors while you're there. For churches and synagogues, practice inside when there are no services. You can practice sitting in a pew or on a chair, being completely quiet, and using quiet voices. You can do something similar when visiting a library. You can even let your child check out a book as a reward if she followed the rules. Give your child multiple opportunities to be successful. With any of these destinations, you should plan on gradually expanding the amount of time you stay until your child demonstrates success. As with other public places, if your child struggles to demonstrate a level of appropriate behavior or cannot be quiet for a reasonable amount of time, be prepared to leave or step outside temporarily so others won't be disturbed. With persistence and practice, your child can learn to be successful in any environment.

fortunately, children's behaviors do not change overnight, but they will change. Giving in and saying "Yes" simply prolongs how long it takes for change to happen.

Use consequences.

Just as it helps to reward children for their positive behavior during or after an outing, there need to be negative consequences associated with inappropriate behavior. Using a set of "progressive" consequences is helpful. By progressive, I mean a continuum of actions you take that include verbal warnings on the front end and concrete actions on the back end. An example of this continuum is providing a reminder to your child about the rules you discussed, followed by a verbal reprimand if they are not followed, and then possibly a consequence (a brief time-out). Using time-out in public can be done in a number of different ways. For example, it can involve taking your child to the restroom and sitting there for a few minutes or using a "time-out mat" (a portable plastic placemat) and having your child sit on it for twenty seconds or until he finishes saying the ABC's. These "mini" time-outs provide a brief break and send a quick message that the behavior was inappropriate. You can use mini time-outs almost anywhere, but if you use a time-out mat in public, you need to teach your child what to do and how it works. This preteaching should be done at home.

If the inappropriate behavior continues to escalate, it may be necessary to leave wherever you happen to be. Leaving the location for a short time to step outside or sit in the car may calm your child and give you an opportunity to review with her what the expectations are. If she calms down, review the rules and then return. Frequently praise her cooperation and positive behavior. Your child also needs to understand that if the negative behavior continues, she, and possibly the entire family, will need to return home. If you do in fact return home, additional consequences may include a time-out and/or a loss of a privilege. If your child has particularly problematic behavior, taking two vehicles (when feasible) may be necessary so other family members won't have to leave, too. Hopefully, if you practiced and rehearsed behavioral skills and praised and reinforced appropriate behaviors in other settings, using a progression of negative consequences will be enough to redirect your child's behavior so you don't have to end an outing. And if your child can regroup and engage in more appropriate behavior, make sure you acknowledge and praise the change in behavior.

These tips and strategies provide a broad foundation to help you make your little one a better-behaved citizen in public. This foundation can be quite helpful if, like most parents, what you really want to know is how to keep your toddler from causing grief in the grocery aisle, creating a ruckus at a restaurant, or acting foolish in front of friends and family. For common, everyday situations like these, there are specific interventions you can practice at home and apply in public to address your child's misbehaviors.

Managing Behaviors When Out and About

This section examines a number of situations that are fairly common and especially problematic for parents and young children. When working with your child on positive behaviors and good habits, it's important to be proactive (teaching appropriate skills and behaviors before going out) and reactive (responding appropriately to misbehaviors). While the following pages focus on situations involving shopping, dining, and socializing, the strategies outlined can be applied in other situations outside the home. Many of the suggestions may seem time consuming, but really they require just a few minutes a day to teach and practice. If you think about the amount of time you spend shopping and dining out or add up the amount of time you have already spent dealing with your child's behavior in public, taking a few minutes each day to teach positive behaviors will pay off in the end. It may seem easier to take a "hope and pray" approach, where you hope for the best behavior and pray you don't see the worst. However, in my experience, such an approach usually doesn't produce a good outcome. It's better if you take the time to teach, shape, and reinforce the skills you want your little one to have and to use.

Shopping

"I was born to shop!" I hear this from time to time from my wife and teenage daughters. Unfortunately, there may be some truth to it. I have yet to see any of them throw a tantrum when asked to go shopping or when they actually shop. (But they have been known to get agitated when they used up their budget or the mall closes!) Regardless, not everyone is born to shop.

Shopping can involve anything from running to the convenience store to pick up a carton of ice cream to spending an entire day at a mall. Before you head out on any shopping excursion, ask yourself if your child has the skills to be a successful shopper. The questions you should ask yourself include:

- Does my child have the physical stamina to walk, ride in a cart, or sit in a stroller for the duration of the shopping trip?
- Will my child be able to walk alongside of me?
- Can my child keep her hands and feet to herself?
- Can my child be redirected or entertained while I shop?

Even if your child demonstrates "perfect" behavior (whatever that is) at home, it's important to ask yourself these and other questions before you take her shopping. Expecting your child to endure a long shopping trip or to walk alongside you, even though it far exceeds her skill or ability, is unreasonable. It almost always guarantees problems. Make sure she has the physical, emotional, and behavioral skills necessary to be successful. As an analogy, you wouldn't run a marathon if you had yet to run a single mile. Likewise, don't expect your child to endure a long or extensive shopping trip if her attention span, physical endurance, or emotional makeup won't allow her to manage it. Whenever there isn't a good match between your child's skills and the demands of a shopping trip, go on your own. Here are several steps you can take to help your child have more behavioral success when shopping:

Create your own "Home Shopping Club" and practice shopping at home.

This is a safe, fun way to teach your child shopping rules and expectations. It also can provide you with a general sense of what problems you might encounter when shopping. By practicing at home, you have much greater control than you do in public if problem behaviors arise. You can create your own retail store by taking the clothes you or your child owns and displaying them. You might even want to attach price tags made from masking tape. Another option is to open up your kitchen's pantry doors or display food items on tables in the kitchen and living area. Once you have the "products" on display, you can review your shopping rules with your child just as you would if you were leaving for the store. Remind your child that he needs to stay by your side and keep his hands and feet to himself. Create a list of what you want to buy and have him help you find the items as you walk through the "store." Frequently praise and reinforce him for staying by your side and keeping his hands and feet to himself. If he breaks a rule, use a consequence, such as a reminder. If he continues breaking rules, use progressively more significant consequences (a verbal reprimand, followed by time-out, and then removal). If he is "successful" with the shopping game, provide a simple reward. The reward can be sitting down and reading a book together, going outside to play, or whatever time allows. I realize you can't completely replicate a retail store in your home, but this is simply a fun exercise your child will enjoy. Besides, playing the game one time takes only a few minutes. By practicing multiple times until you're confident your child understands your rules and can follow them, you will set him up for success when you do "real" shopping. Be careful, however, not to practice so much your child gets bored or has to do everything to your complete satisfaction. If you wait for perfection, you may never go shopping with your child.

Start small.

Take a trip to your nearest convenience mart so your child can practice in a smaller public space (She can only run so far!) yet has just enough items to be distracting and potentially problematic. Before you go, tell your child you're taking her shopping, remind her of the rules, and review the consequences for following and not following the rules. Review the shopping rules as you drive to the store and again as you enter. Give her an instruction, such as asking her to help you push the cart or help you find a specific item. Praise and reinforce her for following the rules. If problems arise (and in some ways you hope they do), use consequences that progressively get more severe (a reprimand, a mini time-out, and removal from the store). Always remember to praise and reinforce your child's success with following the rules. If she succeeds to your satisfaction, provide a small reward.

A reward can be buying a treat at the store or, since you're close to home, doing a special activity there.

One advantage of practicing at a convenience store is that you avoid having a cart full of items. The purpose of the trip is practicing and reinforcing shopping rules with your child, not buying groceries. Another advantage is that you're close to home. If her behavior gets out of control, you can get your child home fairly quickly. If the behavior deteriorates to the point where you need to leave and go home, your child should be placed in time-out as soon as you're home. When your child calms down, briefly review why you returned home and what your expectations are the next time you go shopping. You also may need to do more "home shopping" before returning to the convenience store. It will be important to make several trips to your local convenience store before moving up to larger stores and longer excursions.

Go big.

After you see success at home and in convenience stores, take your child to stores you normally frequent to buy food, clothes, and specialty items. With each outing, make sure you follow the same steps you did when practicing at home and at the convenience store. It may seem like you're being awfully repetitive, but you shouldn't assume your child remembers each step even though you have repeated them over and over. When going to larger stores, it's important to keep your initial trips brief. A large store and thousands of items are too tempting for a young child. He will be much more tempted to sprint down the long, wide aisles of a grocery store than the narrow, short aisles of a convenience mart. And you also have to deal with the dreaded candy and toy aisles. You're much more likely to encounter problems in a large grocery store than you are almost anywhere else. That's why it's best to make the first trip to a large store quick and easy. Simply walk around or grab an item or two. Praise and reinforce your child's success. If he misbehaves, follow the same series of corrective actions and consequences you used at home and in the convenience mart. As your child demonstrates more success, gradually increase the amount of time you spend shopping until you reach the point that matches your child's attention span and tolerance level.

If at any point along the way you encounter frequent behavior problems, move back a step to do more practice. For example, if your son has few problems shopping in a large store for five to ten minutes but acts out when you shop for twenty or thirty minutes, you're probably exceeding his attention span and tolerance level. Go back to a shorter period of time to see if his behavior improves. It's possible he's not ready for thirty-minute shopping. On the other hand, if you think he is over stimulated or struggles in such a big environment, spend more time practicing in the convenience store or wait before going on larger shopping excursions. In general, you want your child's behaviors to determine the expectations you set for shopping. I realize this can be time consuming. However, by providing plenty of training opportunities along the way, you set your child up for more success. There are other issues to keep in mind when working to improve your child's shopping behavior. They include:

Follow through.

It's critical that you use positive and negative consequences to reinforce behavior. Wavering on consequences or giving in to pleas for a toy or piece of candy, when your child's behavior was less than stellar, can undermine your efforts. If you tell your daughter she can have a piece of candy if she does a good job following the rules, reward her if she does a good job. But if she doesn't follow the rules or misbehaves, don't offer a reward. If you give in to her begging, crying, and pleading, you will definitely see a repeat of that inappropriate behavior in the future.

Be willing to leave.

There may be situations where your child is not responding to your efforts to make the public outing successful. If your child's behavior is consistently negative, causing disruptions and irritation for you and those around you, it may be necessary to leave. This is easier to do if you're shopping for a few items but much more difficult if it's an important or time-consuming excursion. If you're concerned your child may have difficulty with an outing, planning ahead can be helpful. This might include taking a second vehicle or having another family member or friend to assist you.

Distinguish between "buying" trips and "looking" trips.

When going to a store, most children want to get something. This is certainly unnecessary and not creating this expectation is reasonable. Some parents tell their children that certain shopping trips are for "buying" and others are for "looking." Before taking your toddler or preschooler on a shopping trip, explain whether it's a "buying" or "looking" trip. It's important that you follow through and not purchase any items for your child when it's a "looking" trip. If your child pleads, begs, or throws a tantrum for something and you're on a "looking" trip, apply a meaningful consequence. Once he understands that looking never means buying, it will help to reduce the whining and other annoying behaviors. This is especially true if your child also learns that when he's on a "buying" trip, his positive behavior will earn him a small item.

Involve your child, within reason.

Let your child help you as much as possible on shopping trips. You can ask her to hand you the blue can of beans or the yellow sweater. By involving your child, you make it more enjoyable. Also, when possible, make it educational. For example, tell your four-year-old that the oranges you're buying are grown on trees or the noodles you're buying are an ingredient in her favorite meal. Sharing information like this can help your child take some interest in the shopping trip.

Dining Out

To dine or not to dine? Young children and restaurants are often a challenging mix. Some do well with limited assistance from their parents while others imitate what they saw at their last trip to the zoo. If your child is one of the latter, it doesn't mean you have to stay home to eat. It does, however, mean you need to be selective about which restaurants you patronize, especially in the beginning. It also means you need to spend some time teaching and training appropriate dining behavior at home and planning ahead before you go to a restaurant. Here are several suggestions to consider before taking your little one to a restaurant:

Watch your child's behavior at the kitchen table.

Before hitting the restaurant circuit, the most important thing you can do is observe your child's mealtime behavior at home. The novel environment of a restaurant provides an opportunity for your child to explore and play. It's also a great opportunity for him to use a straw to make a bubble bath in his soda or stuff an entire dinner roll in his mouth. You should not expect him to use better manners or behave better in a restaurant than he does at home. Use your time at home to work on appropriate table manners and other behaviors you want your child to learn. Practice how to sit at a table, make appropriate requests for condiments and beverages, use appropriate language, and other behaviors. Doing this will give you an idea of how long he can remain seated during a typical situation at home. Going beyond that amount of time when dining out is not likely to be successful.

Practice the restaurant experience at home.

When your child masters basic mealtime behaviors and manners, create a more typical restaurant environment for her to practice in. If you have a formal dining table, this would be an ideal place to practice, especially if you do not regularly eat meals there. This will signify to your child that something is different. By practicing a typical restaurant experience, you can rehearse the dining-out routine. For example, you can begin by having your child wait at the front door until someone, namely you, seats her at the table. Offer water or other drinks and then have her sit and wait a few minutes before a "waiter" takes her order. Again, it would be helpful to wait a reasonable period of time, just as you would in a restaurant, before serving the food. Once the food is served, remind her of your behavioral expectations. Her positive behaviors, including using table manners and talking appropriately, should be acknowledged and praised throughout the meal. When everyone finishes and the dishes are cleared, stay seated a little while and wait for the "bill." The more you can replicate a restaurant experience, the more helpful it will be for your child. After you have practiced a few times, you will have a fairly realistic view about whether it's appropriate to eat out and, if so, where. It's important to pick restaurants that will be a good fit for your family. Regardless of where you eat, you should practice appropriate behaviors at home and then reinforce those behaviors at the restaurant.

Pick an appropriate place.

If you're taking your toddler to a formal, sit-down restaurant where the meal will last an hour or more, I have some advice for you: Prepare for disappointment. This may seem somewhat obvious, but it is surprising how many parents take their children to formal and semi-formal restaurants and expect them to maintain appropriate behavior for what, to the kids and eventually their parents, seems like an eternity. Until your child has the emotional and behavioral skills needed to be successful in this type of environment, it's best to avoid formal dining. Hiring a babysitter or having your child stay with friends or relatives makes much more sense, and it will be more enjoyable for everyone.

Choose restaurants with short waits and informal atmospheres.

Eating in restaurants where the food is served quickly, where entertaining your child isn't frowned upon, and where you can shape and reinforce your child's dining skills are ideal. Also, dining during off-hours, after or before the breakfast, lunch, and dinner crowds, can be less stressful.

Reinforce appropriate behaviors regardless of the setting.

If you're eating at a fast-food restaurant, you should expect the same behaviors and table manners that you enforce at home or in a more formal restaurant. The advantage of a fast-food restaurant, however, is that you always have the option of taking your food and leaving if your child's behavior gets out of control. In any case, it makes for a good place to practice.

Review rules and expectations.

As with shopping, it's important to review behavioral expectations and rules with your child before you go to a restaurant and again when you arrive. Remember to praise and acknowledge your child for doing a nice job following the rules.

Prepare for long waits.

If there's a chance you may have to wait a while before being served your entrees, order an appetizer or bring along a small bag of snack food to help take the edge off your child's appetite while you wait. This is a situation where some minor, controlled "grazing" (see Mealtime Chapter) is acceptable.

Bring along entertainment or a distraction.

This can be especially helpful for toddlers. Many restaurants provide crayons or even small games to occupy a child's time. To be safe, you may want to bring some quiet activity with you that will entertain your child in case nothing is available at the restaurant.

Let your child eat familiar or favorite foods.

This is not the time to have your child try escargot or pheasant-under-glass.

Address inappropriate behavior.

If your child acts out or uses inappropriate manners, remind him of the rule or table manner that is expected. If it happens again, give him a reprimand. If the problem persists, remove your child from the table and take him to a restroom or outside. If his acting out is severe, use time-out by taking him outside or to your car. If you're dining with a spouse or partner, discuss between yourselves a plan of action for dealing with a child (or two) who's throwing a tantrum and being disruptive. One of you may have to sit in the car or the whole family may have to prepare to leave the restaurant.

Be a good role model.

Demonstrate and use the table manners and behaviors you expect to see from your child. Your behavior, and the example you set, is one of the most effective tools you have.

When possible, dine during off-peak hours.

When you dine during off hours, there typically is more staff available so the wait is shorter. And if your child happens to have a meltdown, it may not feel so overwhelming because fewer eyes are on you.

Although there is a fair amount of work involved in teaching these behaviors, the end result will be an enjoyable and relatively worry-free dining experience with your children at the restaurant of your choice. Really!

Visiting Friends and Family

Many parents get nervous just thinking about visiting certain friends and family. Some have friends who don't seem to understand the actions of little ones or how parents manage them. Others have family members who are clueless about what little children do. It doesn't help when so many friends and relatives consider themselves "parenting experts," especially when it comes to other people's children.

Hearing unsolicited advice and opinions can fuel a parent's insecurities and frustrations. Even when someone's intentions are good, it can cause unintended consequences. For example, it seems many grandparents suffer amnesia when it comes to managing children's behaviors. The rules and discipline approaches they used with their children are forgotten when the grandkids visit. Most grandchildren learn sooner or later that the rules at Grandma and Grandpa's house are more relaxed. Even if parents try to step in and manage or control a situation, it's the grandparent who will say, "It's okay, I don't get to see them very often" or "Let them be, they're not hurting anything."

Parental insecurity can be exacerbated when moms and dads want to make a good impression. This is especially true if they are visiting rarely seen friends and family. They don't want to embarrass themselves or have their children "create a scene" that will be "discussed" for months to come. Not surprisingly, it's the parents' behavior, not the children's, that is more likely to change. Moms and dads are less likely to use the same consequences when they're in someone else's home or have visitors to their home. Children are quick to pick up on this change, which encourages them to push the boundaries when they are in someone else's home. They also like to test limits when they return to their homes. Maintaining your parenting approach and using consequences consistently are more challenging when you're a guest in someone else's home. Here are some suggestions to help you have a more successful and enjoyable visit:

Inform your host before the visit if there is a particular skill or behavior you are working on with your child.

Describe the strategies you're using to correct or shape the behavior. It's important to explain you have spent considerable time and effort helping your child with the behavior, and you want him to learn that the behavior is important regardless of where he is.

Pick your battles.

Focus on the behaviors that concern you the most. In order to make the visit as pleasant as possible, try to create a positive environment. If you target every behavior that you do at home, you could end up creating a stressful experience for everyone. Instead, focus on the top one or two behaviors you feel need to be addressed no matter where you are.

Spend time pre-teaching rules and expectations.

Before a visit, explain to your child the rules and behaviors you expect from her when visiting friends or family. Explain the positive outcomes for acting appropriately and the negative consequences for not following the rules. Remind her that even though you are not at home, the same consequences (time-out or the loss of a privilege, for example) apply.

Plan for time-out.

Don't be shy about asking your hosts if they have a location or place you can use for a time-out. You might say something such as, "If I need to put Sasha in time-out, is there a quiet room I can use?" You don't need to go into a lengthy discussion beyond getting permission. Your family and friends most likely will be supportive and happy that you're taking a proactive approach to managing your child's behavior.

When only your child is visiting, talk to the caregiver about your rules and expectations.

Describe your discipline techniques and determine whether or not the caregiver is comfortable using them. For example, is she comfortable using time-out if your child becomes aggressive? You may need to demonstrate or provide some instruction, especially if the caregiver is unfamiliar with your strategies. Providing a written description would also be helpful. Offer to make yourself available to answer questions and provide whatever resources you can. Also review your expectations with your child before he goes on the visit.

Ask your friends and family for help.

What can they do? Probably the most effective thing they can do is praise and reinforce the behaviors your child is trying to improve. Receiving praise and attention from grandparents, cousins, and friends will stand out and go a long way toward reinforcing the importance of those behaviors. This is especially true because the praise is coming from someone besides you and in a relatively novel environment. Grandma's praise for "Good listening" or a friend's reminder that "Dad said 'No,'" will strengthen and reinforce what you taught your child.

When visiting or staying with loved ones, parenting with the same level of consistency and predictability that you do at home will be a challenge. However, remembering these strategies will help you send the appropriate message to your child: You take his behavior seriously and for the most important behaviors, the rules don't change – not even at Grandma's!

chapter 8

Siblings Are Forever: Turning Rivalry into Revelry

It was a stormy day and five-year-old Savannah and her four-year-old brother Shane were sad. Because of the weather, they couldn't play on the new swing set their parents built the day before. As a consolation, the family decided to go to their favorite restaurant for lunch. While Mom and Dad dressed, Savannah sat down to watch television. When Shane walked into the family room, he immediately noticed something was horribly wrong. Savannah was sitting in "his spot," and she had an evil smirk on her face. Shane asked her nicely, and then not so nicely, to get out of "his spot." Savannah shook her head no and said, "I'm never leaving, and this is my spot!" Shane shrieked and ran upstairs to complain to Mom and Dad.

Shane, with Mom in tow, returned to the family room and saw Savannah sitting where she normally sits. Mom asked her what the problem was, and Savannah looked at her quizzically and shrugged her shoulders. Shane then smugly sat in "his spot" but soon realized the TV channel had been changed. He looked around for the remote, but Savannah had hidden it. When he stood up to look for the remote, Savannah ran and sat in "his spot." After a colorful verbal exchange, Shane screamed and stomped his way upstairs to get reinforcements.

When Shane returned, Dad was at his side. By now, however, Savannah had left her brother's spot, placed the remote on the end table, and turned the television to the "correct" channel. Their dad was annoyed and asked, "Why can't you two get along?" Savannah looked at her father and said, "What?" As Dad went back upstairs, Savannah looked at her brother, smiled, and laughed. Shane looked at his sister and said, "I hate you!"

If you were Savannah and Shane's parent, what would you have done?

A. Handle the situation exactly the same way.

B. Ground Savannah and Shane, turn off the TV, and cancel eating out.

C. Ignore them. Children should be seen, not heard.

D. Encourage them to work out their differences on their own, and if they can't, come up with a solution for them.

The interactions between Savannah and Shane are fairly typical and are probably playing out in thousands of households as you read this. Although rivalry between siblings is fairly common, it doesn't need to be tolerated if it negatively affects family relationships or leads to more severe behaviors, such as aggression or abuse. By effectively managing sibling rivalry, you can help your children maintain healthy relationships with one another and empower them to resolve their differences and conflicts in positive ways. For Savannah and Shane, encouraging them to work out their differences on their own before giving them a solution is the best strategy for managing their rivalry.

I am often asked, "What causes sibling rivalry?" The answer is very simple: The birth of your second child. There is not so much a cause for sibling rivalry as much as sibling rivalry is a state of being. In other words, it's a natural, to-be-expected phenomenon that occurs in all families between siblings. The nature and severity of the rivalry between siblings varies between children and within families. Factors such as the number of children, their ages, age differences, and interpersonal characteristics combine with other traits to help determine how significant an issue sibling rivalry will be for parents. Since you have little control over those characteristics, managing sibling rivalry comes back to the one place you probably hope it wouldn't – YOU!

There are a number of steps you can take as a parent to help manage your children's rivalries. You can count on your kids to, at some point, feel jealous, have a certain level of competitiveness against each other, and believe you favor one sibling over another. You also can expect them to have different language skills and behavioral abilities because of age or natural differences. Regardless, if you're proactive and plan ahead, you can do a lot to lessen the degree of sibling rivalry and the negative effects it can have on your children. In this chapter, you will find several strategies to help your children learn how to resolve conflicts, develop positive social skills, and minimize the squabbling and occasional hostility that happens between siblings.

Even though some sibling rivalry is normal, it can become problematic if it undermines the development of normal relationships or causes emotional or physical anguish. For toddlers and preschoolers, sibling rivalry usually flares up under a number of scenarios. One of those is when a new sibling joins the family.

A New Sibling

If your little one is toddler- or preschool-aged, he will be more affected and, in some cases, more distressed by the arrival of a baby brother or sister. At that age, the potential exists for rivalry or resentment to surface because of your toddler's self-centered nature, which is normal at this developmental stage. For an only child, this is especially true. The world no longer revolves solely around him, and he is forced to share his world and accept the fact that much attention will be paid to the newest family member. Fortunately, there are a number of things you can do to minimize rivalry and increase acceptance of a new family member. Here are some strategies you can use:

Announce the baby news a month before the expected arrival.

Waiting has several advantages: Mom can show her belly (which very likely has been noticed) and explain that the baby will arrive in four to five weeks. The time reference won't mean much to a toddler or preschooler, but by waiting until the due date is near, you can reduce how often a little one asks when baby is coming home. Questions about the baby should be answered with short and simple-to-understand responses. To help ease the adjustment, allow your children to have a role in preparing the home. Ask for their suggestions and input on where to put the baby's crib or where to set up the changing table. If you're feeling real generous, you might even ask them to help you pick colors or a theme for the baby's room. Be careful not to overwhelm young children with options. Let them choose between two colors or two themes. Also, if other changes need to be made, such as moving one or more siblings to new bedrooms, make the changes several weeks before your newborn comes home so everyone has enough time to adjust to the changes. Another common change involves the teaching of new skills, such as toilet training. Be aware that if you are working on skills, such as toilet training your toddler, the arrival of a new family member can disrupt the learning process. You may want to delay toilet training until after the baby arrives or start the training well in advance.

Share information.

When your due date approaches, explain to your children that you will be going to the hospital to have the baby. Let them know they will be able to see you, too. When they visit, let them take pictures with their new sibling and have bonding time so they all experience a connection to the larger family.

Have your children help care for the baby.

A toddler, for example, can bring you a diaper, hold your changing bag when you're out in public, or help you prepare bottles. Simple tasks such as these, while helpful to you, also can give your child a sense of pride and importance because she's helping you care for the baby.

Involve your children in decisions.

Take advantage of any opportunities you have to include older siblings in decisions, such as "Should baby wear the blue hat or the white hat?" or "Do you think baby would like to play with the rattle or the binky?" Whenever your toddler or preschooler interacts with the baby, make sure you point out when the baby is smiling or cooing at him. This can help reinforce the positive connections between the two.

Make special time with your other children.

If you have young children, they are probably accustomed to spending a lot of time with you. However, a new baby means some of that time and attention will go away. When possible, set aside time each day (when baby is napping, for example) to do something with your other children, even if it's only for a few minutes. You can do simple activities, such as read books, draw, or play blocks. Any one-on-one time you can find to spend with your other children can prevent or reduce feelings of resentment and disappointment.

Prepare for some resentment.

Everything may not go as smoothly as you would like. Toddlers often experience jealousy, and they often have difficulty controlling their emotions and feelings. As a result, it's not uncommon for them to express their displeasure by taking swipes at or throwing things at their newest siblings. Anytime a sibling becomes aggressive toward a baby, respond immediately. Calmly but firmly explain to your child that such behavior is unacceptable because of the harm it can cause. In some instances, a short time-out also is an appropriate consequence. If the behaviors continue, monitor your toddler closely to make sure he doesn't do anything that could harm the baby. Also, try to model appropriate ways to behave around the baby. For example, some little ones like to give babies "big hugs" just like they do with a parent or grandparent. Bear hugs are obviously not appropriate for infants. Modeling appropriate touch and demonstrating how to interact with the baby is essential. To help your toddler learn appropriate touch, let him practice by taking care of a baby doll. (This is especially helpful if done before the baby's arrival.) The more you prepare and involve your young children in the process, the more you can minimize any sense of disruption they feel or envy they have toward the newest family member.

Take advantage of extended family and friends.

Give your children the opportunity to spend extra time with grandparents, aunts and uncles, or friends so they can feel special and appreciated. Also, when you invite family or friends to your home to see the baby, encourage them to spend time with the other children, not just the baby. You also might ask them to bring something for your other children rather than (or in addition to) a gift for the baby.

Make time for the transition.

If your youngest child needs to move out of the crib to make room for baby, you may need to make this transition well in advance. If your child is still attached to sleeping in the crib or is having a hard time transitioning to his new bed, he may have some added resentment about the baby getting "his" crib. Making the transition a month or two in advance will help reduce any possible resentment

Take a trip down memory lane.

Look through picture albums and scrapbooks with your other children. This can remind, reinforce, and reassure them that they continue to be an important part of the family. Use the opportunity to relive enjoyable activities and events from the past. Show your children their baby pictures and share stories and events that happened when they were infants. This can encourage them to look forward to having a new sibling in the home.

Fortunately, many toddlers and preschoolers are excited and accepting of new siblings. By planning ahead to make the transition as smooth as possible and being aware of any signs that rivalries or resentments are developing, you can proactively take steps to promote acceptance and build positive relationships between all your children.

Managing Sibling Conflicts

The majority of sibling conflicts usually occur once children are old enough to walk and talk. By the time they are toddlers and preschoolers, they also have learned to become somewhat competitive about time with parents and access to certain toys and activities. They also have developed a stronger need for attention from others. These and a large number of other factors set the stage for occasional, and sometimes frequent, conflict between siblings. Although it's not possible to eliminate sibling rivalry, there are a number of strategies you can use to better manage conflicts between your children. They include the following:

Catch your children playing nicely together.

Think of those rare times when your children play quietly

together. You probably peek your head around the corner to make sure they are not "getting into something." After you get over the shock of them actually playing peacefully together, you probably sneak off to get other things done or take a little time to yourself. If this sounds familiar, you're not alone. Imagine, however, if instead of turning around and saying nothing, you actually praised your children for their cooperation. Just as it's important to correct your children when they are fighting and arguing, it's equally important to acknowledge them when they play well together. You can show how much you appreciate their cooperative play by walking into the room, smiling at them, and thanking them for playing well together or commenting about the activity they're doing. Also, there are benefits to praising the cooperative behavior between your child and a friend. This can get the attention of your other children who, hopefully, will then want to earn similar praise when they play with their friends or siblings. When you take the time to acknowledge your children's positive interactions, you provide a necessary and nice contrast to the times when you need to address their negative behaviors.

Think of activities that your children enjoy and can do together.

The developmental differences between toddlers and preschoolers are evident in their motor skills and verbal abilities. The different skill levels mean certain activities or games will be too sophisticated for some while not stimulating enough for others. When possible, find games and toys they can play with together rather than ones done alone. For example, when a three-year old wants to play with her six-year-old sister's toys, the six-year-old might resist. And even if the six-year-old is willing to share, the toy or activity may be too sophisticated or challenging for baby sis, which again can lead to conflict and frustration. Rather than have them fight over the six-year-old's favorite doll, let them color together. It may not always be practical to have siblings do the same activity or game, but when it can be done it creates opportunities for positive interactions and strengthens the bonds between them.

Trust, but verify.

Ronald Reagan popularized this phrase when describing the relationship between the United States and the former Soviet Union.

In your family, some of your children might act like warring nations, too. When a fight breaks out, you can't always trust your children to give you the complete truth. Older children can sometimes resolve their differences without parents being actively involved. However, if there is a significant age difference between the children, you can't always expect a fair resolution if you allow them to solve the problem. Inevitably, an older child may use his superior skills to manipulate a younger sibling into a solution that is not fair. To avoid these problems, there are several steps you can take to promote positive interactions without taking sides or being the referee:

Set ground rules. Establish some clear rules for your children when they are playing together, such as keeping hands and feet to self, taking turns, asking for toys appropriately, and sharing.

Shape and develop social skills. Your children's social abilities will vary. Some simply need more time to develop their social skills while others need you to practice and model certain skills to help them be more successful with their siblings and peers.

Level the playing field. If there is a wide age range between your children (two to six years), there are certain games, activities, and toys that are going to put the youngest children at a disadvantage. You may need to step in and suggest a game or activity that is more suitable for all ages or make adaptations that will allow everyone to participate equally. By doing this, you can reduce the potential for conflicts.

Monitor your children's play and intervene only when needed. When is intervention needed? Intervene if a child breaks the ground rules, takes advantage of another child, or becomes aggressive. You may need to pull the offending child aside and remind her of the expectations, and then give her an opportunity to show you she can follow the rules. Praise her and others when they follow the rules. If a child continually disrupts a game or activity, issue a time-out. Have her sit on the sidelines and watch the others play. Once she returns and is following the rules, praise her.

Allow older children to work out their differences independently, when appropriate. Again, this may require some monitoring and participation on your part. However, your role is not to resolve the issue. Instead, teach your children how to work out their differences. If they can't, offer a solution that is more extreme or less acceptable than any they would have come up with on their own. This can motivate them to be more agreeable with one another in the future.

Don't referee. If you didn't see what happened and can't verify it, don't guess and don't always trust what you hear. If you attempt to resolve a situation by listening to the stories of each of your little attorneys, there will definitely be at least one loser – you. It's nearly impossible to figure out the "truth" in these situations. If you guess and choose a side, the consequences of being wrong are more significant than any benefits you might receive if you're right. You are better off making a decision that resolves the conflict and is equitable to everyone. You might, for example, stop the game, take away the toys, or have your children do another activity. Spending time trying to sort out the matter is almost always a losing proposition.

Listen without judging.

Siblings are naturally going to be frustrated with each other or point out some difference that exists between them. Don't feel as though you need to "fix" one child's frustration with another sibling at that moment or change the perceptions or misperceptions each has about the other. Listen to your children and allow them to vent. Avoid taking sides or debating the merits or weaknesses of their arguments. Typically, angry remarks are temporary and come and go in the lives of most siblings. Sometimes, simply allowing children a chance to express their frustration is the only action you need to take.

Don't allow children to become physically or verbally abusive toward each other.

When your children get physical with each other, step in. Make it clear to them that it's never okay to hit, bite, pinch, punch, shove, or pull hair. Some of these behaviors will happen, and when they do, avoid the blame game between siblings. Stay neutral and remain as impartial as possible. Apply whatever consequences seem appropriate. If the physical aggression was fairly minor, firmly tell your children that such behavior is unacceptable. Give them an opportunity to resolve the dispute on their own. If they can resolve it successfully, let them go on about their day and praise their positive interactions with one another. If the aggression was more severe or repeated, use time-out. Either remove the children from whatever activity they were engaged in or take away their toy or game.

Show appreciation for the unique qualities of each child.

Children, by nature, vary dramatically in regard to their personalities, learning abilities, artistic talents, athletic skills, verbal abilities, and motor skills. Therefore, it's only natural for parents to make comparisons. The different characteristics, attributes, and quirks children possess make them individuals. Parents are interested in or attracted to certain activities or qualities that their children possess or show some promise toward. Although this is understandable, it's important to take time to identify and appreciate the unique qualities in each of your children. This may seem obvious, but it's often a source of frustration, disappointment, and jealousy for children who feel as though they are not measuring up because they're not as smart, athletic, or artistic as their siblings. You can help make each of your children feel secure by providing unconditional love and recognizing all of their unique qualities and attributes. As they get older, this may include helping them develop hobbies or interests that allow them to stand apart from their siblings. Unfortunately, rivalries often flare up when children hear their parents making comparisons. In some instances, the comparisons can be hurtful and diminish a child's sense of self. Remarks such as, "Why can't you be more like your brother?" or "Your sister never did anything that stupid when she was your age" may sound like ones you heard as a child or said yourself as a parent. You might be talking to a friend and say, "You just won't believe what Cassandra did this morning. When her sister was four, she never did anything that ridiculous." If your child overhears statements like this, it can foster resentment toward other siblings and harm your parent-child relationship. Your child might think, "Mom and Dad love my sister more than me." Be aware that your comments carry a lot of weight, and your children might not understand that you were "joking" or didn't mean it as a putdown. To be safe, when talking on the phone or face-to-face with family and friends when your children are around, replace comparisons or criticisms with compliments. When your children overhear compliments, it can have a powerful and positive effect on how they perceive themselves and their status within the family.

Tame the tattling!

Federal and state governments have whistleblower laws protecting workers from repercussions if they report illegal activities or other wrongdoing at their workplaces. These laws are meant for serious transgressions, not the typical grievances an employee may have about day-to-day business operations or the friction that sometimes exists between workers and managers. The government doesn't want to hear the whining and minor complaints of every employee from every company in the country. They are only concerned about illegal and harmful conduct. When it comes to promoting positive interactions between your children, you, too, should have a family whistleblower law or tattling rule. A good and easy one to use with toddlers and preschoolers is the In/Out Rule. Ask your child to think about why he wants to tell on a sibling or friend. If he wants to tell for no other reason than to get someone "in" trouble, he should not tattle. If he wants to tell on someone to keep the person from getting hurt or "out" of trouble, he should tell an adult right away. Describe some of the situations or behaviors that could get someone hurt, such as playing with a lighter or matches, climbing on top of furniture, wandering away from the house, going into the medicine cabinet, fighting, or destroying property.

Using the In/Out Rule early on can reduce the number of minor complaints and problems children bring to you and can help them learn to be more responsible. Unfortunately, young children will not always follow the rule, so you should expect to hear some whining and tattling. Toddlers and preschoolers have an especially hard time determining what is harmful and what is not. From their perspective, every situation requires a parent's assistance. To help reinforce the rule, watch how you react when they tattle on one another. For minor, insignificant behaviors that you want your children to ignore or resolve on their own, give them suggestions on what they can do independently to deal with the situation rather than simply stepping in and solving the problem for them. For example, let's say your three-year-old daughter comes to you and complains her brother is "making faces." It's better to tell your three-year-old to ignore the funny faces or go to another room to play than it is to tell your son to "stop it." Responding to your son's teasing may end up rewarding your three-year-old for tattling. Nothing brings more satisfaction than watching a sibling get a good "chewing out," especially when it's fueled by a brother's or sister's "inside information." If you step in to fix the problem, it only reinforces tattling and increases the rivalry and angst between them. Taking the time to teach and shape appropriate ways for your children to resolve minor conflicts will pay off in the long run. You will (eventually!) hear less whining and tattling. Also, your children will learn to handle minor conflicts more responsibly and be more likely to tell an adult if there is some harmful behavior occurring.

Carve out special time with each child.

Just as it's important to spend additional time with your older children when a new baby arrives, it's equally important to find ways to spend special time with each child on a regular basis. Your children likely have different needs in terms of how much time and attention they demand from you. Whereas one child might be content playing independently and doing his own thing, another may be equally content to always be by your side. All children want to spend some time with their parents. (Enjoy it while it lasts!) Even fairly independent children enjoy hanging around Mom and Dad. Unfortunately, you may not always have enough time to give, especially in a large family. The key is taking the time that you do have and carving out a few minutes with each child during the day to read a story, play, or chat. Sometimes, for reasons beyond your control (a child's health or special needs, for example), you might have to spend significant time with one child. Regardless of the reason, other siblings may feel a certain amount of jealousy or animosity toward that child because of all the attention. They might not always understand that this is not the kind of attention or time you would like to have with their sibling. When you are not able to balance things out evenly, it's all the more important to spend individual time with each of your children. Allow them to feel special and provide the attention and affection they are looking for.

Focus on words versus actions.

Anger is one of the most common emotions associated with sibling rivalry. The anger is usually directed toward a specific behavior or event. The issue isn't that children become angry at each other, it's that they don't know what to do with each other when they become angry. The younger the children, the bigger the challenge. All their raw emotions, including anger, come right to the surface and show themselves in all kinds of interesting ways. Physical aggression is one way. As you have likely observed, when children are not able to resolve their differences, they often start to push, hit, kick, and bite. That's when you need to step in. Once children have crossed the line in terms of their behavior, the best response is using time-out and removing the source of the conflict. This is not the time to sort out what happened or to interrogate them. Provide a quiet place for them to calm down. Once the dust settles (usually hours later when they are calm), explain that hitting, kicking, and biting are never acceptable, and those behaviors will always result in a negative consequence. After you have made that point, discuss what led to the aggressive behavior in a way that will allow you to provide some instruction on how they can avoid escalating similar situations in the future. Providing positive feedback and attention when they are playing cooperatively will help to further reinforce this.

Put the toys in time-out.

At your house, there are probably certain toys or activities that tend to create conflict between siblings or others. To lessen the fighting, you have several options. One is to allow your children access to the toy and work out their differences on their own or with your assistance. Another option involves limiting access to the particular toy or activity. Depending on what is being fought over and the age differences between your children, it may be easier to simply take away the toy or activity than to physically send a child (or children) to time-out or a quiet place in the house. It may even be more effective to tell your children they lost access to the toy or activity because of their arguing, crying, hitting, or fighting. When you take away a toy, redirect your children to another activity and explain how they need to act so they don't lose that toy, too. You might also warn your children that if they cannot resolve their conflicts among themselves, you will solve the problem for them. By giving children an opportunity to work through their problems independently (when the conflicts are minor), they can see the benefits. If they get along, they can enjoy their favorite toy or game. If they fight and argue, they will have to stop playing.

As a side note, a lot of children have certain toys or possessions that are especially important to them. A highly valued item often is the source of conflict when a child is forced to share it with other siblings or friends. Rather than force your child to share every toy, and thereby making the problem worse, it's okay if you let each of your children "exclusively own" one or two games or toys. If they choose to share them with others, that's great. But they don't have to. The choice is theirs.

Focus on the victim.

When sibling rivalry gets out of hand, one child may end up physically or emotionally hurt. If one of your children was undeniably hurt by the actions or words of another, give support and encouragement to the hurting child. As you talk to him, point out how his sibling should have responded. For example, you might say something like, "I'm sorry you were hurt, Sanjay. Your sister should have used her words to tell you she was angry instead of throwing the fire engine at you." Not only does this statement show caring, the child hears what action is appropriate when he is angry or frustrated. Explaining to your children what you want them to do is more informative and effective than simply saying, "Don't hit!" or "Stop throwing toys."

Emphasize cooperation not competition.

Children actually like to compete with one another, whether it's playing a game, racing in the backyard, or seeing who can eat the most doughnuts. There are many benefits to healthy competition. However, not every activity should be a competition. Also, when there is a significant age difference (a three-year-old versus a six-year-old, for example), the older sibling's constant victories are likely to cause the younger child to have emotional meltdowns. If you notice your children having frequent conflicts because they turn daily routines into mini-Olympics, look for ways to promote cooperation. For example, have them team up to see if they can pick up the toys in the family room before you finish getting ready for work, or have them try to "beat the clock" by helping each other clean their rooms. Finding creative ways for siblings to compete together, instead of against each other, can lessen the rivalry and tension that arise from direct competition. In addition, there are other benefits for your children:

- They learn to work together.
- They have more fun teaming up and competing

against someone or something else besides each other.

Model appropriate ways to resolve conflict.

There is no better way for your children to learn how to resolve conflict than to watch you do it. When you have a disagreement or conflict with a spouse, neighbor, or friend, remember there may be many eyes watching you. When your children see you do something, they often think it's okay for them to do it that way, too. Resolving a conflict in a civil and appropriate manner will send a much louder message in a much more appropriate way than if you get over-the-top angry, yell, scream, or throw things. Hopefully, you're good at keeping your emotions in check. But if you see yourself behaving badly, you will likely see your behaviors repeated by your children the next time they have conflicts with one another.

Have family fun time.

When possible, create time for the entire family to do something pleasurable together. It should be an activity that all can participate in, such as playing in a park, bowling, going to the zoo, or working on an art project. The more time siblings can spend together in an enjoyable activity, where fun memories and positive experiences are created, the more likely they are to resolve their differences in positive ways. It's much easier to resolve a conflict with someone you share fond memories with.

Carve out alone time.

Everyone needs a certain amount of time to themselves, even young children. Younger children will often want to play with their older siblings. They follow them around and inject themselves in play activities even when they are not welcome. There will be times when your children will want to do certain things on their own or want time alone. Children, like adults, vary considerably in their need to have alone time. Pay attention to each of your children's need to be alone. Make sure you carve out that time for them. It might mean setting limits, such as allowing a child to play with a friend by herself, without interference from other siblings, or letting a child work alone on an art project. During these times, you may need to redirect your other children to activities they can do on their own or with other siblings. It also may be helpful to set a timer to help your children understand their sibling is off limits until the timer sounds.

Involve your children in making ground rules.

You more than likely have some behavioral rules for your children, such as sharing and taking turns. It's a good idea to periodically sit down with them and review some basic rules as well as give them a chance to make rules that you have talked about in the past. By involving your children, you give them more ownership of their behavior, and the broken rule will have more meaning for them. That is, if they helped make the rule, they may be more likely to follow it.

Teach basic conflict resolution skills.

Children are never too young to learn how to resolve differences among themselves. However, given their youth, they are going to need some instruction from an expert (that would be you). Teaching them how to divide evenly, take turns, share, and use other basic play skills can help eliminate or reduce some conflicts. As your children grow, you will have plenty of opportunities to teach them how to compromise. Eventually, they will learn to do it on their own. Their "compromises" might involve things as simple as agreeing who gets to drink out of the red cup versus the blue cup, who gets to go down the slide first, or whose book gets read first. These compromises will help them learn that "give and take" is a normal part of life and, eventually, they will get "their turn." They also will learn that sometimes things are "not fair" – an important lesson we all need to learn.

From Tattling to Battling

Despite your best efforts, there will be times when your children's rivalries will escalate from civil disagreement to all-out war. The degree to which you need to intervene will depend on the nature and severity of the conflict. Here are a few strategies you can use when your children can't get along:

Use "unique" solutions.

Children love to tattle and point fingers at each other. As I'm sure you've already learned, not even the FBI or CIA can uncover a fraction of the truth in some of these situations. When your children have conflicts, it's important for them to learn how to resolve the problems on their own. They have the ability to resolve conflicts independently, but they just don't know it. After all, you have already discussed, modeled, and taught a number of ways for them to solve most of the conflicts they have. Despite this, they run and scream for the great and wonderful Wizard (you) for help. Let's say, for example, the Scarecrow (your four-year-old) and Tin Man (your six-year-old) come to you with their usual complaints. You have two options: You can listen intently and solve the problem for them, or you can send them away to come up with their own solution. Of course, they might plead with you to solve their dilemma as only a great Wizard can. But don't give in to their pleas. Instead, give them the time and opportunity to resolve the problem, knowing that if they can't solve it, you will give them a solution. The main point you want to make is that **they need to work out a solution**. If they are successful, praise their accomplishment and ability to come up with a workable plan. If they made an effort to resolve the conflict, but need some additional "consultation," provide it. However, if they make no attempt to reasonably resolve their conflict and continue to bicker, then offer a solution. However, your solution should be less than appealing. For example, if your children are fighting about what computer game to play and they can't come to a resolution, even after you give them time to work it out, offer a solution like this, "Kids, I have an answer for you. The computer is off limits for the rest of the day. Go find something else to do." This, of course, is not a solution your children will want to hear. They probably hoped you would have some wonderful, creative, and fair decision that would make them happy. However, the less appealing you make your solution, the more motivation your children will have to actually try to resolve conflicts by themselves. Eventually they will learn that if they don't make an effort to solve their disagreement, you will resolve it, but perhaps not in a way they like. Once they're able to work out solutions, and they will, praise them for being able to compromise.

Try temporary separation, not divorce.

When a conflict between siblings reaches a tipping point (arguing turns into screaming or hitting, for example), you should intervene. There are a number of intervention strategies you can use but acting as a referee should not be one of them. You simply won't learn the truth. Your children have their ideas about how wrong or unfair the other is, and you're not going to sort that out – ever. Instead, explain how disappointed you are in their behavior. Then, because they are unable to play nicely together, have them find other activities they can do by themselves. Send each child to a different part of the house for fifteen minutes (to track time, use a timer). This is not a time-out, and your children are not necessarily being sent into isolation. Rather, they are simply not allowed to be around one another. After fifteen minutes, bring them together and give them a chance to resume their activities. They might choose to do something else, which is fine. If they play together, and nicely, praise their cooperation. However, if their conflict resumes to its previous level, repeat the separation strategy and increase the time apart to thirty minutes. Each time their negative language or behavior crosses the line, increase the length of separation by fifteen minutes. This will accomplish several things:

1. It gives you some peace and quiet. There is no reason why the rest of the family should have to listen to the cat fight.
2. It gives your children some time to calm down and think about better ways to resolve their problems.
3. Most siblings, despite their occasional fights, like to spend time with each other. Time spent apart will be a reminder that if they want to do things together, they need to get along. It's important for your children to understand that certain behaviors can result in losing access to one another or other activities and that finding ways to compromise and get along has its benefits.

Use time-out.

Time-out has its place when children are in conflict. Time-out is certainly an appropriate response anytime you see your children being aggressive toward each other, physically fighting with one another, or being destructive in some way. If you observe one child being destructive or aggressive with another, placing the aggressive child in time-out is warranted. If both children are acting aggressively or being destructive and you're not certain who is responsible, place both of them in time-out.

Take away privileges.

You may have noticed that your children's conflicts often have to do with disagreements over who has access to an electronic device, toy, or activity. If you've taken all the appropriate steps previously described and a compromise has not been reached and the behavior has deteriorated to the point where your involvement is needed, a logical consequence is to eliminate or take away the source of the conflict. For example, if the argument is over who gets to play with the Nintendo Wii, take the game away for a certain amount of time. When the time is up, bring your children together and give them an opportunity to work out a solution. Offer praise if they come up with a workable solution and cooperate with each other. If their negative behavior or fighting resumes, take the game away again. Later, give your children another opportunity to resolve the problem. They will quickly learn that coming up with some resolution will allow them access to the activity they wanted in the first place. Eventually, you will see them compromising and solving their differences in ways that allow them to enjoy each other and their activities. That creates an opportunity for you to comment on how well they play together.

Level the playing field.

In general, you don't need to worry about everything being equal or whether one sibling gets the better end of a deal. However, there can be situations where one child learns to manipulate a sibling rather than compromise or share. This can happen when the sibling uses his superior size, age, or verbal skills to his advantage. If you see this happening, you may need to intervene to make sure your children learn some sense of fairness. Intervening to level the playing field may be necessary until the younger or less verbally and physically skilled child is able to hold his own.

Have structured activities.

One fairly easy way to reinforce all of the qualities you want to promote in your children when they play together is to encourage activities and games that require waiting, sharing, or taking turns. This can best be accomplished through a family activity. Just about any board game or card game can work as well as many electronic games. Before play starts, remind everyone (parents and children) of the rules of the game and the importance of taking turns. You might also have an additional rule that if a player doesn't follow one of the rules, that person loses a turn. When your children wait patiently, take turns, and share (Yes, this actually happens!), provide lots of positive attention and praise. Point out how nicely they take turns or share. In addition, you might intentionally break one of the rules so you lose your turn. You could say, "I have to sit out this round because I didn't follow the rules." Doing these types of activities with your children has many benefits. The most obvious is that you're spending time together as a family. It also allows you, in a structured way, to reinforce all the important behaviors you want to see in your children when they play together without you. By doing this fairly frequently, your children will hopefully be able to generalize their behaviors to other day-to-day activities in the future.

The goal here is not to eliminate rivalry but rather find ways to promote revelry. Siblings have had conflicts with each other since the days of cave dwellers and will continue to have conflicts for many thousands of years in the future. By planning ahead, you can take positive steps to promote behaviors that will allow your children to act responsibly and respectfully. This will help them learn how to interact with each other in healthier ways and to more effectively deal with the inevitable conflicts and rivalries that naturally exist among siblings. You can't control whether rivalry will occur, but you can certainly influence how you and your children respond to and manage the challenges that come with it.

chapter 9

The ABC'S on Getting ZZZ'S

Four-year-old Lakeesha, with help from her mother, got ready for bed. Lakeesha knew it was time to go night-night because she finished her snack, bathed, brushed her teeth, and put on her pajamas. Now she patiently sat on her bed waiting for Mom to read a bedtime story. Mom read one story and then another after her daughter pleaded for one more. When Mom finished reading, she tucked Lakeesha in, gave her a kiss goodnight, turned off the lights, and left the room. Mom let out a big sigh as she sat down in the recliner to read the paper and relax. A few minutes went by before she saw a shadow. It didn't belong to a burglar. It was Lakeesha standing by her side and asking for a drink of water.

Mom took her daughter to the kitchen, got her a drink, and returned her to bed. "Okay Lakeesha, it's time for bed now. Goodnight." Mom returned to her chair. A few minutes later the same shadow reappeared. "Mom, I need to go to the bathroom." Over the next forty-five minutes, Mom responded to multiple requests, including "Can I give you a hug?"; "I'm scared"; "Will you tuck me in again?"; and "I heard a noise." With each interruption, Mom's frustration became evident as her voice and footsteps got louder each time she took Lakeesha back to bed. Lakeesha finally fell asleep, allowing her exhausted mother to go to bed as well.

Compared to your child, how typical is Lakeesha's behavior?

A. You mean some children stay in bed after you put them there?

B. If my child only got out of bed five times each night, I'd be thrilled.

C. This is rare. Most children are too exhausted to get out of bed.

D. I think it's fairly common for some children to get out of bed at least a couple times each night.

It's fairly common for toddlers and preschoolers to have some type of disruption to their sleep. Some estimates suggest that anywhere from thirty to forty percent of children under the age of six will experience some type of sleep disruption. Most parents are absolutely thrilled when their infant learns to sleep through the night. "She's such a good baby" or "He found his thumb" is usually a reference to the fact that a child is now sleeping anywhere from six to eight hours without interruption. For many children, this is simply the calm before the storm. Along with advancing age and development comes the ability for children to use their imaginations, get scared, develop an awareness that Mom is much more comfortable than a pillow, and, most importantly, come up with all kinds of reasons why they cannot sleep. How parents respond to these interruptions will make a tremendous difference in how long and how significant any sleep problem becomes.

The first response from most parents is to provide comfort and to satisfy the needs of their child. This is especially true if a child is scared during a storm or if there is some disruption to the family that requires additional comforting. There are many "normal" disruptions that warrant giving a child additional comfort and support during the night. However, once a disruption passes, it's expected the child will resume his normal sleeping routine without much additional involvement from a parent. Sometimes that happens and sometimes not. For some children, normal disruptions turn into new routines. They simply want additional attention or comfort from their parents during the night. Once they learn they can continue the days' festivities or gain some more attention from their parents at bedtime, the party is on. Unfortunately, it's usually just a party for the little one.

What is the difference between a normal disruption to a child's sleep and a sleep disorder? If your child is not sleeping through the night, you probably don't care what it's called. I will not bore you with the distinction between sleep disruptions and sleep disorders. In general, however, sleep "problems" are usually grouped into three general areas. The first includes children who do not fall asleep within a reasonable amount of time after being put to bed. Some may not have learned how to fall asleep or transition themselves to sleep, while others have the skills but simply do not want to fall asleep. Children who take excessive amounts of time to fall asleep or have considerable difficulty falling asleep represent a common challenge for many parents. The second general group includes those who fall asleep easily and within a reasonable amount of time (fifteen to thirty minutes) but then wake in the middle of the night. These children typically come into a parents' room, cry out during the night, or in some way let Mom and Dad know they're up and unhappy. Of course, Mom and Dad aren't happy either. The third group involves a somewhat smaller percentage of children and includes those who have night terrors, nightmares, or who sleepwalk. (Additionally, there are certain medical conditions that can affect a child's sleep. If your child snores, has some type of breathing difficulty, sweats excessively, or moves excessively during the night, it would be wise to talk to your pediatrician. You might also consult with a pediatrician if your child has repeated night terrors, sleepwalks, or wets the bed.)

A Good Night's Sleep (for Everyone)!

Maintaining good sleep hygiene is an important consideration not only for children but for parents as well. Sleep hygiene refers to the good habits and routines that help a child learn to fall asleep and remain sleeping (or use skills previously learned to sleep peacefully through the night.) Here are some general strategies and tips to help you establish good sleep hygiene for your child:

Set a bedtime and stick to it.

Picking the right bedtime requires spending some time looking at your child's sleep schedule and determining the amount of sleep she **needs**. This will help you determine what time your child should be in bed. Most parents don't want their children sleeping until noon, even if it were possible, because that means they will probably stay up until midnight or later. If your child needs to get up in the morning for daycare or school, there will be a specific time she needs to get up so she's ready for the day. You can set her bedtime by working backwards from when she needs to get up and adding how many hours of sleep she needs. (The bedtime routine should begin thirty to forty-five minutes prior to bedtime.) When you establish a specific bedtime, stick to it. Children do very well with routines. Once they know their bedtime, it provides a predictable marker for parents and ensures children will get the amount of sleep they need. For some working parents, the limited time they have to spend with their children causes them to let their children stay up later than what may be desirable. I understand the importance and need for parents to spend time with their children, especially if they work all day. However, if this means children get less sleep than they need, making them irritable and crabby, it's important to adjust their bedtimes so they get sufficient sleep.

Develop a consistent routine.

Routines are important for all children, but establishing a consistent bedtime routine is probably one of the more important routines you can have. Establishing a consistent routine at bedtime is important for one primary reason: It helps your child prepare for going to sleep. When you follow a consistent bedtime routine, it provides a sense of security and predictability for your child. Each part of the routine is like a link in a chain that ends with turning off the lights and falling asleep. In general, it doesn't matter what routine you follow as long as you have a routine and follow the steps in the same order whenever possible. Your child will quickly learn that one step in the routine is followed by another. For example, your son's bedtime routine could go something like this: take bath, put on pajamas, brush teeth, pick out a bedtime story, read story, take one last sip of water, and turn off the lights. When this routine is followed dozens or hundreds of times, he learns what the steps are and what order they occur. He also knows the final step is turning off the lights and going to sleep. Rearranging the steps or following the routine one night but not another can be disruptive, and your child may not know what steps come next. For you, a bedtime routine can be a relaxing and fun part of the day. This is especially true if you create a routine that your child cooperates with and enjoys.

Set limits with the routine.

As with most routines, children like to vary them. It's important to establish fairly clear limits regarding bedtime routines. You should plan on spending thirty to forty-five minutes going through the routine from start to finish. If you find your children want to modify or change the routine so it lasts an hour or more, you may need to set clear limits for each step. Once you establish limits within the routine, stick to them. For example, if the limit is reading no more than two books, stop reading after the second book. Of course, you can be flexible from time to time if there is a special occasion. Also, if an exception is made, you should be the one who suggests the exception ("How about we read one more book?") not your child. However, these exceptions should only occur if your child understands that it's an exception and the normal routine will return the next night. If your child will have difficulty accepting your exception to a rule, then stick with the limits you set. Limits also should be set for behavior. If your child wants to play with toys or run around the room while you're reading stories, you should set "book reading" boundaries and limit his behavior. He needs to understand that if he wants to enjoy having stories read, he needs to be lying in bed or sitting quietly while you read. If he runs around or becomes disruptive, remind him of the rule and use redirection. If that's unsuccessful, put the books away and turn off the lights. You will need to decide which limits are appropriate. Again, once you have established them, stick to them.

Allow at least an hour for your child to wind down before you expect her to fall asleep.

If given the opportunity, most children would choose to engage in some high-adrenaline activity prior to bedtime. These activities (running, playing basketball, wrestling, jumping on the bed, watching an action movie, playing a video game, or listening to lively music, for example) can stimulate the body and the brain. However, your child needs time for her brain and body to slow down and relax in order to be ready for bed. Reading, doing an art project, or some mildly stimulating activities are better prior to bedtime.

Adjust naps as needed.

Most young children (especially toddlers) need at least one nap per day. A typical nap lasts about one to two hours. As children approach the preschool years, they vary widely in terms of their need for naps. You're probably well aware if your child needs a nap or not. If he does not want to sleep, but needs to have some "rest time," insist he do a quiet activity for an hour during the middle of the day, whether he's at home, daycare, or preschool. Even for children who are not asleep during this time, having an hour of quiet, relaxed time recharges their batteries and helps them be more pleasant and less irritable. If your child naps or takes fairly long naps, and you think it's affecting his ability to fall asleep at night, feel free to shorten his naps as needed.

Anticipate.

All good waiters anticipate their diners' needs. Although you're certainly not a waiter for your child, you might as well expect she will need "something" once you wrap up the bedtime routine. Do what you can to anticipate the need, including asking her if she needs to go to the bathroom one more time, needs an extra hug, or wants a drink of water. This should only take a moment, and it allows you to take away a tool from her bag of tricks after the lights are turned off.

Keep your child moving during the day.

This may seem obvious, but our over-saturated electronic world makes it worth saying again. Toddlers have lots of energy and need opportunities to use it. I can't begin to tell you how many toddlers and preschoolers spend their days plopped in front of a television, computer, or game system. I've seen some preschoolers spend ten or more hours in front of an electronic device during the day. They also are quick to throw a tantrum at the first suggestion they go outside to play or ride a bike. There's nothing wrong with any of the electronic devices available to children. However, like everything else, they should be used in moderation. An hour or two, at most, is sufficient for them. They need to use their imaginations as well as their limbs – climbing, running, playing, and interacting with others – whenever possible. This also helps them get ready for a good night's sleep at the end of the day.

Avoid caffeine.

Make sure your child avoids drinking caffeinated beverages or having anything that includes caffeine before bed. Caffeine is a stimulant that will inhibit sleep.

Keep the bedroom quiet and cozy.

Some children want their overhead light on at night. Others want music playing. Although certain modifications need to be made from time to time, including perhaps a night-light, allowing any type of stimulation that makes it difficult for your child to sleep should be avoided. Even though he may be able to fall asleep with the overhead light on, it's not the type of habit you want him to develop. Having a light on sends a mixed message to your child's brain: It's time to be up, not time to sleep. When there is light, the body makes certain chemicals that help keep us awake. Likewise, when the lights are down or off, it increases the production of other chemicals that promote sleep. Therefore, you want to do everything you can to help your child's body make use of the ingredients that encourage sleep. Even though a dark room is best for sleep, it may be necessary to plug in a small night-light or play soothing music as a compromise. The need for "sleep aids" is usually temporary and can be faded over time.

Don't jump on the bed!

How many times have parents said this over the years? Children frequently hear this refrain from moms and dads because they are concerned about their children's safety, or maybe concerned about the bed. Regardless, it's important that a child's bed not become a toy or place to play. Activities such as watching television or playing games on the bed are certainly not harmful. However, to promote positive sleep habits, it's important your child associate the bed with sleeping. Psychologists sometimes refer to this as "stimulus control." This simply means that individuals learn to engage in certain behaviors in specific environments or situations. For example, your behavior in church is under stimulus control just as your driving behavior changes in the presence of a police officer. If children learn their bed is only used for resting or sleeping, the bed becomes associated with that activity and that activity only. If, on the other hand, it becomes associated with jumping, playing games, or watching television, you lose the benefit of children learning that crawling into bed means it's time for sleep. Establishing the bed as a place for sleep, and only sleep, is helpful to all children. It's especially important for those who have difficulty falling asleep.

Unplug the electronics.

Is your child's bedroom wired for sound or sleep? We live in a high-tech, electronic world. It's nearly impossible to go anywhere without seeing someone talking on a cell phone, listening to an iPod, or playing with a portable game system. Most of these gadgets are very entertaining and even useful, if used at the right time and in the right place. However, it's not unusual for children to have a telephone, game system, television, DVD and/or iPod in their bedrooms. It's somewhat rare when I hear of a child who does not have at least one of these electronic devices in his bedroom. On the other hand, I commonly hear about a child, sometimes as young as two or three, who routinely watches a television program or movie in his bed well into the evening! Most children spend too much time in front of electronics as it is. Having access to these gadgets in their bedrooms, especially at a young age, works against their ability to develop good sleep habits, not to mention inhibiting their creative and imaginative play. When it comes to most electronics in the bedroom, I have one simple piece of advice: Get them out. If you don't place a television or DVD player in your child's room, it certainly won't traumatize him. For the best sleep (and for many other benefits) keep bedrooms TV-free zones.

Make transition objects available.

Many children enjoy having a stuffed animal or special blanket with them in bed. This routine usually starts very early in life and carries over into early childhood. Transition objects play an important role for children when it comes to sleep. Since parents are not available to sleep with them (hopefully), children can be comforted by reaching out for that favorite stuffed animal or blanket. This provides a sense of security and comfort in the middle of the night, especially when they wake. Promoting the use of a transition object early on will help promote a better sleep routine and better sleep hygiene. It's also important to remember that the transition object should remain in your child's bed and not be carried around throughout the house, into the car, or out in public. Exceptions might include traveling on a long trip or staying overnight with family or friends. The transition object will have more value if it's associated with sleep and remains in your child's bedroom.

Using some or all of these tips and strategies will help establish a lifetime of good sleep habits. At the very least, it may help prevent small disruptions in your child's sleep routine from turning into more significant problems.

Behavioral Interventions for Sleep Problems

Many children experience sleep difficulties. If your child has sleep difficulties, there are several behavioral interventions you can use to address them. Most of these strategies are effective for problems associated with falling asleep, including not staying in bed, because that is the most common problem for children and parents.

When it comes to sleep, one of the challenges parents have with toddlers and preschoolers is that, unlike infants, they no longer have a captive audience. Toddlers and preschoolers can crawl out of bed and come find you. Their internal GPS system takes them directly to you at anytime of the night. Parents are understandably excited to see their young children take their first steps and learn to walk. They are far less excited when they see them walk downstairs for the tenth time in thirty minutes after being put to bed. Children at this age also have learned to call out to their parents with all kinds of excuses as to why they can't go to sleep.

Let's review some of the strategies you can use to help your child not only stay in bed but actually fall asleep. These techniques are focused on bedtime but also can be used for naps. In fact, trying them out during naptime can help you fine-tune whatever approaches work best for your child.

Planned Ignoring

What parents haven't heard their children calling out from their rooms, pleading for another drink or one more kiss goodnight, or making a legal argument as to why they need to tell you something **really** important? At some point (much sooner than you might think), the whining and pleading needs to be ignored. There are a number of ways to do this, including one called planned ignoring. This technique works just the way it sounds. First, make sure your child is safe and in no danger. Next, make it clear to her that you will no longer respond to her cries and requests. Then ignore her whining, crying, and calling out to you. If you're able to follow through with the ignoring, it can be very effective. The problem, however, is that most parents have a difficult time ignoring their child long enough for the ignoring to work its charm. It's also complicated by the fact that if the child does not get a response, the child often gets out of bed to find Mom and Dad. Ignoring works well for infants who can't get out of their cribs. Babies eventually learn their whimpering and crying are no longer effective. This helps them learn to fall asleep on their own. They discover they don't need Mom or Dad to hold them or perform some other action to help them fall asleep. You want your toddler to learn the same thing.

Ignoring typically does not work as effectively as it could primarily because parents eventually get frustrated. They yell something from another room, go back into the room "one more time" to calm their child, or respond in some other way. Of course, this is exactly what the child wants. The child is not calling out because she actually **needs** something. She **wants** something – more attention. Any form of attention, positive or negative, tends to reward her for crying and whining and encourages her to use the same behaviors the next night.

If you think your child will remain in bed and you can effectively ignore her requests or demands night after night, she will eventually learn her behavior is not effective. She will eventually fall asleep on her own, and, believe it or not, her requests and complaints will eventually end. In general, there are three simple steps to using planned ignoring:

1. Once you put your child to bed, explain to him that you will no longer answer his questions or respond in any way.
2. Do not respond, in any way, to his calls, requests, or complaints.
3. If he leaves his room, immediately return him back to bed with no discussion of any kind.

For many parents, following this technique to its conclusion is very difficult. Most children are able to push a button or two, causing their parents to react in some way that usually results in the nighttime disruptions continuing much longer than most parents can tolerate. Because of that, there are several variations of planned ignoring you can use to make it more effective and help your child fall asleep more quickly. They include the following:

The Quick Check

One alternative to planned ignoring is the "quick check." Bradley's parents heard an old familiar song, "Mom? Dad? I need to tell you something. I need to go to the bathroom. I'm thirsty. I'm scared. I'm…." Very soon, they heard the pitter-patter of Bradley's feet. As they had done for the past ten nights, they said nothing to Bradley, escorted him back to his bed, and left his room. The song continued. They had been trying to ignore Bradley's requests, pleas, and cries for the past ten nights. The longer they ignored him, the more awake and energetic he seemed to become. The planned ignoring didn't seem to be doing the trick. Even if it was going to be effective eventually, they weren't sure if they could keep this up. The sleep specialist they were working with suggested they modify the planned ignoring strategy by using a technique called the "quick check."

This is a variation on completely ignoring your child once he's in bed. It simply involves telling your child that you will check on him as long as he stays in bed. The checks mean you very quickly look in on your child. The length of the check should be measured in seconds. This is not a time to sit on the edge of his bed to talk or comfort. This technique is designed to let you check on your child for your own comfort and peace of mind. At the same time, your child knows that you haven't forgotten and are keeping a close eye on him. Most importantly, your child learns that he needs to be in bed in order for you to check on him. You can decide how often you check-in, but you should gradually increase the time between check-ins to give your child an opportunity to fall asleep on his own. Again, any time your child leaves his bed or bedroom, he should be escorted back. You should avoid any conversation, and leave his room as quickly as possible. The check-ins should only occur if your child is in his bed and quiet. Any talking, crying, or screaming between checks should be ignored.

The advantages of the quick check over planned ignoring include the following:

- Your child is less likely to leave his bed since you are checking on him rather than him checking on you.
- The increased time spent in bed, waiting for you to check in, increases the likelihood that he will fall asleep.
- You spend much less time "checking in" compared to the time you spend returning him to his bed every time he leaves.

To implement the quick check, follow these steps:

1. Complete your bedtime routine and explain to your child that you will "check back," but only if he is in bed and quiet.
2. Leave your child's room and check back quickly, in a minute or less. Praise him for being in bed. Spend no more than ten to fifteen seconds in your child's room.
3. Continue to do very brief check-ins while gradually increasing the time between check-ins until they are at least ten minutes apart.
4. Ignore any noises, requests, or crying.
5. If your child leaves his bed at anytime, return him. Provide no attention or have any discussion. Remind him that you will only return if he stays in bed and is quiet.
6. Continue this process until your child is asleep.
7. Once your child understands the process, you can lengthen the time between check-ins from the start.

This process works best if you keep the time spent during check-ins brief, gradually lengthen the time between check-ins, and offer no reinforcement to your child if he calls out to you or leaves his bed.

The "Excuse Me" Drill

Another technique that many parents find helpful is the "Excuse Me" drill. This strategy is helpful for children who have difficulty separating from their parents at the end of the bedtime routine. It's especially effective for fairly needy children who require more of their parents' time, at least early on when parents try to change their sleep hygiene and self-calming skills. This technique involves spending some additional time at the end of the bedtime routine helping your child calm down and prepare for sleep. This might mean sitting by the edge of the bed, rubbing your child's back, or talking quietly. The "Excuse Me" portion of the drill involves saying something such as, "Excuse me, I need to check on something, I'll be right back." You then step away from your child's bedside before she can engage in some type of disruptive behavior. Initially, you should only leave for a few seconds. Again, you repeat the drill and gradually increase the length of time you're out of the room. Each time you return, it's important to praise your child's positive behaviors, such as staying in bed, lying still, keeping her eyes closed, or remaining quiet. If your child becomes disruptive, cries, or complains, tell her you will give her some time to calm down, and you'll return after she has quieted down and calmed herself. When she calms down, immediately go in and provide some additional attention. Repeat the process until your child understands you will leave for gradually longer periods of time but that you do eventually return. As you gradually extend the length of time away from your child, she not only learns you will return at some point but also that she needs to be quiet and calm for you to return. This also gives your child increasingly more time to learn to fall asleep on her own.

Graduated Ignoring

Heidi, a three-year-old bundle of energy, was finally learning to stay in bed after her parents said good night and turned off the lights.

The quick check technique helped Heidi learn that her parents would return, as long as she was in bed. Whenever she left, her parents took her back without saying a word. She liked it better when they came back into her room, smiled, and said "Good night." Although Heidi's parents were happy she was staying in bed, they felt they were going into her room too frequently. They worried Heidi might be staying awake longer than she should, waiting to see when they would return. They needed a way to gradually spread out the time between checks, giving Heidi a better chance to fall asleep without them. They had read several books on sleep and decided to try a technique called graduated ignoring (sometimes referred to as the Ferber Technique).

Graduated ignoring is very similar to the quick check technique with one exception. The check-ins happen at a specific time. Using this technique, you ignore your child's whining and crying for a specific amount of time (one minute, for example). When the time is up, you go into your child's room, briefly check on him, tell him goodnight, and leave the room. It's important that the amount of interaction you have with your child is limited. You continue to check on your child, but the time between check-ins gradually becomes lon-

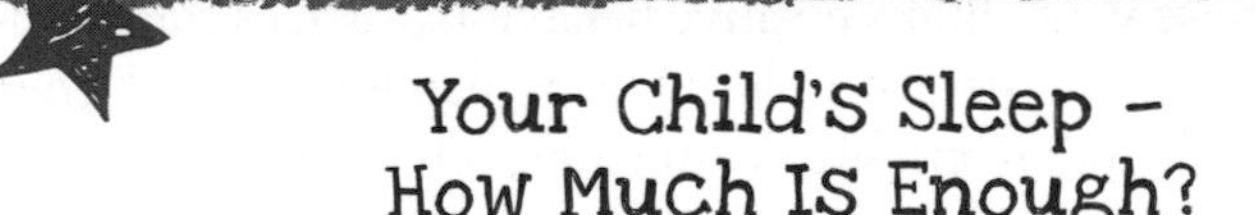

Your Child's Sleep – How Much Is Enough?

Children's sleep needs vary from day to day depending on their activity level and changes to their daily routines. In general, most toddlers need anywhere from twelve to fourteen hours of sleep. Most preschoolers need eleven to thirteen hours of sleep. This is the total amount of sleep needed and includes time spent napping (for those who nap). These numbers can vary by an hour or two for any given child. However, this should provide you with a general rule of thumb regarding how much sleep your child should be getting. If your little one is getting significantly less sleep than this (two or three hours), you may want to consult with a pediatrician. Your pediatrician can determine whether there is any benefit to working with a sleep specialist.

ger and longer. For example, the second check-in is two minutes after the first, and the third check-in is five minutes after the second, and so on. Set a time interval that you're comfortable with, and check on your child until he falls asleep. You might set ten or fifteen minutes as the maximum amount of time between check-ins because that fits your comfort level. The advantage of this particular technique is that it allows you to establish a specific schedule for checking on your child, while gradually extending the amount of time between check-ins. As with the other strategies, it allows your child to use his own skills and abilities to put himself to sleep. Also, by checking on him in a systematic and scheduled way, you are reassured your child is safe and not in danger.

With this particular technique, it's especially important that you gradually increase the length of time between check-ins. If the intervals are too short, you will only reinforce your child's whining and crying. Your child needs more and more time to learn to fall asleep on his own and use his self-soothing skills to fall asleep, while getting reassurance but minimal contact from you. Many parents find that having a set schedule to check on their child prevents them from checking too often. A schedule for returning to your child's room might be as follows: On the first night, you check-in after one minute, with subsequent check-ins occurring after two-, three-, four-, and five-minute intervals until your child is asleep. You could follow this schedule for a few nights and then increase the time between check-ins to intervals of two, four, six, eight, and ten minutes. The time intervals can be adjusted to your preference. The important thing is that you follow a schedule and gradually increase the intervals over time.

This approach is sometimes modified to discourage children from leaving their rooms. If your child is constantly leaving his room, you could follow a schedule similar (but shorter) than the one just described with one exception: The interval applies to how long your child's door is closed. Using this approach, your child learns that if he wants his door open, he needs to remain in bed. This will result in, at least initially, you checking on him periodically. If he leaves his room, return him to the bedroom and close the door for a specific amount of time (per the schedule) before opening it. Closing the door provides a negative consequence for leaving the bed and motivation to remain there. Remind your child that the door will stay open as long as he stays in bed. Using a schedule where the door is closed for a specific amount of time provides limits for you, and your child knows that each time he leaves his room, the door will be closed a little longer but not indefinitely.

If you use this technique, be prepared to respond to your child's crying and fussing, and the likelihood he will open the door once it's shut. Following through with the consequence of shutting the door if he leaves his bed will be important. Also, remind him the door will be opened only after he has been in bed for a certain length of time. If you feel you won't be able to follow through with this approach from start to finish, you should not start it.

Scheduled Awakening

Have you ever thought about actually waking your child up in the middle of the night? Sounds crazy, huh? Many children wake up in the middle of the night for a variety of reasons. They then like to wake their parents – usually from a dead sleep. If you have had this experience, I'm guessing it's probably not your favorite way to wake up. Parents can usually pin down the time their child is most likely to wake. If your child wakes at a fairly predictable time, you can schedule a time to check on him beforehand. By scheduling "an awakening," you can briefly wake your child into a semi-conscious state, letting him know you've checked on him. Then allow him to fall back to sleep. This usually takes away the need for your child to wake and come find you in the middle of the night. Is your child a good candidate for this technique? To find out, keep track of how often he wakes in the middle of the night and at what times. If it's often and you see a clear pattern, you may be able to use this technique to reduce and eventually eliminate his waking up at night. To use the technique, wake your child ten or fifteen minutes before he typically wakes. When he's awake, provide some comfort for a brief time and then help him back to sleep. Again, you want to provide the least amount of interaction as possible. The purpose of this strategy is to reduce your child's need to leave his bed or call out to you during the night. By checking on him before he checks on you, you can hopefully eliminate his need to get up again. Also, by having your child remain in bed, you're teaching him that there is no need to leave his bedroom.

If the scheduled awakenings are effective, you can gradually "fade" them. Fading simply means you wait longer and longer periods of time between each awakening, which lengthens the amount of time your child needs to sleep without getting your attention. Should your child spontaneously wake in the middle of the night, immediately return him back to bed. When doing so, it's important to have limited interaction. Simply take him back to bed and then return to your own bed. Providing additional attention after your child is up tends to reward the behavior and increase the likelihood that he will wake up again. The idea behind scheduled awakenings is to have a "preemptive strike," taking away your child's need to come find you whenever he wakes in the middle of the night.

Rewarding Good Sleep

As children approach school age, they may benefit from some simple reward-based strategies. This is possible, in part, because they are better able to delay gratification to some extent. If your child is able to count to twenty and can delay gratification for twenty-four to forty-eight hours, the following ideas can help.

Dominic's parents were pleased that he seemed to **finally** be learning to sleep through the night. He had just finished preschool and was excited about starting kindergarten in a few months. Although Dominic had made excellent progress with his sleep routine, he still left his room once or twice a night. He would find his parents and have the usual excuses. Dominic's parents returned him back to bed whenever he left his room, but he seemed to lack the motivation to stay there. Mom and Dad noticed he seemed to work extra hard to earn stickers and other rewards at preschool. They had just read Dr. Pat Friman's book, ***Good Night, Sweet Dreams, I Love You***, and wondered if their son would benefit from having a bedtime pass.

The Bedtime Pass

As I've mentioned, most children have sleep difficulties that involve falling asleep at the beginning of the night. Some children also have difficulty remaining in bed if they wake during the night. A technique called the bedtime pass can help children who experience problems with sleep onset and/or have difficulty sleeping through the

night. To use the bedtime pass, start by creating an object that can be used for the pass. You can create the pass with your child or, better yet, have her create her own. Allow her to create and decorate the pass any way she likes. The pass is "worth" one chance to leave the bedroom after bedtime. Your child might decide to use the pass to give you another hug, ask you a question, or get a sip of water. Once she uses the pass, she can no longer call out to you or leave her room. Any attempts to do so should be ignored by you. (Return your child to her room if she leaves.)

Most parents discover that their children often fall asleep before they use the pass. The children may be thinking, "I better not use my pass now. What if I **really** need it later?" As a result, the loud, disruptive behaviors exhibited by most children at bedtime tend to disappear. Some parents also offer a reward for not using the pass. If a child elects not to use the pass, he can exchange it in the morning for a favorite breakfast cereal or a chance to watch his favorite video or cartoon. As a concept, the bedtime pass may be a little too complicated for most toddlers to comprehend, so it's better suited for preschool-aged children.

Three Strikes and You're Out

This strategy often serves as a fresh start for children who have not been successful with the bedtime pass. This is a strategy in which a child starts the night with three tokens and earns a reward for having at least one left in the morning. Here is how you can explain it to your child: Tell him you're going to put three nickels, marbles, poker chips, or some other similar token in a dish beside his bed. Each time he gets out of bed and leaves his room, you will take him back to his bed and take one of the tokens. (When you have to return your child to his bed, give him as little attention as possible.) If he wants to earn a special reward in the morning, he will need to have at least one token left beside his bed. If all the tokens are gone, the special reward won't be available.

The special reward can be whatever you choose, but it should be something your child can obtain immediately (eating a special breakfast or doing an activity, for example). Some parents like to offer "mystery prizes," which often involve wrapping up small toys and displaying them in a basket. They let their child choose between picking a wrapped (mystery) gift or having a non-mystery reward, such as a favorite breakfast cereal.

The advantage of using three tokens is that it gives your child multiple opportunities, at least initially, to ask questions or go to the bathroom. This is important for children who are unsuccessful at staying in bed after they use up their one bedtime pass. Once your child understands how this "game" works and starts to enjoy its benefits, you can gradually reduce the number of tokens until you're down to one. At that point, you can replace the tokens with a bedtime pass. Also, I have found that some children, when they reach school age, start to understand the concept of money. Some parents who use nickels, dimes, or pennies as tokens will take the coins that are left each morning and place them in a jar. When the jar fills with coins, they let their children spend the money. This serves as a long-term goal or reward for children, in addition to the daily rewards they receive.

As you can see, there is a wide range of approaches that can be used to help manage your child's sleep difficulties. The basic message is fairly simple: Children need support, want to know they're safe, and have parents available. Children also need to be given the opportunity and the motivation to use their skills and abilities to calm and soothe themselves. As a parent, you need to gradually but steadily reduce and remove your involvement and presence so your child can become more independent and transition himself to sleep. I've seen hundreds of parents be very successful with these types of approaches, and I'm confident you will be, too.

When Two (or Three) Is a Crowd

Using good sleep routines and habits, along with one or a combination of the strategies previously described, will hopefully allow you and your child to sleep well – in your own beds. Still, children sometimes find their way into a parent's bed. This may be due to general insecurity, a bad dream, fear of a storm, or something similar. Some parents also find comfort in having their child sleep next to them, and many children certainly enjoy this, too. However, what sometimes starts out as a single event can eventually turn into a nightly routine.

Some children understand that sleeping in a parent's bed during a bad storm or after a bad dream is the exception, and they will be expected to return to their own bed the next night. In fact, most children do this willingly. However, some children learn fairly quickly that they enjoy sleeping next to Mom or Dad, finding it far superior to sleeping alone. This can set the stage for them to become more resistant to sleeping in their own beds and more persistent about sleeping in Mommy and Daddy's bed. Many of these children are successful in their efforts because their parents are too tired to return them to their bedrooms. Understandably, the parents need their sleep, too. There also are parents who are completely unaware that a child has entered their room and climbed into bed with them. In any respect, if your goal is to have your child sleep in his own bed or to get him out of your bed, here are a few suggestions:

Set rules before problems occur.

If your child has yet to venture into your bed to sleep, establishing a strict rule against sleeping in your bed will save you the time, trouble, and hassle of eventually having to remove him or dealing with his nightly visits to your bedroom. If your child is or has been sleeping in your bed, establish a rule that he can only sleep in his bed. Communicate the rule to your child, and take steps to enforce the rule.

Comfort children in their own beds.

Children often need comfort in thc middlc of the night. They may feel sick, can't sleep, had a bad dream, think they saw "monsters," or simply want reassurance. There are a few good, but mostly hundreds of not-so-good, reasons why your child is up and out of her bed in the middle of the night. Regardless of the reason, the best place to provide comfort and reassurance, if she really needs it, is in her own bed. Therefore, if she needs reassurance and support in the middle of the night, is sick, or there is a severe storm, take her back to her bedroom and provide any needed reassurance there. If she is ill and you need to watch her, do so in her bedroom not yours. This helps reestablish the expectation that your child will sleep in her own bed. It also reduces the association of her feeling comforted and reassured in the confines of your bedroom versus hers. Let me explain further. Most nights, your child sleeps calmly and peacefully without any disruptions. On rare occasions, a bad dream, storm, or illness wakes your child. He is fearful and naturally comes to you for support and reassurance. If that support and reassurance is always provided in your bedroom or bed, your child learns that he can go from a sometimes frightening and fearful state to a very calm and relaxed state when he's in your bed or bedroom. It's much better if he experiences your comfort in his own bed. Your child then associates his bed and the surroundings of his bedroom with a reduction in fear and worry.

Return children to their own beds.

In general, if your child comes into your room after she is put to bcd, rcturn her immediately and have very limited interaction. Unless there is a legitimate reason (and there are very few) to spend time with her, return her to bed with limited or no interaction. You don't want to give her any reason to get out of bed again. It's not uncommon for parents to tell me they wake up in the morning and find their child or children sleeping in bed with them. If you're a sound sleeper (Congratulations!) and are unaware that your kids are coming into your room (Condolences!), there are a few things you can do to increase your awareness. One option is to simply close and lock your door. Doing this means a child will have to knock to wake you. Although you certainly don't want to hear a knock on your door in the middle of the night, it will let you know your child is up and needs to be returned to bed. If you don't want to lock your door, you can place an inexpensive contact alarm on the door that will sound when the door opens. Another simple and inexpensive solution is to place a bell or similar item around the door handle that will make a noise when someone opens the door.

Many parents find themselves in a situation where their child has slept in their bed for months or maybe years. They assumed, or hoped, their child would eventually outgrow the behavior or want to move to his own bed. (You, too, may be hoping your child will graduate from your bed before graduating from high school.) Parents oftentimes offer all kinds of enticements – a new bed or bedspread, the chance to paint his room any color he likes, a new toy, or a trip to Disney World – to get their child into his own bed. However, after the room is painted fire engine red and half a dozen trips are made to Orlando, they still find their little one sleeping next to them.

As I discussed in other chapters, long-term gratification isn't very effective with toddlers and preschoolers. Once they have enjoyed the comfort of sleeping next to a parent, it's difficult to find some reward or incentive that will compete with that. So what should you do if you find yourself in this situation but want your child to sleep in his own bed? The first and most direct approach is to establish a specific date when you will return your child to his bed. Selecting a date that coincides with a long weekend is ideal. Explain to your child that he can no longer sleep in your bed, and he now has to sleep in his own room. (This won't make your child cheer and clap.) Clearly state that after the bedtime routine, you will tuck him into his bed, and he has to remain there. If he leaves, he will be taken back to his bed.

You can use any of the previously described strategies to help him remain in his own bed. I would also recommend identifying some reward your child can have first thing in the morning if he wakes up in his own bed. This will not be motivation enough for him to sleep in his bed versus yours, but it will, at the very least, provide minor motivation to stay in his bed. You should fully expect resistance from your child, and you should plan on wearing out the carpet between the two bedrooms. The reason why I suggest you do this over a long weekend is because it's likely you won't get much sleep. However, after several nights of consistently following this routine, most children respond fairly favorably. Your child's insistence and persistence about sleeping in your bed will decline fairly dramatically. The reward offered for sleeping in his own bed then becomes somewhat more valuable, especially when he realizes he's not going to have any success sleeping with you.

An alternative to this abrupt approach is to take it more gradually. You use the same general techniques previously described, but you do them in a series of steps. The first step is to move your child from your bed to a blowup mattress or sleeping bag on your bedroom floor. Again, your child will resist sleeping on the mattress or in the sleeping bag. However, some children are less resistant to sleeping on a mattress or the floor if they're still in the parents' bedroom. Of course, they would prefer to be in the bed but being in the room is better than nothing. (One issue to be aware of is that your child may attempt to crawl into your bed during the night.)

Step two involves moving the sleeping bag or blowup mattress out of your room. You can give your child the option of sleeping in the hallway (if it's between both bedrooms) or her bedroom, but not your room. You also can give her the option of sleeping on the mattress or in the sleeping bag (if she wants to be in the hallway) or in her own bed. Neither option is likely to be attractive to her. She will likely plead and insist that she sleep in your room. Again, you will need to deal with your child's resistance to this new arrangement and be prepared to escort her from your room on a fairly regular basis for several nights. If your child elects to sleep in the hallway, this will be temporary. Once she realizes she will not be sleeping in your room, she will move to the comfort of her bed.

The key to your success when you decide to put forth the effort to move your child from your bed to her bedroom is persistence. The worst thing you can do is give in to your child's insistence that she sleep in your bed after several nights of consistently returning her to her bedroom. This would only teach your child that she needs to keep coming to your bedroom to eventually get what she wants. This will strengthen your child's resolve to sleep in your room, making it much more difficult to stop the practice in the future. Thus, once you start this process, you must finish it.

Nightmare/Terror Table

	Nightmare (scary dream)	Night Terror
What is my child's reaction?	Frightened, racing heart, eyes open, awake and alert, aware of parents' presence	Eyes open but asleep, possibly screaming, sweating and breathing fast, unaware of parents' presence, difficult to awaken
When is it most likely to occur?	Near the end of sleep	Around the start of sleep
Is my child awake and alert?	Yes	No
Will my child remember the event in the morning?	Yes	No
When the event is over, will my child return to peaceful sleep?	Maybe	Yes
How will my child react to my presence?	Will reach for parent, seek comfort and support	Little awareness of parent, may push parent away
What is the appropriate parental response?	Offer comfort and support, and discuss event if child mentions it.	Ensure safety and gently comfort child back to sleep. Do not discuss event in the morning.

Nightmare or Night Terror?

Has your child ever awoken in the middle of the night, eyes wide open, screaming, and sweating? If so, it was probably more frightening for you than your child. It's typical to assume your child had a bad dream or a nightmare. But it's also possible your child experienced a night terror. Parents often have a difficult time determining the difference between a nightmare and a night terror. This isn't surprising since they appear similar. In both events, children often scream, appear panicked, are wide-eyed, and frightened. The first reaction of most parents, of course, is to comfort and support their child. Although providing comfort and support to a child who had a nightmare is certainly important, it's not necessary for night terrors. In fact, it may be counterproductive.

There are a few basic differences between nightmares and night terrors. With a nightmare, children typically wake up and are alert. They will seek comfort (reach out for a parent) and be able to describe what scared them. With a night terror, children are not awake and alert. Although their eyes are open, they are not fully awake. They typically don't reach out for a parent, and they are not responsive or alert enough to interact or describe the "bad dream" they had.

When your child wakes up in the morning after having a nightmare, she probably can remember her bad dream. She almost certainly remembers you providing some comfort during the night. On the other hand, if your child had a night terror, she probably went back to sleep and doesn't remember anything when she wakes up. If you ask her about the bad dream, she will have a puzzled look and wonder what you're talking about.

With nightmares, it's important to provide immediate comfort and reassurance. Once your child calms down, put him back in bed. If your child has a night terror, avoid restraining or holding him. This may cause him to become combative or thrash about. Some parents attempt to wake their child during a night terror. This tends to make matters worse. Since the child is not fully awake and not aware of the night terror, waking him may result in him sitting in the middle of the bed, screaming, perspiring, and having a racing heart. Then he'll wonder why his heart is racing and why you're sitting in the bed with him. Now your child is, in fact, frightened. As you might imagine, when it's time to go to bed the next night, he's certainly going to worry and wonder if he's going to have another "bad dream." This sometimes leads to additional sleep problems that didn't exist before. Therefore, if your child is having a night terror, don't restrain or hold him. Allow him to get through the episode until he calms himself into a peaceful sleep. Your main role is to remove any dangers and make sure your child is safe. Once the night terror passes, you can help him go back to sleep. In the morning, don't mention the episode. Your child won't remember the event and bringing it up will only cause him to worry over what might happen tonight.

Approximately five percent of children will experience night terrors. Most of these occur between the ages of two and five. Others tend to appear periodically and unpredictably. Your child may have several night terrors over a one- or two-week period and then not experience any for some time or ever again. Night terrors are not associated with significant emotional concerns. Seeking professional assistance is usually not necessary unless the night terrors are occurring on a regular basis or seem to be increasing in intensity and length.

Sleepwalking is another area of concern for some parents. Sleepwalking occurs for many of the same reasons as night terrors and should be managed in much the same way. However, there is one caveat: Some children have been known to actually leave their homes while sleepwalking. If you have this concern, place locks beyond your child's reach so he cannot open any door that leads outside. You also could place inexpensive contact alarms on outside doors to alert you if someone is trying to leave in the middle of the night. Again, there are no significant psychological concerns associated with either night terrors or sleepwalking. The same is generally true for nightmares. Most of these events will come and go. If you see a trend develop in your child and you're concerned about the frequency of such events, contact your pediatrician.

Finally, there are some excellent resources available for parents. One of the best books and resources for parents who have children with sleep difficulties is ***Good Night, Sweet Dreams, I Love You: Now Get into Bed and Go to Sleep!*** by Dr. Pat Friman. It provides an excellent overview of the types of sleep difficulties parents' experience with children as well as some excellent strategies to solve sleep problems with children of all ages. Another good resource is ***Solve Your Child's Sleep Problems*** by Dr. Richard Ferber. (Both books are included in the resource list on pages 251-252.)

chapter 10

Time-Out: It's Not Just for Athletes

Four-year-old Jalen was playing with his action figures when he heard his Dad say, "Jalen, please pick up your action figures and put them in the toy box." Jalen ignored him. He was having too much fun. A few minutes later, Dad walked into the room and said, "Jalen, we need to leave for the game. Please put the action figures in the toy box now." Jalen replied, "No, I don't want to." He then chucked a transformer at his father, who then said, "No throwing. Time-out!"

Dad took Jalen to time-out, a beanbag chair facing a corner in the dining room, and Jalen threw himself down. Jalen's dad set a timer for three minutes and walked away. Jalen screamed, cried, and protested. His father did not respond. Jalen screamed louder and yelled, "You're not the boss of me!" Again, Dad did nothing. Jalen couldn't take it anymore. He got up from the time-out chair and went looking for his father. When Dad saw Jalen, he said nothing. He escorted him back to the time-out chair, reset the timer, and walked away. Jalen continued yelling but soon quieted down. When Dad heard the timer sound, he walked over to Jalen and repeated, "No throwing." He then said, "You need to pick up your action figures and put them in the toy box now, please." With a scowl, Jalen walked over to the action figures and put them away. Jalen and his family then left for the game.

If you had to give Jalen's father advice on how he used time-out with his son, which of these suggestions would you offer?

A. The length of the time-out should have matched Jalen's age – one minute for each year.

B. Time-out should not have started until Jalen was quiet.

C. Time-out should have been done in Jalen's room.

D. All of the above.

First of all, Jalen's father did an excellent job using time-out. He clearly explained why Jalen was going to time-out, ignored his protests, returned him to time-out and reset the timer after he left early, and made sure Jalen finished picking up his toys. You might be thinking, "Shouldn't the time-out have lasted four minutes to match his son's age?" There would have been nothing wrong with a four-minute time-out, or even a ten-minute one. There is no science that says the length of a time-out has to match a child's age. Time-out simply needs to last long enough to get a child's attention and make him understand that negative behaviors result in negative consequences.

You also might be wondering if it was okay for Jalen to be so loud during time-out. As a parent, you can decide what behaviors are acceptable from your child during time-out. If you can ignore the whining and crying, fine. If you want your child to learn to be completely quiet during time-out, that's also fine. Decide what the rule is for your child and stay with it. What about the location? Wouldn't Jalen's bedroom make a better spot for time-out? Depending on what's in a child's room, a time-out can turn into playtime instead. A corner, step, or other quiet, distraction-free location is best.

You may have tried time-out before and felt it didn't work. If so, chances are you didn't use it in a way that was meaningful to your child because time-out can be a very effective discipline technique. It also may be the most used, misused, and discussed parenting technique for young children. Time-out has taken on a variety of different names, including "think time" and "quiet time." The "traditional" time-out chair also goes by other names, including "naughty step" and "safe seat." Regardless of what name is used, the concept of time-out is easy to understand. When a child misbehaves, he sits alone in a quiet place away from the action. While sitting in time-out, **nothing** happens. It's similar to when a football coach calls timeout because things are going badly on the field. When a child's behavior isn't going well, a parent can call time-out. Time-out gives the parent and child time to calm down. It also sends a signal to the child that his behavior was inappropriate or unacceptable. Just like a football player on the bench who wants to get into the game, your little one wants to play instead of sit alone. And in case you haven't noticed, toddlers can be very effective and creative at letting everyone know they want to be in the action, not sitting in a corner.

Time-out can be confusing for parents because they don't always know what behaviors warrant such a consequence, what to do when their child does not "go willingly," or how to respond when their child doesn't stay in time-out. In the following pages, I'll answer some of the most common questions and concerns parents have about time-out, including how you can make time-out as effective as possible.

There's No Time-Out without Time-In

The official name for time-out is "time out from reinforcement." Reinforcement is "time-in" and refers to all the fun stuff kids do and participate in throughout their day. This includes playing games, watching television, coloring, reading independently or with a parent, playing with siblings and friends, climbing on play equipment in the backyard, tossing a ball to the family dog, playing with dolls and trucks, riding a tricycle, or any number of other enjoyable activities. It also includes all the positive interactions that parents and others have with them. This includes everything from smiles and hugs to kisses and gentle touches. It includes parents acting surprised after their child has colored the same picture for the twentieth time or giving a high-five after he eats all of his green beans. It also includes the thousands of times a child hears "Nice job," "I love you," "Well done," "Great," and "I knew you could do it."

For time-out to work, you have to create a time-in environment. If you read through the list of positive activities and interactions (the essence of time-in) and thought to yourself, "Hmm, I don't do much of that" or "I could do a whole lot more of that," there is no time like the present. Creating a positive, nurturing, and loving environment is important for children, regardless of how it affects discipline techniques. The truth is, time-out is much more effective when it's used in an environment that also includes attention and praise for a child's positive behaviors. To highlight this point, imagine two different work scenarios. In one scenario, your boss and coworkers frequently tell you what a wonderful job you do. They acknowledge the projects you complete on time and appreciate your positive attitude. They don't take your day-to-day work for granted, and they take every opportunity to show you how much they value you and your work. Your boss offers constructive criticism but much more frequently acknowledges all of your accomplishments and contributions. In the second scenario, imagine nothing in the first scenario happens. The only time you hear from your boss or coworkers is if you're a minute late, they need extra help with a project, or you didn't meet their expectations. You rarely hear words of encouragement. You know very well that if you make a mistake, you will hear about it. As long as you do your job, you know you can keep your boss off your back. If not, you will be criticized or disciplined.

Think about those two situations. Which workplace would you rather go to each morning? Which work environment makes feedback from others more meaningful to you? My guess is that you would be much more motivated to work in scenario one's environment. The positive encouragement and recognition from your coworkers and boss would encourage you to work even harder. Also, when your boss provides critical feedback or some form of discipline, it may sting a bit more because you can contrast that with all the positives you receive when you do your job or do it especially well. On the other hand, if you're getting little or no positive feedback, as in scenario two, all the negative comments, at worst, cause you to be angry or cynical, and at best, do nothing to change your behavior. When negative feedback becomes the norm, you essentially work to earn a paycheck and avoid negative criticisms and evaluations. So, time-out is much more effective if you have a positive, nurturing time-in environment.

Creating a time-in environment means you can't take your child's positive behaviors for granted because that's what she "is supposed to do." A simple acknowledgment, whether it's a smile, nod, or simple "Nice job," goes a long way toward establishing a healthy, nurturing time-in environment. As a general rule, you should make three positive gestures or comments for every negative one. If you can make this ratio higher, by all means do it. Positive gestures and comments are just one way of creating time-in. You also can create time-in by carving out time together to play, talk, or work on projects you both enjoy.

Answering Time-Out Questions

Even though time-out is a fairly simple technique, parents often have many questions about how to do it properly. Here are some answers to commonly asked questions:

What is time-out?

First of all, time-out is an experience, **not** a location. It's more important to focus on the experience your child has during time-out than where it occurs. To put it simply, time-out means putting your child in a boring place (no fun stuff, attention, or interactions from others) for a brief period of time. When your child misbehaves, a time-out gives him a certain amount of time to cool off and helps him understand that his behavior was unacceptable. Time-out is essentially a penalty box where he's expected to sit until the time is up. While in the "penalty box," everyone else continues to have fun and enjoy various games, activities, and electronics. He, on the other hand, should experience as much nothingness as possible. That's one of the reasons why time-out should be in a fairly isolated location, so your child cannot be entertained in some way, such as watching television, talking to others, or looking out a window. If he has access to fun stuff and people, it's not "time out from reinforcement."

You experienced a form of time-out if you were ever stuck in traffic or stood in a long line. There is nothing you can do or say to make the traffic or line move faster. You're stuck! Pretty frustrating isn't it? Maybe that's why we always scope out the shortest lines at a concession stand or listen to traffic reports before we head to work. Time-out is not fun, and it's not supposed to be.

Is my child too old or too young for time-out?

When your child can communicate with you in simple, three- or four-word sentences and understands basic statements and instructions, she's ready for time-out. This typically happens around age two. However, children as young as twelve months can learn by association. For example, a one-year-old child who repeatedly finds herself alone in her play pen after pulling the cat's tail will eventually learn to stop pulling Tiger's tail. In general, time-out is most effective for children in the two- to six-year age range, but it can certainly work with children who are elementary-school age. However, when children reach the later elementary school years, a wider range of consequences are available. Also, because there is a fairly limited number of consequences one can use with toddlers and preschoolers, time-out is an excellent consequence for common misbehaviors, such as aggression, destruction of property, and inappropriate language.

Why not just spank?

Many of today's parents grew up in environments where spanking and corporal punishment were a way of life. In today's world, the phrase "This is going to hurt me more than it's going to hurt you" is echoed much less. To some degree, though, the expression is true. Parents often tell me they feel guilty when they resort to spanking but then they quickly add, "It doesn't work anyway." One problem with corporal punishment is that it suppresses (puts on hold) a behavior without teaching a new, more appropriate skill or behavior. We have all had an experience where we did something that caused us discomfort or pain. We didn't spend a lot of time thinking about why it was painful or what caused the pain, we simply stopped whatever we were doing because it hurt. A young child who touches a hot stove, for example, doesn't need to understand how heat is conducted or how electricity works to know that touching a hot stove can cause severe pain. The painful association of touching the stove is lesson enough. Does this mean the child should never use a stove or go near one as long as he lives? Of course not. The lesson learned from a hot stove and physical punishments are similar: A behavior is followed by physical pain. If one doesn't like the pain that follows the behavior, the behavior stops. Unfortunately for many children, spanking does not suppress a behavior well enough to change it in any meaningful way and little is taught in the process. The other problem is that research shows corporal punishment can lead to negative side effects, including aggressive behavior. Children who experience corporal punishment as a primary method of discipline can become more aggressive toward others.

The benefit of a non-physical punishment, such as time-out, is that it more effectively suppresses a behavior and allows parents to show their children that negative actions take them away from positive, nurturing environments. It also gives children time to think about their behaviors and associate their choices with the fact that they're now sitting alone and not having any fun. Using time-out consistently to associate negative behaviors with the temporary loss of an enriching environment may take longer to change behavior (compared to physical punishment), but the behavior change tends to be longer lasting. Another reason to use time-out over spanking is that it's less likely to be emotionally upsetting to you. If spanking or corporal punishment upsets you, you're less likely to use them consistently. You may even be more likely to use them out of anger. If you spank when you're angry, you put yourself and your child at greater risk (emotionally and physically).

How can I introduce time-out to my child?

Needless to say, children are not born with an understanding of time-out. They can learn what time-out is through experience, or, if you prefer, you can teach them what it is. To introduce the concept before actually using it, start by briefly explaining the general rules. Tell your child that when he misbehaves (hits, kicks, or throws things, for example), he will need to have a time-out. Show him the location you chose for time-out, which could be a step, hallway, or chair facing a corner. Tell him that time-out means sitting quietly by himself for a short time. (I recommend showing him a timer and explaining that when it sounds, time-out is over.) Then review with him the four rules of time-out:

1. If he misbehaves (give examples), he will go directly to time-out and a timer will be set.
2. If he leaves time-out before the timer sounds, he will be returned and the timer will be reset.

3. During time-out, no one will talk to him or interact with him in any way.
4. Once the timer sounds, time-out is over.

After you review the rules, practice. You can even start by putting yourself in time-out. For example, pick up a toy and toss it to the floor. Then say, "We don't throw toys, do we? I need to go to time-out." Go to the designated time-out spot, sit down, and set the timer for thirty seconds. Tell your child you're in time-out, so he can't play with or talk to you. Ask him to step far enough way so he can see you but not touch you (for demonstration purposes). When the timer sounds, let your child know that means you can get up. Now have your child practice. Set the timer for five or ten seconds, have him sit on a step or seat, and remind him again that he can't get up until the timer sounds. Then leave the area. You may have to go back and forth during the practice until your child grasps each concept. After you finish, practice again and review the time-out rules. I recommend practicing time-out until your child can sit comfortably and cooperatively for at least thirty seconds. This is a good starting point when you begin to use time-out for real. You can gradually extend the length of time-out until it reaches a point that is meaningful and effective for your child.

What behaviors deserve a time-out?

In general, I would use time-out whenever your child engages in the following:

- **Aggressive behaviors,** such as hitting, kicking, pinching, and biting.
- **Destructive behaviors,** such as breaking toys, throwing objects, and pushing things over.
- **Noncompliant behaviors** (when guided listening and Grandma's Rule, explained in Chapter 2, are ineffective). Generally speaking, I prefer parents use guided listening or Grandma's Rule with noncompliance, especially with children who are approaching school age. If your child becomes aggressive during guided listening, then time-out is appropriate. It's okay to start with a time-out first

if your child is noncompliant so long as you have your child complete the requested task. You may have to go back and forth between the time-out and the completion of the task, meaning you may have to use multiple time-outs if your child continues to have fits while following your instructions. (For more explanation, see Chapter 2.)

- **Inappropriate language.** This is especially important if you hear your child use inappropriate words in a conversation or call other people names. Sometimes your child may use negative language when he's being disciplined for some other behavior. When this happens, ignore the language for the time being and stay focused on the demand you made or the consequence you applied. Addressing your child's inappropriate language when he's angry can take the focus away from the behavior you're trying to manage, complicating the entire situation. Addressing two or three behaviors (including language) at the same time increases the

Quick Facts about Time-Out

- Time-out is a way of disciplining your child without yelling, screaming, or spanking.
- Time-out can be used for most toddler and preschooler behaviors.
- Making use of a timer will help you and your child keep track of the length of time-out.
- Time-out is most effective if there is a lot of "time-in."
- Time-out is easiest to use at home but can be used almost anywhere.
- When possible, time-out should occur in a quiet, isolated area away from the fun stuff.
- During time-out, children should receive no attention or interactions from others.

likelihood that you will pile on one consequence after another, and you will lose the opportunity to drive home a point on a particular behavior. It's better to address the inappropriate language later, after your child is calm. On the other hand, if your child uses inappropriate language that he picked up at school or in the neighborhood (certainly not from you), it's important to address it. This includes demeaning or hurtful language ("Idiot" or "You're fat," for example) or any profanity. You can start by giving him warnings the first time you hear the inappropriate language. Let him know his language is unacceptable, and provide him with other language to use, or to say nothing at all. For example, if your son is angry at his sister and calls her an idiot, give him a warning and provide more appropriate suggestions for expressing frustration ("You make me angry."). If the bad language persists and your child ignores your warnings and instructions, use time-out. Repeated uses of inappropriate language in the future should result in immediate time-outs and no warnings.

What steps do I follow to use time-out effectively?

To apply a time-out after a negative behavior, follow these steps:

1. Select a spot for time-out. Remember, this should be a quiet, isolated part of your home. Good locations include a corner that is away from windows and televisions or a step that is away from the main activity of the house.
2. When a negative behavior occurs, briefly explain to your child what the negative behavior was before going to time-out. For example, you can say, "No hitting, time-out." Don't scold, lecture, or yell. Also, once your child understands that certain behaviors will result in time-out, don't provide warn-

ings. This just gives her permission to engage in a negative behavior at least once.

3. Send your child to the time-out location. If she is resistant, gently guide her to the time-out spot. If necessary, you may have to carry her. If resistance continues to be a problem whenever you issue a time-out or your child frequently leaves before time expires, have more practices when she is calm. However, it's important to show resolve and not end time-out early. Maintain the requirement that your child remain in time-out, either sitting or standing.

4. Once your child is in the time-out location, set the timer. Initially, set it for a short time (thirty seconds) to increase the odds she will stay in time-out. This also will make it easier for you to follow through with the time-out requirements since the time is so brief. Once your child understands the routine and is cooperatively following it, you can gradually increase the length of time-out. You will need to adjust the length of time-out up or down based on how the time affects your child's behavior. For example, if your child's negative behavior is decreasing when time-out is a certain length, continue with that time. If not, gradually increase the length of the time-out. Also, you need to think about what behavior you expect from your child before starting time-out. Some parents want their child to be standing or seated quietly before the timer is set. The child is told that time-out will not start until he is quiet. Other parents start the timer immediately, as long as the child is either standing or seated in the time-out location, regardless of the child's other behaviors (whining, complaining, stomping, or crying). Initially, I recommend you do the latter. Start the timer immediately, as long as your child is staying in the time-out location. If you add too many behavioral requirements to the time-

out experience, you may get more resistance and opposition, which decreases the likelihood you will use time-out as consistently as you should. You can always change the behavioral expectations (requiring him to be seated, quiet, or both) once he understands the process better.

5. Once your child is in time-out, walk away and completely ignore him. Do not talk to him, look at him, or respond to anything he says or does (except if he leaves time-out). Feel free to read a newspaper, look at a book, or busy yourself with some activity by yourself or with others. The important thing is that your child receives absolutely no attention or interaction from you or anybody else in the family (including pets). If other siblings are present, they should be reminded that he's in time-out and off limits.
6. If your child leaves the time-out location before the timer sounds, return her to time-out and reset the timer. Remind her that she is not allowed to leave time-out until the timer sounds. Walk away and ignore any pleading or promising she makes until the time-out ends.
7. Once the timer sounds, time-out is over. The slate is clean. One exception to this is if you sent your child to time-out because she refused to follow a demand or an instruction ("Pick up your toys" or "Put away your clothes," for example). In this case, your child needs to complete the chore or task immediately after leaving time-out. Refusing to do so should result in a return to time-out. This process should continue until the task is completed. If time becomes an issue, you can tell your child she has one final opportunity to complete the task. Refusing to do so will result in the loss of privileges, such as no television or computer time, for a set period of time (hours).

8. Remember not to lecture your child about his negative behavior once time-out is over. In fact, look for opportunities to catch your child being good. Praise him for some positive behavior as soon as time-out ends. You provided a negative consequence for his inappropriate behavior, and it's equally important to praise and acknowledge positive behaviors as soon as you can.

How long should time-out last?

Remember, time-out is an experience. In general, you want time-out to last long enough so your child recognizes that he has been removed from an enjoyable activity or environment and that each time he engages in a particular negative behavior, he will find himself sitting in time-out and away from his favorite things. Time-out also needs to last long enough to get your child's attention so he sees the contrast between time spent doing fun things and time spent doing nothing. If time-out is too short, it will have little effect on behavior. If it's too long, he may focus more on how long it is rather than the negative behavior that earned him a time-out in the first place. Time-out needs to be long enough to get your child's attention and drive home the point that negative behaviors are going to result in losing access to all the fun that happens in the rest of the house.

Practically every parent has heard the rule of thumb that the length of time-out should match a child's age – one minute for each year. So, if your child is three years old, the time-out lasts three minutes. This is an easy-to-recall guideline to help parents remember how long a time-out should last. But this is just a general guideline. For some children, thirty seconds to a minute may be long enough, while ten minutes may not be enough time for others. You can best determine the appropriate length of a time-out by starting at thirty seconds and gradually increasing the time by thirty seconds until the time-out starts motivating behavioral change. Once you find an ideal time, stay with it. Adjust the length (usually longer) as needed.

Can I use time-out away from home?

Yes, you can. But it's much easier to use the technique in your home because, for example, you won't have dozens of people leaning over their restaurant booths staring at you or Aunt Millie spouting her sage advice on child development at the family reunion. However, you don't want to restrict your use of time-out just to your home. It's possible your child will learn that he can get away with certain negative behaviors when he's in public or visiting friends and family. For example, if your son is routinely sent to time-out for pulling his sister's hair when he's at home but only gets a stern look or verbal reprimand at Grandpa's house or in a restaurant, he will learn time-out isn't going to happen away from home. This may actually cause the behavior to get worse as your son enjoys the power and pleasure of pestering his sister away from home without any real negative outcome. On the other hand, if you're able to use time-out in many different situations, you take the wind out of your child's sails and send a consistent message that a negative behavior will earn him the same consequence no matter where you are.

To use time-out outside your home, you have to prepare and make adjustments to your routine. For example, it's a good idea to give your hosts (friends or family) a heads up that you're working on certain behaviors with your child. Because you want to maintain consistency, you may need to use a bathroom or an isolated part of their home for a brief time-out. Some parents even bring along a plastic placemat or something similar that fits in a bag to use as a time-out spot when they're in a store or out shopping. They put the mat on the floor and have their child sit there for a "mini" time-out, a concept I will explain shortly. When dining out, parents can use the restroom as a time-out spot or take their child to the car. This works better if there is another adult available who can watch any other children, if necessary. If you think and plan ahead, you can almost always find a workable spot for time-out. Doing so will give you a better sense of control and provide a predictable, consistent message to your child as you teach and shape his behaviors.

Where should time-out be located?

Even though time-out is an experience, it has to occur somewhere and the mantra "location, location, location" definitely applies. Most often, time-out will happen in your home. The key is to make sure it happens in a quiet, somewhat isolated area where little entertainment can be found. I prefer children sit on the floor or in a chair facing a corner so they cannot look out a window, watch a television, or see other family members in the home. Standing in the time-out location is acceptable as well. Whatever spot you choose, make sure you can see your child so you know she's safe and not leaving time-out early. From your child's vantage point, she should not be able to see other siblings playing or entertaining themselves. Remember, it's time-out from reinforcement. That's why you should avoid using your child's bedroom as a time-out location. Many parents prefer to send their children to their bedrooms for time-out. But that's like sending a starving man to a buffet and asking him not to eat. Most children have too many toys and entertainment options in their rooms. Also, some children use time-out to "rearrange" their bedrooms, adding one more chore to their chore list (cleaning up). Sending your child to his room may seem convenient because it gets him out of your hair but it will not serve as a time-out. Save yourself the trouble and stick to a semi-isolated corner, chair, or step.

What should I do while my child is in time-out?

The most important thing to do is avoid interacting or responding to your child in any way, other than if he leaves time-out. During time-out, you can read, clean, or do an activity with your other children. When your child realizes he cannot be part of the family's great time, it will put an exclamation point on the drudgery of time-out. It's also essential that other family members, visitors, friends, and even pets do not interact with the child who's in time-out. Remember, the more the time-out experience feels like being stuck on a deserted island, the better.

What do I do if my child talks back to me when I put her in time-out?

I have met very few children who enjoy time-out. To use an old expression, "They enjoy the crime, but don't like doing the time." I feel more confident about the effectiveness of time-out when I hear parents say their children whine or fuss on the way to time-out. This tells me that their little ones are leaving a fairly enriching and reinforcing environment and are not looking forward to "doing time." Of course, we want children to learn that they need to go to time-out cooperatively, but that is often not the case, at least in the beginning. Also, some children head directly to time-out with a smile on their face that implies, "I don't mind time-out. In fact, I like it." Don't be fooled! If you have created a reinforcing and enriching environment, they are simply looking for a button to push to convince you otherwise. Now, back to my point. If your child uses inappropriate words on her way to time-out, simply ignore it. Stay focused on why she is going to time-out. For example, when she is yelling how much she hates you and wants to "buy new parents," simply respond with "You know the rule. No hitting [or whatever the transgression was]. Time-out." When you put your child in time-out, walk away. Now is not the time to talk about her inappropriate language. Later in the day, when you're both calm, would be an appropriate time to have that discussion, if it requires any discussion at all. You will have to decide whether your child's language warrants further discussion. If the language is not too severe, simply let it go. If the language persists or worsens, an additional consequence outside of time-out can be added.

What if my child won't stay in time-out?

Believe me, your child won't be the first to "break out" of time-out. For time-out to be effective, your child obviously has to stay there. Unfortunately, this may require some time and effort on your part. The bottom line is this: If your child leaves time-out, he needs to be returned. Once he is back in time-out, reset the timer. Explain to him that you will be setting the timer and that he is not allowed to leave the time-out location until he hears the timer sound. Here are a few reasons why using a timer is helpful:

- You will know exactly how long your child has been in time-out.
- It provides a definitive indication to you and your child that time-out is over.
- It prevents you from losing track of time. You're responsible for telling your child time-out is over, but it can be easy to forget when you actually put your child in time-out. If you forget, your child might call out to you or look for you because he doesn't know if time-out is over (and sometimes it is). When this happens, your child learns that if he persists long enough, asks enough questions, or comes looking for you, that time-out ends. You don't want your child to wrongly assume his plead-

> ing and questioning ended the time-out. A timer prevents you from losing track of time and provides a clear indication as to when time-out is over.

Another option to consider if your child has trouble remaining in time-out is using a beanbag chair. A beanbag chair can be very effective because it's difficult to get out of. Again, you should place the beanbag chair in a corner. Have your child sit in the beanbag facing a wall. If he attempts to get out, remind him that he's not allowed to leave time-out until the timer sounds. Gently place your hand on his shoulder and guide him back to the beanbag. This requires very little effort on your part and allows you to help your child remain in time-out with very little struggle. Also, remember to reset the timer and remind him that each time he attempts to leave, the timer will be reset.

Finally, there are times when a child is so persistent about leaving time-out that you need a back-up plan. For example, you may have to take your child to another quiet and safe location, such as a bathroom or bedroom, where he can spend time alone calming down. Once he calms down, return him to the time-out location, reset the timer, and have him finish the time-out. Consistently using this routine will quickly teach your child to remain in time-out. It also reinforces the importance of teaching him how time-out works and what rules apply.

What should I do when time-out is over?

Once your child has successfully completed time-out, tell her that it's okay to leave. If she was sent to time-out because she was not following instructions or a request, she needs to successfully complete that task before time-out is officially over. In other words, time-out successfully ends once the task is completed. At that point, she is free to play and go back to whatever activity she desires. Also, telling your child that it's okay for her to get up should be the last conversation you have about the behavior that resulted in the time-out. In other words, don't nag or make comments such as, "If this happens again…" or "Why did you do that?" When time-out is over, the slate is clean. There should be no more discussion about your child's behavior. Should the behavior occur again, shortly after the time-out ends, the time-out routine should resume. Perhaps the most important thing you can do is catch your child being good as soon as possible following a time-out. Praising her for playing nicely, sharing, or keeping her hands and feet to herself will reinforce the benefits of positive behaviors and provide a contrast to being in time-out for negative behaviors.

The Mini Time-Out

There may be situations where your child's behavior requires your attention but does not require a "full" time-out. This can involve behaviors such as shaking his head "No" when you make a request, rolling his eyes, or sticking out his tongue at a sibling. A mini time-out can be an appropriate consequence for a variety of relatively minor negative behaviors. A mini time-out is exactly what it sounds like. It's a shortened version of time-out, and it doesn't require a special time-out location. Wherever your child happens to be at the moment can be where the mini time-out starts. Here are the steps to using a mini time-out for minor misbehaviors:

1. Tell your child, in clear language, what he did to earn a mini time-out (rolled his eyes or stuck out his tongue, for example).
2. Say to your child, "Mini time-out" or "Mini," provided he's aware of what "mini" means.
3. Have your child sit on the floor wherever he happens to be.
4. Make the mini time-out brief. One option is to have it last as long as it takes him to say or sing the ABC's or count to twenty, if he knows the alphabet or can count. Have your child sing or count to himself (or do so quietly). Otherwise, you can simply count quietly to yourself and let him know when the "mini" is over.
5. Say or indicate when the "mini" is over and let your child go back to his activity. Praise cooperative and acceptable behavior. If the behavior happens again, use another mini time-out. If the behavior worsens, send your child to time-out.

A mini time-out provides an effective alternative to always saying "No" or using some other verbal reprimand in response to an unacceptable behavior. The primary reason to use this technique for minor behaviors at home is that it provides good training when you use a mini time-out in public, such as restaurants, stores, or the homes of friends and family.

Some parents carry plastic placemats or other small mats for their children to sit on during mini time-outs. The mats provide a clean surface and help children associate the mats with time-out, helping them understand there are certain behavioral expectations when they are on the mat.

Another advantage of using mini time-outs in public is that it provides a wakeup call to your child about her minor behaviors, making it less likely more severe behaviors will occur. If you're constantly providing verbal reprimands and reminders to her in public, that suggests she's learned to ignore you because she doesn't think you will take any action in public. Using a mini time-out may stop her "chain" of behaviors from continuing and, hopefully, make your public outings or time spent with friends and family more enjoyable. Remember, mini time-outs will be more effective if you practice and establish a routine at home before using them in public.

Time-out is a common discipline technique that should be an important part of your overall parenting and discipline strategy. It should not be the only technique you use but one of your many tools. You will benefit from taking the time to decide how you're going to use time-out and for which behaviors. Teaching the technique to your child and using it consistently will not only make positive improvements in your child's behavior, it will reduce everyone's frustration.

Helpful Resources for Parents

Books for Parents

Common Sense Parenting of Toddlers and Preschoolers, by Bridget A. Barnes and Steven M. York (2001). Boys Town Press: Boys Town, NE.

Good Night, Sweet Dreams, I Love You: Now Get into Bed and Go to Sleep!, by Patrick C. Friman, (2005). Boys Town Press: Boys Town, NE.

How to Get Your Kid to Eat: But Not Too Much, by Ellyn Satter (1987). Bull Publishing Company: Boulder, CO.

I Brake for Meltdowns: How to Handle the Most Exasperating Behavior of Your 2- to- 5-Year-Old, by Michelle Nicholasen and Barbara O'Neal (2008). Da Capo Press: Cambridge, MA.

Little People, by Edward R. Christophersen, (1998). Westport Publishers: Kansas City, MO.

Poor Eaters: Helping Children Who Refuse to Eat, by Joel Mach (2002). Da Capo Press: Cambridge, MA.

Setting Limits with Your Strong-Willed Child: Eliminating Conflict by Establishing Clear, Firm, and Respectful Boundaries, by Robert J. MacKenzie (2001). Prima Publishing: Roseville, CA.

Solve Your Child's Sleep Problems: New, Revised and Expanded Edition, by Richard Ferber, (2006). Simon & Schuster: New York.

Picture Books for Children

Parents can teach and reinforce concepts like controlling anger, listening, sharing, and other social skills by reading entertaining books with children that demonstrate these skills.

The WORST Day of My Life EVER! My Story about Listening and Following Instructions...or Not!, by Julia Cook (2011). Boys Town Press: Boys Town, NE.

My Mouth Is a Volcano!, by Julia Cook (2006). National Center for Youth Issues: Chattanooga, TN.

It's Hard to Be a Verb!, by Julia Cook (2008). National Center for Youth Issues: Chattanooga, TN.

A Bad Case of Tattle Tongue, by Julia Cook (2005). National Center for Youth Issues: Chattanooga, TN.

It's You and Me Against the PEE... and the POOP Too!, by Julia Cook and Laura Jana, M.D. (2011). National Center for Youth Issues: Chattanooga, TN.

Hands Are Not for Hitting, by Martine Agassi, Ph.D. (2000). Free Spirit Publishing: Minneapolis, MN.

Words Are Not for Hurting, by Elizabeth Verdick (2004). Free Spirit Publishing: Minneapolis, MN.

Learning to Get Along Picture Books, by Cheri J. Meiners, M.Ed. Free Spirit Publishing: Minneapolis, MN.

Be Honest and Tell the Truth (2007)
Be Polite and Kind (2004)
Cool Down and Work Through Anger (2010)
Join In and Play (2004)
Know and Follow Rules (2005)
Respect and Take Care of Things (2004)
Share and Take Turns (2003)
Talk and Work It Out (2005)
When I Feel Afraid (2003)

ParentSmart/KidHappy Books, by Stacey R. Kaye. Free Spirit Publishing: Minneapolis, MN.

Ready for Bed! (2008)
Ready for the Day! (2008)
Ready to Play! (2009)

Kindness to Share from A to Z, by Todd and Peggy Snow (2008). Maren Green Publishing: Oak Park Heights, MN.

Manners Are Important for You and Me, by Todd Snow (2007). Maren Green Publishing: Oak Park Heights, MN.

You Are Helpful, by Todd Snow (2008). Maren Green Publishing: Oak Park Heights, MN.

Index

C

D

E

P

R

S

T

U

V

W

Y

CHAPTER 1

Clarke

The door slid open, and Clarke knew it was time to die.

Her eyes locked on the guard's boots, and she braced for the rush of fear, the flood of desperate panic. But as she rose up onto her elbow, peeling her shirt from the sweat-soaked cot, all she felt was relief.

She'd been transferred to a single after attacking a guard, but for Clarke, there was no such thing as solitary. She heard voices everywhere. They called to her from the corners of her dark cell. They filled the silence between her heart-beats. They screamed from the deepest recesses of her mind. It wasn't death she craved, but if that was the only way to silence the voices, then she was prepared to die.

She'd been Confined for treason, but the truth was far worse than anyone could've imagined. Even if by some miracle she was pardoned at her retrial, there'd be no real reprieve. Her memories were more oppressive than any cell walls.

The guard cleared his throat as he shifted his weight from side to side. "Prisoner number 319, please stand." He was younger than she'd expected, and his uniform hung loosely from his lanky frame, betraying his status as a recent recruit. A few months of military rations weren't enough to banish the specter of malnutrition that haunted the Colony's poor outer ships, Walden and Arcadia.

Clarke took a deep breath and rose to her feet.

"Hold out your hands," he said, pulling a pair of metal restraints from the pocket of his blue uniform. Clarke shuddered as his skin brushed against hers. She hadn't seen another person since they'd brought her to the new cell, let alone touched one.

"Are they too tight?" he asked, his brusque tone frayed by a note of sympathy that made Clarke's chest ache. It'd been so long since anyone but Thalia—her former cell mate and her only friend in the world—had shown her compassion.

She shook her head.

"Just sit on the bed. The doctor's on his way."

"They're doing it here?" Clarke asked hoarsely, the words

scraping against her throat. If a doctor was coming, that meant they were forgoing her retrial. It shouldn't have come as a surprise. According to Colony law, adults were executed immediately upon conviction, and minors were Confined until they turned eighteen and then given one final chance to make their case. But lately, people were being executed within hours of their retrial for crimes that, a few years ago, would have been pardoned.

Still, it was hard to believe they'd actually do it in her cell. In a twisted way, she'd been looking forward to one final walk to the hospital where she'd spent so much time during her medical apprenticeship—one last chance to experience something familiar, if only the smell of disinfectant and the hum of the ventilation system—before she lost the ability to feel forever.

The guard spoke without meeting her eyes. "I need you to sit down."

Clarke took a few short steps and perched stiffly on the edge of her narrow bed. Although she knew that solitary warped your perception of time, it was hard to believe she had been here—alone—for almost six months. The year she'd spent with Thalia and their third cell mate, Lise, a hard-faced girl who smiled for the first time when they took Clarke away, had felt like an eternity. But there was no other explanation. Today had to be her eighteenth birthday, and the only present waiting for Clarke was a syringe that would paralyze her muscles until her heart stopped beating. Afterward, her lifeless body would be released into space, as was the custom on the Colony, left to drift endlessly through the galaxy.

A figure appeared in the door and a tall, slender man stepped into the cell. Although his shoulder-length gray hair partially obscured the pin on the collar of his lab coat, Clarke didn't need the insignia to recognize him as the Council's chief medical advisor. She'd spent the better part of the year before her Confinement shadowing Dr. Lahiri and couldn't count the number of hours she'd stood next to him during surgery. The other apprentices had envied Clarke's assignment, and had complained of nepotism when they discovered that Dr. Lahiri was one of her father's closest friends. At least, he had been before her parents were executed.

"Hello, Clarke," he said pleasantly, as if he were greeting her in the hospital dining room instead of a detention cell. "How are you?"

"Better than I'll be in a few minutes, I imagine."

Dr. Lahiri used to smile at Clarke's dark humor, but this time he winced and turned to the guard. "Could you undo the cuffs and give us a moment, please?"

The guard shifted uncomfortably. "I'm not supposed to leave her unattended."

"You can wait right outside the door," Dr. Lahiri said with exaggerated patience. "She's an unarmed seventeen-year-old. I think I'll be able to keep things under control."

The guard avoided Clarke's eyes as he removed the handcuffs. He gave Dr. Lahiri a curt nod as he stepped outside.

"You mean I'm an unarmed eighteen-year-old," Clarke said, forcing what she thought was a smile. "Or are you turning into one of those mad scientists who never knows what year it is?" Her father had been like that. He'd forget to program the circadian lights in their flat and end up going to work at 0400, too absorbed in his research to notice that the ship's corridors were deserted.

"You're still seventeen, Clarke," Dr. Lahiri said in the calm, slow manner he usually reserved for patients waking up from surgery. "You've been in solitary for three months."

"Then what are you doing here?" she asked, unable to quell the panic creeping into her voice. "The law says you have to wait until I'm eighteen."

"There's been a change of plans. That's all I'm authorized to say."

"So you're authorized to *execute* me but not to talk to me?" She remembered watching Dr. Lahiri during her parents' trial. At the time, she'd read his grim face as an expression of his disapproval with the proceedings, but now she wasn't sure. He hadn't spoken up in their defense. No one had. He'd simply sat there mutely as the Council found her parents—two of Phoenix's most brilliant scientists—to be in violation of the Gaia Doctrine, the rules established after the Cataclysm to ensure the survival of the human race. "What about my parents? Did you kill them, too?"

Dr. Lahiri closed his eyes, as if Clarke's words had transformed from sounds into something visible. Something grotesque. "I'm not here to kill you," he said quietly. He opened his eyes and then gestured to the stool at the foot of Clarke's bed. "May I?"

When Clarke didn't reply, Dr. Lahiri walked forward and sat down so he was facing her. "Can I see your arm, please?"

Clarke felt her chest tighten, and she forced herself to breathe. He was lying. It was cruel and twisted, but it'd all be over in a minute.

She extended her hand toward him. Dr. Lahiri reached into his coat pocket and produced a cloth that smelled of antiseptic. Clarke shivered as he swept it along the inside of her arm. "Don't worry. This isn't going to hurt."

Clarke closed her eyes.

She remembered the anguished look Wells had given her as the guards were escorting her out of the Council chambers. While the anger that had threatened to consume her during the trial had long since burned out, thinking about Wells sent a new wave of heat pulsing through her body, like a dying star emitting one final flash of light before it faded into nothingness.

Her parents were dead, and it was all his fault.

Dr. Lahiri grasped her arm, his fingers searching for her vein.

See you soon, Mom and Dad.

His grip tightened. This was it.

Clarke took a deep breath as she felt a prick on the inside of her wrist.

"There. You're all set."

Clarke's eyes snapped open. She looked down and saw a metal bracelet clasped to her arm. She ran her finger along it, wincing as what felt like a dozen tiny needles pressed into her skin.

"What is this?" she asked frantically, pulling away from the doctor.

"Just relax," he said with infuriating coolness. "It's a vital transponder. It will track your breathing and blood composition, and gather all sorts of useful information."

"Useful information for who?" Clarke asked, although she could already feel the shape of his answer in the growing mass of dread in her stomach.

"There've been some exciting developments," Dr. Lahiri said, sounding like a hollow imitation of Wells's father, Chancellor Jaha, making one of his Remembrance Day speeches. "You should be very proud. It's all because of your parents."

"My parents were executed for treason."

Dr. Lahiri gave her a disapproving look. A year ago, it would've made Clarke shrink with shame, but now she kept her gaze steady. "Don't ruin this, Clarke. You have a chance to do the right thing, to make up for your parents' appalling crime."

There was a dull crack as Clarke's fist made contact with the doctor's face, followed by a thud as his head slammed against the wall. Seconds later, the guard appeared and had Clarke's hands twisted behind her back. "Are you all right, sir?" he asked.

Dr. Lahiri sat up slowly, rubbing his jaw as he surveyed Clarke with a mixture of anger and amusement. "At least we know you'll be able to hold your own with the other delinquents when you get there."

"Get where?" Clarke grunted, trying to free herself from the guard's grip.

"We're clearing out the detention center today. A hundred lucky criminals are getting the chance to make history." The corners of his mouth twitched into a smirk. "You're going to Earth."

CHAPTER 2

Wells

The Chancellor had aged. Although it'd been less than six weeks since Wells had seen his father, he looked years older. There were new streaks of gray by his temples, and the lines around his eyes had deepened.

"Are you finally going to tell me why you did it?" the Chancellor asked with a tired sigh.

Wells shifted in his chair. He could feel the truth trying to claw its way out. He'd give almost anything to erase the disappointment on his father's face, but he couldn't risk it—not before he learned whether his reckless plan had actually worked.

Wells avoided his father's gaze by glancing around the

room, trying to memorize the relics he might be seeing for the last time: the eagle skeleton perched in a glass case, the few paintings that had survived the burning of the Louvre, and the photos of the beautiful dead cities whose names never ceased to send chills down Wells's spine.

"Was it a dare? Were you trying to show off for your friends?" The Chancellor spoke in the same low, steady tone he used during Council hearings, then raised an eyebrow to indicate that it was Wells's turn to talk.

"No, sir."

"Were you overcome by some temporary bout of insanity? Were you on drugs?" There was a faint note of hopefulness in his voice that, in another situation, Wells might've found amusing. But there was nothing humorous about the look in his father's eyes, a combination of weariness and confusion that Wells hadn't seen since his mother's funeral.

"No, sir."

Wells felt a fleeting urge to touch his father's arm, but something other than the handcuffs shackling his wrists kept him from reaching across the desk. Even as they had gathered around the release portal, saying their final, silent good-byes to Wells's mother, they'd never bridged the six inches of space between their shoulders. It was as if Wells and his father were two magnets, the charge of their grief repelling them apart.

"Was it some kind of political statement?" His father winced slightly, as though the thought hit him like a physical blow. "Did someone from Walden or Arcadia put you up to it?"

"No, sir," Wells said, biting back his indignation. His father had apparently spent the past six weeks trying to recast Wells as some kind of rebel, reprogramming his memories to help him understand why his son, formerly a star student and now the highest-ranked cadet, had committed the most public infraction in history. But even the truth would do little to mitigate his father's confusion. For the Chancellor, nothing could justify setting fire to the Eden Tree, the sapling that had been carried onto Phoenix right before the Exodus. Yet for Wells, it hadn't been a choice. Once he'd discovered that Clarke was one of the hundred being sent to Earth, he'd had to do something to join them. And as the Chancellor's son, only the most public of infractions would land him in Confinement.

Wells remembered moving through the crowd at the Remembrance Ceremony, feeling the weight of hundreds of eyes on him, his hand shaking as he removed the lighter from his pocket and produced a spark that glowed brightly in the gloom. For a moment, everyone had stared in silence as the flames wrapped around the tree. And even as the guards rushed forward in sudden chaos, no one had been able to miss whom they were dragging away.

"What the hell were you thinking?" the Chancellor asked, staring at him in disbelief. "You could've burned down the whole hall and killed everyone in it."

It would be better to lie. His father would have an easier time believing that Wells had been carrying out a dare. Or perhaps he could try to pretend he *had* been on drugs. Either of those scenarios would be more palatable to the Chancellor than the truth—that he'd risked everything for a girl.

The hospital door closed behind him but Wells's smile stayed frozen in place, as if the force it had taken to lift the corners of his mouth had permanently damaged the muscles in his face. Through the haze of drugs, his mother had probably thought his grin looked real, which was all that mattered. She'd held Wells's hand as the lies poured out of him, bitter but harmless. *Yes, Dad and I are doing fine.* She didn't need to know that they'd barely exchanged more than a few words in weeks. *When you're better, we'll finish* Decline and Fall of the Roman Empire. They both knew that she'd never make it to the final volume.

Wells slipped out of the hospital and started walking across B deck, which was mercifully empty. At this hour, most people were either at tutorials, work, or at the Exchange. He was supposed to be at a history lecture, normally his favorite subject. He'd always loved stories about ancient cities like Rome and New York, whose dazzling triumphs were matched only by the magnitude of their downfalls. But he couldn't spend two hours surrounded by the same tutorial mates who had filled his message queue with vague, uncomfortable condolences. The only person he could talk to about his mother was Glass, but she'd been strangely distant lately.

Wells wasn't sure how long he'd been standing outside the door before he realized he'd arrived at the library. He allowed the scanner to pass over his eyes, waited for the prompt, and then pressed his thumb against the pad. The door slid open just long enough for Wells to slip inside and then closed behind him with a huffy thud, as if it had done Wells a great favor by admitting him in the first place.

Wells exhaled as the stillness and shadows washed over him. The books that been evacuated onto Phoenix before the Cataclysm were kept in tall, oxygen-free cases that significantly slowed the deterioration process, which is why they had to be read in the library, and only then for a few hours at a time. The enormous room was hidden away from the circadian lights, in a state of perpetual twilight.

For as long as he could remember, Wells and his mother had spent Sunday evenings here, his mother reading aloud to him when he was little, then reading side by side as he got older. But as her illness progressed and her headaches grew worse, Wells had started reading to her. They'd just started volume two of *Decline and Fall of the Roman Empire* the evening before she was admitted to the hospital.

He wove through the narrow aisles toward the English Language section and then over to History, which was tucked into a dark back corner. The collection was smaller than it should've been. The first colonial government had arranged for digital text to be loaded onto Phoenix, but fewer than a hundred years later, a virus wiped out most of the digital archives, and the only books left were those in private collections—heirlooms handed down from the original colonists to their descendants. Over the past century, most of the relics had been donated to the library.

Wells crouched down until he was eye level with the *G*s. He pressed his thumb against the lock and the glass slid open with a hiss, breaking the vacuum seal. He reached inside to grab *Decline and Fall* but then paused. He wanted to read on so he'd be able to tell his mother about it, but that would be tantamount to arriving in her hospital room with her memorial plaque and asking for her input on the wording.

"You're not supposed to leave the case open," a voice said from behind him.

"Yes, thank you," Wells said, more sharply than he'd meant. He rose to his feet and turned to see a familiar-looking girl staring at him. It was the apprentice medic from the hospital. Wells felt a flash of anger at this blending of worlds. The library was where he went to forget about the sickening smell of antiseptic, the beep of the heart monitor that, far from a sign of life, seemed like a countdown to death.

The girl took a step back and cocked her head, her light hair falling to one side. "Oh. It's you." Wells braced for the first swoon of recognition, and the rapid eye movements that meant she was already messaging her friends on her cornea slip. But this girl's eyes focused directly on him, as if she were looking straight into his brain, peeling back the layers to reveal all the thoughts Wells had purposefully hidden.

"Didn't you want that book?" She nodded toward the shelf where *Decline and Fall* was stored.

Wells shook his head. "I'll read it another time."

She was silent for a moment. "I think you should take it now." Wells's jaw tightened, but when he said nothing, she continued. "I used to see you here with your mother. You should bring it to her."

"Just because my father's in charge of the Council doesn't mean I get to break a three-hundred-year rule," he said, allowing just a shade of condescension to darken his tone.

"The book will be fine for a few hours. They exaggerate the effects of the air."

Wells raised an eyebrow. "And do they exaggerate the power of the exit scanner?" There were scanners over most public doors on Phoenix that could be programmed to any specifications. In the library, it monitored the molecular composition of every person who exited, to make sure no one left with a book in their hands or hidden under their clothes.

A smile flickered across her face. "I figured that out a long time ago." She glanced over her shoulder down the shadowy aisle between the bookcases, reached into her pocket, and extracted a piece of gray cloth. "It keeps the scanner from recognizing the cellulose in the paper." She held it out to him. "Here. Take it."

Wells took a step back. The chances of this girl trying to embarrass him were far greater than the odds of her having a piece of magical fabric hidden in her pocket. "Why do you have this?"

She shrugged. "I like reading other places." When he didn't say anything, she smiled and extended her other hand. "Just give me the book. I'll sneak it out for you and bring it to the hospital."

Wells surprised himself by handing her the book. "What's your name?" he asked.

"So you know to whom you'll be eternally indebted?"

"So I know who to blame when I'm arrested."

The girl tucked the book under her arm and then extended her hand. "Clarke."

"Wells," he said, reaching forward to shake it. He smiled, and this time it didn't hurt.

"They barely managed to save the tree." The Chancellor stared at Wells, as if looking for a sign of remorse or glee—anything to help him understand why his son had tried to set fire to the only tree evacuated from their ravaged planet. "Some of the council members wanted to execute you on the spot, juvenile or not, you know. I was only able to spare your life by getting them to agree to send you to Earth."

Wells exhaled with relief. There were fewer than 150 kids in Confinement, so he had assumed they'd take all the older teens, but until this moment he hadn't been sure he would be sent on the mission.

His father's eyes widened with surprise and understanding as he stared at Wells. "That's what you wanted, isn't it?"

Wells nodded.

The Chancellor grimaced. "Had I known you were this desperate to see Earth, I could have easily arranged for you to join the second expedition. Once we determined it was safe."

"I didn't want to wait. I want to go with the first hundred."

The Chancellor narrowed his eyes slightly as he assessed Wells's impassive face. "Why? You of all people know the risks."

"With all due respect, you're the one who convinced the Council that nuclear winter was over. *You* said it was safe."

"Yes. Safe enough for the hundred convicted criminals who were going to die anyway," the Chancellor said, his voice a mix of condescension and disbelief. "I didn't mean safe for my *son*."

The anger Wells had been trying to smother flared up, reducing his guilt to ashes. He shook his hands so the cuffs rattled against the chair. "I guess I'm one of them now."

"Your mother wouldn't want you to do this, Wells. Just because she enjoyed dreaming about Earth doesn't mean she'd want you to put yourself in harm's way."

Wells leaned forward, ignoring the bite of the metal digging into his flesh. "She's not who I'm doing this for," he said, looking his father straight in the eye for the first time since he'd sat down. "Though I do think she'd be proud of me." It was partially true. She'd had a romantic streak and would have commended her son's desire to protect the girl he loved. But his stomach writhed at the thought of his mom knowing what he'd really done to save Clarke. The truth would make setting the Eden Tree on fire seem like a harmless prank.

His father stared at him. "Are you telling me this whole debacle is because of that girl?"

Wells nodded slowly. "It's my fault she's being sent down there like some lab rat. I'm going to make sure she has the best chance of making it out alive."

The Chancellor was silent for a moment. But when he spoke again, his voice was calm. "That won't be necessary." The Chancellor removed something from his desk drawer and placed it in front of Wells. It was a metal ring affixed with a chip about the size of Wells's thumb. "Every member of the expedition is currently being fitted with one of these bracelets," his father explained. "They'll send data back up to the ship so we can track your location and monitor your vitals. As soon as we have proof that the environment is hospitable, we'll begin recolonization." He forced a grim smile. "If everything goes according to plan, it won't be long before the rest of us come down to join you, and all this"—he gestured toward Wells's bound hands—"will be forgotten."

The door opened and a guard stepped over the threshold. "It's time, sir."

The Chancellor nodded, and the guard strode across the room to pull Wells to his feet.

"Good luck, son," Wells's father said, assuming his trademark brusqueness. "If anyone can make this mission a success, it's you."

He extended his arm to shake Wells's hand, but then let it fall to his side when he realized his mistake. His only child's arms were still shackled behind him.

CHAPTER 3

Bellamy

Of course the smug bastard was late. Bellamy tapped his foot impatiently, not caring about the echo that rang throughout the storeroom. No one came down here anymore; anything valuable had been snatched up years ago. Every surface was covered with junk—spare parts for machines whose functions had been long forgotten, paper currency, endless tangles of cords and wires, cracked screens and monitors.

Bellamy felt a hand on his shoulder and spun around, raising his fists to block his face as he ducked to the side.

"Relax, man," Colton's voice called out as he switched on his flashbeam, shining it right in Bellamy's eyes. He surveyed Bellamy with an amused expression on his long, narrow face.

"Why'd you want to meet down here?" He smirked. "Looking for caveman porn on broken computers? No judgments. If I were stuck with what passes for a girl down on Walden, I'd probably develop some sick habits myself."

Bellamy ignored the jab. Despite his former friend's new role as a guard, Colton didn't stand a chance with a girl no matter what ship he was on. "Just tell me what's going on, okay?" Bellamy said, doing his best to keep his tone light.

Colton leaned back against the wall and smiled. "Don't let the uniform fool you, brother. I haven't forgotten the first rule of business." He held out his hand. "Give it to me."

"You're the one who's confused, Colt. You know I always come through." He patted the pocket that held the chip loaded with stolen ration points. "Now tell me where she is."

The guard smirked, and Bellamy felt something in his chest tighten. He'd been bribing Colton for information about Octavia since her arrest, and the idiot always seemed to find twisted pleasure in delivering bad news.

"They're sending them off today." The words landed with a thud in Bellamy's chest. "They got one of the old dropships on G deck working." He held out his hand again. "Now come on. This mission's top secret and I'm risking my ass for you. I'm done messing around."

Bellamy's stomach twisted as a series of images flashed before his eyes: his little sister strapped into an ancient metal cage, hurtling through space at a thousand kilometers an hour. Her face turning purple as she struggled to breathe the toxic air. Her crumpled body lying just as still as—

Bellamy took a step forward. "I'm sorry, man."

Colton narrowed his eyes. "For what?"

"For this." Bellamy drew his arm back, then punched the guard right in the jaw. There was a loud crack, but he felt nothing but his racing heart as he watched Colton fall to the ground.

Thirty minutes later, Bellamy was trying to wrap his mind around the strange scene in front of him. His back was against the wall of a wide hallway that led onto a steep ramp. Convicts streamed by in gray jackets, led down the incline by a handful of guards. At the bottom was the dropship, a circular contraption outfitted with rows of harnessed seats that would take the poor, clueless kids to Earth.

The whole thing was completely sick, but he supposed it was better than the alternative. While you were supposed to get a retrial at your eighteenth birthday, in the last year or so, pretty much every juvenile defendant had been found guilty. Without this mission, they'd be counting down the days until their executions.

Bellamy's stomach clenched as his eyes settled on a second ramp, and for a moment, he worried that he'd missed

Octavia. But it didn't matter whether he saw her board. They'd be reunited soon enough.

Bellamy tugged on the sleeves of Colton's uniform. It barely fit, but so far none of the other guards seemed to notice. They were focused on the bottom of the ramp, where Chancellor Jaha was speaking to the passengers.

"You have been given an unprecedented opportunity to put the past behind you," the Chancellor was saying. "The mission on which you're about to embark is dangerous, but your bravery will be rewarded. If you succeed, your infractions will be forgiven, and you'll be able to start new lives on Earth."

Bellamy barely suppressed a snort. The Chancellor had some nerve to stand there, spewing whatever bullshit helped him sleep at night.

"We'll be monitoring your progress very closely, in order to keep you safe," the Chancellor continued as the next ten prisoners filed down the ramp, accompanied by a guard who gave the Chancellor a crisp salute before depositing his charges in the dropship and retreating back up to stand in the hallway. Bellamy searched the crowd for Luke, the only Waldenite he knew who hadn't turned into a total prick after becoming a guard. But there were fewer than a dozen guards on the launch deck; the Council had clearly decided that secrecy was more important than security.

He tried not to tap his feet with impatience as the line of prisoners proceeded down the ramp. If he was caught posing as a guard, the list of infractions would be endless: bribery, blackmail, identity theft, conspiracy, and whatever else the Council felt like adding to the mix. And since he was twenty, there'd be no Confinement for him; within twenty-four hours of his sentencing, he'd be dead.

Bellamy's chest tightened as a familiar red hair ribbon appeared at the end of the hallway, peeking out from a curtain of glossy black hair. Octavia.

For the past ten months, he'd been consumed with agonizing worries about what was happening to her in Confinement. Was she getting enough to eat? Was she finding ways to stay occupied? Stay sane? While Confinement would be brutal for anyone, Bellamy knew that it'd be infinitely worse for O.

Bellamy had pretty much raised his younger sister. Or at least he'd tried. After their mother's accident, he and Octavia had been placed under Council care. There was no precedent for what to do with siblings—with the strict population laws, a couple was never allowed to have more than one child, and sometimes, they weren't permitted to have any at all—and so no one in the Colony understood what it meant to have a brother or sister. Bellamy and Octavia lived in different group homes for a number of years, but Bellamy had always looked out for her, sneaking her extra rations whenever he "wandered" into one of the restricted storage facilities, confronting the tough-talking older girls who thought it'd be fun to pick on the chubby-cheeked orphan with the big blue eyes. Bellamy worried about her constantly. The kid was special, and he'd do anything to give her a chance at a different life. Anything to make up for what she'd had to endure.

As Octavia's guard led her onto the ramp, Bellamy suppressed a smile. While the other kids shuffled passively along as their escorts led them toward the dropship, it was clear Octavia was the one setting the pace. She moved deliberately, forcing her guard to shorten his stride as she sauntered down the ramp. She actually looked *better* than the last time he'd seen her. He supposed it made sense. She'd been sentenced to four years in Confinement, until a retrial on her eighteenth birthday that would very well lead to her execution. Now she was being given a second chance at a life. And Bellamy was going to make damn sure she got it.

He didn't care what he had to do. He was going to Earth with her.

The Chancellor's voice boomed over the clamor of footsteps and nervous whispers. He still held himself like a soldier, but his years on the Council had given him a politician's gloss. "No one in the Colony knows what you are about to do, but if you succeed, we will all owe you our lives. I know that you'll do your very best on behalf of yourselves, your families, everyone aboard this ship: the entire human race."

When Octavia's gaze settled on Bellamy, her mouth fell open in surprise. He could see her mind race to make sense of the situation. They both knew he'd never be selected as a guard, which meant that he had to be there as an impostor. But just as she began to mouth a warning, the Chancellor turned to address the prisoners who were still coming down the ramp. Octavia reluctantly turned her head, but Bellamy could see the tension in her shoulders.

His heart sped up as the Chancellor finished his remarks and motioned for the guards to finish loading the passengers. He had to wait for just the right moment. If he acted too soon, there'd be time to haul him out. If he waited too long, Octavia would be barreling through space toward a toxic planet, while he remained to face the consequences of disrupting the launch.

Finally, it was Octavia's turn. She turned over her shoulder and caught his eye, shaking her head slightly, a clear warning not to do anything stupid.

But Bellamy had been doing stupid things his whole life, and he had no intention of stopping now.

The Chancellor nodded at a woman in a black uniform. She turned to the control panel next to the dropship and started pressing a series of buttons. Large numbers began flashing on the screen.

The countdown had begun.

He had three minutes to get past the door, down the ramp, and onto the dropship, or else lose his sister forever.

As the final passengers loaded, the mood in the room shifted. The guards next to Bellamy relaxed and began talking quietly among themselves. Across the deck on the other ramp, someone let out an obnoxious snort.

2:48 . . . 2:47 . . . 2:46 . . .

Bellamy felt a tide of anger rise within him, momentarily overpowering his nerves. How could these assholes *laugh* when his sister and ninety-nine other kids were being sent on what might be a suicide mission?

2:32 . . . 2:31 . . . 2:30 . . .

The woman by the control panel smiled and whispered something to the Chancellor, but he scowled and turned away.

The real guards had begun trudging back up and were filing into the hallway. Either they thought they had better things to do than witness humanity's first attempt to return to Earth, or they thought the ancient dropship was going to explode and were headed to safety.

2:14 . . . 2:13 . . . 2:12 . . .

Bellamy took a deep breath. It was time.

He shoved his way through the crowd and slipped behind a stocky guard whose holster was strapped carelessly to his belt, leaving the handle of the gun exposed. Bellamy snatched the weapon and charged down the loading ramp.

Before anyone knew what was happening, Bellamy jabbed his elbow into the Chancellor's stomach and threw an arm around his neck, securing him in a headlock. The launch deck exploded with shouts and stamping feet, but before anyone had time to reach him, Bellamy placed the barrel of the gun against the Chancellor's temple. There was no way he'd actually shoot the bastard, but the guards needed to think he meant business.

1:12 . . . 1:11 . . . 1:10 . . .

"Everyone back up," Bellamy shouted, tightening his hold. The Chancellor groaned. There was a loud beep, and the flashing numbers changed from green to red. Less than a minute left. All he had to do was wait until the door to the dropship started to close, then push the Chancellor out of the way and duck inside. There wouldn't be any time to stop him.

"Let me onto the dropship, or I'll shoot."

The room fell silent, save for the sound of a dozen guns being cocked.

In thirty seconds, he'd either be heading to Earth with Octavia, or back to Walden in a body bag.

CHAPTER 4

Glass

Glass had just hooked her harness when a flurry of shouts rose up. The guards were closing in around two figures near the entrance to the dropship. It was difficult to see through the shifting mass of uniforms, but Glass caught a flash of suit sleeve, a glimpse of gray hair, and the glint of metal. Then half the guards knelt down and raised their guns to their shoulders, giving Glass an unobstructed view: The Chancellor was being held hostage.

"Everyone back up," the captor yelled, his voice shaking. He wore a uniform, but he clearly wasn't a guard. His hair was far longer than regulation length, his jacket fit badly, and his awkward grip on the gun showed that he'd never been trained to use one.

No one moved. "I said back *up*."

The numbness that had set in during the long walk from her cell to the launch deck melted away like an icy comet passing the sun, leaving a faint trail of hope in its wake. She didn't belong here. She couldn't pretend they were about to head off on some historic adventure. The moment the dropship detached from the ship, Glass's heart would start to break. *This is my chance*, she thought suddenly, excitement and terror shooting through her.

Glass unhooked her harness and sprang to her feet. A few other prisoners noticed, but most were caught up watching the drama unfolding atop the ramp. She dashed to the far side of the dropship, where another ramp led back up to the loading deck.

"I'm going with them," the boy shouted as he took a step backward toward the door, dragging the Chancellor with him. "I'm going with my sister."

A stunned silence fell over the launch deck. *Sister.* The word echoed in Glass's head but before she had time to process its significance, a familiar voice pulled her from her thoughts.

"Let him go."

Glass glanced at the back of the dropship and froze, momentarily stunned by the sight of her best friend's face. Of course, she'd heard the ridiculous rumors that Wells had been Confined, but hadn't given them a second thought. What was he doing here? As she stared at Wells's gray eyes, which were trained intently on his father, the answer came to her: He must have tried to follow Clarke. Wells would do anything to protect the people he cared about, most of all Clarke.

And then there was a deafening crack—*a gunshot?*—and something inside of her snapped. Without stopping to think, to breathe, she dashed through the door and began sprinting up the ramp. Fighting the urge to look back over her shoulder, Glass kept her head down and ran as fast as she'd ever run in her life.

She'd chosen just the right moment. For a few seconds, the guards stood still, as if the reverberation from the gunshot had locked their joints in place.

Then they caught sight of her.

"Prisoner on the run!" one of them shouted, and the others quickly turned in her direction. The flash of movement activated the instincts drilled into their brains during training. It didn't matter that she was a seventeen-year-old girl. They'd been programmed to look past the flowing blond hair and wide blue eyes that had always made people want to protect Glass. All they saw was an escaped convict.

Glass threw herself through the door, ignoring the angry shouts that rose up in her wake. She hurtled down the passageway that led back to Phoenix, her chest heaving, her breath coming in ragged gasps. "You! Stop right there!" a guard shouted, his footsteps echoing behind her, but she didn't pause. If she ran fast enough, and if the luck that had been eluding her all her life made a final, last-minute appearance, maybe she could see Luke one last time. And maybe, just maybe, she could get him to forgive her.

Gasping, Glass staggered down a passageway bordered by unmarked doors. Her right knee buckled, and she grabbed on to the wall to catch herself. The corridor was beginning to grow blurry. She turned her head and could just make out the shape of an air vent. Glass hooked her fingers under one of the slats and pulled. Nothing happened. With a groan, she pulled again and felt the metal grate give. She yanked it open, revealing a dark, narrow tunnel full of ancient-looking pipes.

Glass pulled herself onto the small ledge, then scooted along on her stomach until there was room to bring her knees up to her chest. The metal felt cool against her burning skin. With her last milligram of strength, she crept deeper into the tunnel and closed the vent behind her. She strained her ears for signs of pursuit, but there was no more shouting, no more footsteps, only the desperate thud of her heart.

Glass blinked in the near darkness, taking stock of where she was. The cramped space extended straight in both directions, thick with dust. It had to be one of the original air shafts, from before the Colony built their new air circulation and filtration systems. Glass had no idea where it would lead, but she was out of options. She started to crawl forward.

After what felt like hours, her knees numb and her hands burning, she reached a fork in the tunnel. If her sense of direction was right, then the tunnel on the left would lead to Phoenix, and the other would run parallel to the skybridge—onto Walden, and toward Luke.

Luke, the boy she loved, who she'd been forced to abandon all those months ago. Who she'd spent every night in Confinement thinking about, so desperate for his touch that she'd almost felt the pressure of his arms around her.

She took a deep breath and turned to the right, not knowing if she was headed toward freedom or certain death.

Ten minutes later, Glass slid quietly out of the vent and lowered herself to the floor. She took a step forward and coughed as a plume of dust swirled around her face, sticking to her sweaty skin. She was in some kind of storage space.

As her eyes adjusted to the darkness, shapes began to materialize on the wall—writing, Glass realized. She took another few steps forward, and her eyes widened. There were *messages* carved into the walls.

Rest in peace

In memoriam

From the stars to the heavens

She was on the quarantine deck, the oldest section of Walden. As nuclear and biological war threatened to destroy Earth, space had been the only option for those lucky enough to survive the first stages of the Cataclysm. But some infected survivors fought their way onto the transport pods—only to find themselves barred from Phoenix, left to die on Walden. Now, whenever there was the slightest threat of illness, anyone infected was quarantined, kept far from the rest of the Colony's vulnerable population—the last of the human race.

Glass shivered as she moved quickly toward the door, praying that it hadn't rusted shut. To her relief, she was able to wrench it open and began dashing down the corridor. She peeled off her sweat-soaked jacket; in her white T-shirt and prison-issue pants, she could pass for a worker, someone on sanitation duty, perhaps. She glanced down nervously at the bracelet on her wrist. She wasn't sure whether it would work on the ship, or if it was only meant to transmit data from Earth. Either way, she needed to figure out a way to get it off as soon as possible. Even if she avoided the passages with retina scanners, every guard in the Colony would be on the lookout for her.

Her only hope was that they'd be expecting her to run back to Phoenix. They'd never guess that she would come here. She climbed up the main Walden stairwell until she reached the entrance to Luke's residential unit. She turned into his hallway and slowed down, wiping her sweaty hands on her pants, suddenly more nervous than she'd been on the dropship.

She couldn't imagine what he'd say, the look he'd give her when he saw her on his doorstep after her disappearance more than nine months earlier.

But maybe he wouldn't have to say anything. Perhaps, as soon as he saw her, as soon as the words began to pour out of her mouth, he would silence her with a kiss, relying on his lips to tell her that everything was okay. That she was forgiven.

Glass glanced over her shoulder and then slipped out the door. She didn't think anyone had seen her, but she had to be careful. It was incredibly rude to leave a Partnering Ceremony before the final blessing, but Glass didn't think she'd be able to spend another minute sitting next to Cassius, with his dirty mind and even fouler breath. His wandering hands reminded Glass of Carter, Luke's two-faced roommate whose creepiness only slithered out of the darkness when Luke was out on guard duty.

Glass climbed the stairs toward the observation deck, taking care to lift the hem of her gown with each step. It'd been foolish to waste so many ration points collecting the materials for the dress, a piece of tarp that she'd painstakingly sewn into a silver slip. It felt utterly worthless without Luke there to see her in it.

She hated spending the evening with other boys, but her

mother refused to let Glass be seen at a social event without a date, and as far as she knew, her daughter was single. She couldn't understand why Glass hadn't "snatched up" Wells. No matter how many times Glass explained that she didn't have those types of feelings for him, her mother sighed and muttered about not letting some badly dressed scientist girl steal him away. But Glass was happy that Wells had fallen for the beautiful if slightly over-serious Clarke Griffin. She only wished she could tell her mother the truth: that she was in love with a handsome, brilliant boy who could never escort her to a concert or a Partnering Ceremony.

"May I have this dance?"

Glass gasped and spun around. As her eyes locked with a familiar pair of brown ones, her face broke into a wide smile. "What are you doing here?" she whispered, looking around to make sure they were alone.

"I couldn't let those Phoenix boys have you all to themselves," Luke said, taking a step back to admire her dress. "Not when you look like this."

"Do you know how much trouble you'll get in if they catch you?"

"Let them try to keep up." He wrapped his arms around Glass's waist, and as the music from downstairs swelled, he spun her through the air.

"Put me down!" Glass half whispered, half laughed as she playfully hit his shoulder.

"Is that how young ladies are taught to address gentlemen admirers?" he asked, using a terrible, fake Phoenix accent.

"Come on," she said, giggling as she grabbed his hand. "You really shouldn't be here."

Luke stopped and pulled her to him. "Wherever you are is where I'm supposed to be."

"It's too risky," she said softly, bringing her face up to his.

He grinned. "Then we better make sure it's worth our while." He placed his hand behind her head and brought his lips to hers.

Glass raised her hand to knock a second time when the door opened. Her heart skipped a beat.

There he was, his sandy hair and deep-brown eyes exactly as she remembered them, exactly as they'd appeared in her dreams every night in Confinement. His eyes widened in surprise.

"Luke," she breathed, all the emotion of the past nine months threatening to break through. She was desperate to tell him what had happened, why she'd broken up with him and then disappeared. That she'd spent every minute of the nightmarish last six months thinking of him. That she never stopped loving him. "Luke," she said again, a tear sliding down her cheek. After the countless times she'd broken down in her cell, whispering his name in between sobs, it felt surreal to say it to him.

But before she had a chance to grab hold of any of the words flitting through her mind, another figure appeared in the door, a girl with wavy red hair.

"Glass?"

Glass tried to smile at Camille, Luke's childhood friend, a girl who'd been as close to him as Glass was to Wells. And now she was here . . . in Luke's flat. *Of course*, Glass thought with a strained kind of bitterness. She'd always wondered if there was more to their relationship than Luke had admitted.

"Would you like to come in?" Camille asked with exaggerated politeness. She wrapped her hand around Luke's, but Glass felt as if Camille's fingers had plunged into her heart instead. While Glass had spent months in Confinement pining for Luke until his absence felt like a physical ache, he'd moved on to someone else.

"No . . . no, that's okay," Glass said, her voice hoarse. Even if she managed to find the words, it would be impossible to tell Luke the truth now. Seeing them together made it all the more ridiculous that she'd come so far—risked so much—to see a boy who had already moved on.

"I just came to say hello."

"You came to say *hello*?" Luke repeated. "After almost a year of ignoring my messages, you thought you'd just *drop by*?" He wasn't even trying to hide his anger, and Camille dropped his hand. Her smile hardened into a grimace.

"I know. I'm—I'm sorry. I'll leave you two alone."

"What's really going on?" Luke asked, exchanging a look with Camille that made Glass feel both desperately foolish and terribly alone.

"Nothing," Glass said quickly, trying and failing to keep her voice from trembling. "I'll talk to you . . . I'll see you . . ." She cut herself off with a weak smile and took a deep breath, ignoring her body's furious plea to stay close to him.

But just as she turned, she saw a flash of a guard uniform out of the corner of her vision. She inhaled sharply and turned her face as the guard passed.

Luke pressed his lips together as he looked at something just beyond Glass's head. He was reading a message on his cornea slip, Glass realized. And from the way his jaw was tightening, she got the sickening sense it was about her.

His eyes widened with understanding, and then horror. "Glass," he said hoarsely. "You were Confined." It wasn't a question. Glass nodded.

He shifted his gaze back to Glass for a moment, then sighed and reached out to place his hand on her back. She could feel the pressure of his fingers through the fabric of her thin T-shirt, and despite her anxiety, her skin thrilled at his touch. "Come on," he said, pulling her toward him. Camille stepped to the side, looking annoyed, as Glass stumbled into the flat. Luke quickly shut the door behind them.

The small living area was dark—Luke and Camille had been inside with the lights off. Glass tried to push the implications of that fact out of her head as she watched Camille sit down in the armchair that Luke's great-grandmother had found at the Exchange. Glass shifted uncomfortably, unsure whether to take a seat. Being Luke's ex-girlfriend somehow felt odder than being an escaped convict. She'd had six months in Confinement to come to terms with her criminal record, but Glass had never imagined what it would be like to stand in this flat feeling like a stranger.

"How did you escape?" he asked.

Glass paused. She had spent all her time in Confinement imagining what she would say to Luke if she ever got the chance to see him again. And now she had finally made her way back to him, and all the speeches she'd practiced felt flimsy and selfish. He was doing fine; she could see that now. Why should she tell him the truth, except to win him back and make herself feel less alone? And so, in a shaky voice, Glass quickly told him about the hundred and their secret mission, the hostage situation, and the chase.

"But I still don't understand." Luke shot a glance over his shoulder at Camille, who had given up pretending that she wasn't paying attention. "Why were you Confined in the first place?"

Glass looked away, unable to meet his eyes as her brain

raced for an explanation. She couldn't tell him, not now, not when he'd moved on. Not when it was so obvious he didn't feel the same way for her.

"I can't talk about it," she said quietly. "You wouldn't underst—"

"It's fine." Luke cut her off sharply. "You've made it clear that there are lots of things I can't understand."

For the briefest of moments, Glass wished she'd stayed on the dropship with Clarke and Wells. Although she was standing next to the boy she loved, she couldn't imagine feeling any lonelier on the abandoned Earth than she did right now.

CHAPTER 5

Clarke

For the first ten minutes, the prisoners were too rattled by the shooting to notice that they were floating through space, the only humans to leave the Colony in almost three hundred years. The rogue guard had gotten what he wanted. He'd pushed the Chancellor's limp body forward just as the dropship door was closing, and then stumbled into a seat. But from the shocked expression on his pale face, Clarke gathered that gunfire had never been part of the plan.

Yet for Clarke, watching the Chancellor get shot was less alarming than what she'd seen in the moments beforehand.

Wells was on the dropship.

When he'd first appeared in the door, she'd been sure it

was a hallucination. The chance of her losing her mind in solitary was infinitely higher than the chance of the Chancellor's son ending up in Confinement. She'd been shocked enough when, a month after her own sentencing, Wells's best friend, Glass, had appeared in the cell down the row from her. And now Wells, too? It seemed impossible, but there was no denying it. She'd watched him jump to his feet during the standoff, then crumple back into his seat as the real guard's gun went off and the imposter burst through the door, covered in blood. For a moment, an old instinct gave her the urge to run over and comfort Wells. But something much heavier than her harness kept her feet rooted to the floor. Because of him, she'd watched her parents be dragged off to the execution chamber. Whatever pain he was feeling was no less than he deserved.

"*Clarke.*"

She glanced to the side and saw Thalia grinning at her from a few rows ahead. Her old cell mate twisted in her seat, the only person in the dropship not staring at the guard. Despite the grim circumstances, Clarke couldn't help smiling back. Thalia had that effect. In the days after Clarke's arrest and her parents' execution, when her grief felt so heavy it was difficult to breathe, Thalia had actually made Clarke laugh with her impression of the cocky guard whose shuffle turned into a strut whenever he thought the girls were looking at him.

"Is that him?" Thalia mouthed now, tilting her head toward Wells. Thalia was the only person who knew everything—not just about Clarke's parents, but the unspeakable thing that Clarke had done.

Clarke shook her head to signal that now wasn't the time to talk about it. Thalia motioned again. Clarke started to tell her to knock it off when the main thrusters roared to life, shaking the words from her lips.

It had really happened. For the first time in centuries, humans had left the Colony. She glanced at the other passengers and saw that they had all gone quiet as well, a spontaneous moment of silence for the world they were leaving behind.

But the solemnity didn't last long. For the next twenty minutes, the dropship was filled with the nervous, overexcited chatter of a hundred people who, until a few hours ago, had never even thought about going to Earth. Thalia tried to shout something to Clarke, but her words were lost in the din.

The only conversation Clarke could follow was that of the two girls in front of her, who were arguing over the likelihood of the air on Earth being breathable. "I'd rather drop dead right away than spend days being slowly poisoned," one said grimly.

Clarke sort of agreed, but she kept her mouth shut. There was no point in speculating. The trip to Earth would be short—in just a few more minutes, they'd know their fate.

Clarke looked out the windows, which were now filling with hazy gray clouds. The dropship jerked suddenly, and the buzz of conversation gave way to a flurry of gasps.

"It's okay," Wells shouted, speaking for the first time since the doors closed. "There's supposed to be turbulence when we enter Earth's atmosphere." But his words were overpowered by the shrieks filling the cabin.

The shaking increased, followed by a strange hum. Clarke's harness dug into her stomach as her body lurched from side to side, then up and down, then side to side again. She gagged as a rancid odor filled her nose, and she realized that the girl in front of her had vomited. Clarke squeezed her eyes shut and tried to stay calm. Everything was fine. It'd all be over in a minute.

The hum became a piercing wail, punctuated by a sickening crush. Clarke opened her eyes and saw that the windows had cracked and were no longer full of gray.

They were full of flames.

Bits of white-hot metal began raining down on them. Clarke raised her arms to protect her head, but she could still feel the debris scorching her neck.

The dropship shook even harder, and with a roar, part of the ceiling tore off. There was a deafening crash followed by a thud that sent ripples of pain through every bone in her body.

As suddenly as it began, it was all over.

The cabin was dark and silent. Smoke billowed out of a hole where the control panel had been, and the air grew thick with the smell of melting metal, sweat, and blood.

Clarke winced as she wiggled her fingers and toes. It hurt, but nothing seemed to be broken. She unhooked her harness and rose shakily to her feet, holding on to the scorched seat for balance.

Most people were still strapped in, but a few were slumped over the sides or sprawled on the floor. Clarke squinted as she scanned the rows for Thalia, her heart speeding up each time her eyes landed on another empty seat. A terrifying realization cut through the confusion in Clarke's mind. Some of the passengers had been thrown outside during the crash.

Clarke limped forward, gritting her teeth at the pain that shot up her leg. She reached the door and pulled as hard as she could. She took a deep breath and slipped through the opening.

For a moment, she was aware of only colors, not shapes. Stripes of blue, green, and brown so vibrant her brain couldn't process them. A gust of wind passed over her, making her skin tingle and flooding her nose with scents Clarke couldn't begin to identify. At first, all she could see were the trees. There were hundreds of them, as if every tree on the planet had come to welcome them back to Earth. Their enormous branches were lifted in celebration toward the sky, which was a joyful blue. The ground stretched out in all directions—ten times farther than the longest deck on the ship. The amount of space was almost inconceivable, and Clarke suddenly felt light-headed, as if she were about to float away.

She became vaguely aware of voices behind her and turned to see a few of the others emerge from the dropship. "It's beautiful," a dark-skinned girl whispered as she reached down to run her trembling hand along the shiny green blades of grass.

A short, stocky boy took a few shaky steps forward. The gravitational pull on the Colony was meant to mimic Earth's, but faced with the real thing it was clear they hadn't gotten it quite right. "Everything's fine," the boy said, his voice a mixture of relief and confusion. "We could've come back ages ago."

"You don't know that," the girl replied. "Just because we can breathe now, doesn't mean the air isn't toxic." She twisted around to face him and held her wrist up, gesturing with her bracelet. "The Council didn't give us these as jewelry. They want to see what happens to us."

A smaller girl hovering next to the dropship whimpered as she pulled her jacket up over her mouth.

"You can breathe normally," Clarke told her, looking around to see if Thalia had emerged yet. She wished she had something more reassuring to say, but there was no way to tell how much radiation was still in the atmosphere. All they could do was wait and hope.

"We'll be back soon," her father said as he slipped his long arms into a suit jacket Clarke had never seen before. He walked over to the couch where she was curled up with her tablet and ruffled her hair. "Don't stay out too late. They've been strict about curfew lately. Some trouble on Walden, I think."

"I'm not going anywhere," Clarke said, gesturing toward her bare feet and the surgical pants she wore to sleep. For the most famous scientist in the Colony, her father's deductive reasoning left something to be desired. Although he spent so much time wrapped up in his research, it was unlikely he'd even know that scrubs weren't currently considered high fashion among sixteen-year-old girls.

"Either way, it'd be best if you stayed out of the lab," he said with calculated carelessness, as if the thought had only just crossed his mind. In fact, he'd said this about five times a day since they'd moved into their new flat. The Council had approved their request for a customized private laboratory, as her parents' new project required them to monitor experiments throughout the night.

"I promise," Clarke told them with exaggerated patience.

"It's just that it's dangerous to get near the radioactive materials," her mother called out from where she stood in front of the mirror, fixing her hair. "Especially without the proper equipment."

Clarke repeated her promise until they left and she was finally able to return to her tablet, though she couldn't help wondering idly what Glass and her friends would say if they knew that Clarke was spending Friday night working on an essay. Clarke was normally indifferent toward her Earth Literatures tutorial, but this assignment had piqued her interest. Instead of another predictable paper on the changing view of nature in pre-Cataclysmic poetry, their tutor had asked them to compare and contrast the vampire crazes in the nineteenth and twenty-first centuries.

Yet while the reading was interesting, she must have dozed off at some point, because when she sat up, the circadian lights had dimmed and the living space was a jumble of unfamiliar shadows. She stood up and was about to head to her bedroom when a strange sound pierced the silence. Clarke froze. It almost sounded like screaming. She forced herself to take a deep breath. She should have known better than to read about vampires before bed.

Clarke turned around and started walking down the hallway, but then another sound rang out—a shriek that sent shivers down her spine.

Stop it, Clarke scolded herself. She'd never make it as a doctor if she let her mind play tricks on her. She was just unsettled by the unfamiliar darkness in the new flat. In the morning, everything would be back to normal. Clarke waved her palm across the sensor on her bedroom door and was about to step inside when she heard it again—an anguished moan.

Her heart thumping, Clarke spun around and walked down

the long hallway that led to the lab. Instead of a retinal scanner, there was a keypad. Clarke brushed her fingers over the panel, briefly wondering if she'd be able to guess the password, then crouched down and pressed her ear to the door.

The door vibrated as another sound buzzed through Clarke's ear. Her breath caught in her throat. *That's impossible.* But when the sound came again, it was even clearer.

It wasn't just a scream of anguish. It was a word.

"Please."

Clarke's fingers flew over the keypad as she entered the first thing that came to her head: *Pangea*. It was the code her mother used for her protected files. The screen beeped and an error message appeared. Next she entered *Elysium*, the name of the mythical underground city where, according to bedtime stories parents told their children, humans took refuge after the Cataclysm. Another error. Clarke tore through her memory, searching for words she'd filed away. Her fingers hovered above the keypad. *Lucy.* The name of the oldest hominid remains Earthborn archaeologists ever discovered. There was a series of low beeps, and the door slid open.

The lab was much bigger than she'd imagined, larger than their entire flat, and filled with rows of narrow beds like in the hospital.

Clarke's eyes widened as they darted from one bed to another. Each contained a *child.* Most of the kids were lying there asleep, hooked up to various vital monitors and IV stands, though a few were propped up by pillows, fiddling with tablets in their laps. One little girl, hardly older than a toddler, sat on the floor next to her bed, playing with a ratty stuffed bear as clear liquid dripped from an IV bag into her arm.

Clarke's brain raced for an explanation. These had to be sick children who required round-the-clock care. Maybe they were suffering from some rare disease that only her mother knew how to cure, or perhaps her father was close to inventing a new treatment and needed twenty-four-hour access. They must've known that Clarke would be curious, but since the illness was probably contagious, they'd lied to Clarke to keep her safe.

The same cry that Clarke had heard from the flat came again, this time much louder. She followed it to a bed on the other side of the lab.

A girl her own age—one of the oldest in the room, Clarke realized—was lying on her back, dark-blond hair fanned out on the pillow around her heart-shaped face. For a moment, she just stared at Clarke.

"Please," she said. Her voice trembled. "Help me."

Clarke glanced at the label on the girl's vital monitor. SUBJECT 121. "What's your name?" she asked.

"Lilly."

Clarke stood there awkwardly, but when Lilly scooted back on her pillows, Clarke lowered herself to sit on the bed next to her. She'd just started her medical training and hadn't interacted with patients yet, but she knew one of the most important parts of being a doctor was bedside manner. "I'm sure you'll get to go home soon," she offered. "Once you're feeling better."

The girl pulled her knees to her chest and buried her head, saying something too muffled for Clarke to make out.

"What was that?" she asked. She glanced over her shoulder, wondering why there wasn't a nurse or a medical apprentice covering for her parents. If something happened to one of the kids, there'd be no one to help them.

The girl raised her head but looked away from Clarke. She chewed her lip as the tears in her eyes receded, leaving a haunting emptiness in their wake.

When she finally spoke, it was in a whisper. "No one ever gets better."

Clarke suppressed a shudder. Diseases were rare on the ship; there hadn't been any epidemics since the last outbreak they'd quarantined on Walden. Clarke looked around the lab for something to indicate what her parents were treating, and her eyes settled on an enormous screen on the far wall. Data flashed across it, forming a large graph. *Subject 32. Age 7. Day 189. 3.4 Gy. Red count. White count. Respiration. Subject 33. Age 11. Day 298. 6 Gy. Red count. White count. Respiration.*

At first Clarke thought nothing of the data. It made perfect sense for her parents to monitor the vitals of the sick children in their care. Except that *Gy* had nothing to do with vital signs.

A *Gray* was a measure of radiation, a fact she well knew as her parents had been investigating the effects of radiation exposure for years, part of the ongoing task to determine when it'd be safe for humans to return to Earth.

Clarke's gaze settled on Lilly's pale face as a chilling realization slithered out of a dark place in the back of Clarke's mind. She tried to force it back, but it coiled around her denial, suffocating all thoughts except a truth so horrifying, she almost gagged.

Her parents' research was no longer limited to cell cultures. They'd moved onto human trials.

Her mother and father weren't curing these children. They were killing them.

They'd landed in some kind of clearing, an L-shaped space surrounded by trees.

There weren't many serious injuries, but there were enough to keep Clarke busy. For nearly an hour, she used torn jacket sleeves and pant legs as makeshift tourniquets, and ordered the few people with broken bones to lie still until she found a way to fashion splints. Their supplies were scattered across the grass, but although she'd sent multiple people to search for the medicine chest, it hadn't been recovered.

The battered dropship was at the short end of the clearing, and for the first fifteen minutes, the passengers had clustered around the smoldering wreckage, too scared and stunned to move more than a few shaky steps. But now they'd started milling around. Clarke hadn't spotted Thalia, or Wells, either, although she wasn't sure whether that made her more anxious or relieved. Maybe he was off with Glass. Clarke hadn't seen her on the dropship, but she had to be here somewhere.

"How does that feel?" Clarke asked, returning her attention to wrapping the swollen ankle of a pretty, wide-eyed girl with a frayed red ribbon in her dark hair.

"Better," she said, wiping her nose with her hand, unintentionally smearing blood from the cut on her face. Clarke had to find real bandages and antiseptic. They were all being exposed to germs their bodies had never encountered, and the risk of infection was high.

"I'll be right back." Clarke flashed her a quick smile and rose to her feet. If the medicine chest wasn't in the clearing, that meant it was probably still in the dropship. She hurried back to the still-smoking wreck, walking around the perimeter as she searched for the safest way to get back inside. Clarke reached the back of the ship, which was just a few meters from the tree line. She shivered. The trees grew so closely together on this side of the clearing, their leaves blocked most of the light, casting intricate shadows on the ground that scattered when the wind blew.

Her eyes narrowed as they focused on something that didn't move. It wasn't a shadow.

A girl was lying on the ground, nestled against the roots of a tree. She must have been thrown out of the back of the dropship during the landing. Clarke lurched forward, and felt a sob form in her throat as she recognized the girl's short, curly hair and the smattering of freckles on the bridge of her nose. *Thalia.*

Clarke hurried over and knelt beside her. Blood was gushing from a wound on the side of her ribs, staining the grass beneath her dark red, as if the earth itself were bleeding. Thalia was breathing, but her gasps were labored and shallow. "It's going to be okay," Clarke whispered, grabbing on to her friend's limp hand as the wind rustled above them. "I swear, Thalia, it's all going to be okay." It sounded more like a prayer than a reassurance, although she wasn't sure who she was praying to. Humans had abandoned Earth during its darkest hour. It wouldn't care how many died trying to return.

CHAPTER 6

Wells

Wells shivered in the late afternoon chill. In the few hours since they'd landed, the air had grown colder. He moved closer to the bonfire, ignoring the snide glances of the Arcadian boys on either side of him. Every night he'd spent in Confinement, he'd fallen asleep dreaming about arriving on Earth with Clarke. But instead of holding her hand while they gazed at the planet in wonder, he'd spent the day sorting through burned supplies and trying to forget the expression that crossed Clarke's face when she spotted him. He hadn't expected her to throw her arms around him, but nothing could've prepared him for the look of pure loathing in her eyes.

"Think your father kicked the bucket already?" a Walden boy a few years younger than Wells asked as the kids around him snickered.

Wells's chest tightened, but he forced himself to stay calm. He could take one or two of the little punks without breaking a sweat. He'd been the undisputed champion of the hand-to-hand combat course during officer training. But there was only one of him and ninety-five of them—ninety-six if you counted Clarke, who was arguably less of a Wells fan than anyone on the planet at the moment.

As they'd loaded onto the dropship, he'd been dismayed not to see Glass there. To the shock of everyone on Phoenix, Glass had been Confined not long after Clarke, though no matter how many times he pressed his father, Wells had never discovered what she'd done. He wished he knew why she hadn't been selected for the mission. Although he tried to convince himself that she could've been pardoned, it was far more likely that she was still in Confinement, counting down the days until her fast-approaching eighteenth birthday. The thought made his stomach twist.

"I wonder if Chancellor Junior thinks he gets first dibs on all the food?" asked an Arcadian boy whose pockets were bulging with nutrition packs he'd collected during the mad scramble after the crash. From what Wells could see, it looked like they'd been sent down with less than a month's worth of food, which would disappear quickly if people kept pocketing everything they found. But that couldn't be possible—there had to be more in a container somewhere. They would come across it once they finished sorting through the wreckage.

"Or if he expects us to make his bed for him." A petite girl with a scar on her forehead smirked.

Wells ignored them, looking up at the endless stretch of deep-blue sky. It really was astonishing. Even though he'd seen photographs, he had never imagined the color would be quite so vivid. It was strange to think that a blanket of blue—made of nothing more substantial than nitrogen crystals and refracted light—separated him from the sea of stars and the only world he'd ever known. He felt his chest ache for the three kids who hadn't survived long enough to see these sights. Their bodies lay on the other side of the dropship.

"Beds?" a boy said with a snort. "You tell me where we'll find a *bed* in this place."

"So where the hell are we supposed to sleep?" the girl with the scar asked, looking around the clearing as if she expected sleeping quarters to magically appear.

Wells cleared his throat. "Our supplies included tents. We just need to finish sorting through the containers and collect all the pieces. In the meantime, we should send a few scouts to look for water so we know where to set up camp."

The girl made a show of glancing from side to side. "This looks good to me," she said, prompting more snickers.

Wells tried to force himself to stay calm. "The thing is, if we're near a stream or a lake, it'll be easier to—"

"Oh, good." A low voice cut him off. "I'm just in time for the lecture." Wells glanced to the side and saw a boy named Graham walking toward them. Aside from Wells and Clarke, he was the only other person from Phoenix, yet Graham appeared to know most of the Waldenites and Arcadians by name, and they all treated him with a surprising amount of respect. Wells didn't want to imagine what he'd had to do to earn it.

"I wasn't *lecturing* anyone. I'm just trying to keep us alive."

Graham raised an eyebrow. "That's interesting, considering that your father keeps sentencing our friends to death. But don't worry, I know you're on our side." He grinned at Wells. "Isn't that right?"

Wells glanced at him warily, then gave a curt nod. "Of course."

"So," Graham went on, his friendly tone at odds with the hostile glint in his eyes, "what was your infraction?"

"That's not a very polite question, is it?" Wells tried for what he hoped was a cryptic smile.

"I'm so sorry." Graham's face took on an expression of mock horror. "You have to forgive me. You see, when you've spent the past 847 days of your life locked in the bottom of the ship, you tend to forget what's considered polite conversation on Phoenix."

"847 days?" Wells repeated. "I guess we can assume you weren't Confined for miscounting the herbs you probably stole from the storehouse."

"No," Graham said, taking a step toward Wells. "I wasn't." The crowd fell silent, and Wells could see a few people shifting uncomfortably while others leaned in eagerly. "I was Confined for murder."

Their eyes locked. Wells kept his expression carefully devoid of emotion, refusing to give Graham the satisfaction of seeing the shock on his face. "Oh?" he said carelessly. "Who'd you kill?"

Graham smiled coldly. "If you'd spent any time with the rest of us, you'd know that *that* isn't considered a very polite question." There was a moment of tense silence before Graham switched gears. "But I already know what you did anyway. When the Chancellor's son gets locked up, word travels fast. Figures you wouldn't fess up. But now that we're having a nice little chat, maybe you can tell us exactly what we're doing down here. Maybe you can explain why so many of our *friends* keep getting executed after their retrials." Graham was still smiling, but his tone had grown low and dangerous. "And why now? What made *your father* decide to send us down all of a sudden?"

His father. All day, absorbed in the newness of being on Earth, Wells had almost been able to convince himself that the scene on the launch deck—the sharp sound of the gunshot, the blood blooming like a dark flower on his father's chest—had been a terrifying dream.

"Of course he's not going to tell us," Graham scoffed. "Are you, soldier?" he added with a mock salute.

The Arcadians and Waldenites who'd been watching Graham turned eagerly to Wells, the intensity of their gazes making his skin prickle. Of course, he knew what was going on. Why so many kids were being executed on their eighteenth birthdays for crimes that might have been pardoned in the past. Why the mission had been hastily thrown together and put in motion before there'd been time to plan properly.

He knew better than anyone, because it was all his fault.

"When will we get to go home?" asked a boy who didn't look much older than twelve. Wells felt an unexpected pang of pity for the brokenhearted mother who was still somewhere on the ship. She had no idea that her son had been hurtled through space onto a planet the human race had left for dead.

"We *are* home," Wells said, forcing as much sincerity as he could into the words.

If he said it enough times, perhaps he'd start to believe it himself.

He'd almost skipped the concert that year. It had always been his favorite event, the one evening musical relics were taken out of their oxygen-free preservation chambers. Watching the performers, who spent most of their time practicing on simulators, coax notes and chords out of the relics was like witnessing a resurrection. Carved and welded by long-dead hands, the only instruments left in the universe produced the same soaring melodies that had once echoed through the concert halls of ruined civilizations. Once a year, Eden Hall was filled with music that had outlasted humanity's tenure on Earth.

But as Wells entered the hall, a large, oval room bordered by a curved panoramic window, the grief that had been drifting through his body for the past week solidified in his stomach. He normally found the view incredibly beautiful, but that night the glittering stars that surrounded the cloud-shrouded Earth reminded him of candles at a vigil. His mother had loved music.

It was crowded as usual, with most of Phoenix buzzing around excitedly. Many of the women were eager to debut new dresses, an expensive and potentially maddening feat depending on what sort of textile scraps you found at the Exchange. He took a few steps forward, sending a ripple of whispers and knowing glances through the crowd.

Wells tried to focus on the front of the room where the musicians were gathering under the tree for which Eden Hall was named. The legend was that the sapling had miraculously survived the burning of North America and had been carried onto Phoenix right before the Exodus. Now it reached to the very top of the hall, its slender branches stretching out more than ten meters in each direction, creating a canopy of leaves that partially obscured the performers with a veil of green-tinged shadows.

"Is that the Chancellor's son?" a woman behind him asked. A new wave of heat rose to his already flushed cheeks. He'd never grown immune to the comet tail of double takes and curious glances he dragged behind him, but tonight it felt unbearable.

He turned and started walking toward the door, but froze as a hand grabbed his arm. He spun around and saw Clarke giving him a quizzical look. "Where are you running off to?"

Wells smiled grimly. "Turns out I'm not in the mood for music."

Clarke looked at him for a moment, then slipped her hand into his. "Stay. As a favor to me." She led him toward two empty seats in the back row. "I need you to tell me what we're listening to."

Wells sighed as he settled down next to Clarke. "I already told you they were performing Bach," he said, shooting a longing glance at the door.

"You know what I'm talking about." Clarke interlocked her fingers with his. "This movement, that movement." She grinned. "Besides, I always clap at the wrong time."

Wells gave her hand a squeeze.

There was no need for any sort of introduction or announcement. From the moment the first notes burst forward, the crowd fell silent, the violinist's bow slicing through their chatter as it swept across the strings. Then the cello joined in, followed by the clarinet. There were no drums tonight, but it didn't matter. Wells could practically hear the thud of two hundred hearts beating in time to the music.

"This is what I always imagined a sunset would sound like," Wells whispered. The words slipped out of his mouth before he had time to think, and he braced for an eye roll, or at least a look of confusion.

But the music had also cast its spell on Clarke. "I'd love to see a sunset," she murmured, resting her head on his shoulder.

Wells absently ran his hand through her silky hair. "I'd love to see a sunset with you." He bent down and kissed her forehead. "What are you doing in about seventy-five years?" he whispered.

"Cleaning my dentures," Clarke said with a smile. "Why?"

"Because I have an idea for our first date on Earth."

The light was fading, the bonfire flickering across the faces standing around Wells.

"I know this all seems strange and intimidating and, yes, unfair, but we're here for a reason," he told the crowd. "If we survive, everyone survives."

Nearly a hundred heads turned to him, and for a moment, he thought perhaps his words had chipped away at the layers of calcified defiance and ignorance. But then a new voice crashed into the silence.

"Careful there, Jaha."

Wells twisted around and saw a tall kid in a bloodstained guard uniform. The boy who'd forced his way onto the dropship—who'd held Wells's father hostage. "Earth is still in recovery mode. We don't know how much bullshit it can handle."

Another wave of snickers and snorts rippled around the fire, and Wells felt a rush of sudden, sharp anger. Because of this kid, his father—the person responsible for protecting the entire human race—had been *shot*, and he had the nerve to stand there and accuse *Wells* of bullshit?

"Excuse me?" Wells said, lifting his chin to give the boy his best officer's stare.

"Cut the crap, okay? Just say what you really mean. If we do exactly what you say, then you won't report us to your father."

Wells narrowed his eyes. "Thanks to you, my father is probably in the hospital." *Being given the best possible care, and on his way to a swift recovery*, Wells added silently. He hoped it was true.

"If he's even alive," Graham interjected, and laughed. For a second, Wells thought he saw the other boy wince.

Wells took a step forward, but then another voice yelled

out from the crowd, stopping him. "So you're not a spy?"

"A *spy*?" Wells almost laughed at the accusation.

"Yeah," the impostor guard agreed. "Spying on us just like these bracelets, right?"

Wells looked at the kid in the ill-fitting guard uniform more closely. Had he been told about the purpose of the bracelets, or had he figured it out on his own? "If the Council wanted to spy on you," he said, ignoring the comment about the transponders, "don't you think they'd choose someone a bit less obvious?"

The boy in the bloody uniform smirked. "We can discuss the pros and cons of your father's administration some other time. But for now, just tell us: If you're not a spy, what the hell are you doing here? There's no way anyone will believe you were actually Confined."

"I'm sorry," Wells said in a tone that conveyed anything but regret. "You appeared in a stolen guard's uniform and held my father hostage in order to break onto this ship. I think *you're* the one who owes us an explanation."

The boy's eyes narrowed. "I did what I had to do to protect my sister."

"Your *sister*?" Wells repeated. People broke the population laws more often on Walden than on Phoenix. But Wells had never heard of anyone having a sibling, not since the Cataclysm.

“That’s right.” The boy crossed his arms and met Wells’s eyes with a challenging stare. “Now I’m going to ask you one more time, what are you really doing here?”

Wells took a step forward. He didn’t owe anyone an explanation, let alone this criminal, who was probably lying about having a sister and who knew what else. But then a flash of movement caught his eye. Clarke was heading toward the fire from the other side of the clearing, where she’d been tending to the injured passengers.

Wells turned back to the tall boy and sighed, his anger draining away. “I’m here for the same reason you are.” His eyes darted toward Clarke, who was still out of earshot. “I got myself Confined to protect someone I care about.”

The crowd fell silent. Wells turned his back on them and started walking, not caring if their eyes followed him as he made his way toward Clarke.

For a moment, the sight of her overwhelmed his brain. The light in the clearing had changed as the sky grew darker, making the flecks of gold in her green eyes appear to glow. She was more beautiful on Earth than he’d ever seen her.

Their eyes locked, and a chill traveled down his spine. Less than a year ago, he’d been able to tell what she was thinking just by looking at her. But now her expression was inscrutable.

"What are you doing here, Wells?" she asked, her voice strained and weary.

She's in shock, Wells told himself, forcing his mind to wrap around the ill-fitting explanation. "I came for you," he said softly.

Her face assumed an expression that broke through the barriers, a mixture of sorrow, frustration, and pity that seemed to travel from Clarke's eyes straight into his chest.

"I wish you hadn't." She sighed and pushed past him, striding off without another glance.

Her words knocked the air out of him, and for a moment, all Wells could think about was remembering how to breathe. Then he heard a chorus of murmurs from the bonfire behind him, and turned, curious despite himself. Everyone was pointing upward at the sky, which was turning into a symphony of color.

First, orange streaks appeared in the blue, like an oboe joining a flute, turning a solo into a duet. That harmony built into a crescendo of colors as yellow and then pink added their voices to the chorus. The sky darkened, throwing the array of colors into even sharper relief. The word *sunset* couldn't possibly contain the meaning of the beauty above them, and for the millionth time since they'd landed, Wells found that the words they'd been taught to describe Earth paled in comparison to the real thing.

Even Clarke, who hadn't stopped moving since the crash, froze in her tracks, her head tilted up to better appreciate the miracle taking place overhead. Wells didn't have to see her face to know that her eyes would be widened in awe, her mouth slightly parted with a gasp as she watched something she had only ever dreamed about. Something *they* had only ever dreamed about, Wells corrected himself. He turned away, unable to look at the sky any longer, pain hardening into something dense and sharp in his chest. It was the first sunset humans had witnessed in three centuries, and he was watching it alone.

CHAPTER 7

Bellamy

Bellamy squinted up at the sunrise. He'd always assumed those ancient poets had been full of shit, or at least had much better drugs than he'd ever tried. But they were right. It was crazy to watch the sky go from black to gray and then explode into streaks of color. It didn't make him want to break out into song or anything, but then again, Bellamy had never been the artistic type.

He leaned over and pulled Octavia's blanket up over her shoulder. He'd spotted it sticking out of one of the supply containers the night before and had practically knocked out some kid's tooth in the ensuing tussle. Bellamy exhaled, watching as his breath crystallized in front of him, lingering far longer than it would on the ship, where the ventilation system practically sucked the air out of your lungs before it had a chance to leave your mouth.

He looked around the clearing. After that Clarke girl had finished evaluating Octavia and determined she only had a sprained ankle, Bellamy had carried her over toward the trees where they'd spent the night. They were going to keep their distance until he figured out how many of these kids were real criminals and how many had just been in the wrong place at the wrong time.

Bellamy squeezed his sister's hand. It was his fault she'd been Confined. It was his fault she was here. He should've known she'd been planning something; she'd been talking for weeks about how hungry some of the children in her unit had been. It had been only a matter of time before she did something to feed them—even if it meant stealing. His selfless little sister was sentenced to die for having too big of a heart.

It was his job to protect her. And for the first time in her life, he'd failed.

Bellamy threw his shoulders back and raised his chin. He was tall for a six-year-old, but that didn't stop people from staring as he made his way through the crowd at the distribution center. It wasn't against the rules for children to come on their own, but it was rare. He went over the list his mother had made him repeat back to her three times before she'd let him leave their flat. *Fiber meal—two credits. Glucose packets—one credit. Dehydrated grain—two credits. Tuber flakes—one credit. Protein loaf—three credits.*

He darted around two women who'd stopped to grumble in front of some white things that looked like brains. Bellamy rolled his eyes and kept moving. Who cared that Phoenix got all the good stuff from the solar fields? Anyone who wanted to eat vegetables probably had little, mushy white brains themselves.

Bellamy cupped his hands under the fiber dispenser, caught the packet that slid out, and tucked it under his arm. He started to make his way over to the tuber section when something bright and shiny caught his eye. Bellamy turned and saw a pile of red, round fruit inside a display case. Normally, he didn't care about the expensive things they locked away—twisted carrots that reminded Bellamy of orange witch fingers, and ugly mushrooms that looked more like brain-sucking black-hole zombies than food. But these were different. The fruit was a rosy pink, the same color that his neighbor Rilla turned when they played alien invasion in the corridor. Or used to play before Rilla's father was taken away by the guards and Rilla was sent to live in the care center.

Bellamy stood on his tiptoes to read the number on the data

panel. Eleven credits. That sounded like a lot, but he wanted to do something nice for his mother. She hadn't gotten out of bed for three days. Bellamy couldn't imagine being that tired.

"Do you want one?" an irritated voice asked. He looked up and saw a woman in a green uniform glaring at him. "Order it or step aside."

Heat rose to Bellamy's cheeks, and for a moment, he considered running away. But then a surge of indignation washed over his embarrassment. He wasn't going to let some sour-faced distribution worker stop him from getting his mother the treat she deserved. "I'll take *two*," he said in the haughty voice that always made his mother roll her eyes and ask, *I wonder who you got that from?* "And don't rub your fingers all over them," he added pointedly.

The woman raised her eyebrow before glancing at the guards behind the transaction table. No one on Walden liked the guards, but his mother seemed particularly afraid of them. Lately, she'd grab Bellamy's hand and turn in the other direction whenever she saw a patrol team approaching. Could she have done something wrong? Were the guards going to come take her away like they'd taken Rilla's father? *No*, he told himself. *I won't let them.*

He took his apples and marched over to the transaction table. Another distribution worker scanned his card, staring for a moment at the information on the panel before shrugging her shoulders and waving him forward. One of the guards shot him a curious look, but Bellamy kept his eyes straight ahead. He forced himself to walk until he'd left the distribution center and then broke into a run, clutching his packets to his chest as he tore down the walkway leading to his residential unit.

He palmed into their flat and shut the door carefully behind him. He couldn't wait to show his mother what he'd brought her. He stepped into the living space, but the lights didn't turn on. Was the sensor broken again? His stomach tightened slightly. His mother hated entering maintenance requests. She didn't like having strangers in their home. But how long could they spend in the dark?

"Mom!" Bellamy called, dashing into her room. "I'm back! I did it!" The lights were working here, and they buzzed to life as Bellamy ran through the door. But the bed was empty.

Bellamy froze as a wave of terror washed over him. She was gone. They'd taken her. He was all alone. But then a muffled stomp from the kitchen reached his ears. He sighed as his panic was quickly replaced by relief, then excitement. She was out of bed!

He ran into the kitchen. His mother was facing the small, round window that looked out into the dark staircase. One hand was placed on her lower back, as if it was hurting her. "Mom!" he called. "Look what I got you."

His mother inhaled sharply but didn't turn around. "Bellamy," she said, as though he were a neighbor dropping by for an unexpected visit. "You're back. Leave the food on the table and go to your room. I'll be right there."

Disappointment pressed down on him, weighing his feet to the floor. He wanted to see the look on his mother's face when she saw the fruit. "Look!" he urged, stretching his arms forward, unsure what she could see in the reflection of the dark, dusty window.

She twisted her head to look at him over her shoulder. "What are those?" She narrowed her eyes. "Apples?" She pressed her lips together and rubbed the side of her head like she used to do when she came home from work. Before she got sick. "How much did they—never mind. Just go to your room, okay?"

Bellamy's palms had begun to sweat as he placed the packets on the table near the door. Had he done something wrong? The lights flickered and then went out. "*Damn it*," his mother muttered as she looked up at the ceiling. "Bellamy, *now*," she commanded. Or at least, he thought it was his mother. She was facing away from him again, and her voice swirled through the darkness until it didn't sound like her anymore.

As he slunk away, Bellamy shot a quick glance over his shoulder. His mother didn't even look like herself. She'd turned to the side, and her stomach appeared huge and round, like she was hiding something under her shirt. He blinked and scampered off, convinced that his eyes had been playing tricks on him, ignoring the chill traveling down his spine.

"How's she doing?"

Bellamy glanced up to see Clarke standing above him, looking uneasily from him to his sleeping sister. He nodded. "I think she's okay."

"Good." She raised a slightly singed eyebrow. "Because it'd be a shame if you followed through on your threat from last night."

"What did I say?"

"You told me that if I didn't save your sister, you'd blow up the goddamn planet and everyone on it."

Bellamy smiled. "Good thing it's only a sprained ankle." He cocked his head to the side and surveyed Clarke quizzically. The skin under her eyes was bruised with exhaustion, but the purple shadows just made them look greener. He felt a twinge of guilt for being such a jerk to her the night before. He'd pegged her as another self-absorbed Phoenix girl who was training as a doctor because it gave her something to brag about at parties. But the strain in her delicate face and the blood matted in her reddish-gold hair made it clear she hadn't stopped to rest since they'd landed.

"So," Bellamy continued, remembering Wells's declaration at the bonfire yesterday, and the way Clarke had stomped away from him, "why were you so mean to little Chancellor Junior?"

Clarke looked at him with a mixture of shock and indignation. For a moment, he thought she might actually hit him, but then she just shook her head. "That's none of your business."

"Is he your boyfriend?" Bellamy pressed.

"No," Clarke said flatly. But then her mouth twitched into a questioning smile. "Why do you care?"

"Just taking a census," Bellamy replied. "Specifically, to determine the relationship status of all the pretty girls on Earth."

Clarke rolled her eyes, but then she turned back to Octavia and the playfulness drained from her face.

"What is it?" Bellamy looked from Clarke to his sister.

"Nothing," Clarke said quickly. "I just wish I had some antiseptic for that cut on her face. And some of the others are going to need antibiotics."

"So we don't have *any* medicine?" Bellamy asked, frowning in concern.

Clarke looked at him, startled. "I think the medical supplies kits were thrown out of the dropship in the crash. We'll be fine, though," she said quickly, the lie shooting out of her mouth before she had time to make her features match it. "We'll be okay for a while. The human body has a remarkable ability to heal itself. . . ." She trailed off as her eyes settled on the bloodstains on his stolen uniform.

Bellamy grimaced as he glanced down, wondering if she was thinking about the Chancellor. Bellamy hoped he'd survived—he had enough blood on his hands already. But it probably didn't matter one way or another. Whoever the Council sent down with the next group would most certainly be authorized to execute Bellamy on the spot, regardless of the fact that the Chancellor's injury had been an accident. As soon as Octavia was well enough to move, she and Bellamy would be out of there. They'd hike for a few days, put some distance between themselves and the group, and eventually find somewhere to settle down. He hadn't spent months poring over those ancient survival guides he'd discovered on B deck for nothing. He'd be ready for whatever was waiting for them in those woods. It couldn't be worse than what was going to come hurtling down from the sky.

"How long until she'll be able to walk on it?"

Clarke turned back to Bellamy. "It's a pretty bad sprain, so I'd say a few days until she can walk, a week or two until it's fully healed."

"But possibly sooner?"

She tilted her head to the side and gave him a small smile

that, for a moment, made him forget that he was marooned on a potentially toxic planet with ninety-nine juvenile delinquents. "What's the rush?"

But before he had time to respond, someone called Clarke's name and she was gone.

Bellamy took a deep breath. To his surprise, the simple act cleared his head, leaving him more awake and alert. It'd probably turn out to be toxic, but every time he inhaled, he sensed something unnamable but intriguing, like a mysterious girl who wouldn't meet your eyes but passed closely enough for you to catch a whiff of her perfume.

He took a few steps closer to the trees, anxious for a better look but unwilling to stray too far from Octavia. They didn't look like any species he recognized, but then again, the only Earth botany book he'd been able to find had been about plants native to Africa, and he thought he'd heard Wells say they were on the East Coast of what had once been the United States.

A twig snapped next to him. Bellamy whipped around and saw a girl with a long, narrow face and stringy hair. "Can I help you?"

"Wells says everyone who's not hurt should collect wood."

A thread of irritation coiled around Bellamy's stomach, and he gave the girl a tight smile. "I don't think Wells is in any position to be giving orders, so if it's all right with you, I'm going to worry about myself, okay?" She shifted uneasily for a moment before shooting a nervous glance over her shoulder. "Off you go," Bellamy said, motioning her forward with his hands. He watched her scurry off with satisfaction.

He craned his neck and stared up at the sky, his eyes drinking in nothing but emptiness in all directions. It didn't matter where they were. Any spot on this planet was going to be infinitely better than the world they'd left behind.

For the first time in his life, he was free.

CHAPTER 8

Glass

Glass spent the rest of the night on Luke's couch, grateful that Camille didn't ask why she refused to sleep in Carter's old room. They'd decided that it was best for Glass to stay hidden in Luke's flat until the shift change at 0600, when there would be fewer guards on patrol.

She'd tossed and turned all night. Every time she rolled over, the bracelet dug into her skin, a painful reminder that while she was in danger, Wells was hundreds of kilometers away, fighting to survive on a planet that hadn't been able to support life for centuries. It'd always been his dream to see Earth, but not like this. Not when it might still be toxic. Not after seeing his father shot right in front of him.

As she lay staring at the ceiling, she couldn't keep her ears from searching for sounds in the darkness. The faintest murmur from the other side of Luke's door was enough to turn her stomach. The silence was even worse.

Just as the circadian lights began to creep under the front door, Luke's bedroom door opened, and both he and Camille staggered out wearily. Clearly, neither of them had slept much either. Luke was already dressed in off-duty civilian clothes, but Camille wore only one of Luke's old undershirts, the hem of which skimmed the tops of her slender thighs. Glass blushed and looked away.

"Good morning." The formality in Luke's voice made Glass wince. The last time Luke had said those words to her, the two of them had been in his bed, and he'd whispered them in her ear.

"Good morning," she managed, shoving the memory out of her head.

"We need to get that bracelet off." Luke gestured toward her wrist.

Glass nodded and rose from the couch, shifting uneasily as Camille looked back and forth between her and Luke. Finally, she crossed her arms and turned to him. "Are you sure this is a good idea? What if someone sees you?"

Luke's expression darkened. "We talked about this." He spoke quietly, but Glass heard the note of frustration in his voice. "If we don't help her, they're going to *kill* her. It's the right thing to do."

The right thing to do, Glass thought. That was all she meant to him anymore, a life he didn't want on his conscience.

"Better her than you," Camille said, her voice trembling.

Luke leaned over and kissed the top of her head. "It's going to be fine. I'll take her back to Phoenix and then come straight home."

Camille sighed and tossed Glass a shirt and a pair of pants. "Here," she said. "I know it's not up to your Phoenix standards, but you'll look a bit more believable in this. You aren't going to pass for a sanitation worker with that hair." She gave Luke's arm a squeeze and then slipped back into his bedroom, leaving Glass and Luke alone.

Glass stood holding the clothes awkwardly in her arms, and for a moment, they just stared at each other. The last time she'd seen Luke, she'd have thought nothing of changing in front of him. "Should I . . ." She trailed off, gesturing toward Carter's room.

"Oh," Luke said, reddening slightly. "No, I'll just . . . I'll be right back." He retreated to his bedroom. Glass changed as quickly as she could, trying to ignore the whispers that escaped through the door, stinging her skin like pinpricks.

When Luke returned, Glass was dressed in a pair of loose gray pants that barely clung to her hips and a rough blue

T-shirt that chafed her skin. Luke surveyed her critically. "Something's still off," he said. "You don't look like a prisoner, but you definitely don't look like a Waldenite."

Glass began to smooth the sides of her wrinkled trousers self-consciously, wondering whether Luke preferred being with a girl who looked at home in these clothes. "It's not that," he said. "It's your hair. Girls don't wear it that long here."

"Why?" she asked, realizing with a small measure of guilt that she'd never even noticed.

Luke had turned and began rummaging through a small storage bin against the wall. "Probably because it'd be too hard to take care of. We don't get the same water allotment on Walden that you do on Phoenix." He turned around with a look of triumph on his face and produced an ancient-looking stained cap.

Glass gave him a weak smile. "Thanks." She took the hat from Luke, their hands brushing, and placed it on her head.

"I don't think we're quite there yet," he said, surveying her with a frown. He stepped toward her and removed the hat with one hand, and with his other, reached over her shoulder to gather her hair, gently twisting it into a knot on top of her head. "There," he said in satisfaction, placing the cap on top.

The silence stretched between them. Slowly, Luke reached up and tucked a few stray strands behind Glass's ear. His rough fingers lingered on her neck, and he looked into her eyes, unblinking.

"Ready?" Glass asked, breaking the spell as she stepped to the side.

"Yes. Let's go." Luke stepped back stiffly and led her out into the hallway.

There weren't as many circadian lights on Walden as there were on Phoenix, so although it was technically dawn, the corridors were mostly dark. Glass couldn't tell where Luke was leading her, and she clenched her hands to keep herself from reaching for his.

Finally, Luke stopped in front of the faint outline of a door. He dug into his pocket, producing something Glass couldn't see and holding it up to the scanner. The door beeped and slid open. Glass's insides twisted as she realized that wherever Luke took her, he'd leave a trail of log-ins and access codes. She couldn't bear to think what would happen when the Council figured out that he'd helped an escaped criminal.

But there was no other option. After she said one last good-bye to her mother, she'd wait for the guards to find her. She wouldn't try to see Luke again. She couldn't ask him to risk his safety for her. Not after what she'd done.

A faint light flickered wearily to life, casting a dirty, yellowish glow over machinery Glass didn't recognize. "Where are we?" she asked, her voice echoing strangely.

"One of the old workshops. This is where they used to

repair the Earthmade equipment, before it was all replaced. I came here for some of my training."

Glass started to ask why the guards would train here, but bit back the question. She always forgot that Luke had already started his mechanical apprenticeship when he was accepted into the engineering corps of the guards. He rarely spoke about that part of his life. Looking back, Glass was ashamed that she hadn't tried harder to learn about Luke's world; it was no wonder he'd turned to Camille.

Luke stood next to an enormous machine, pushing different buttons, his brow furrowed in concentration. "What is *that*?" Glass asked when it started to hum ominously.

"A laser cutter," Luke said without glancing up.

Glass hugged her wrist protectively to her chest. "No way."

Luke gave Glass a look that was equal parts amusement and irritation. "No arguing. The sooner we get that thing off of you, the better your chances of hiding."

"Can't we just figure out how to unlock it?"

Luke shook his head. "It has to be cut off." When she didn't move, he held out his hand with a sigh. "Come here, Glass," he said, beckoning her over.

Glass's feet locked into the floor. Although she'd spent the last six months imagining Luke calling to her, she'd never thought that a piece of deadly machinery would be involved. Luke raised an eyebrow. "Glass?"

Glass took a tentative step forward. It wasn't like she had anything to lose. Better to have Luke slice her wrist off than a medic inject poison into her vein.

Luke tapped a flat surface in the middle of the machine. "Just put your hand here." He flipped a switch and the whole machine began to vibrate.

Glass trembled as her skin made contact with the cold metal.

"It'll be okay," Luke said. "I promise. Just hold still."

Glass nodded, too afraid to speak. The humming continued and was soon accompanied by a high-pitched screech.

Luke made a few more adjustments, then came to stand next to her. "Ready?"

She swallowed nervously. "Yes."

Luke placed his left hand over her arm, and with his right, started to move another lever toward her. To her horror, she saw that it was emitting a thin red line of light that pulsed with dangerous energy.

She started to shake, but Luke gripped her arm tighter. "It's okay," he murmured. "Just stay still."

The light was getting closer. Glass could feel the heat on her skin. Luke's face tensed with concentration, his eyes fixed on Glass's wrist as he moved the laser steadily along.

Glass closed her eyes, bracing herself for the searing pain, the screaming of her nerves as they lost contact with her hand.

"Perfect." Luke's voice cut through her terror. Glass looked down and saw the bracelet had been split into two neat pieces, freeing her wrist.

She sighed, her breath ragged. "Thank you."

"You're welcome." He smiled at her, his hand still clutching her arm.

Neither of them spoke as they slipped out of the workshop and began to wind their way back up toward the skybridge.

"What's wrong?" Luke whispered as he guided Glass around a corner and up another flight of stairs, narrower and darker than anything on Phoenix.

"Nothing."

In the past, Luke would've reached over, taken her chin in his hand, and looked her in the eye until she giggled. *You're a terrible liar, Rapunzel*, he'd say, a reference to the fairytale about the girl whose hair grew a foot anytime she fibbed. But this time, Glass's lie evaporated into the air.

"So how have you been?" she asked finally, when she couldn't bear the weight of the silence any longer.

Luke glanced over his shoulder and raised an eyebrow. "Oh, you know, apart from being dumped by the girl I loved and then having my best friend executed for a bullshit infraction, I'd say not too bad."

Glass cringed as his words landed in her chest. She'd never heard that kind of bitterness in Luke's voice before.

"But at least I had Camille. . . ."

Glass nodded, but as she stole a glance at Luke's familiar profile, shards of indignation gathered, sharp and dangerous, in her mind. What did he think she had done to be Confined? Why wasn't he more curious or surprised? Did he think she was such a terrible person that she would have committed an infraction?

Luke stopped abruptly, causing Glass to stumble into him. "Sorry," she muttered, scrambling to regain her balance.

"Does your mother know what happened?" Luke asked, turning to face her.

"No," Glass said. "I mean, she knew I was Confined, but she can't have known about the Earth mission." The Chancellor had made it clear that the operation was top secret. Their parents wouldn't be informed until it was certain their children had survived the journey—or until the Council was sure they'd never return.

"It's good that you're going to see her."

Glass said nothing. She knew he was thinking of his own mother, who'd died when he was only twelve, which was why he'd ended up living with his then-eighteen-year-old neighbor Carter.

"Yeah," Glass said in a shaky voice. She'd been desperate to see her mother, but even without the bracelet, it wouldn't take the guards long to find her. What was more important?

Saying good-bye? Or sparing her mother the pain of seeing her daughter being dragged away toward certain death? "We should keep going."

They crossed the bridge in silence as Glass drank in the sight of the twinkling stars. She hadn't realized how much she loved the view from the skybridge until she'd been locked in a tiny, windowless cell. She stole a glance at Luke, not sure whether to be hurt or relieved that he didn't turn to look at her.

"You should go back," Glass said as they reached the Phoenix checkpoint, which was, as Luke had promised, free of guards. "I'll be okay."

Luke's jaw tightened and he gave her a bitter smile. "You're an escaped convict, and I'm *still* not good enough to meet your mother."

"That's not what I meant," she said, thinking of the scan trail he'd already left behind. "It's not safe for you to help me. I can't let you risk your life. You've already done so much."

Luke took a breath as if to say something, then nodded. "Okay, then."

She forced what she hoped was a smile, holding back tears. "Thank you for everything."

Luke's face softened slightly. "Good luck, Glass." He started to lean in, and Glass couldn't help tipping her head up, out of habit—but then he stepped back, wrenching his eyes from her with an almost physical force. Without a word, Luke turned and moved soundlessly back the way they'd come. Glass watched him go, her lips aching for the good-bye kiss they'd never feel again.

When she reached the entrance to her flat, Glass raised her fist and tapped lightly. The door opened and Glass's mother, Sonja, peered around it. A symphony of emotions played across her face in an instant—surprise, joy, confusion, and fear.

"Glass?" she gasped, reaching for her daughter, as if she wasn't sure she was really there. Glass leaned gratefully into her mother's hug, drinking in the smell of her perfume. "I thought I'd never see you again." She gave Glass one more squeeze before pulling her inside and closing the door. Sonja stepped back and stared at her daughter. "I was just counting down the days." Her voice faded into a whisper. "You turn eighteen in three weeks."

Glass grabbed her mother's clammy hand and led her to the couch. "They were going to send us to Earth," Glass told her. "A hundred of us." She took a deep breath. "I was supposed to be one of them."

"Earth?" Sonja repeated slowly, holding the word almost at a distance, as if trying to get a better look. "Oh my god."

"There was an altercation at the launch. The Chancellor . . ." Glass's head swam as she recalled the scene from the launch deck. She sent up a silent prayer that Wells was okay down there on Earth, that he was with Clarke and didn't have to grieve alone. "In the chaos, I was able to get away," Glass continued. The details weren't important right now. "I just came to say I love you."

Her mother's eyes widened. "So that's how the Chancellor was shot. Oh, Glass," she whispered, wrapping her arms around her daughter.

The thud of footsteps echoed out in the hallway, and Glass flinched. She looked warily at the door before turning back to face her mother. "I can't stay long," she said, rising shakily to her feet.

"Wait!" Sonja jumped up and clutched Glass's arm, pulling her back to the couch. Her fingers tightened around her wrist. "The Chancellor is on life support, which means that Vice Chancellor Rhodes is in charge. You shouldn't go yet." She paused. "He has a very different approach to . . . governing. There's a chance that he'll pardon you. He can be convinced." Sonja stood and gave Glass a smile that did little to illuminate her glistening eyes. "Just wait here."

"Do you have to go?" Glass asked, her voice small. She couldn't bear to say another good-bye. Not when every goodbye could be forever.

Her mother bent down and kissed Glass's forehead. "I won't be long."

She watched Sonja apply a hurried layer of lipstick and slip out into the still-empty corridor, then pulled her knees into her chest and hugged them tightly, as if trying to keep everything inside her from spilling out.

Glass wasn't sure how long she slept, but curled up on the cushions that still remembered the shape of her body, it seemed possible that the past six months had been a nightmare. That she hadn't actually been imprisoned in a cell that contained nothing besides two metal cots, a silent, seething Arcadian cell mate, and the ghosts of sobs that remained long after her tears dried up.

When she opened her eyes her mother was sitting next to her on the couch, stroking Glass's matted hair. "It's all taken care of," she said softly. "You've been pardoned."

Glass rolled over to look up at her mother's face. "How?" she asked, the surprise shocking her out of her sleep, chasing away the images of Luke that lingered on her eyelids when she first woke up. "Why?"

"People are growing restless," her mother explained. "None of the convicted juveniles have made it past their retrials in the last year, and it makes the justice system look anything but just. You're going to be the exception—the proof that the system's still working how it's supposed to, that those who can contribute to society are given the chance to return to it. It took a little convincing, but eventually Vice Chancellor Rhodes saw my side of things," her mother finished, sinking back into the couch, looking exhausted but relieved.

"Mom—I can't—I don't—thank you." Glass didn't know what else to say. She smiled as she pushed herself up into a seated position and rested her head against her mother's shoulder. She was free? She almost couldn't comprehend the meaning of the word.

"You don't need to thank me, sweetheart. I'd do anything for you." Sonja pushed a piece of Glass's hair behind her ear and smiled. "Just remember, you're not to tell anyone about the Earth mission—I mean it."

"But what happened to the others? Is Wells okay? Can you find out?"

Sonja shook her head. "As far as you're concerned, there was no mission. What's important is that you're safe now. You have a second chance," her mother murmured. "Just promise me you won't do anything foolish."

"I promise," Glass said finally, shaking her head in disbelief. "I promise."

CHAPTER 9

Clarke

Clarke slipped through the flap of the designated infirmary tent and stepped into the clearing. Even without the luxury of windows, she sensed that it was dawn. The sky erupted with color, and the pungent air stimulated sensors in her brain Clarke had never realized existed. She wished she could share the experience with the two people who had made her yearn to see Earth in the first place. But Clarke would never have that chance.

Her parents were gone.

"Good morning."

Clarke stiffened. It was almost unfathomable that Wells's voice had once been her favorite sound in the universe. He was the reason her parents were dead, their bodies floating through the depths of space, moving farther and farther from everything they'd known and loved. In a moment of weakness, Clarke had confided a secret that wasn't hers to share. And even though he'd sworn not to tell a soul, Wells hadn't even waited twenty-four hours before skipping off to his father, so desperate to be the perfect son, Phoenix's golden child, that he betrayed the girl he'd pretended to love.

She turned to face Wells. There was nothing to keep her from lunging at him, but she wanted to avoid any confrontation that would prolong the exposure.

As she strode past him, Wells grabbed her arm. "Hold on a second, I just wanted to—"

Clarke spun around and wrenched herself free. "Don't *touch* me," she hissed.

Wells took a step back, his eyes wide. "I'm sorry," he said. His voice was steady, but she could see the hurt on his face. Clarke had always been able to tell what Wells was feeling. He was a terrible liar, which was how she'd known, in that brief moment, that his promise to keep her secret had been sincere. But something had changed his mind, and it was Clarke's parents who had paid the price.

Wells didn't move. "I just wanted to make sure you were doing okay," he said quietly. "We're going to finish sorting through the wreckage today. Is there anything in particular you need for your patients?"

"Yes. A sterile operating room, IVs, a full-body scanner, *real* doctors . . ."

"You're doing an incredible job."

"I'd be doing even better if I'd spent the past six months training at the hospital instead of in Confinement." This time, Wells had braced for the barb, and his face remained impassive.

The sky was growing brighter, filling the clearing with an almost golden light that made everything look like it'd been polished overnight. The grass seemed greener, glistening with tiny drops of water. Purple blossoms began unfurling from what had seemed like an unremarkable shrub. The long, tapered petals stretched toward the sun, twisting in the air as if dancing to music only they could hear.

Wells seemed to read her mind. "If you hadn't been Confined, you'd never have come here," he said quietly.

She whipped her head back to face him. "You think I should be grateful for what you did? I've seen kids *die*, kids who never wanted to come here but had to because some little shit like you turned them in just to feel important."

"That's not what I meant." Wells sighed and met her gaze straight on. "I'm so sorry, Clarke. I can't tell you how sorry. But I didn't do it to *feel important*." He started to step forward, but then seemed to think better of it and shifted his weight back. "You were suffering, and I wanted to help. I couldn't bear it, seeing you like that. I just wanted to help make the pain go away."

The tenderness in his voice made Clarke's stomach twist. "They killed my parents," she said quietly, imagining the scene as she had so many times before. Her mother bracing for the prick of a needle, her body systematically shutting down until those final dreadful moments when only her brain was left. Had they been offered the customary last meal? Clarke's heart twinged as she imagined her father's lifeless body in a release capsule, his fingers stained red from the berries he'd eaten alone. "That kind of pain never goes away."

For a moment, they just stared at each other, the silence taking on a physical weight. But then Wells broke eye contact and turned his head up toward the trees above them. There were faintly musical sounds coming from the leaves.

"Do you hear that?" Wells whispered without looking at her.

The song was both haunting and joyful, the first few notes an elegy for the fading stars. Yet just when Clarke was sure her heart would break with the bittersweet loveliness, the melody soared, trumpeting the arrival of the dawn.

Birds. Real birds. She couldn't see them, but she knew they were there. She wondered if the first colonists had heard birds singing as they'd boarded the final ship. Would the music have been a song of farewell? Or had the creatures already joined their voices together in a requiem for the dying Earth?

"It's incredible," Wells said, turning to look at her with a smile she recognized from long ago. Clarke shivered. It was like seeing a ghost—a specter of the boy to whom she'd been foolish enough to give her heart.

Clarke couldn't suppress a smile as she watched Wells shift from side to side outside her front door. He always got nervous about kissing her in public, but it had gotten worse since he'd started officer training. The idea of making out with his girlfriend while in uniform seemed to make him uncomfortable, which was unfortunate because the sight of him in his uniform made her want to kiss him even more than usual.

"I'll see you tomorrow." Clarke turned to press her thumb to the scanner.

"Wait," Wells said, glancing over his shoulder before grabbing hold of her arm.

Clarke sighed. "Wells," she started as she tried to wiggle out of his grasp. "I need to go."

He grinned as he tightened his grip. "Are your parents home?"

"Yes." She inclined her head toward the door. "I'm late for dinner."

Wells stared at her expectantly. He much preferred eating with her family to sitting across from his father in silence, but she couldn't invite him to join them. Not tonight.

Wells cocked his head to the side. "I won't make a face this time, no matter what your father added to the protein paste. I've been practicing." His face broke into a comically bright smile as he nodded emphatically. "Wow. This is delicious!"

Clarke pressed her lips together for a moment before responding. "I just need to have a private conversation with them."

Wells's face grew serious. "What's going on?" He released her arm and brought his hand to her cheek. "Is everything okay?"

"It's fine." She stepped to the side and tilted her head so her eyes wouldn't betray her by sending distress signals from behind the lies. She needed to confront her parents about their experiments, and she couldn't put it off any longer.

"Okay, then," he said slowly. "See you tomorrow?"

Instead of kissing her on the cheek, Wells surprised Clarke by wrapping his arms around her waist and pulling her close. His lips pressed against hers, and for a moment, she forgot about everything except the warmth of his body. But by the time she'd closed the door, the tingle of Wells's touch on her skin had been replaced by a prickle of dread.

Her parents were sitting on the couch. Their heads turned to her. "Clarke." Her mother rose to her feet, smiling. "Was that Wells with you outside? Does he want to join us for din—"

"No," Clarke said, more sharply than she'd meant to. "Can you sit down? I need to talk to you." She crossed the room and settled on a chair facing her parents, trembling as two violent forces waged war for control of her body: burning fury and desperate hope. She needed her parents to admit what they'd done to justify her anger, but she also prayed they'd have a good excuse. "I figured out the password," she said simply. "I've been in the lab."

Her mother's eyes widened as she sank back onto the couch. Then she took a deep breath, and for a moment, Clarke hoped she'd try to explain, that she had the words to make it all better. But then she whispered the phrase Clarke had been dreading. "I'm sorry."

Her father took his wife's hand, his eyes on Clarke. "I'm sorry you had to see that," he said quietly. "I know it's . . . shocking. But they don't feel any pain. We make sure of that."

"How could you?" The question felt flimsy, incapable of supporting the weight of her accusation, but she couldn't think of anything else to ask. "You're experimenting on people. On *children*." Saying it aloud made her stomach churn. Bile crept up her throat.

Her mother closed her eyes. "We didn't have a choice," she said softly. "We've spent years trying to test radiation levels in other ways—you know that. When we reported back to the Vice Chancellor there was no way to gather conclusive evidence without human studies, we thought he understood it was a dead end. But then he insisted that we . . ." Her voice cracked. Clarke didn't need her to finish the sentence. "We had no choice," she repeated desperately.

"We always have a choice," Clarke said, trembling. "You could have said no. I would have let them *kill* me before I agreed to that."

"But he didn't threaten to kill us." Her father's voice was infuriatingly quiet.

"Then what the hell are you doing this for?" Clarke asked shrilly.

"He said he would kill *you*."

The birdsong trailed off, leaving a charged silence in its wake, as if the music had seeped into the stillness, imbuing the air with melody. "Wow," Wells said softly. "That was amazing." He was still facing the trees, but he'd extended his arm toward her, as if reaching through time to hold the hand of the girl who used to love him.

The spell was broken. Clarke stiffened and, without a word, headed back toward the infirmary.

It was dark inside the tent. Clarke almost tripped as she stepped in, making a mental note to change the bandages on one boy's leg, fix the sloppy stitches she'd given the girl with the gash on her thigh. She'd finally found a container with real bandages and surgical thread, but there wasn't going to be much more she could do if they didn't find the actual medicine chest. It hadn't turned up in the wreckage, most likely thrown from the dropship during the crash and destroyed.

Thalia was lying on one of the cots. She was still asleep, and the newest bandage seemed to be holding up. Clarke had already changed the wrappings three times since she'd found Thalia after the crash, blood pouring out of an ugly gash in her side.

The memory of stitching up the wound made Clarke's stomach churn, and she hoped that her friend remembered even less. Thalia had passed out from the pain and had been fading in and out of consciousness ever since. Clarke knelt down and brushed a strand of damp hair back from her friend's brow.

"Hi," she whispered as Thalia's eyes fluttered open. "How are you feeling?"

The injured girl forced a smile that seemed to drain the energy from the rest of her body. "I'm just great," Thalia said, but then winced, the pain flashing in her eyes.

"You used to be a much better liar."

"I never *lied*." Her voice was hoarse but still full of mock indignation. "I just told the guard that I had a neck problem and needed an extra pillow."

"And then convinced him that black-market whiskey would keep you from singing in your 'sleep,'" Clarke added with a smile.

"Yeah. . . . It's too bad Lise wasn't willing to play along."

"Or that you can't carry a tune to save your life."

"That's what made it so great!" Thalia protested. "The night guard would've done anything to shut me up at that point."

Clarke shook her head with a smile. "And you say that Phoenix girls are lunatics." She gestured toward the thin blanket draped over Thalia. "May I?"

Thalia nodded, and Clarke pulled it back, trying to keep her face neutral as she unwrapped the bandage. The skin around the wound was red and swollen, and pus was forming in the gaps between the stitches. The wound itself wasn't the problem, Clarke knew. While it looked bad, it was the kind of injury they wouldn't bat an eye at in the medical center. The infection was the real threat.

"That bad?" Thalia asked quietly.

"Nah, you look great," Clarke said, the lie falling smoothly from her lips. Her eyes slid involuntarily toward the empty cot where a boy who died the day before had spent his final hours.

"That wasn't your fault," Thalia said quietly.

"I know." Clarke sighed. "I just wished he hadn't been alone."

"He wasn't. Wells was here."

"What?" Clarke asked, confused.

"He came to check on him a few times. I think the first time he came into the tent, he was looking for you, but once he saw how badly that boy was hurt . . ."

"Really?" Clarke asked, not quite sure whether to trust the observations of a girl who'd spent most of the past day unconscious.

"It was definitely him," another voice called. Clarke looked over and saw Octavia sitting up, a playful smile on her face. "It's not every day Wells Jaha comes and sits by your bed."

Clarke looked at her in disbelief. "How do you even know Wells?"

"He visited the care center with his father a few years ago. The girls were talking about it for weeks. He's kind of a supernova."

Clarke smiled at the Walden slang as Octavia continued. "I asked him if he remembered me. He said he did, but he's too much of a gentleman to say no." Octavia gave an exaggerated sigh and placed the back of her hand against her forehead. "Alas. My one chance at love."

"Hey, what about me?" A boy Clarke had thought was asleep shot Octavia an injured look, and she blew him a kiss.

Clarke just shook her head and turned back to Thalia,

her eyes traveling from her friend's face back to the infected wound.

"That's not a good sign, is it?" Thalia asked quietly, fatigue beginning to tug at the ragged edges of her voice.

"It could be worse."

"Your lying skills are slipping as well. What's going on?" She managed to raise an eyebrow. "Is love making you soft?"

Clarke stiffened and snatched her hand back from Thalia's blanket. "Are your injuries making you delirious?" She glanced over her shoulder and was relieved to see Octavia absorbed in conversation with the Arcadian boy. "You *know* what he did to me." She paused as her stomach churned with revulsion. "What he did to my *parents*."

"Of course I know." Thalia looked at Clarke with a mixture of frustration and pity. "But I also know what he risked to come here." She smiled. "He loves you, Clarke. The kind of love most people spend their whole lives looking for."

Clarke sighed. "Well, I hope, for your sake, that you never find it."

CHAPTER 10

Bellamy

It was crazy how much their surroundings could change throughout the day. In the mornings, everything felt crisp and new. Even the air had a sharpness to it. Yet in the afternoon, the light mellowed and the colors softened. That's what Bellamy liked best about Earth so far—the unexpectedness. Like a girl who kept you guessing. He'd always been drawn to the ones he couldn't quite figure out.

Laughter rose up from the far side of the clearing. Bellamy turned to see two girls perched on a low tree branch, giggling as they swatted at the boy attempting to climb up and join them. Nearby, a bunch of Walden boys were playing a game of keep-away with an Arcadian girl's shoe, the owner of which was laughing as she skidded barefoot across the grass. For a moment, he felt a twinge of regret that Octavia still wasn't well enough to join in—she'd had so little fun in her life. But then again, it was probably best that she didn't form any real attachments. As soon as her ankle healed, she and Bellamy would be off for good.

Bellamy tore open a crumpled nutrition pack, squeezed half the contents into his mouth, then slipped the carefully folded wrapper back into his pocket. After sorting through the remainder of the wreckage, they'd discovered what they'd all feared: The few weeks' worth of nutrition packets they'd found when they first landed was all they'd been sent with. Either the Council had assumed the hundred would figure out how to live off the land after a month . . . or they didn't plan on them surviving that long.

Graham had strong-armed most people into handing over any packs they'd salvaged and had supposedly put an Arcadian named Asher in charge of distributing them, but there was already a fledgling black market; people were trading nutrition packs for blankets and taking on extra water shifts in exchange for reserved spots inside the crowded tents. Wells had spent the day trying to get everyone to agree to a more formal system, and while some people had seemed interested, it hadn't taken Graham long to shut him down.

Bellamy turned as the laughter at the short end of the clearing gave way to shouts.

"Give that to me!" one of the Waldenites cried, trying to wrench something away from another. As Bellamy hurried over, he realized it was an ax. The first boy was holding the handle with both hands and was trying to swing it out of reach while the second boy attempted to grab on to the blade.

Others began to descend on the boys, but instead of pulling them apart, they darted between the trees, scooping items into their arms. Tools were scattered on the ground—more axes, knives, even spears. Bellamy smiled as his eyes landed on a bow and arrow.

Just this morning, he'd found animal prints—goddamn real tracks, leading into the trees. His discovery had caused a huge commotion. At one point, there'd been at least three dozen people gathered around, all making intelligent, helpful observations like *It's probably not a bird* and *It looks like it has four legs*. Finally, Bellamy had been the one to point out that they were hooves, not paws, which meant that it was probably an herbivore, and therefore something they could conceivably catch and eat. He'd just been waiting for something to hunt with, and now, in his first stroke of good luck on Earth, he had it. Hopefully he and Octavia would be long gone before the nutrition packets ran out, but he wasn't taking any chances.

"Hold it, everyone," a voice rang out over the crowd. Bellamy glanced up as Wells reached the tree line. "We can't just let random people carry weapons. We need to sort and organize these, and *then* decide who should have them."

A flurry of snorts and defiant glares rose up from the crowd.

"That guy took the Chancellor hostage," Wells went on, pointing at Bellamy, who'd already swung the bow and arrows over his shoulder. "Who knows what else he's capable of. You want someone like *him* walking around carrying a deadly weapon?" Wells raised his chin. "We should at least put it to a vote."

Bellamy couldn't help but laugh. Who the hell did this kid think he was, anyway? He reached down, picked a knife up off the ground, and began walking toward Wells.

Wells stood his ground, and Bellamy wondered if he was trying not to flinch, or if maybe Wells was less of a pushover than Bellamy had thought. Just when it seemed like he might stab Wells in the chest, Bellamy flipped the weapon so that the handle faced Wells, and pushed it into his hand.

"Breaking news, pretty boy." Bellamy winked. "We're all criminals here."

But before he had time to respond, Graham sauntered over. As he looked from Wells to Bellamy, a wry smile flickered across his face.

"I agree with the right honorable mini-Chancellor," Graham said. "We should lock up the weapons."

Bellamy took a step back. "What? And put you in charge of those as well?" He ran his finger along the bow. "No way. I'm ready to hunt."

Graham snorted. "And what exactly did you hunt back on Walden except for girls with low standards and even lower self-esteem?"

Bellamy stiffened but didn't say anything. It was a waste of time to rise to Graham's bait, but he could feel his fingers clenching.

"Or maybe you don't even have to chase after them," Graham continued. "I suppose that's the benefit to having a sister."

With a sickening crunch, Bellamy's fist sank into Graham's jaw. Graham staggered back a few steps, too stunned to raise his arms before Bellamy landed another punch. Then he righted himself and struck Bellamy with a powerful, well-aimed shot to the chin. Bellamy lunged forward with a growl, using his whole body weight to send Graham flying backward. He landed on the grass with a heavy thud, but just when Bellamy was about to deliver a swift kick, Graham rolled to the side and knocked Bellamy's legs out from under him.

Bellamy thrashed around, trying to sit up in time to gain leverage over his opponent, but it was too late. Graham had him pinned to the ground and was holding something just above his face, something that glinted in the sun. A knife.

"That's *enough*," Wells shouted. He grabbed Graham by the collar and flung him off Bellamy, who rolled over onto his side, wheezing.

"What the hell?" Graham bellowed, scrambling to his feet.

Bellamy winced as he rose onto his knees and then slowly stood up and walked over to pick up the bow. He shot a quick glance at Graham, who was too busy glaring at Wells to notice.

"Just because the Chancellor used to tuck you into bed doesn't mean you're automatically in charge," Graham spat. "I don't care what Daddy told you before we left."

"I have no interest in being in *charge*. I just want to make sure we don't *die*."

Graham exchanged a glance with Asher. "If that's your concern, then I suggest you mind your own business." He reached down and scooped up the knife. "We wouldn't want there to be any accidents."

"That's not how we're going to do things here," Wells said, holding his ground.

"Yeah?" Graham raised his eyebrows. "And what makes you think you have any say over that?"

"Because I'm not an idiot. But if you're anxious to become the first thug to try to kill someone on Earth in centuries, be my guest."

Bellamy exhaled as he crossed the clearing toward the area where he'd seen the animal tracks. He didn't need to get pulled into a pissing contest, not when there was food to find. He swung the bow over his shoulder and stepped into the woods.

As he'd learned at a young age, if you wanted to get something done, you had to do it yourself.

Bellamy had been eight years old during the first visit.

His mother hadn't been home, but she'd told him exactly what to do. The guards rarely inspected their unit. Many of them had grown up nearby, and while the recruits liked showing off their uniforms and hassling their former rivals, investigating their neighbors' flats felt like crossing the line. But it was obvious the officer in charge of this regiment wasn't a local. It wasn't just his snooty accent. It was the way he'd looked around their tiny flat with a mixture of surprise and disgust, like he couldn't imagine human beings living there.

He'd come in without knocking while Bellamy had been trying to clean the breakfast dishes. They only had running water a few hours a day, generally while his mother was working in the solar fields. Bellamy was so startled, he dropped the cup he was cleaning and watched in horror as it bounced on the floor and rolled toward the closet.

The officer's eyes darted back and forth as he read something off his cornea slip. "Bellamy Blake?" he said in his weird Phoenix accent that made it sound like his mouth was full of nutrition paste. Bellamy nodded slowly. "Is your mother home?"

"No," he said, working hard to keep his voice steady, just like he'd practiced.

Another guard stepped through the door. After a nod from the officer, he began asking questions in a dull, flat tone that suggested he'd given the same speech a dozen times already that day.

"Do you have more than three meals' worth of food in your residence?" he droned. Bellamy shook his head. "Do you have an energy source other than . . ."

Bellamy's heart was beating so loudly, it seemed to drown out the guard's voice. Although his mother had drilled him countless times, practicing any number of scenarios, he never imagined the way the officer's eyes would move around their flat. When his eyes landed on the dropped cup then moved to the closet, Bellamy thought his chest was going to explode.

"Are you going to answer his question?"

Bellamy looked up and saw both men staring at him. The officer was scowling impatiently, and the other guard just looked bored.

Bellamy started to apologize, but his "Sorry" came out like a wheeze.

"Do you have any permanent residents other than the two people registered for this unit?"

Bellamy took a deep breath. "No," he said, forcing the word out. He finally remembered to affect the annoyed expression his mother had him practice in the mirror.

The officer raised one eyebrow. "So sorry to have wasted your time," he said with mock cordiality. With a final glance around the flat, he strode out, followed by the guard, who slammed the door shut behind him.

Bellamy sank to his knees, too terrified to answer the question rattling through his mind: What would have happened if they'd looked in the closet?

CHAPTER 11

Glass

As she trailed behind Cora and Huxley on their way to the Exchange, Glass found herself wishing that her mother had waited a few more days before spreading the news of her pardon. At first, she'd been overjoyed to see her friends. When they'd walked through her door that morning, all three girls had burst into sobs. But now, watching Cora and Huxley exchange knowing smiles as they passed a boy Glass didn't recognize, she felt more alone than she ever had in her cell.

"I bet you have a ton of points saved up," Huxley said as she wrapped her arm around Glass. "I'm jealous."

"All I have is what my mother transferred to me this

morning." Glass gave her a weak smile. "The rest were eliminated after my arrest."

Huxley shuddered dramatically. "I still can't believe it." She lowered her voice. "You never did tell us why you were Confined."

"She doesn't want to talk about that," Cora said as she glanced nervously over her shoulder.

No, you *don't want to talk about that,* Glass thought as they turned onto the main B deck corridor, a long, wide passage bordered by panoramic windows on one side and benches tucked between artificial plants on the other. It was midday, and most of the benches were occupied by women her mother's age talking and sipping sunflower root tea. Technically, you were supposed to use ration points at the tea stand, but Glass couldn't remember the last time she'd been asked to scan her thumb. It was just one of the many small luxuries of life on Phoenix that she'd never given a second thought until she started spending time with Luke.

As the girls strode down the corridor, Glass could feel nearly every pair of eyes turn to her. Her stomach twisted as she wondered what had been more shocking—the fact that she'd been Confined or the fact that she'd been pardoned. She held her head up high and tried to look confident as she walked past. Glass was supposed to be an example of the Colony's sense of justice, and she would have to keep face as though her life depended on it. Because this time, it did.

"Do you think there's any chance Clarke will get pardoned too?" Huxley asked as Cora shot her a warning look. "Did you guys ever like, hang out, while you were in Confinement?"

"Oh my god, Huxley, will you give it a rest?" Cora said, touching Glass's arm in a supportive gesture. "Sorry," she said. "It's just that, when Clarke was sentenced just after you, nobody could believe it: two Phoenix girls in a few months? And then when you came back, there were all these rumors. . . ."

"It's fine," Glass said, forcing a smile to signal that she was okay talking about it. "Clarke got put into solitary pretty quickly, so I didn't see her much. And I don't know whether she'll be pardoned," she lied, remembering her mom's imperative that she not talk about the Earth mission. "I'm not sure when she turns eighteen—my case was reevaluated since it's almost my birthday."

"Oh, right, your birthday!" Huxley squealed, clapping her hands. "I forgot it's coming up. We'll have to find you something at the Exchange."

Cora nodded, seeming overjoyed to have found their way back to such an acceptable topic, as the girls approached their destination.

The Phoenix Exchange was in a large hall at the end of

B deck. In addition to panoramic windows, it held an enormous chandelier that had supposedly been evacuated from the Paris Opera house hours before the first bomb fell on Western Europe. Whenever Glass heard the tale, she felt a twinge of sadness for the people who might've been saved instead, but she couldn't deny that the chandelier was breathtaking. Dancing with reflected light from the ceiling and the windows, it looked like a small cluster of stars, a miniature galaxy spinning and shimmering overhead.

Huxley let go of Glass's arm and dashed over to a display of ribbons, oblivious to the nearby group of girls who'd fallen silent at Glass's arrival. Glass blushed and hurried after Cora, whose eyes were trained on a textile booth near the back wall.

She stood awkwardly next to Cora while her friend rummaged through the fabric, quickly reducing the orderly stack into a messy pile while the Walden woman behind the table gave her a tight smile. "Look at all this crap," Cora muttered as she flung a piece of burlap and a few strips of fleece to the side.

"What are you looking for?" Glass asked, running her finger along a tiny scrap of pale-pink silk. It was beautiful, even with the rust marks and water stains along the edges, but it would be impossible to find enough matching pieces for a small evening bag, let alone a dress.

"I've spent a million years collecting scraps of blue satin, and I finally have enough for the slip, but I need to layer something over it so it doesn't look too patchworky." Cora wrinkled her nose as she examined a large piece of clear vinyl. "How much is this?"

"Six," the Walden woman said.

"You're not serious." Cora rolled her eyes at Glass. "It's a *shower curtain*."

"It's Earthmade."

Cora snickered. "Authenticated by who?"

"How about this?" Glass asked, holding up a piece of blue netting. It looked like it had once been part of a storage bag, but no one would be able to tell once it was applied to the dress.

"Oooh," Cora cooed, snatching it out of Glass's hand. "I like it." She held it against her body to check the length, then smiled up at Glass. "Good thing your time in Confinement didn't affect your fashion sense." Glass stiffened but said nothing. "So, what are you going to wear?"

"To what?"

"To the viewing party," she said, enunciating her syllables as one might do with a small child. "For the comet?"

"Sorry." Glass shrugged. Apparently, spending six months in Confinement was no excuse for failing to keep up with the Phoenix social calendar.

"Your mother didn't tell you about it when you got back?" Cora continued, holding the netting around her waist like a petticoat. "There's a comet on track to pass right by the ship—the closest any has come since the Colony was founded."

"And there's a viewing party?"

Cora nodded. "On the observation deck. They've been making all sorts of exceptions so there can be food, drinks, music, everything. I'm going with Vikram." She grinned, but then her face fell. "I'm sure he won't mind if you come along. He knows there are, well, extenuating circumstances." She gave Glass a sympathetic smile and turned back to the Walden woman. "How much?"

"Nine."

Suddenly, Glass's head began to pound. She murmured an excuse to Cora, who was still negotiating with the shop-keeper, and wandered off to look at the display of jewelry on a nearby table. She brushed her fingers absently along her bare throat. She'd always worn a necklace chip, the device some girls on Phoenix chose as an alternative to earbuds or cornea slips. It was fashionable to have the chip embedded in a piece of jewelry, if you were lucky enough to have a relic in the family or managed to find something at the Exchange.

Her eyes traveled over the glittering assemblage and a glint of gold caught her eye—an oval locket on a delicate chain. Glass inhaled sharply as a wave of pain crashed over her, filling every inch of her body with a throbbing mix of grief and sorrow. She knew she should turn away and keep walking, but she couldn't help it.

Glass reached out a trembling arm and picked up the necklace. The outline blurred as tears filled her eyes. She ran her finger carefully over the carving in the back, knowing without having to look that it was an ornate cursive *G.*

"Are you sure you don't mind spending your birthday on Walden?" Luke asked, leaning his head back next to hers on the couch. The look of concern on his face was so sincere, it almost made her laugh.

"How many times do I have to tell you?" Glass swung her legs up so they were lying across Luke's. "There's nowhere else I'd rather be."

"But didn't your mom want to throw you some fancy party?"

Glass rested her head on her shoulder. "Yes, but what's the point if you can't be there?"

"I don't want you giving up your whole life just because I can't be a part of it." Luke ran his fingers down Glass's arm, suddenly serious. "Do you ever wish we hadn't stopped you that night?"

As a member of the prestigious mechanical engineering unit, Luke wasn't normally assigned to checkpoint duty, but he'd been called in one evening when Glass had been hurrying back from studying with Wells.

"Are you kidding?" She raised her head to kiss his cheek. The taste of his skin was enough to make her whole body tingle, and she moved her lips down, tracing the line of his jaw up to his ear. "Breaking curfew that night was the best decision I've ever made," she whispered, smiling as he shuddered slightly.

The curfew wasn't strictly enforced on Phoenix, but she'd been stopped by a pair of guards. One of them had given Glass a hard time, forcing her to provide a thumb scan and then asking hostile questions. Eventually, the other guard had stepped in and insisted on escorting Glass the rest of the way.

"Walking you home was the best decision I ever made," he murmured. "Although it was torture trying to keep myself from kissing you that night."

"Well, then, we'd better make up for lost time now," Glass teased, moving her lips back to his. Her kisses grew more urgent as he placed his hand on the back of her head and wove his fingers through her hair. Glass shifted until she was sitting mostly in Luke's lap, feeling his other arm move down to her waist to keep her from falling.

"I love you," he whispered in her ear. No matter how many times she heard the words, they never ceased to make her shiver.

She pulled away just long enough to breathe, "I love you too," then kissed him again, running her hand lightly down his side and then resting her fingers on the sliver of skin between his shirt and his belt.

"We should take a break," Luke said, gently pushing her hand to the side. Over the past few weeks, it'd become increasingly difficult to keep things from progressing too far.

"I don't want to." Glass gave him a coy smile and returned her lips to his ear. "And it's *my* birthday."

Luke laughed, then groaned as he rose to his feet with Glass in his arms.

"Put me down!" Glass giggled, kicking her feet in the air. "What are you doing?"

Luke took a few steps forward. "Taking you to the Exchange. I'm trading you in for a girl who won't try so hard to get me in trouble."

"*Hey.*" She huffed with mock indignation, then started pounding her fists into his chest. "Put me down!"

He turned away from the door. "Are you going to behave yourself?"

"What? It's not *my* fault you're too hot to keep my hands off of."

"Glass," he warned.

"Fine. Yes, I promise."

"Good." He walked back to the couch and laid her gently back down. "Because it'd be a shame if I couldn't give you your present."

"What is it?" Glass asked, pushing herself up into a seated position.

"A chastity belt," Luke said gravely. "For me. I found it at the Exchange. It cost a fortune, but it's worth it to protect—"

Glass smacked him in the chest. Luke laughed and wrapped his arms around her. "Sorry," he said with a grin. He reached into his pocket then paused. "It's not wrapped or anything."

"That's okay."

He pulled something out of his pocket and extended his arm toward her. A gold locket glittered on his palm.

"Luke, it's beautiful," Glass whispered, reaching out to take the locket. Her eyes widened as her fingers ran along its delicate edges. "This is Earthmade." She looked up at him in surprise.

He nodded. "Yes, at least, it's supposed to be, according to the records." He picked it up out of her hand. "May I?"

Glass nodded, and Luke stepped behind her to fasten the clasp. She shivered at the touch of his hand on her neck as he brushed her hair to the side. She could only imagine how much something like this cost—Luke must have used his entire savings on it. Even as a guard, he didn't have many ration points to spare.

"I love it," Glass said, running her finger along the chain as she turned to face him.

His smile lit up his whole face. "I'm so glad." Luke ran his hand down her neck and turned the locket over, revealing a *G* etched into the gold.

"Did you do that?" Glass asked.

Luke nodded. "Even in a thousand years, I want people to

know that it belonged to you." He pressed his finger against the locket, pushing the metal against her skin. "Now you just have to fill it with your own memories."

Glass smiled. "I know what memory I want to start with." She looked up, expecting to see Luke roll his eyes, but his face was serious. Their eyes met, and for a long moment, the flat was silent except for the sound of their beating hearts.

"Are you sure?" Luke asked, his brow furrowing slightly as he ran a finger along the inside of her arm.

"More sure than I've been of anything in my life."

Luke took Glass's hand, and a current of electricity shot through her. He squeezed his fingers around hers and, without a word, led her toward his bedroom.

Of course he'd traded it, Glass told herself. It'd be ridiculous to keep such a valuable item, especially after she'd broken his heart. Yet the thought of her discarded necklace languishing alone in the Exchange unleashed a pang of grief that threatened to rip her heart in two. A prickle on the back of her neck pulled Glass from her thoughts. She braced herself, expecting to see another vague acquaintance staring at her with open suspicion. But when she turned around, her eyes landed on someone else entirely.

Luke.

He stared at her just long enough for Glass to blush, then

broke away as his eyes flitted toward the table. An odd expression crossed his face as his gaze landed on the necklace. "I'm surprised no one's snatched it up yet," he said quietly. "It's so beautiful." His arm dropped back to his side, and he turned around to give her a small, sad smile. "But then again, the beautiful ones can hurt you the most."

"Luke," Glass began, "I—" But then she noticed a familiar figure behind Luke. Camille stood behind the counter of the paper texts stall, her eyes fixed on Glass.

Luke glanced over his shoulder and then turned back to Glass. "Camille's covering for her father. He's been sick."

"I'm sorry," Glass said. But before she had time to say anything else, she was distracted by the sound of raised voices.

Glass turned and saw Cora shouting at the Walden woman. "If you refuse to charge me a reasonable price, then I'll have no choice but to report you for fraud." The woman paled and said something Glass couldn't hear, but apparently, it was to Cora's liking, because she smiled and held her thumb up to be scanned.

Glass grimaced, embarrassed by her friend's behavior. "Sorry—I should go."

"Don't," Luke pleaded, touching her arm. "I've been worried about you." He lowered his voice. "What are you doing here? Is it safe?"

The concern in his voice filled some of the smaller cracks

in her battered heart, but not enough to make the pain go away. "It's safe. I was pardoned, actually," Glass said, trying hard to keep her voice steady.

"Pardoned?" His eyes widened. "Wow. I never thought . . . That's incredible." He paused, as if unsure how to go on. "You know, you never told me why you were Confined in the first place."

Glass cast her eyes toward the ground, fighting an overwhelming urge to tell Luke the truth. *He deserves to be happy*, she reminded herself firmly. *He's not yours anymore.*

"It doesn't matter," she said finally. "I just want to put it all behind me."

Luke stared at her, and for a moment Glass wondered if he could see straight through her. "Well, take care of yourself," he said finally.

Glass nodded. "I will." She knew she was doing the right thing, for once. She just wished it didn't hurt so much.

CHAPTER 12

Clarke

Clarke sat in the dark infirmary tent, watching nervously as Thalia tossed and turned in her sleep, restless from the fever that set in as the infection grew worse.

"What do you think she's dreaming about?"

Clarke turned and saw Octavia sitting up, staring at Thalia wide-eyed.

"I'm not sure," Clarke lied. From the expression on Thalia's face, Clarke could tell she was thinking about her father again. She'd been Confined for trying to steal medicine after the Council had weighed against treating him; with limited medical supplies, they'd deemed his prospects too grim to be worth the resources. Thalia still didn't know what happened to him—whether he'd succumbed to his disease after her arrest, or whether he was still clinging to life, praying that he'd get to see his daughter again someday.

Thalia moaned and curled into a ball, reminding Clarke of Lilly on one of her bad nights, when Clarke would sneak into the lab so her friend wouldn't have to be alone. Although no one was keeping Clarke from helping Thalia, she felt just as frantic, just as helpless. Unless they found the medicine that had been flung from the dropship, there was nothing she could do to ease her suffering.

The flap flew open, flooding the tent with light and cool, pungent air, and Bellamy tumbled in. He had a bow slung over his shoulder, and his eyes were bright. "Good afternoon, ladies," he said with a grin as he strode over to Octavia's cot. He stooped down to ruffle her hair, which was still secured with a neatly tied red ribbon. He was close enough that Clarke couldn't help but notice the faint smell of sweat clinging to his skin, blending with another scent she couldn't identify but that made her think of trees.

"How's the ankle?" he asked Octavia, making an exaggerated show of squinting and examining it from all angles.

She flexed it gingerly. "Much better." She turned to Clarke. "Am I ready to leave yet?"

Clarke hesitated. Octavia's ankle was still fragile, and there was no way of making an effective brace. If she put too much pressure on it, she'd sprain it all over again, or worse.

Octavia sighed, then stuck her bottom lip out in a pleading expression. "Please? I didn't come all the way to Earth to sit in a *tent*."

"*You* didn't have a choice," Bellamy said. "But *I* certainly didn't risk my ass coming here just to watch you get gangrene."

"How do you know about gangrene?" Clarke asked, surprised. No one would ever have developed that kind of infection back on the Colony, and she doubted many other people read ancient medical texts for fun.

"You disappoint me, Doctor." He raised an eyebrow. "I didn't take you for one of those."

"One of those what?"

"One of those Phoenicians who assume all Waldenites are illiterate."

Octavia rolled her eyes as she turned to Bellamy. "Not *everything* is an insult, you know."

Bellamy opened his mouth, but then thought better of it and folded his lips into a smirk. "You better watch it, or I'll leave without you." He adjusted the bow on his shoulder.

"Don't leave me," she said, suddenly serious. "You know how I feel about being trapped inside."

A strange expression flashed across Bellamy's face, and Clarke wondered what he was thinking about. Finally, he smiled. “Okay. I’ll take you outside, but just for a little bit. I want to try hunting again before it gets dark.” He turned to Clarke. “That is, if the doctor says it’s okay.”

Clarke nodded. “Just be careful.” She gave him a quizzical look. “Do you really think you’ll be able to *hunt*?” No one had seen a mammal yet, let alone tried to kill one.

“Someone has to. Our nutrition packs won’t last a week at the rate they’re going.”

She gave him a small smile. “Well, best of luck.” Clarke walked over to Octavia’s cot and helped Bellamy lift her to her feet.

“I’m fine,” Octavia said, balancing on one foot as she clutched Bellamy’s arm. She hopped forward, pulling him toward the flap. “Let’s go!”

Bellamy twisted to look back over his shoulder. “Oh, by the way, Clarke, I found some debris from the crash when I was out in the woods. Any interest in checking it out tomorrow?”

Clarke inhaled as her heart sped up. “You think it could be the missing supplies?” She took a step forward. “Let’s go now.”

Bellamy shook his head. “It was too far away. We wouldn’t make it back before dark. We’ll go tomorrow.”

She glanced at Thalia, whose face was still contorted in pain. “Okay. First thing in the morning.”

“Let’s wait until the afternoon. I’ll be hunting in the

morning. That's when the animals are out looking for water." Clarke suppressed the urge to ask him where he'd learned that, although she couldn't quite mask the surprise on her face. "Until tomorrow, then?" Bellamy asked, and Clarke nodded. "Great." He grinned. "It's a date."

She watched them lumber out of the tent, then went back over to Thalia. Her friend's eyes fluttered open. "Hi," she said weakly.

"How are you feeling?" Clarke asked, moving to check Thalia's vital signs.

"Great," she croaked. "Just about ready to join Bellamy on his next hunting expedition."

Clarke smiled. "I thought you were sleeping."

"I was. Off and on."

"I'm just going to take a quick look, okay?" Clarke asked, and Thalia nodded. Clarke pushed the blanket aside and lifted Thalia's shirt. Streaks of red radiated out from the oozing wound, suggesting that the infection was making its way into her bloodstream.

"Does it hurt?"

"No," Thalia said hollowly. They both knew she wasn't getting any better.

"Can you believe they're really siblings?" Clarke asked, purposefully changing the subject as she replaced Thalia's blanket.

"Yeah, it's crazy to think about." Thalia's voice grew slightly stronger.

"What's crazy is pulling a stunt like that on the launch deck," Clarke said. "But it was really brave. They would've killed him if they'd caught him." She paused. "They'll kill him when they come down."

"He's done a lot to keep her safe," Thalia agreed, turning her face away from Clarke in an attempt to hide a grimace as a new wave of pain washed over her. "He really loves you, you know."

"Who? *Bellamy?*" Clarke asked, startled.

"No. Wells. He came to *Earth* for you, Clarke."

She pressed her lips together. "I didn't ask him to."

"We've all done things we're not proud of," Thalia said, her voice quiet.

Clarke shuddered and closed her eyes. "I'm not asking anyone for forgiveness."

"That's not what I mean, and you know it." Thalia paused to catch her breath. The effort it took to speak was wearing her out.

"You need to rest," Clarke said, reaching over to pull the blanket up over her friend's shoulders. "We can talk about this tomorrow."

"*No*!" Thalia exclaimed. "Clarke, what happened wasn't your fault."

"Of course it was my fault." Clarke refused to meet her friend's gaze. Thalia was the only one who knew what Clarke had really done, and Clarke couldn't bear to face that right now, to see the memory reflected in her friend's dark, expressive eyes. "And what does it have to do with Wells anyway?"

Thalia closed her eyes and sighed, ignoring the question. "You need to let yourself be happy. Or else, what's the point of anything?"

Clarke opened her mouth to launch a retort, but the words disappeared as she watched Thalia lean over, suddenly coughing. "It'll be okay," Clarke whispered, running her hand through her friend's sweat-dampened hair. "You'll be okay."

This time, the words weren't a prayer but a declaration. Clarke refused to let Thalia die, and nothing was going to stop her. She wouldn't let her best friend join the chorus of ghosts in her head.

CHAPTER 13

Wells

Wells looked up at the star-filled sky. He never imagined how homesick it would make him to stare at the familiar scene from hundreds of kilometers away. It was unsettling to see the moon so tiny and featureless, like waking up to find that your family's faces had been erased.

Sitting at the campfire around him, the others were grumbling. They'd been on Earth less than a week, and already their rations were dwindling. The fact that they had no medicine was troubling, but right now the bigger concern was the food supply. Either the Colony miscalculated their provisions, or Graham and his friends had been hoarding more than he'd realized. Either way, the effects were already beginning to show. It wasn't just the hollows forming under their cheekbones—there was a hunger in their eyes that terrified Wells. He could never let himself forget that they'd all been Confined for a reason, that everyone surrounding him had done something to endanger the Colony.

Wells most of all.

Just then, Clarke emerged from the infirmary tent and walked toward the campfire, her eyes skimming the circle as she searched for a spot. There was an empty space next to Wells, but her gaze skipped right over him. She sat beside Octavia, who was perched on a log, her injured leg stretched out in front of her.

Wells sighed as he turned to look around the clearing, the flames flickering on the dark forms of the three tents they'd finally built—the infirmary, a structure to hold supplies, and Wells's personal favorite, a ditch for collecting water, in case it ever rained. At least their camp wasn't turning out to be a complete failure. His father would be impressed when he joined them on Earth.

If he joined them. It was becoming harder and harder to convince himself that his father was fine, that the bullet wound was only superficial. His chest tightened painfully as he thought of his father clinging to life in a hospital bed, or worse, his body floating somewhere through space. His father's words still rang in his ears: *If anyone can make this mission a success, it's you.* After a lifetime of urging Wells to work harder and do better, he wondered if the Chancellor might have given his last order to his son.

A strange noise came from the trees. Wells sat up straighter, all his senses on the alert. There was a cracking sound, followed by a rustling. The murmurs by the fire turned to gasps as a strange shape materialized out of the shadows, part human, part animal, like something from the ancient myths.

Wells leapt to his feet. But then the creature moved past the tree line and into the light.

Bellamy stood with an animal carcass draped over his shoulders, a trail of blood in his wake.

A deer. Wells's eyes traveled over the lifeless animal, taking in its soft brown fur, spindly legs, delicately tapered ears. As Bellamy moved toward them, the deer's head swayed back and forth from its limp neck—but it never made a full arc, because each time it swung back, it knocked against something else.

It was another head, swinging from another slender neck. *The deer had two heads.*

Wells froze as everyone around the fire scrambled to their feet, some of them inching forward for a better look, others backing up in terror. "Is it safe?" one girl asked.

"It's safe." Clarke's voice came from the shadows, and then

she stepped into the light. "The radiation might have mutated the genetic material hundreds of years ago, but there wouldn't be any trace of it now."

Everyone fell silent as Clarke stretched out her hand to stroke the creature's fur. Standing in a pool of moonlight, she never looked so beautiful.

Clarke turned to Bellamy with a smile that made Wells's stomach twist. "We're not going to starve." Then she said something Wells couldn't hear, and Bellamy nodded.

Wells exhaled, willing his resentment to drain away. He took another deep breath before walking toward Bellamy and Clarke. She stiffened as he approached, but Wells forced himself to keep his eyes on Bellamy. "Thank you," Wells said. "This will feed a lot of people."

Bellamy stared at him questioningly as he shifted his weight from one foot to the other.

"I mean it," Wells said. "Thanks."

Finally, Bellamy nodded. Wells went back to his place by the fire, leaving Bellamy and Clarke to talk quietly, their heads bowed together.

The observation deck was completely empty. Staring out into the immeasurably vast sea of stars, Wells could easily imagine that they were the only two living things in the entire universe. He tightened his arm around Clarke. She pressed her head against his chest and exhaled, sinking closer to him as the air left her body. As if she was happy to let him breathe for them both.

"How'd it go today?" she murmured.

"Fine," Wells said, not sure why he was bothering to lie when Clarke was pressed against his chest. She could read his heartbeat like it was Morse code.

"What happened?" she asked, concern flickering in her large green eyes.

His officer training entailed periodic trips to Walden and Arcadia to monitor the guards. Today, he'd observed them seize a woman who'd gotten pregnant with an unregistered child. There'd be no chance at lenience. She would be Confined until she gave birth, the child would be placed in the Council's care, and the mother would be executed. The law was harsh but necessary. The ship could only support a certain number of lives, and allowing anyone to disrupt the delicate balance would jeopardize the entire race. But the look of panic in the woman's eyes as the guards had dragged her away was burned into Wells's brain.

Surprisingly, it'd been his father who helped Wells make sense of what he'd seen. That night at dinner, he'd sensed something was wrong, and Wells had told him about the incident, trying to sound soldierly and detached. But his father had seen through the act and, in a rare gesture, put his hand over Wells's across the table. "What we do isn't easy," he'd told his son, "but it's crucial.

We can't afford to let our feelings keep us from doing our duty—keeping the human race alive."

"Let me guess," Clarke said, interrupting his thoughts. "You arrested some criminal mastermind for stealing books from the library."

"Nope." He swept a piece of hair behind her ear. "She's still at large. They're forming a special task force as we speak."

She smiled, and the flecks of gold in her eyes seemed to sparkle. He couldn't imagine a prettier color.

Wells turned his attention back to the enormous window. Tonight, the clouds covering Earth didn't remind him of a shroud—they were merely a blanket. The planet hadn't died, it'd only slipped into an enchanted sleep until the time came for it to welcome humanity home.

"What are you thinking about?" Clarke asked. "Is it your mom?"

"No," he said slowly. "Not really." Wells reached out and absentmindedly wrapped a lock of Clarke's hair around his finger, then let it fall back to her shoulder. "Though I guess, in a way, I'm always thinking about her." It was hard to believe that she was really gone.

"I just want to make sure she's proud of me, wherever she is," Wells continued, a chill passing over him as he glanced toward the stars.

Clarke squeezed his hand, transferring her warmth to him.

"Of course she's proud of you. Any mother would be proud of a son like you."

Wells turned back to Clarke with a grin. "Just mothers?"

"I imagine you're a hit with grandparents, too." She nodded gravely, but then giggled when Wells playfully smacked her shoulder.

"There's someone else I want to make proud."

Clarke raised an eyebrow. "She'd better watch her back," she said, reaching out to wrap her hands behind Wells's head. "Because I'm not very good at sharing."

Wells grinned as he leaned forward and closed his eyes, brushing his lips against hers for a teasing kiss before moving down to her neck. "Neither am I," he whispered into her ear, feeling her shiver as his breath tickled her skin. She pulled him closer, her touch melting away the tension until he forgot about his day, forgot that he'd have to repeat it all tomorrow and the day after that. All that mattered was the girl in his arms.

The smell of the roasting deer was foreign and intoxicating. There was no meat on the Colony, not even on Phoenix. All the livestock had been eliminated in the middle of the first century.

"How do we know when it's done?" an Arcadian girl named Darcy asked Wells.

"When the outside starts to crisp and the inside turns pink," Bellamy called without turning his head.

Graham snorted, but Wells nodded. "I think you're right."

After the meat cooled, they chopped it into smaller pieces and began passing it around the fire. Wells carried some to the other side of the circle, distributing it to the crowd.

He handed a piece to Octavia, who held it in front of her as she looked up at Wells. "Have you tried it yet?"

Wells shook his head. "Not yet."

"Well, *that's* not fair." She raised her eyebrows. "What if it turns out to be disgusting?"

He glanced around the circle. "Everyone else seems to be okay with it."

Octavia pursed her lips together. "I'm not like everyone else." She looked at him for a moment, as if waiting for him to speak, then smiled and pushed her piece toward him. "Here, you take the first bite and tell me what you think."

"I'm okay, thanks," Wells said. "I want to make sure everyone else—"

"Come on." She giggled as she tried to slip it into his mouth. "Take a bite."

Wells snuck a quick glance around the circle to make sure Clarke hadn't been watching. She wasn't—she was caught up in conversation with Bellamy.

Wells turned back to Octavia. "Okay," he said, taking the

piece of meat from her hands. She looked disappointed not to feed it to him, but Wells didn't care. He took a bite. The outside was tough, but as his teeth sank in, the meat released a flood of flavor unlike anything Wells had tasted before, simultaneously salty and smoky and faintly sweet. He chewed some more and then swallowed, bracing for his stomach to reject the alien substance. But all he felt was warmth.

The kids who'd eaten first had risen from the fire and begun milling around the clearing, and for a few minutes, the soft hum of their conversation merged with the crackling of the flames. But then the sound of confused murmurs began to rise to the surface, making the skin on the back of Wells's neck prickle. He rose to his feet and walked over to where a group was standing near the tree line.

"What's going on?" he asked.

"*Look*." One of the girls pointed to something in the trees.

"What?" Wells squinted into the darkness.

"There," another girl said. "Did you see it?"

For a moment, Wells thought they were playing a trick on him, but then something caught his eye. A flash of light, so brief that he might have imagined it. There was another flash a few feet away, then another, this one a little higher up. He took a step toward the edge of the clearing, which was now ablaze with glowing lights, as if invisible hands had decorated it for a party. His eyes landed on the closest orb, a ball of light hanging from the lowest branch of a nearby tree.

There was something moving inside. A creature. It was some sort of insect, with a tiny body and disproportionately large, delicate wings. The word fluttered to Wells's lips. *Butterfly.*

Some of the others had followed him into the forest and were now staring in wonder alongside him. "Clarke," he whispered into the darkness. She needed to see this. He tore his eyes away and spun around, ready to go run and find her. But she was already there.

Clarke stood a few feet away, utterly transfixed. A soft glow lit up her face, and the tense, worried expression that had clung to her features since the crash had fallen away.

"Hey," Wells said softly, not wanting to disrupt the stillness. He expected Clarke to scowl at him, or silence him, or walk away. But she didn't move. She stood right where she was, staring up at the luminous butterflies.

Wells didn't dare move or say another word. The girl he thought he'd lost was still in there, somewhere, and in that instant, he knew: He could make her love him again.

CHAPTER 14

Bellamy

Bellamy didn't know why the ancient humans even bothered doing drugs. What was the point of shooting junk into your veins when walking through the forest had the same effect? Something happened each time he crossed the tree line. As he moved away from the camp in the early morning sunlight, setting out on another hunting expedition, he began taking deeper breaths. His heart pounded with strong, slow, steady beats, his organs marching in time to a pulse in the ground. It was like someone had hacked into his brain and cranked up his senses to a setting Bellamy hadn't known existed.

But the best part was the quiet. The ship had never been completely silent. There was always a low hum of background noise: the drone of the generators, the buzz of the lights, the echo of footsteps in the hallway. It had freaked him out the first time he entered the forest, not having anything to drown out his thoughts. But the more time he spent here, the quieter his mind became.

Bellamy scanned the ground, his eyes skipping over the rocks and damp patches as they searched for clues. There were no tracks to follow as there'd been yesterday, but something told Bellamy to turn right, and go deeper into the forest where the trees grew thicker, covering the ground with strange shadows. That's where he would go if he were an animal.

He reached behind his shoulder to grab one of the arrows from the sling he'd constructed. Although it was terrible to watch them die, his aim had vastly improved over the past few days, so he knew the animals didn't suffer much. He'd never forget the pain and fear in the first deer's eyes as it staggered across the ground. Yet shooting an animal was less of a crime than a lot of the crap the other kids had done to end up here. While he might be cutting the creature's life short, Bellamy knew that it had lived every moment of that life completely free.

The hundred prisoners might have been promised their freedom, but Bellamy knew he wouldn't be afforded the same privilege, not after what he'd done to the Chancellor. If he was still around when the next ship landed, the first person off it would probably shoot him on the spot.

Bellamy was done with all of it—the punishments, the stations, the system. He was through following other people's rules. He was sick of having to fight to survive. Living in the forest wouldn't be easy, but at least he and Octavia would be free.

Holding his arms out for balance, he half shuffled, half skidded down the slope, trying his best to not make any noise that could scare an animal away. He landed at the bottom with a thud, mud squelching under his tattered boots. Bellamy winced as water sloshed through the gap above the soles. It would be uncomfortable walking back to camp with wet socks, something he'd learned the hard way. He wasn't sure why that wasn't mentioned in any of the books he read. What was the point of knowing how to build a snare out of vines, or which plants to use to treat burns, if you couldn't walk?

Bellamy laid his socks over a branch to dry, then dipped his feet into the stream. It was already hotter out than it had been when he left camp, and the cold water felt incredible on his skin. He rolled his pants up to his knees and waded in farther, grinning like a complete doofus as the water swirled around his calves. It was one of his favorite things about Earth, how mundane stuff like washing your feet suddenly felt like a huge deal.

The trees weren't as dense by the stream, and the sun shone brighter. Bellamy's face and arms suddenly felt unbearably hot. He pulled off his T-shirt, crumpled it into a ball, and tossed it onto the grass before reaching down to scoop water into his hands and splash it over his face. He smiled, still blown away by the revelation that water could have a *taste*. They'd always made crude jokes about the ship's recycled water supply, how you were basically drinking your great-grandfather's piss. Yet now he realized that the centuries of filtration and purification had stripped the liquid until it was no more than a collection of hydrogen and oxygen molecules. He reached down and cupped another handful. If he'd had to describe it, he would say it tasted like a combination of Earth and sky—and then he'd punch whoever laughed at him for it.

A crack sounded from inside the woods. Bellamy spun around so quickly, he lost his balance and fell backward with a splash. He quickly scrambled to his feet, rocks and mud shifting beneath his bare toes as he turned to look for the source of the sound.

"Sorry, I didn't mean to scare you."

Bellamy pushed his hair back and saw Clarke standing on the grass. It was startling to see someone else in the woods, which he'd come to think of as belonging exclusively to him. But the flash of irritation he was expecting never came. "You couldn't wait till afternoon?" he asked, making his way back to the bank.

Clarke blushed. "We need that medicine," she said as she looked away from his bare chest. She was so tough most of the time, it was easy to forget that she grew up in a world of fancy concerts and lecture parties. Bellamy grinned as he shook his head, sending droplets of water flying.

"*Hey*," she shouted, jumping backward as she tried to flick the water off. "We haven't tested this stream yet. That could be toxic."

"Since when did our badass surgeon become such a priss?" He sat down in a sunny patch of grass and patted the spot next to him in invitation.

"A *priss*?" Clarke lowered herself to the ground with a huff. "You could barely hold the knife last night, your hand was shaking so badly."

"Hey, I *killed* the deer. I think I did more than my fair share. Besides"—he paused as he lay back on the grass—"you're the one who's trained to cut things open."

"I'm not, really."

Bellamy brought his hands behind his head and tilted his face toward the sun, exhaling as the warmth seeped into his skin. It was almost as nice as being in bed with a girl. Maybe even better, because the sun would never ask him what he was thinking. "Sorry to insult you," he said, stretching out the words as a relaxed heaviness settled in his limbs. "I know you're a doctor, not a butcher."

"No, I mean I was Confined before I finished my apprenticeship."

The note of sorrow in her voice reverberated strangely in Bellamy's gut. He gave her a weak smile. "Well, you're doing a great job for a quack."

She stared at him, and for a second, he worried he'd offended her. But then she nodded and stood up. "You're right," she said. "Which is why we need to find that medicine. Come on."

Bellamy rose to his feet with a groan, slipped into his shoes and socks, then slung his shirt over his shoulder.

"I'd recommend putting your shirt back on."

"Why? Are you worried you won't be able to control yourself? Because if you're concerned about my virtue, I have to tell you, I'm not—"

"I meant"—she cut him off with a small smile—"there are some poisonous plants out here that could make that pretty back of yours erupt with pus-filled boils."

He shrugged. "For all I know, that might be your thing, doctor girl. I'll take my chances."

She laughed for what Bellamy was pretty sure was her first time on Earth. He felt a surprising flicker of pride that he'd been the one to make it happen.

"Okay," he said lightly, pulling his shirt over his head and smiling to himself when he caught Clarke's eyes on his stomach. "The wreckage was farther west. Let's go." He started walking up the slope, then turned to look at Clarke. "The direction the sun sets in."

She ran a few steps to catch up to him. "You taught yourself all of this?"

"I guess. There aren't a lot of lectures on Earth's geography on Walden." The statement didn't carry the bitterness it might have, had it been directed at Wells or Graham. "I'd always been interested in that stuff, and then when I found out they were planning on sending Octavia to Earth . . ." He paused, not sure how much it was safe to share. But Clarke was looking at him expectantly, her green eyes full of curiosity and something else he couldn't quite identify. "I figured, the more I knew, the better equipped I'd be to keep her safe."

They reached the top of the slope, but instead of heading back toward camp, Bellamy led them deeper into the woods. The trees grew so close together that their leaves blocked most of the sun. What little light made it through dappled the ground in golden pools. Bellamy smiled as he saw Clarke taking care to step around them, like a little kid trying to avoid the lines crossing the skybridge.

"This is how I imagined Sherwood Forest," she said, her

voice full of reverence. "I almost expect to see Robin Hood pop out from behind a tree."

"Robin Hood?"

"You know." She stopped to look at him. "The exiled prince who stole medicine to give to the orphans?" Bellamy stared at her blankly. "With the enchanted bow and arrows? You kind of remind me of him, now that I think about it," she added, smiling.

Bellamy ran his hand along a vine-covered branch that shimmered slightly in the dim light. "We don't get a lot of story time on Walden," he said stiffly. But then his voice softened. "There aren't many books, so I used to make up fairy tales for Octavia when she was little. Her favorite was about an enchanted trash can." He snorted. "It was the best I could do."

Clarke smiled. "It was brave, what you did for her," she said.

"Yeah, well, I'd say the same thing about you, but I have a feeling you're not exactly here by choice."

She held up her wrist, which, like all the others', was still encased in the monitor bracelet. "What gave it away?"

"I'm sure he deserved it," Bellamy said with a grin. But instead of laughing, Clarke turned away. He'd meant it as a joke, but he should have known that he couldn't be so glib with her—with anyone who was here, really. They were all hiding something. Bellamy most of all.

"Hey, I'm sorry," he said. He apologized so rarely, the word felt strange in his mouth. "We'll find the medicine chest. What's in it, anyway?"

"Everything. Sterile bandages, painkillers, antibiotics . . . things that could make all the difference to . . ." She paused for a moment. "To the injured people."

Bellamy knew she was thinking about the one girl she was always watching over, her friend.

"You really care about her, don't you?" He held out his hand to help her over a moss-covered log blocking their path.

"She's my best friend," Clarke said, taking his hand. "The only person on Earth who knows the real me."

She shot an embarrassed smile at Bellamy, but he nodded. "I know what you mean." Octavia was the only person in the world who truly knew him. There was no one else he really cared about ever seeing again.

But then he glanced over at Clarke, who was leaning over to breathe in the scent of a bright-pink flower, the sun catching the gold strands in her hair, and suddenly he wasn't so sure.

CHAPTER 15

Clarke

Bellamy led Clarke down a steep hill bordered by slender trees whose branches wove together to form a sort of archway. The silence felt ancient, as if even the wind hadn't dared to disturb the solitude of the trees for centuries.

"I'm not sure I ever thanked you for what you did for Octavia," Bellamy said, breaking the spell.

"Does this count as a thank-you?" Clarke teased.

"I think it's the closest you're going to get." He shot her a sidelong look. "I'm not the best at stuff like that."

Clarke opened her mouth, but before she could launch a retort, she stumbled over a rock. "Whoa there," Bellamy said with a laugh, grabbing Clarke's hand to steady her. "And apparently, you're not the best at stuff like *walking*."

"This isn't walking. This is *hiking*—something no human has done for hundreds of years, so give me a break."

"It's okay. It's all about division of labor. You keep us alive, and I'll keep you on two feet." He gave her a playful squeeze, and Clarke felt her face flush. She hadn't realized she was still clutching his hand.

"Thanks," she said, letting her arm fall to her side.

Bellamy paused as they reached the point where the ground flattened out again. "This way," he said, gesturing to the left. "So, how did you end up becoming a doctor?"

Clarke's eyebrows knit in confusion. "I wanted to. Didn't you choose to . . ." She trailed off, realizing, to her embarrassment, that she had no idea what Bellamy had done back on the ship. Clearly he hadn't been a guard.

He stared at her, as if trying to determine whether or not she was joking. "It doesn't work that way on Walden," he said slowly, stepping deeper into the green-tinged shade. "If you've got a great record and you get lucky, you can become a guard. Otherwise you just do whatever job your parents had."

Clarke tried to keep the surprise from registering on her face. Of course she knew only certain jobs were available to Waldenites, but she hadn't realized they had no choice at all. "So what were you?"

"I was . . ." He pressed his lips together. "You know what? It doesn't matter what I did back there."

"I'm sorry," Clarke said quickly. "I didn't mean that—"

"It's fine," Bellamy cut her off, taking a step forward. They continued walking, although now, the silence had an edge to it.

"Hold on," Bellamy whispered, reaching out a hand to block her path. In one fluid motion, he pulled out one of the arrows tucked into his sling and raised his bow. His eyes fixed on a spot where the trees were so dense, it was almost impossible to distinguish the shrubs from the shadows. Then she saw it—a flash of motion, a glint of light reflected in an eye. Clarke held her breath as an animal emerged, small and brown with long, tapered ears that flicked back and forth. A rabbit.

She watched the creature spring forward, its tail almost twice as long as its body, twitching curiously. *Aren't rabbits supposed to have little, fluffy tails?* she wondered. But before she could remember her old notes from Biology of Earth class, Clarke saw Bellamy's elbow draw back, chasing every thought out of her head.

Her gasp caught in her throat as Bellamy's arrow shot forward, landing with a terrible thwack right in the creature's chest. For a second, Clarke wondered if she could save it—run over, remove the arrow, and stitch it back up.

Bellamy grabbed her arm, squeezing it just hard enough to convey both assurance and warning. That rabbit was going to help keep them alive, Clarke knew. It would give Thalia a little strength. She tried to close her eyes, but they remained locked on the animal.

"It's okay," Bellamy said quietly. "I got it through the heart. He won't suffer for long." He was right. The rabbit stopped twitching and slowly fell to the forest floor, then went still. Bellamy turned to her. "Sorry. I know it's not easy to watch someone suffer."

A chill passed over her that had nothing to do with the dead rabbit. "Someone?"

"Some*thing*." He corrected himself with a shrug. "Anything."

Clarke watched Bellamy jog over to the rabbit, extract the arrow, and swing the creature over his shoulder. "Let's go this way," he said, inclining his head.

The tension seemed to have drained away, Bellamy's mood visibly bolstered by his successful kill. "So, what's the story with you and Wells?" he asked, shifting the rabbit over to his other shoulder.

Clarke braced for a rush of indignation at his nosiness, but it never came. "We dated for a little bit, a while ago, but it didn't work out."

Bellamy snickered. "Yeah, well, that part was obvious."

He paused, waiting for Clarke to continue. "So," he prodded, "what happened?"

"He did something unforgivable."

Instead of making a joke or using the opportunity to make a jab at Wells, Bellamy grew serious. "I don't think anything's unforgivable," he said quietly. "Not if it's done for the right reasons."

Clarke didn't say anything, but couldn't help wondering whether he was talking about what Octavia had done to be Confined, or something else.

Bellamy glanced up, as if the treetops had caught his attention, then looked back at Clarke. "I'm not saying he didn't do something terrible, whatever it was. All I mean is that I sort of understand where he's coming from." He reached out to run his finger along the bright-yellow moss spiraling up the trunk of a tree. "Wells and I are the only two people who *chose* to be here, who came for a reason."

Clarke started to reply, but realized that she wasn't sure what to say. They were so different on the surface—Wells, whose belief in structure and authority had resulted in her parents' execution, and Bellamy, the hotheaded Waldenite who'd held the Chancellor at gunpoint. But they were both willing to do anything to get what they wanted. To protect the people they cared about.

"Maybe you're right," she said quietly, surprised by his insight.

Bellamy paused, then increased his stride, suddenly excited by whatever he saw. "It was up here," he said, pulling her up another shallow slope into a clearing. The grass was dotted with white flowers, except for a spot about halfway down that was burned black. Pieces of the dropship lay scattered about like bones. Clarke broke into a run.

She heard Bellamy call her name but didn't bother to look back. She stumbled forward, hope blooming in her chest. "Come on, come on, come *on*," she muttered to herself as she began rummaging through the wreckage with a manic frenzy.

Then she saw them. The metal boxes that had once been white but were now discolored by the dirt and flames. She grabbed the closest one and held it up, her heart pounding so fast it became difficult to breathe. Clarke fumbled with the misshapen clasp. It wouldn't open. The heat had welded the hinges shut. Frantically, she shook the box, praying that the medicine had survived.

The sound of pill bottles rattling around inside was the sweetest thing she had ever heard.

"Is that it?" Bellamy asked, skidding to a breathless stop next to her.

"Can you open this?" Clarke shoved the box at his chest.

He held it up, squinting at the clasp. "Let me see." He removed a knife from his pocket, and with a few quick movements, pried the chest open.

Exhilaration fizzed through Clarke's body. Before she realized what she was doing, she had thrown her arms around Bellamy. He joined in her laughter as he staggered backward, and wrapped his arms around her waist, lifting her up and spinning her through the air. The colors of the clearing swirled, green and gold and blue all blurring until there was nothing in the world but Bellamy's smile, lighting up his eyes.

Finally, he set her down gently on the ground. But he didn't loosen his hold. Instead, he pulled her even closer, and before Clarke had time to catch her breath, his lips were on hers.

A voice in the back of her brain told her to stop, but it was overpowered by the smell of his skin and the pressure of his touch.

Clarke felt like she was melting into his arms, losing herself in the kiss.

He tasted like joy, and joy tasted better on Earth.

CHAPTER 16

Glass

"I don't know," Sonja said slowly, squinting at her daughter in the dim light of the bedroom. "What if we take the skirt off that one and combine it with the green bodice?"

Glass forced herself to take a deep, calming breath. She'd been trying on gowns for two hours, and they were no closer to picking one for the comet viewing party than when they'd started. "Whatever you think, Mom," she said, hoping her smile didn't look as strained as it felt.

"I'm not sure." Glass's mother sighed. "It'll be hard to have it ready in time, but we'll just have to do our best."

Glass reminded herself that her mother was only trying to help. She saw the comet viewing party as the perfect moment for Glass to reenter Phoenix society, armed with the official pardon and dressed to perfection. Glass knew the Vice Chancellor would be there, and that it was essential to play her part; she'd gotten back her life in exchange for giving him a better image, which was a more than fair trade-off. Still, Glass felt anxious about making herself the center of attention.

"Or maybe we should go back to the tulle?" Her mother gestured to the pile of discarded gowns. "Just put it back on and we can—" She was cut off by the beep of a message alert from the kitchen.

"I'll get it," Glass said quickly, hurrying from the room before her mother had time to protest. It wouldn't be for her, of course. Her friends only contacted each other via chips; message screens were generally reserved for pointless updates from sanitation, or slightly more ominous alerts from the Council. But it would at least provide a brief respite from dress talk. Glass projected the message queue in the air in front of her. Her breath caught in her chest as she saw the blinking name at the top. It was from Luke.

Dear Miss Sorenson,

Security recovered a missing item of yours near the solar fields. It will be held at the checkpoint until 1600 today.

She had to read it several times before the message sank in. She and Luke had created this system long ago, before she got her chip, in case her mother ever snooped through her messages. He wanted her to meet him by the solar fields that afternoon.

"Glass?" Sonja called from the other room. "What was it?"

She deleted the message quickly. "Just a reminder about the comet viewing, as if we could forget!" She glanced at the clock and sighed. It was only 1015. The next few hours were going to pass more slowly than they had in Confinement.

"Oh," Glass's mother gasped when Glass stepped back into the bedroom. "Maybe this is the one after all. You look beautiful."

Glass turned hesitantly toward the mirror. She saw what her mother meant. But it wasn't the dress. Her cheeks were flushed, her eyes bright with anticipation.

She looked like a girl in love.

At 1540, Glass climbed the endless flight of stairs up to the solar fields that covered the top of Walden. The plants themselves were off-limits to everyone except scientists and gatherers, but there was a small, enclosed deck overlooking the fields. It must've been designed for supervising the workers but had fallen out of use and was almost always empty.

When she reached the top, Glass moved to the edge of the

platform and sat down against the railing, her legs dangling over the side. She felt her body relax as her eyes traveled over the rows of plants stretching their leaves toward the solar panels. The far side of the field was bordered by an enormous window that made it look as though the crops were growing right out of the stars. She and Luke used to meet here all the time. It was safer than him sneaking onto Phoenix, or having Glass wander through his residential unit.

"Hey."

Glass turned to see Luke standing stiffly behind her. She started to get to her feet, but he shook his head. "Can I join you?" She nodded and moved her legs to the side to make room, and he lowered himself to the ground. "Thanks for coming," he said awkwardly. "Your mom didn't suspect anything, did she?"

"It's fine. She was too busy trying to solve a dress crisis."

Luke surprised Glass with a smile, then cleared his throat. "Glass, I . . . I haven't been able to stop thinking about what happened," he said, and her whole body tensed. She kept her eyes trained carefully on the ground. "I mean, what someone like you could possibly be Confined for. But then I remembered—a few months after we broke up, I heard a rumor about a girl on Phoenix who was arrested for . . ." His voice broke as he trailed off. Glass turned back to face him and saw that his eyes were glistening. "The timing made sense. But I never believed it could be you." Luke stared straight ahead, as if looking at something far in the distance. "I told myself that you'd never keep something like that a secret from me. I needed to believe that you trusted me more than that."

Glass bit her lip, trying to hold back the flood of words welling up in her throat. She so desperately wanted to tell him, but what good would come from admitting the truth? Better to let him think she was just a silly, spoiled Phoenix girl who'd broken his heart. He was happy with Camille right now—and he deserved to be happy.

But then Luke reached over and cupped her chin in his hand, and all her thoughts faded away.

Glass woke up smiling. Although it'd been a few weeks since the night she and Luke had spent together, she couldn't stop thinking about it. But just as she began to replay the events in her head, a wave of nausea rolled over her.

She tumbled out of bed and staggered through the hallway to the bathroom, grateful that the lights were working, probably thanks to her mother's new "friend," the head of the Resource Board.

Glass sank to the cold floor of the bathroom and quickly shut the door behind her, her brain battling with her stomach. She forced herself to breathe, trying to keep quiet. The last thing she needed was for her mother to drag her off to the medical center.

Her stomach won out, and Glass leaned over the toilet just in time. She gagged, tears stinging her eyes, then slumped back against the wall. There was no way she'd be able to meet Wells for lunch, although she felt terrible standing him up again. She'd been spending all her time with Luke, and hadn't been much of a friend to Wells lately. She missed him. He never seemed to resent her flakiness, which somehow made her feel worse. Especially after everything that had happened with his mother, and now Clarke was apparently acting strange . . . She really needed to catch up with him.

"Glass?" her mother called out from the other side of the door. "What's going on in there?"

"Nothing," Glass said, trying to keep her voice light.

"Are you ill?"

Glass groaned softly. Their new flat had no privacy. She missed their old, spacious flat with the windows full of stars. She still didn't understand why they'd had to downgrade just because her father had made the unusual and mortifying decision to sever his marriage contract and move out.

"I'm coming in," her mother's voice called from the other side of the door. Glass hastily wiped her mouth and tried to rise to her feet but slid back down as another wave of nausea sent her stomach into revolt. The door opened and Glass saw her mother, dressed for an evening out despite the fact that it wasn't even noon. But before she had a chance to ask where she was going—or where she was coming *from*—her mother's eyes widened, and she visibly paled under her generously applied blush. "What's going on?"

"Nothing," Glass said, try to shake the haze from her mind long enough to come up with an explanation that would get her mother to leave her alone. Stomach viruses were rare on Phoenix, and anyone who seemed vaguely contagious was required to spend the duration of their illness in quarantine. "I'm fine."

"Were you"—Sonja looked behind her and lowered her voice, which was ridiculous considering they were the only two people in the flat—"throwing up?"

"Yes, but I'm fine. I think I just—"

"Oh my god," her mother said, closing her eyes.

"I'm not sick, I promise. I don't need to be quarantined. I've just been nauseous the past few mornings, but it goes away by the afternoon."

When her mother opened her eyes, she didn't look any less worried. The room started to spin, and Sonja's voice grew faint, as if she were speaking from somewhere far away. Glass could barely make out her question, something about how long it'd been since her last—

Suddenly, Glass's confusion hardened into a ball of dread. She looked up at Sonja and saw the terrifying realization reflected in her mother's eyes.

"Glass." Sonja's voice was hoarse. "You're pregnant."

Staring at Luke's face, full of sympathy and understanding, Glass felt her last bit of self-control shatter. "I'm sorry." Her breath caught in her throat as she tried to stifle a sob. "I should've told you, I just—I didn't see any reason for both of us to die."

"Oh, Glass." Luke reached out and wrapped his arms tight around her. She nestled gratefully into his familiar embrace, her tears spilling onto the jacket of his guard uniform. "I can't believe it," he murmured. "I can't believe you did this all on your own. I knew you were brave, but I never thought . . . What happened?" he asked finally, and Glass knew what he meant. Who he was referring to.

"He—" She swallowed as she struggled to breathe. It felt like her heart was about to break apart, unable to contain both the grief and relief pouring into her chest. Finally, she just shook her head. There were no words.

"Oh my god," he whispered, grabbing her hand and lacing his fingers between hers, squeezing it tight. "I'm so sorry." He sighed. "Why didn't you tell me any of this the night you escaped? I had no idea." He closed his eyes as if to shut out the memory.

"You were with Camille. I knew she was a good friend of yours, and I figured . . . you'd finally found someone who made you happy." Glass smiled and wiped away the tears that were still running down her face. "You deserved it, after everything I put you through."

Luke reached out to brush a strand of hair behind her ear. "There's only one person in the universe who can make me happy, and she's sitting right here with me." He stared at her, as if drinking her in. "From the moment I saw you again, I knew it wasn't Camille—she's a great friend, always will be, but that's all she is to me now, and I've told her that. I love you, Glass. I never stopped loving you. And I never will."

He leaned forward and brushed his lips against hers, lightly at first, as if giving their mouths a chance to become reacquainted. For a moment it felt like their first kiss all over again. But a moment was all it took.

He pressed against Glass, her lips parting as his mouth sank into hers. She was vaguely aware of his hand tangling in her hair, then slipping down her back, pulling her closer to him as he wrapped his other arm around her waist.

Finally, Glass shifted back and let her lips break away from his. "I love you," she whispered, needing desperately to say it. *I love you I love you I love you* throbbed through her body as Luke smiled and pulled her back to him.

CHAPTER 17

Wells

It was nearly noon, and Clarke had been gone for hours. One of the Arcadian girls had seen her head into the woods earlier that morning, and it had taken all of Wells's self-control to keep from running after her. The thought of her venturing off on her own made his stomach feel like a punching bag for his imagination. But he had to accept that, of all the people in camp, Clarke knew how to take care of herself. He also knew how important it was to find the missing medicine. Just yesterday, they'd dug another grave.

He wandered toward the de facto cemetery that had cropped up on the far side of the clearing. Over the past few days, Wells had arranged for wooden markers to be placed at the head of each mound, something he remembered from old photographs. He'd wanted to carve the names onto the crosses, but he only knew the names of three of the five kids sleeping beneath the soil, and it didn't seem right to leave the others blank.

He shuddered and turned back to the graves. The concept of burying the dead had initially struck him as repulsive, but there hadn't seemed to be any alternative. The thought of burning the bodies was even worse. But although the normal practice of releasing corpses into space was certainly tidier, there was something reassuring about gathering the dead together. Even in death, they'd never be alone.

It was also strangely comforting to have a place to visit, to say the things you couldn't say to people you could see. Someone, possibly a Walden girl he'd seen flitting near the trees, had gathered fallen branches and rested them along the wooden markers. In the evening, the pods still glowed to life, casting a soft light over the cemetery that gave it an almost unearthly beauty. It would have been nice to have somewhere on the ship where it wouldn't have seemed strange to talk to his mother.

Wells glanced up at the darkening sky. He had no idea if the Colony lost contact with the dropship when it crashed, but he hoped that the monitors in the bracelets were still transmitting data about their blood composition and heart rates. They must have collected enough information to prove that Earth was safe, and would surely begin sending groups of citizens down soon. For a moment he dared to let himself hope that his father and Glass would be among them.

"What are you doing over here?"

Wells turned and saw Octavia moving toward him slowly. Her ankle was healing quickly; her limp was starting to look like a saunter.

"I don't know. Paying my respects, I suppose." He gestured toward the graves. "But I was just leaving," he added quickly as he watched her toss her dark hair over her shoulder. "It's my turn to go for water."

"I'll go with you." Octavia smiled, and Wells looked away uncomfortably. The long lashes that made her look so innocent when she was sleeping in the infirmary tent now lent a feral gleam to her enormous blue eyes.

"Are you sure that's a good idea with your ankle? It's a long walk."

"I'm *fine*," she said, her voice full of playful exasperation as she fell into stride next to him. "Though you're very sweet to be concerned. You know," she went on, increasing her pace to catch up with Wells, who hadn't noticed he'd lengthened his step, "it's ridiculous that everyone hangs on to Graham's every word. You know so much more than he does."

Wells grabbed one of the empty jugs next to the supply

tent and turned toward the forest. They'd discovered a stream not far from camp, and everyone strong enough to carry a full container took turns going for water. At least, they were *supposed* to take turns. He hadn't seen Graham go for days.

Octavia paused as Wells stepped across the tree line. "Are you coming?" he asked, throwing a glance over his shoulder.

She tilted her head back, her eyes widening as she scanned the shadowy outlines of the trees in the fading light. "I'm coming." Her voice grew quiet as she darted to Wells's side. "I haven't been in the woods yet."

Wells softened. Even he, who'd spent most of his life dreaming about coming to Earth, found it frightening at times—the vastness, the unfamiliar sounds, the sense that anything could be hiding beyond the light of the campfire. And he'd had time to prepare. He could only imagine what it was like for the others, who were snatched from their cells and shoved onto the dropship before they had time to process what was going on, that they were being sent to a foreign planet that had never been more to them than an empty word.

"Careful," he said, pointing at a tangle of roots hidden by a mass of purple leaves. "The ground gets pretty uneven here."

Wells took Octavia's small hand and helped her climb over a fallen tree. It was strange to think that something without a pulse could die, but the soggy, peeling bark was decidedly corpse-like.

"So is it true?" Octavia asked as they began walking down the slope that led to the stream. "Did you really get yourself Confined so you could come with Clarke?"

"I suppose it is."

She sighed wistfully. "That's the most romantic thing I've ever heard."

Wells gave her a wry smile. "Trust me, it's not."

"What do you mean?" Octavia asked, cocking her head to one side. In the shadows of the forest, she looked almost childlike again.

Wells glanced away, suddenly unable to look her in the eye. He wondered grimly what Octavia would say if she knew the truth.

He wasn't the brave knight who'd come to rescue the princess. He was the reason she'd been locked away in the dungeon.

Wells glanced at his collar chip for the fourteenth time since he'd sat down two minutes earlier. The message Clarke had sent him earlier that day had sounded anxious, and she'd been acting strange for the past few weeks. Wells had barely seen her, and the few times he managed to track her down, she'd been practically twitching with nervous energy.

He couldn't help but worry that she was about to break up with him. The only thing that kept the anxiety from burning a hole through his stomach was the knowledge that she probably wouldn't have chosen the library to dump him. It'd be cruel to tarnish the spot they both loved best. Clarke wouldn't do that to him.

He heard footsteps and rose to his feet as the overhead lights flickered back on. Wells had been still for so long that the library had forgotten his presence, the dim safety lights on the floor providing the only light. Clarke approached, still wearing her scrubs, which normally made him smile—he loved that she didn't spend hours stressing over her appearance, like most girls on Phoenix—but the blue top and pants fell too loosely from her frame, and there were dark circles under her eyes.

"Hey," he said, stepping forward to kiss her lightly in greeting. She didn't move away, but she didn't kiss him back. "Are you okay?" he asked, even though he knew full well that she wasn't.

"Wells," she said, her voice breaking. She blinked back tears. His eyes widened in alarm. Clarke never cried.

"Hey," he murmured, putting his arm around her to lead her to the couch. Her legs seemed to buckle beneath her. "It'll be okay, I promise. Just tell me what's going on."

She stared at him, and he could see her urge to confide in him battling her fear. "I need you to promise me that you won't say anything about this to anyone."

He nodded. "Of course."

"I'm serious. This isn't gossip. This is real, life-or-death."

Wells squeezed her hand. "Clarke, you know you can tell me anything."

"I found out . . ." She took a breath, closed her eyes for a moment, and then started again. "You know about my parents' radiation research." He nodded. Her parents were in charge of a massive ongoing study meant to determine when, if ever, it would be safe for humans to return to Earth. Whenever his father had spoken of an Earth mission, Wells had thought of it as a distant possibility, more of a hope than a real plan. Still, he knew how important the Griffins' work was to the Chancellor and to the whole Colony. "They're doing human trials," Clarke said softly. A chill traveled down Wells's spine, but he said nothing, just tightened his grasp on her hand. "They're experimenting on children," Clarke finally said, her voice barely a whisper.

Her voice was hollow, as if the thought had been circulating for so long, it no longer held any meaning. "What children?" he asked, his brain racing to understand.

"Unregistereds," Clarke said, her tear-filled eyes flashing with sudden anger. "Children from the care center whose parents were executed for violating the population laws." He could hear the unspoken accusation. *People your father killed.*

"They're so young. . . ." Clarke's voice trailed off. She sank back and seemed to shrink, as if the truth had taken some part of her with it.

Wells slid his arm behind her, but instead of recoiling as she'd done every day over the past few weeks, she leaned into him and rested her head against his chest. "They're all so sick." He could feel her tears seeping through his shirt. "Some of them have already died."

"I'm so sorry, Clarke," he murmured as he searched for something to say, anything to make her pain go away. "I'm sure your parents are doing their best to make sure it's . . ." He paused. There weren't any words that could make it better. He had to do something, to put a stop to it before the guilt and horror destroyed her. "What can I do?" he asked, his voice becoming firm.

She bolted upright and stared at him, a different kind of terror filling her eyes. "Nothing," she said with a resolve that took him by surprise. "You have to promise me that you'll do *nothing*. My parents made me swear not to tell anyone. They didn't want to do this, Wells. It wasn't their choice. Vice Chancellor Rhodes is *making* them. He threatened them." She grabbed Wells's hands. "Promise me you won't say anything. I just . . ." She bit her lip. "I just couldn't keep it from you anymore. I had to tell someone."

"I promise," he said, though his skin was growing warm with fury. The slimy bastard had no right to go around the Chancellor like that. He thought of his father, the man who had an unflinching sense of right and wrong. His father never would have approved human trials. He could put a stop to it immediately.

Clarke stared at him, searching his eyes, and then gave him a small, trembling smile that vanished almost as quickly as it had appeared. "Thank you."

She returned her head to Wells's chest, and he wrapped his arm around her. "I love you," he whispered.

An hour later, after he'd walked Clarke home, Wells headed back along the observation deck alone. He needed to *do* something. If something didn't change soon, the guilt would destroy her, and he refused to stand by and watch.

Wells had never broken a promise before. It was something his father had impressed upon him from an early age—a leader never goes back on his word. But then he thought of Clarke's tears, and knew he didn't have a choice.

He turned around and began walking toward his father's office.

They filled the water jug at the stream and started to make their way back to the camp. After giving enough one-word answers, Wells had gotten Octavia to stop asking about Clarke, but now she was walking along sullenly, and he felt guilty. She was a sweet girl, and he knew she meant well. How had she wound up here?

"So," Wells said, breaking the silence, "what could you have possibly done to end up in Confinement?"

Octavia looked at him in surprise. "Haven't you heard my brother talking about it?" She gave him a tight smile. "He loves telling people about how I was caught stealing food for the younger kids in the care center—the little ones who are always bullied into giving up their rations—and how the monsters on the Council Confined me without batting an eye."

Something in Octavia's voice gave him pause. "Is that really how it happened?"

"Does it matter?" she asked with a weariness that suddenly made her seem older than fourteen. "We're all going to think what we want about each other. If that's the story Bellamy needs to believe, then I'm not going to stop him."

Wells stopped to rearrange the heavy water jug. Somehow, they'd ended up in a different part of the woods. The trees grew even closer together here, and he could see far enough ahead to tell how far they'd strayed.

"Are we lost?" Octavia glanced from side to side, and even in the dim light he could see the panic flash across her face.

"We'll be fine. I just need to—" He stopped as a sound shuddered through the air.

"What was that?" Octavia asked. "Are we—"

Wells cut her off with a shush and took a step forward. It sounded like a twig snapping, which meant that something was moving just behind the trees. He kicked himself for not bringing a weapon. It would've been nice to bring back his own kill, to show that Bellamy wasn't the only one who could learn how to hunt. The sound came again, and Wells's frustration turned to fear. Forget catching dinner—if he wasn't careful, he and Octavia might become dinner themselves.

He was about to grab her hand and run away when something caught his eye. A glint of reddish gold. Wells lowered the water jug and took a few steps forward. "Stay here," he whispered.

Just ahead, he could see an open space beyond the trees. Some kind of clearing. He was about to shout the name hovering on his lips when he froze, skidding to a stop.

Clarke was standing in the grass, locked in an embrace with none other than *Bellamy*. As she brought her lips up to the Waldenite, fury tore through Wells. Heat shot up through his chest to settle in his racing heart.

Somehow, he managed to wrench his eyes away and stagger back into the trees before a wave of nausea sent his head spinning. He grabbed on to a branch for balance, gasping as he tried to force air into his lungs. The girl he'd risked his life to protect wasn't just kissing someone else—she was kissing the hothead who may have gotten his father killed.

"Whoa." Octavia's voice came from beside him. "Their walk looks a lot more fun than ours."

But Wells had already turned and begun walking in the other direction. He was vaguely aware of Octavia scampering after him, asking something about a medicine chest, but her voice was drowned out by the pulsing of blood in his head. He didn't care whether they'd found the missing medicine. There was no drug strong enough to repair a broken heart.

CHAPTER 18

Clarke

By the time Clarke and Bellamy returned to camp with the medicine, darkness had fallen. She'd only been in the woods for a few hours, but as they stepped through the tree line into the clearing, it felt like she'd left a lifetime ago.

They'd spent most of the walk back in silence, but every time Clarke's arm accidentally brushed against Bellamy's, electricity seemed to dance across her skin. She'd been mortified after their kiss, and had spent the next five minutes stammering an apology while he grinned. Eventually, he cut her off with a laugh and told her not to worry about it. "I know you're not the type of girl to make out with random guys in the woods," he'd said with a mischievous grin, "but maybe you should be."

But as they approached the clearing, all thoughts of the kiss were pushed aside by the shadowy outline of the infirmary tent. Clarke took off with the medicine tucked under her arm.

The tent was empty except for a delirious, feverish Thalia, and to Clarke's surprise, Octavia, who was just settling back in her old cot. "The other tent is just so *small*," Octavia was saying, but Clarke couldn't do more than nod.

She flung the medicine chest onto the floor, filled a syringe, and plunged the needle into Thalia's arm. Then Clarke turned back to the box, searching for painkillers. She quickly gave Thalia a dose and smiled as her friend's face relaxed in sleep.

Clarke knelt next to Thalia for a few more minutes, breathing a deep sigh of relief at her steady pulse. For a moment, she looked down at the bracelet on her wrist and wondered if, somewhere up in the sky, someone was monitoring her own heart rate. Dr. Lahiri, perhaps, or another of the Colony's top doctors, reading the hundred's vital signs like the day's news. Surely they had seen that five people had died already. . . . She wondered if they'd chalk the deaths up to radiation poisoning and rethink their colonization efforts, or if they'd be smart enough to realize they'd been killed because of the rough landing. She wasn't sure which scenario she preferred. She certainly wasn't ready for the Council to extend its jurisdiction to Earth. And yet her mother and father had devoted their lives to helping humanity return home. A permanent settlement would mean, in a way, that her parents had succeeded too. That they hadn't died for nothing.

Finally, she scooped the medicine back into the chest and placed it in the corner of the tent. Tomorrow, she'd find a place to lock it up, but for now, Clarke felt like she could finally rest. If someone was indeed monitoring their body count up in space, she was going to make damn sure they didn't drop below ninety-five.

She took a few shaky steps and collapsed on her cot without even bothering to take off her shoes.

"Is she going to be okay?" Octavia asked. Her voice sounded far away.

Clarke murmured yes. She could barely open her eyelids.

"What other medicine was in there?"

"Everything," Clarke said. Or at least, she tried to say it. By the time the word reached her lips, exhaustion had numbed her brain. The last thing she remembered was hearing Octavia rise from her cot before falling into a deep, dreamless sleep.

When Clarke awoke the next morning, Octavia was gone, and bright light was streaming in through the tent flap.

Thalia lay on her side, still asleep. Clarke rose with a

groan, her muscles stiff from their hike yesterday. But it was a good kind of pain; she'd walked through a forest that hadn't been seen by a single human being in three hundred years. Her stomach squirmed as she thought about another distinction she'd inadvertently earned—the first girl to kiss a boy on Earth since the Cataclysm.

Clarke smiled as she hurried over to Thalia. She couldn't wait until she was well enough to hear all about it. She pressed the back of her hand against her friend's forehead and was relieved to feel that it was cooler than it had been last night. She gently pulled back the blanket to look at Thalia's stomach. Her skin still showed signs of an infection, but it hadn't spread any farther. As long as Thalia had a full course of antibiotics, she'd make a full recovery.

It was hard to know exactly, but based on the strength of the light, she guessed that at least eight hours had passed since Thalia's last dose. She turned and walked over to the corner where she'd stashed the medicine chest, frowning slightly as she realized it was open. Clarke crouched down and inhaled sharply, blinking to make sure her eyes weren't playing tricks on her.

The chest was empty.

All the antibiotics, the painkillers, even the syringes—they were all gone. "No," Clarke whispered. There was nothing. "No," she said again, scrambling to her feet. She ran over to the nearest cot and started to throw the bedding aside, then did the same with her own.

Her eyes landed on Octavia's cot, and her panic momentarily hardened into suspicion. She hurried over and began rummaging through the pile of blankets. "Come on," she muttered to herself, but her hands came up empty.

"*No.*" She kicked the ground. The medicine wasn't in the tent, that much was clear. But whoever had taken it couldn't have gone far. There were fewer than a hundred human beings on the planet, and Clarke wasn't going to rest until she found the thief who was jeopardizing Thalia's life. She probably wouldn't have to look very far.

After a quick search of the flat to make sure her parents weren't home, Clarke hurried to the lab and entered the code. She kept expecting her parents to change the password, but either they didn't know how often she visited the kids, or they didn't want to stop her. Perhaps they liked knowing that Clarke was keeping them company.

As she made her way toward Lilly, Clarke smiled at the others, though her chest tightened when she saw how few were awake. Most were growing sicker, and there were more empty beds than there'd been the last time.

She tried to force this thought out of her head as she approached Lilly, but as her eyes locked on her friend, her hands began to tremble.

Lilly was dying. Her eyes barely fluttered open when Clarke whispered her name, and even when her lips moved, she didn't have the strength to turn the shapes into words.

There were more flaky red patches on her skin, although fewer of them were bleeding, as Lilly no longer had the energy to scratch them. Clarke sat there, fighting a wave of nausea as she watched the irregular rise and fall of her friend's chest. The worst part was that she knew this was only the beginning. The other subjects had lingered on for weeks, their symptoms growing increasingly gruesome as the radiation poisoning progressed through their bodies.

For a moment, Clarke imagined carrying Lilly to the medical center, where they could at least put her on high-intensity pain medication even if it was too late to save her. But that would be tantamount to asking the Vice Chancellor to execute her parents. Then he'd just find someone else to finish what her mother and father had started. All Clarke hoped was that their research proved conclusive so that the experiments could stop, so that these test subjects wouldn't have suffered in vain.

Lilly's translucent eyelids fluttered open. "Hey, Clarke," she croaked, the beginnings of a smile flickering on her face before a new wave of pain washed them away.

Clarke reached over and grasped Lilly's hand, giving it a gentle squeeze. "Hey," she whispered. "How are you feeling?"

"Fine," Lilly lied, wincing as she struggled to sit up.

"It's okay." Clarke placed a hand on her shoulder. "You don't need to sit."

"No, I want to." The girl's voice was strained.

Clarke gently helped her sit, then adjusted the pillows behind her. She suppressed a shudder as her fingers brushed against Lilly's back. She could feel every vertebra poking out from her sallow skin.

"How did you like the Dickens anthology?" Clarke asked, glancing under Lilly's bed, where they kept the books Clarke had stolen from the library.

"I only read the first story, the one about Oliver Twist." Lilly gave Clarke a weak smile. "My vision is . . ." She trailed off. They both knew that once the subjects had trouble seeing, the end wasn't far. "But I didn't like it, anyway. It reminded me too much of the care center."

Clarke hadn't asked any questions about Lilly's life before this. She'd gotten the sense that Lilly didn't want to talk about it. "Was it really that bad?" she said carefully.

Lilly shrugged. "We all looked out for one another. We didn't have anyone else. Well, except this one girl. She had a *brother*, a real-life older brother." She looked down, suddenly blushing. "He was . . . nice. He used to bring her things—extra food, pieces of ribbon . . ."

"Really?" Clarke asked, pretending to believe the comment

about a girl with a brother as she brushed a lock of hair off Lilly's damp forehead. Even this far along in her sickness, Lilly had a flair for the dramatic.

"He sounds nice," Clarke said vaguely as her eyes flitted toward the bald patches on Lilly's head, which were becoming difficult to ignore.

"Anyway," Lilly said, her voice strained, "I want to hear about your birthday. What are you going to wear?"

Clarke had almost forgotten that her birthday was next week. She didn't feel much like celebrating. "Oh, you know, my best scrubs," she said lightly. "I'd rather hang out here with you than go to some silly party, anyway."

"Oh, Clarke," Lilly groaned in mock exasperation. "You have to do *something*. You're starting to be seriously boring. Besides, I want to hear about your birthday dress." She winced suddenly, doubling over in pain.

"Are you okay?" Clarke asked, her hand on Lilly's fragile arm.

"It hurts," Lilly gasped.

"Can I get you anything? Do you want some water?"

Lilly opened her eyes, which were now pleading. "You can make it stop, Clarke." She was cut off by a groan. "Please make it stop. It's only a matter of time. . . ."

Clarke turned her head to the side so Lilly wouldn't see her tears. "It'll be okay," she whispered, forcing a fake smile. "I promise."

Lilly whimpered before falling silent again, then leaned back and closed her eyes.

Clarke pulled the blankets up over her friend's chest, trying to ignore the demon that was clawing its way to the front of her mind. She knew what Lilly was asking for. And it wouldn't be difficult. She was so frail at this point, it would take just a few well-combined painkillers to ease her into a coma. She'd slip away painlessly.

What am I thinking? Clarke asked herself, drawing back in horror. The blood on her parents' hands had spread to her own. This whole nightmare had infected her, turned her into a monster. Or maybe it wasn't her parents' fault. Maybe she'd always had this darkness inside of her, waiting to rise to the surface.

Just as she was about to leave, Lilly spoke again. "Please," she begged. "If you love me, please." Her voice was quiet but contained an edge of desperation that terrified Clarke. "Just make it all stop."

Bellamy was chopping wood on the far side of the clearing. Although the morning was cool, his T-shirt was already soaked through with sweat. Clarke tried not to notice how it clung to his muscular chest. When he saw her running toward him, he lowered his ax to the ground and turned to face her with a grin.

"Well, hello there," he said as she came to a stop and

paused to catch her breath. "Couldn't stay away, could you?" He stepped forward and placed his hand on her waist, but Clarke swatted his arm away.

"Where's your sister?" she asked. "I can't find her anywhere."

"Why?" Urgency shoved the playfulness out of his voice. "What's wrong?"

"The medicine we found is missing." Clarke took a deep breath, bracing herself for her next words. "And I think Octavia took it."

"*What?*" His eyes narrowed.

"She was the only other person in the tent last night, and she seemed really fixated on the drugs—"

"*No,*" Bellamy snapped, cutting her off. "Of all the criminals on this goddamn planet, you think *my sister* is the thief?" He stared at her, his eyes burning with anger. But when he spoke again, his voice was quiet. "I thought you were different. But I was wrong. You're just another stupid Phoenix bitch who thinks she knows better than everyone else."

He kicked the handle of the ax, then pushed past her without another word.

For a moment, Clarke stood rooted to the ground, too stunned by Bellamy's words to move. But then she felt something inside her tear, and suddenly she was running toward the trees, staggering into the shade of the forest canopy. Her throat raw, she slumped onto the ground, wrapping her arms around her knees to keep the anguish from flowing out of her chest.

Alone in the shadows, Clarke did something else on Earth for the first time. She cried.

CHAPTER 19

Bellamy

Bellamy paused to adjust the bird that he'd slung over his shoulder. The confrontation with Clarke had left him so agitated that he'd grabbed his bow and stormed off into the woods without a second thought. Only after shooting this bird near the stream had he started to calm down. It was a good kill—his first bird, much harder than animals on the ground—and its feathers would be perfect for the new arrows he'd been working on, to take with them when he and Octavia headed out on their own. As he stepped back into camp, he realized that he hadn't seen Octavia since early that morning, and felt a twinge of concern. He should have checked on her before he left.

The fire was already built up, and a dozen faces turned to look at Bellamy as he approached. But no one was smiling. He shifted the bird over to his other shoulder to give them a better view of his kill. Why the hell were they staring at him like that?

An angry shout pulled his attention to a group at the far end of the clearing, near the wreckage of the dropship. They were clustered in a circle around something on the ground. He inhaled sharply as the shape on the ground moved.

Then he saw her, and his confusion erupted into a rage unlike anything he'd ever felt.

It was *Octavia*.

He threw the bird on the ground and broke into a run.

"Out of my way," Bellamy shouted as he forced his way inside the circle.

Octavia was on the ground, tears streaming down her cheeks. Graham and a few of the Arcadians stood over her, a deranged gleam in their eyes.

"*Get away from her*," Bellamy bellowed as he charged forward. But before he could reach Octavia, an arm hooked around his neck, nearly crushing his windpipe. Bellamy wheezed and looked around frantically. Wells was standing in front of him, his expression cold and firm. "What the *hell?*" Bellamy sputtered. "Get out of my way."

When Wells didn't move, Bellamy gritted his teeth and

lunged at him, but someone else had a hold on his collar and jerked him back. "Get off of me!" Bellamy spat, shooting his elbow back with enough force to make whoever was behind him grunt and let go.

Octavia was still on the ground, her eyes wide with terror as she looked from Bellamy to Graham, who was standing over her. "You better tell me what's going on, *right now*," Bellamy said through clenched teeth.

"I heard you and Clarke talking about the missing medicine earlier," Wells said with infuriating calmness. "No one besides Octavia knew about it. She must have taken it."

"I didn't take *anything*." Octavia sobbed. She wiped her face with the back of her hand and sniffed. "They've all gone crazy." She rose shakily to her feet and started to take a step toward Bellamy.

"You're not going anywhere," Graham snapped, grabbing Octavia's wrist and wrenching her back.

"Let *go* of her!" Bellamy bellowed. He dove for Graham, but Wells stepped in front of him, and someone else wrenched his arm behind his back. "Get off of me!" Bellamy thrashed wildly as he tried to wrench himself free, but there were too many sets of hands holding him down, locking him in place.

"Look," Bellamy continued, trying in vain to keep his voice steady, "she's been injured ever since we landed. Do you really think she was up to stealing medicine and dragging it off somewhere outside of camp?"

"She was up to following me into the woods yesterday," Wells answered calmly. "We walked pretty far together."

Bellamy thrashed against the arms holding him, unable to quell his rage as the implication of Wells's words sank in. If he so much as laid a hand on his sister . . .

"Just take it easy," Wells said. He nodded at a Walden boy, who stepped forward with a coil of rope.

"Then tell that creep to take his disgusting hands off my sister," Bellamy spat.

Clarke suddenly appeared, pushing her way through the crowd. "What's going on?" she asked, her eyes wide when they landed on Octavia. "Are you okay?" Octavia shook her head, tears streaming down her face.

"We just need Octavia to tell us where the medicine is," Wells said calmly, "and then we'll get this all sorted out."

"I *don't have it*." Octavia's voice had grown ragged.

"We know you're lying," Graham hissed. Octavia yelped as he tightened his hold on her wrist, and Bellamy struggled against the hands that held him. "You're only making things worse."

"So what are you going to do?" Bellamy spat at Wells. "Keep us both tied up?"

"Exactly," Wells said, his jaw tightening. "We'll keep

Octavia locked up until she tells us where she hid the medicine, or we find evidence pointing to another suspect."

"Lock her up?" Bellamy made a show of looking around the clearing. "And how do you propose to do that?"

Clarke stepped forward, a tense look on her face. "I spend most of the day in the infirmary tent, anyway," she said curtly. "Octavia can stay there. I'll keep an eye on her and make sure she doesn't sneak off."

"Are you serious?" Graham snorted. "She stole the medicine from under your nose, and your plan is to *keep an eye on her*?"

Clarke turned to Graham with a scowl. "If that's not good enough for you, Graham, you can post a guard outside the door."

"This is ridiculous." Bellamy's whole body was beginning to shake as his anger smoldered into exhaustion. "Look at her," he said weakly. "She's obviously not a danger to anyone. Just untie her and I promise I won't let her out of my sight." He scanned the crowd that had assembled around them, scouring the audience for a sympathetic face. Surely someone else saw that this whole thing was complete bullshit. But no one was willing to meet his eyes.

"You're all insane." His mouth curled into a snarl as he turned back to face Graham. "You set her up. *You* stole those meds."

Graham snickered and shot a look at Asher. "I told you he was going to say that."

The sky was growing dark, the clouds weaving into a blanket of gray. Bellamy took a deep breath. "Fine. Believe whatever you want. Just untie Octavia and let us go. We'll leave camp for good. We won't even take any of your precious supplies." He glanced at his sister, but she didn't look happy at the idea; her features seemed frozen in shock. "You'll never have to think about us again."

A fleeting look of pain crossed Clarke's face before she retreated behind her mask of steely resolve. *She'll get over it*, Bellamy thought bitterly. She'd find someone else to go traipsing through the woods with her.

"I don't think so," Graham said, sneering. "Not until we get back the meds. We can't let anyone else die just because your little sister's a drug addict."

The accusation made every nerve in Bellamy's body sizzle until his fingers itched to close around Graham's neck.

"Enough," Clarke said, shaking her head at Graham and raising a hand. "I want the medicine back more than anyone, but you're not helping."

"Fine," Bellamy snapped. "But *I'm* taking her into the tent. And *no one* is going to put their hands on her again."

He wrenched free from his captors and strode over to Octavia, grabbing her hand as he locked eyes with Graham.

"You're going to regret this," Bellamy said in a low, dangerous voice. He wrapped his arm around his trembling sister and led her toward the infirmary tent, a grim determination overtaking him.

He'd do whatever it took to protect her. He always had.

It was the third guard visit in the last few months. They had been coming more often that year, and Octavia was getting bigger. Bellamy tried not to think about what would happen next time, but even he knew they wouldn't be able to hide her forever.

"I can't believe they looked in the closet," his mother said hoarsely, staring at Octavia, whom Bellamy had carried to the couch. "Thank god she didn't cry."

Bellamy looked over at his toddler sister. Everything about her was miniaturized, from her tiny sock-clad feet to her impossibly small fingers. Everything except her round cheeks and enormous eyes, which always glistened with tears she never seemed to shed. Was it normal for a two-year-old to be so quiet? Did she somehow know what would happen if someone found her?

Bellamy walked over and sat down next to Octavia, who turned her head to stare at him with her deep-blue eyes. He reached forward to touch one of her dark, glossy curls. She looked just like that doll head he'd found while scavenging for relics in the storage room. He'd thought about taking it home to Octavia, but decided the ration points he'd get for it at the Exchange were more important. He also hadn't been sure whether it was right to give a baby a disembodied doll's head, no matter how pretty it was.

He grinned as Octavia grabbed his finger with her tiny fist. "Hey, give that back," he said, pretending to wince. She smiled but didn't giggle. He couldn't remember ever hearing her laugh.

"It was too close," his mother was muttering to herself as she paced back and forth. "Too close . . . too close . . . too close."

"Mom. Are you okay?" Bellamy asked, feeling his panic return. She walked over to the sink, which was still spilling over with dishes despite the fact that this morning had been their water hour. He hadn't been able to finish before the guards came. It would be another five days before they'd have the chance to wash them again.

There was a faint crash down the hallway, followed by a peal of laughter. His mother gasped and looked around the flat. "Get her back in the closet."

Bellamy put his arm in front of Octavia. "It's fine," he said. "The guards were just here. They're not going to be back for a while."

His mother took a step forward. Her eyes were wide and full of terror. "Get her out of here!"

"*No,*" Bellamy said, sliding off the couch and standing in front of Octavia. "That wasn't even the guards. It was just someone messing around. She doesn't need to go back in yet."

Octavia whimpered but fell silent as their mother fixed her with a wild-eyed stare.

"Oh no, oh no, oh no," their mother was muttering, running her hands distractedly through her already disheveled hair. She leaned back against the wall and slid down to the floor, landing with a sharp thud.

Bellamy glanced at Octavia, then walked slowly over to his mother, kneeling carefully beside her. "Mom?" A new kind of fear welled up inside him, different from what he'd felt during the inspection. This fear was cold and seemed to be creeping out from his stomach, turning his blood to ice.

"You don't understand," she said faintly, staring at something just behind Bellamy's head. "They're going to kill me. They're going to take you and they're going to kill me."

"Take me where?" Bellamy asked, his voice quivering.

"You can't have both," she whispered, her eyes growing even larger. "You can't have both." She blinked and refocused her gaze on Bellamy. "You can't have a mother and a sister."

CHAPTER 20

Glass

Glass swept up the final flight of stairs and turned into her corridor. She wasn't worried about being stopped by the guards for violating curfew. She felt like she was floating, her steps featherlight as she skimmed silently down the hallway. She raised her hand to her lips, where the memory of Luke's kiss still lingered, and smiled.

It was a little after three in the morning; the ship was empty, the lights in the hallway a dim glow. Tearing herself away from Luke made her ache with an almost physical pain, but she knew better than to risk getting caught by her mother. If she fell asleep quickly enough, she might be able to trick her mind into thinking that she was still with Luke, his warm, sleeping form curled up next to her.

She pressed her thumb against the key panel on the door and slipped inside.

"Hello, Glass." Her mother's voice came from the sofa.

Glass gasped and started stammering. "Hi, I was . . . I . . ." She fumbled for words, trying to come up with a plausible reason for why she'd been out in the middle of the night. But she couldn't lie; not anymore, not about this.

They stood in silence for a long moment, and although she couldn't make out the expression on her mother's face, Glass could feel her confusion and anger radiating through the darkness. "You were with *him*, weren't you?" Sonja finally asked.

"Yes," Glass said, relieved to be telling the truth at last. "Mom, I love him."

Her mother took a step forward, and Glass realized that she was still wearing a black evening dress, the outline of faded lipstick on her mouth, dying traces of her perfume in the air.

"Where were *you* tonight?" Glass asked wearily. It was like last year all over again. Ever since her father had left them, her mother had barely been around, staying out all hours of the night and sometimes sleeping through the day. Now Glass didn't have the energy to be embarrassed, or even angry, about her mother's behavior. All she could feel was a faint pang of sadness.

Sonja's lips twisted into a gruesome approximation of a smile. "You have no idea what I've done to protect you" was all she said. "You need to stay away from that boy."

"That *boy*?" Glass cringed. "I know you think he's just—"

"That's *enough*," her mother snapped. "Don't you realize how lucky you are to even be here? I'm not going to let you die for some Walden trash who seduces Phoenix girls and then abandons them."

"He's not like that!" Glass exclaimed, her voice growing shrill. "You don't even know him."

"He doesn't care about you. You were ready to *die* to save him. While you were in Confinement he'd probably forgotten all about you."

Glass winced. It was true that Luke had started seeing Camille while Glass was in Confinement. But she couldn't blame him, not after the cruel things she'd said when she broke up with him in a desperate attempt to keep him safe.

"Glass." Sonja's voice quivered with the strain of trying to remain calm. "I'm sorry to be harsh. But with the Chancellor still on life support, you need to be careful. If he wakes up and has any reason, any reason at all, to revoke your pardon, he will." She sighed. "I can't let you risk your life again. Have you already forgotten what happened last time?"

But of course Glass hadn't forgotten. The memory of it was as permanent as the scars from the bracelet on her skin, something she would carry with her the rest of her life.

And her mother didn't even know the whole truth.

Glass ignored the guards' strange looks as she passed the checkpoint and began crossing the skybridge toward Walden. Let them think she was off to buy drugs if they wanted. No punishment they gave her could possibly hurt more than what she was about to do.

It was late afternoon, and the corridors were thankfully empty. Luke would be back from his morning shift by now, but Carter would still be at the distribution center, where he worked sorting nutrition packets. Glass knew it was foolish—Carter hated her, and he would hate her even more once he found out that she had broken Luke's heart—but she couldn't bear to break up with Luke with Carter in the other room.

She paused at the door, absently bringing her hand to her stomach. She had to do it now. She'd already put this off so many times. She'd muster the courage to break up with him, then hesitate as the terrible words rose to her mouth. *Next time*, she always promised herself. *I just need to see him one more time.*

But now her stomach was growing noticeably rounder. Even on half rations, it was getting harder and harder for Glass to disguise her weight gain under the shapeless dresses that prompted snickers from Cora. Soon she would start to show. And once she did, there would be questions. The Council would demand to know who the father was. If she was still in touch with Luke, he would find out, and volunteer himself in some misguided attempt to save her that would only end in both of their deaths.

You're saving his life, Glass told herself as she knocked on the door, realizing that this was the last time she would ever stand in this spot. The last time she'd see Luke smile at her like she was the only girl in the universe. Her own words of encouragement sounded hollow to her ears.

But when the door opened, it wasn't Luke standing there. It was Carter, wearing nothing but a pair of plain work pants.

"He's not here," he growled, his eyes narrowing as he took in her flushed cheeks.

"Oh, sorry," Glass said, taking an involuntary step back. "I'll come back later."

But Carter surprised her by reaching out and grabbing her arm, his hand clamping painfully over her wrist.

"What's the hurry?" he asked with a sudden grin that made her stomach churn. "Come on in and wait. I'm sure he just got held up."

Glass winced, rubbing her wrist, as she followed Carter inside. She'd forgotten how tall he was.

"Did you not have work today?" she asked in her most polite

voice, perching on the edge of the couch where she and Luke usually sat. Her heart cramped as she realized she'd never be able to curl up against his shoulder again, or run her fingers through his curls as he lay with his head in her lap.

"I wasn't in the mood," Carter said with a careless shrug.

"Oh," Glass said, biting back a criticism. If Carter wasn't careful, he'd get demoted yet again, and the only position below the distribution center was sanitation duty. "I'm sorry," she added, because she wasn't sure what else to say.

"No, you're not," Carter said, taking a pull of an unmarked bottle. Glass wrinkled her nose. Black-market whiskey. "You're just like all the other assholes on Phoenix. All you care about is yourself."

"You know what, I should be going," Glass said, moving quickly across the living space toward the door. "Tell Luke I'll see him later."

"Hold it," Carter called. Glass ignored him and grabbed the handle without turning around, but before she could open the door, Carter reached over her shoulder and leaned forward to slam it shut.

"Let me go," Glass ordered, turning to face him.

Carter's grin widened, sending chills down Glass's spine. "What's the problem?" he asked, reaching down to rub his hands over her arms. "We both know how much you like slumming it down on Walden. Don't pretend to be all choosy."

"What are you talking about?" Glass spat, wincing as she tried unsuccessfully to break his grip.

He frowned, digging his fingers painfully into her arms. "You think you're being so rebellious, sneaking around with Luke. But I've known plenty of Phoenix girls like you. You're all the same." Still holding one of her arms, he reached his other hand around and started to fumble with the waistband of her pants.

"Stop," Glass said, trying to push him away, horror spreading rapidly through her veins. Then, more loudly, "Stop it! Let me *go*!"

"It's okay," Carter murmured, yanking her closer to him and wrenching her arms above her head. Glass tried to move away, but he weighed more than twice what she did and she couldn't wriggle free. She thrashed around wildly, trying to jab her knee into his stomach, but she was trapped.

"Don't worry," Carter said, filling her ear with his sour breath. "Luke won't mind. He owes me this, after all I've done for him. Besides, we share *everything*."

Glass opened her mouth to scream, but Carter had pushed himself up against her chest, and there was no air in her lungs. Black spots danced before her vision, and she felt herself losing consciousness.

Then the door opened, and Carter jumped back so quickly, Glass lost her balance and fell to the floor.

"Glass?" Luke asked, stepping inside. "Are you okay? What's going on?"

Glass tried to catch her breath, but before she had time to answer, Carter called out from the couch, where he was already reclined in an attitude of calculated carelessness, "Your girlfriend was just showing me the latest Phoenix dance move." He snorted. "I think she needs a little more practice."

Luke tried to catch Glass's gaze, but she looked away. Her heart thumped wildly with fear-fueled adrenaline and rage.

"Sorry I was late—I got caught up talking to Bekah and Ali," Luke said as he reached down to help her up, naming two of his friends from the engineering corps who had always been nice to Glass. "Hey, what's wrong?" he asked quietly when she didn't take his hand.

After what had just happened, all she wanted to do was throw herself into Luke's arms, to allow the warmth of his body to convince hers that everything was okay. But she'd come here for a reason. She couldn't let him comfort her.

"Are you okay? Should we go talk in my room?"

Glass glanced over at Carter, summoning her anger and hatred for him to the surface, letting it boil her blood. She stood up.

"I'm not going into your room," she said, forcing an edge into her voice she didn't recognize. "Ever again."

"What? What's wrong?" Luke asked. He gently pulled on her

hand but she snatched it away. "Glass?" The confusion in his voice was enough to make her heart throb.

"It's over," she said, shocked at the coldness in her own voice. A strange numbness spread through her, as if her nerves were shutting down to protect her from the grief that would surely destroy her. "Did you really think it was going to last?"

"Glass." Luke's voice was low and strained. "I'm not sure what you're talking about, but could we continue this conversation in my room?" He reached out to place his hand on her arm, and she recoiled from his touch.

"*No.*" She pretended to shudder in horror, looking away so that he couldn't see the tears in her eyes. "I can't believe I let you take me in there in the first place."

Luke fell silent, and Glass couldn't help glancing back at him. He was staring at her, his eyes full of hurt. He had always worried that he wasn't good enough for Glass—that he was keeping her from a better life on Phoenix. And now here she was, using the same fears she had once dismissed to turn Luke against her. "Is that really how you feel?" he asked finally. "I thought we—Glass, I love you," he said helplessly.

"I never loved you." She forced the words out of her mouth with such intensity, they seemed to tear out her very soul. "Don't you see? This was all just a *game* to me, seeing how long I could go on before I got caught. But I'm done now. I'm bored."

Luke reached up to take her chin, turning her face up so that their eyes met. She could feel him searching her for some sign that the real Glass was hidden deep inside. "You don't mean that." His voice cracked. "I don't know what's going on, but this isn't you. Glass, talk to me. Please."

For a brief moment, Glass wavered. She could tell him the truth. Of course he would understand; he would forgive all the terrible things she'd just said. She would lean her head on his shoulder and pretend that everything would be okay. They could face this together.

But then she thought of Luke being executed—the lethal injection shutting down his body before it was released into the cold emptiness of space.

The only way to save Luke's heart was to break it.

"You don't even *know* me," she said, jerking away from his touch, the pain of her grief slicing sharp and hot through her chest. "Here," she finished, blinking back tears as she reached behind her neck to unhook the clasp of her locket. "I don't want this anymore."

As she dropped it into Luke's hand he stared at her wordlessly, shock and hurt etched in sharp lines across his face.

She was only vaguely aware of running out of the door and slamming it shut, and then she was racing down the hall, concentrating on the thud of her steps across the skybridge. Left, right, left, right. *Just get home*, Glass told herself. *Just get home, and then you can cry.*

But the moment she turned the corner, she staggered and slid to the floor, both hands clutching her stomach. "I'm sorry," Glass whispered softly, uncertain whether she was speaking to the baby, or Luke, or her own bruised and damaged heart.

CHAPTER 21

Clarke

The tension in the infirmary tent was so thick, Clarke could practically feel it pressing against her chest when she breathed.

She hovered wordlessly at Thalia's side, trying in vain to battle the infection that had already claimed her kidneys and seemed hell-bent on taking her liver next, seething in silent fury at Octavia's selfishness. How could she sit there, watching Thalia slip in and out of consciousness, and not return the stolen medicine?

But then she glanced over to the corner, where Octavia lay curled up. The sight of her round cheeks and thick lashes made her look painfully young, and Clarke's anger was replaced by doubt and guilt. Maybe Octavia hadn't done it. But if not, who had?

Her eyes lowered to the bracelet that encased her wrist. If Thalia could just hold on until the next wave of colonists arrived, she'd be okay. But there was no knowing when that would be. The Council would wait until they had conclusive data on the radiation levels, regardless of what was happening on Earth.

Thalia's death, she knew, would matter as little to the Council as Lilly's had. Orphans and criminals didn't count.

As she watched Thalia's labored breathing, Clarke felt a surge of white-hot fury. She refused to sit here and just wait for her friend to die. Hadn't humans cured illnesses for millennia before the discovery of penicillin? There had to be *something* in the woods that fought infection. She tried to remember what little she'd learned about plants in Biology of Earth class. Who knew if those plants were even around anymore—everything seemed to have evolved strangely after the Cataclysm. But she had to at least try.

"I'll be back," she whispered to her sleeping friend. Without a word to the Arcadian boy standing guard outside, Clarke hurried out of the infirmary and began to walk toward the trees, not bothering to grab anything from the supply tent lest she attract any unwanted attention. But she didn't manage to go more than ten meters without a familiar voice scratching at her eardrums.

"Where are you going?" Wells asked as he fell in step next to her.

"Looking for medicinal plants." She was too tired to lie to Wells, and it didn't matter anyway; he always saw through her lies. Somehow, the self-righteousness that blinded him to the most glaring truths didn't prevent him from reading the secrets in her eyes.

"I'll come with you."

"I'm fine on my own, thanks," Clarke said, increasing her pace, as if that could possibly deter the boy who'd traveled across the solar system to be with her. "You stay here in case they need someone to lead an angry mob."

"You're right. Things got a little out of hand last night," he said with a frown. "I didn't mean for anything bad to happen to Octavia. I only wanted to help. I know you need that medicine for Thalia."

"You *only wanted to help*. I've heard that one before." Clarke whipped around to face Wells. She didn't have the time or the energy to deal with his need for redemption right now. "Guess what, Wells. Someone ended up Confined this time too."

Wells stopped in his tracks, and Clarke jerked her head away, unable to look at the hurt in his eyes. But she refused to let him make her feel guilty. Nothing she could say to him could begin to approximate the pain he'd caused her.

Clarke stared straight ahead as she strode into the trees, still half expecting to hear the thud of footsteps behind her. But this time there was only silence.

By the time she reached the creek, the fury Clarke had carried into the woods had been replaced by despair. The scientist in her was mortified by her own naïveté. It was foolish to think that she would somehow recognize a plant from a class she'd taken six years ago, let alone that it would even look the same after all this time. But she refused to turn back, restrained partly by her own stubborn pride and partly by a desire to avoid Wells for as long as possible.

It was too chilly to wade through the water, so she climbed up the slope and walked along the ridge to cross over to the other side. This was the farthest she'd ever been from camp, and it felt different out here; the air even *tasted* somehow different than it did closer to the clearing. She closed her eyes, hoping that it would help her identify the strange swirl of scents that she had no words to describe. It was like trying to recall a memory that hadn't been hers to begin with.

The ground was flatter here than she'd seen elsewhere in the woods. Up ahead, the gap between the trees grew even wider, and the trees themselves seemed to part into straight lines on either side, as if they could sense Clarke's presence and had stood aside to let her pass.

Clarke started to pull a star-shaped leaf from a tree, then froze as a glint of light caught her eye. Something nestled in between two enormous trees was reflecting the fading sunlight.

She took another step forward, her heart racing.

It was a window.

Clarke began walking toward it slowly, feeling as though she were moving through one of her own dreams. The window was framed by two trees, which must have grown out of the ruins of the structure, whatever it had been. But the glass wasn't clear. As she got closer, she saw that the window was actually made from different pieces of colored glass that had been arranged to create an image, although there were too many cracks to tell what it had once been.

She reached forward and gently brushed her finger against the glass, shivering as the cold seeped into her fingers. It was like touching a corpse. For a moment, she found herself wishing Wells was with her. No matter how angry she was with him, she'd never deprive him of the chance to see one of the ruins he'd spent his whole life dreaming about.

She turned and walked around one of the large trees. There was another window, but this one had been smashed, sharp fragments of glass glittering on the ground. Clarke stepped forward and crouched down to peer inside. The jagged opening was almost large enough to crawl through. The sun was only beginning to set, and the orange rays seemed to shine right into the opening, revealing what looked like a wooden floor. Every instinct in Clarke's brain was shouting at her to keep away, but she couldn't bring herself to stop.

Taking care not to let her skin touch the glass, Clarke reached her arm through the opening of the window and brushed her hand against the wood. Nothing happened. She clenched her fingers into a fist and rapped on it, coughing as a cloud of dust rose into the air. It felt solid. She paused, considering. The building had survived this long. Surely the floor would be able to hold her weight.

Carefully, she slid one leg through the opening, then the other. She held her breath, but nothing happened.

When she looked up and around her, Clarke sucked in her breath.

The walls soared on all sides, converging in a point many meters above her head, higher than even the roof above the solar fields. It wasn't as dark as she'd expected. There were windows along the other wall that she hadn't been able to see. These were made of clear glass, but they weren't broken. Beams of sunlight shone through, illuminating millions of dust particles dancing through the air.

Clark rose slowly to her feet. There was a railing up ahead that ran parallel to the floor at about waist height. She took a few hesitant steps toward it and gasped, startling herself again as the sound echoed far above her head.

She was standing on a balcony overlooking an enormous open space. It was almost completely dark, probably because most of the building was now underground, but she could just make out the outline of benches. She didn't dare venture any closer to the edge for a better look, but as her eyes adjusted to the darkness, more shapes sharpened into focus.

Bodies.

At first she thought she'd only imagined it, that her mind was using the shadows to play tricks on her. She closed her eyes and willed herself not to be such a fool. But when she turned back, the shapes were the same.

Two skeletons were draped over one of the benches, and another, smaller one lay at their feet. Although there was no knowing whether the bones had been disturbed, from what she could tell, these people had died huddled together. Had they been trying to keep warm as the skies darkened and nuclear winter set in? How many people had been left at that point?

Clarke took another small step forward, but this time, the wood creaked dangerously. She froze and started to inch her way back. But a loud crack sang out through the silence, and with a sudden lurch, the floor fell out from underneath her.

She waved her hands wildly, grabbing hold of the balcony

edge as the railing and floor tumbled through the air. Her legs dangled over a vast, open space as the pieces landed with a thud on the stone far below.

She screamed, a loud, wordless cry that rose up toward the ceiling and then faded away, joining the ghosts of whatever other screams still lingered in the dust. Her fingers started to slide.

"*Help!*" Using every ounce of strength in her body, she tried to pull herself up, her arms shaking with the effort, but her grip was failing. She started to scream again, but there was no more air left in her lungs, and the word died on her lips before she realized it had been Wells's name.

CHAPTER 22

Wells

Wells broke into a sprint as Clarke's scream ignited every nerve in his body. It had been difficult following Clarke through the woods, especially since he had to keep his distance—she would have been furious if she'd spotted him. But now he was flying over the grass and could barely feel his boots hitting the ground. He had just reached the stained-glass window when a second, louder scream filled the air.

"Clarke!" he yelled, sticking his head through the gap in the broken glass. It was dark inside the ruin, but there was no time to take out his flashbeam. Up ahead, he could just make out fingers clinging to a ledge. Wells ducked inside, landing with a thud on a wooden platform, and then slid forward on his stomach, reaching over the edge to wrap one hand around Clarke's wrist while he grabbed on to the stone wall for leverage. "I've got you," he said.

But he spoke too soon. One of her hands disappeared, and he was now supporting her entire weight. He could feel himself slipping toward the edge. "*Clarke!*" he screamed again. "Hold on!"

With a grunt, he managed to pull himself up into a sitting position, then pressed one foot against the wall. His hand was sweating, and he could feel himself losing his grip. "*Wells*," she shrieked. Her voice echoed through the cavernous space, making it sound like there were a hundred Clarkes in peril.

He gritted his teeth and pulled, gasping with relief and exhaustion when Clarke's other hand regained its hold. "You're almost there. Come on."

She placed her elbows on the wooden platform, and he reached over to grab her upper arm, heaving the rest of her body up over the ledge. They collapsed into a heap against the stone wall.

Clarke was sobbing as she struggled to catch her breath. "It's okay," Wells said, wrapping his arm around her. "You're okay." He waited for her to recoil from his touch, but instead, she buried herself in his arms. Wells tightened his hold.

"What are you doing here?" she asked from inside his embrace, her voice muffled. "I thought . . . I hoped . . ."

"I followed you—I was worried," Wells spoke into her hair. "I could never let anything happen to you. No matter what." He spoke without thinking, but as the words left his lips he knew that they were true. Even if she kissed someone else—even if she wanted to be with someone else—he would always be there for her.

Clarke didn't say anything, but she stayed in his arms.

Wells held her there, terrified to say anything else and end this moment too soon, his relief expanding into joy. Maybe he had a chance to win her back. Maybe, here in the ruins of the old world, they could start something new.

CHAPTER 23

Bellamy

He'd start with letting the bastards starve. Then, maybe when they were all so weak with hunger that they had to *crawl* over to him and beg for forgiveness, then he'd consider going out to hunt. But they'd have to make do with a squirrel or something else small—no way was he killing another deer for them.

Bellamy had spent the night unable to sleep, watching the infirmary tent in order to make damn sure no one got anywhere *near* his sister. Now that it was morning, he'd resorted to pacing around the perimeter of the camp. He had too much energy to sit still.

Bellamy stepped over the tree line, feeling his body relax slightly as the shadows washed over him. Over the past few weeks, he'd discovered that he enjoyed the company of trees more than people. He shivered as a breeze swept across the back of his neck, and looked up. The patches of sky visible through the branches were beginning to turn gray, and the air suddenly felt different—almost damp. He lowered his head and kept walking. Perhaps Earth had had enough of their bullshit already and was initiating a second nuclear winter.

He turned and began drifting in the direction of the stream, where there were usually animal tracks to follow. But then a flash of movement in a tree a few meters away caught his attention, and he paused.

Something bright red was waving in the wind. It might've been a leaf, except there wasn't anything else close to that shade nearby. Bellamy squinted, then took a few steps forward, feeling a strange prickle on the back of his neck. It was Octavia's hair ribbon. It made absolutely no sense—she hadn't been out in the woods for days—but he'd recognize it anywhere. There were some things you could never forget.

The halls were dark as Bellamy scurried up the stairs to their flat. It had been worth staying out after curfew, as long as he didn't get caught. He'd broken through an old air shaft, too small for anyone but a child to crawl through, into an abandoned storage room he'd heard about on C deck. It was full of all kinds of treasures:

a brimmed hat topped with a funny-looking bird; a box that said EIGHT MINUTE ABS on it, whatever that meant; and a red ribbon he'd found wrapped around the handle of a strange wheeled bag. Bellamy had traded his other discoveries in exchange for ration points, but he'd kept the ribbon, even though it would have fed them for a month. He wanted to give it to Octavia.

He pressed his thumb to the scanner and carefully opened the door, then froze. Someone was moving inside. His mother was normally asleep by now. He took a silent step forward, just enough to hear better, and felt himself relax as a familiar sound filled his ears. His mother was singing Octavia's favorite lullaby, something she used to do all the time, sitting on the floor and singing through the door of the closet until Octavia fell asleep. Bellamy sighed with relief. It didn't sound like she was in the mood to scream at him, or worse, have one of her endless crying fits that made Bellamy want to hide in the closet with his sister.

Bellamy smiled as he crept into the main room and saw his mother kneeling on the floor. "Hush, little baby, don't you cry, mama's gonna buy you a star in the sky. And if that star can't carry a tune, mama's going buy you a piece of the moon." Another sound drifted through the darkness, a faint wheeze. Was the ventilation system acting up again? He took a step forward. "And if the moon ever loses its shine, mama's gonna buy you—"

Bellamy heard the sound again, although this time, it sounded more like a gasp.

"Mom?" He took another step. She was crouched over something on the floor. "*Mom*," he bellowed, lunging forward.

His mother had her hands around Octavia's neck, and even in the darkness, Bellamy could see that his sister's face was blue. He knocked his mother to the side and scooped Octavia into his arms. For one heart-stopping second, he was sure she was dead, but then she twitched and started coughing. Bellamy exhaled, and his heart began thumping wildly.

"We were just playing a game," his mother said faintly. "She couldn't sleep. So we were playing a game. . . ."

Bellamy held Octavia close, making soothing noises, staring at the wall as a strange feeling came over him. He wasn't sure what his mother had been doing, but he was sure she was going to try again.

Bellamy rose onto the balls of his feet and stretched his arm toward the ribbon. His fingers wrapped around the familiar satin, but as he tried to pull it down, he realized the ornament wasn't just caught on the branch—it had been tied there.

Had someone found the ribbon and tied it to the tree for safekeeping? But why wouldn't they just have brought it back to camp? He absentmindedly ran his hand down the branch, letting the rough bark dig into his skin as he traced a line from the branch down to the trunk. But then he froze. His fingers were hovering on the edge of a dip in the trunk, where a chunk of wood had been scooped out. There was something sticking out—a bird's nest, maybe?

Bellamy grabbed on to the edge and pulled, watching in horror as the medicine he and Clarke had discovered came tumbling out. The pills, syringes, bottles—all of it was scattered in the grass by his feet. His brain raced for an explanation, anything to staunch the panic welling up in his chest.

He sank to the grass with a groan and closed his eyes.

It was true. Octavia *had* taken the medicine. She'd hidden it in the tree and used her hair ribbon as a marker so she could find it again. But he couldn't think why she'd done it. Had she worried about what would happen if one of them had gotten sick? Maybe she'd been planning to take the supplies with them when they set out on their own.

But then Graham's words rang in his ears. *We can't let anyone else die just because your little sister's a drug addict.*

The boy assigned to stand guard outside the infirmary tent had fallen asleep. He barely managed to scramble to his feet and mumble a quick "Hey, you can't go in there" before Bellamy burst through the flap. He jerked his head around, confirming that it was empty except for Clarke's sleeping sick friend, then strode over to where Octavia was sitting cross-legged on her cot, braiding her hair.

"What the hell do you think you're doing?" he hissed.

"What are you talking about?" Her voice was a mixture of boredom and irritation, as if he were pestering her about schoolwork like he always used to when checking up on her in the care center.

Bellamy threw the hair ribbon down on her cot, wincing as he saw horror rush to Octavia's face. "I didn't . . . ," she stammered. "It wasn't . . ."

"Cut the bullshit, O," he snapped. "Now you can finish braiding your goddamn hair while a girl is dying in front of you."

Octavia's eyes darted to Thalia, then shifted down. "I didn't think she was really that sick," she said softly. "Clarke had already given her medicine. By the time I realized she needed more, it was too late. I can't confess now. You saw how they were. I didn't know what they'd do to me." When she looked up again, her deep-blue eyes were filled with tears. "Even you hate me now, and you're my brother."

Bellamy sighed and sat down next to his sister. "I don't hate you." He grabbed her hand and gave it a squeeze. "I just don't understand. Why'd you do it? The truth this time, please."

Octavia fell silent, and he could feel her skin growing clammy as she began to tremble. "O?" He released her hand.

"I needed them," she said, her voice small. "I can't sleep

without them." She paused and closed her eyes. "At first, it was just at night. I kept having these terrible dreams, so the nurse at the care center gave me medicine to help me sleep, but then it got worse. There were times when I couldn't breathe, when it felt like the whole universe was closing in on me, crushing me. The nurse wouldn't give me any more medicine, even when I asked, so I started stealing pills. It was the only thing that made me feel better."

Bellamy stared at her. "*That's* what you were caught stealing?" he asked slowly, the realization overtaking him. "Not food for the younger kids in the care center. *Pills*."

Octavia didn't say anything, just nodded, her eyes full of tears.

"O," Bellamy sighed. "Why didn't you tell me?"

"I know how much you worry about me." She took a deep breath. "I know how you want to protect me all the time. I didn't want you to feel like you'd failed."

Bellamy felt pain radiating out from a spot behind his heart. He didn't know which hurt more: that his sister was a drug addict, or that she hadn't told him the truth because he'd been so blinded by his insane need to watch over her. When he finally spoke, his voice was hoarse. "So what do we do now?" he asked. For the first time in his life, he had no idea how to help his sister. "What will happen when we give the medicine back?"

"I'll be okay. I just need to learn how to live without them. It's already easier here." She reached out and took his hand, giving him a strange, almost pleading look. "Do you wish you hadn't come here for me?"

"No," Bellamy said firmly, shaking his head. "I just need some time to process everything." He rose to his feet, then looked back at his sister. "But you need to make sure Clarke gets the medicine. *You* have to be the one to tell her. I'm serious, O."

"I know." She nodded, then turned to look at Thalia and seemed to deflate a little. "I'll do it tonight."

"Okay." Sighing, Bellamy strode out of the tent and into the clearing. When he reached the tree line, he took a deep breath, allowing the damp air to seep through his lungs into his aching chest. He tilted his head back to let the wind wash over his flushed skin. Now that the sky was unobstructed by trees, it looked even darker, almost black. Suddenly, a line of jagged light flashed across the sky, followed by a violent, resounding crack that made the earth shudder. Bellamy jumped, and screams filled the clearing. But they were quickly drowned out by another deafening boom, this one louder than the first, like the sky was about to tumble to Earth.

Then something did start to fall. Drops of liquid were cascading down his skin, dripping off his hair, and quickly seeping into his clothes. *Rain*, Bellamy realized, real rain. He tilted his face up toward the sky, and for a moment, his wonder drowned out all the rest—his anger at Graham and Wells and Clarke, his concern for his sister, the screams of the idiot kids who didn't know that rain was harmless. He closed his eyes, letting the water wash away the dirt and sweat caked on his face. For a second, he let himself imagine that the rain could wash everything away: the blood, the tears, the fact that he and Octavia had failed each other. They could have a clean start, try again.

Bellamy opened his eyes. He was being ridiculous, he knew. The rain was only water, and there was no such thing as a clean start. That was the thing about secrets—you had to carry them with you forever, no matter what the cost.

CHAPTER 24

Glass

As she walked across the skybridge, the terrible realization that her mother was right hung like a weight on Glass's heart. She couldn't risk a single misstep—not for her sake, but for Luke's. What if the Chancellor woke up and revoked her pardon, and then Luke did something stupid and admitted the truth about the pregnancy? It was like history was repeating itself, and yet she knew she'd always make the same choice. She would always choose to protect the boy she loved.

She'd been avoiding Luke for several days, though he'd been summoned for so many emergency shifts lately that she wasn't sure he'd even noticed. She'd finally arranged to meet at his flat this evening, and the thought of him greeting her with a smile made her chest ache. At least this time, there'd be no tricks, no lies. She'd simply tell him the truth, no matter how difficult. Maybe he'd seek comfort in Camille again, and then things would truly come full circle. The thought came with a knife-sharp pang, but Glass ignored it and kept walking.

As she approached the far end of the skybridge, her eyes landed on a small group gathered near the checkpoint. A few guards stood speaking in a tight circle, while a number of civilians whispered and pointed at something through the long, star-filled window that bordered the walkway. Glass suddenly recognized a few of the guards—they were Luke's team, members of the elite guard's engineering corps. The woman with graying hair who was moving her fingers rapidly through the air, manipulating a holo-diagram in front of her face, was Bekah. Next to her was Ali, a boy with dark skin and bright-green eyes fixed intently on the image Bekah was creating.

"Glass!" Ali exclaimed warmly, looking up as she approached. He jogged forward a few steps and clasped her hands in his. "It's great to see you. How are you?"

"I'm . . . good," she stammered, confused. How much did they know? Were they greeting her as Luke's ex, the snotty Phoenix girl who'd broken his heart, or as Luke's escaped-convict girlfriend? Either way, Ali was being much kinder than she deserved.

Bekah shot Glass a quick smile and then returned to her

diagrams, frowning as she rotated a complicated-looking three-dimensional blueprint. "Where's Luke?" Glass asked as she glanced from side to side. If they were still on duty, he wouldn't be home yet either.

Ali gestured out the window with a grin. "Look outside."

Glass turned slowly, every atom in her body turning to ice. She knew already what she would see. Two figures in space suits were floating outside, each tethered to the ship by a thin cord. They had tool kits strapped to their backs and were using their gloved hands to move along the skybridge.

As if in a trance, Glass moved slowly forward and pressed her face against the window. She watched in horror as the two figures nodded at each other, then disappeared under the skybridge. Luke's unit was responsible for crucial repairs, but he'd only been a junior member of the team when they were dating last year. She knew he'd been promoted, but she had no idea he would be out on spacewalks this soon.

The thought of him outside—nothing separating him from the cold emptiness of space but a laughably thin cord and a pressurized suit—made Glass feel dizzy. She grabbed on to the railing to steady herself, sending up a silent prayer to the stars to keep him safe.

She hadn't left the flat in two weeks. Not even her loosest clothes could mask the bump that had emerged with alarming suddenness. Glass wasn't sure how much longer her mother would be able to make excuses for her. She'd stopped responding to her friends' messages, and eventually, they'd stopped sending them. Everyone except for Wells, who contacted her every day without fail.

Glass pulled up her message queue to reread the note he'd sent her that morning.

I know something must be wrong, and I hope you know that I'm always here for whatever you need. But even if you don't (or can't) write back, I'm going to keep filling your queue with my stupid ramblings because, no matter what happened, you're still my best friend and I'll never stop wishing you were here.

The rest of the note went on to talk about Wells's frustrations with officer training, then ended with a few cryptic allusions to something about Clarke. Glass hoped there was nothing seriously wrong—Clarke needed to realize how good she had it. She would never find a sweeter, smarter boy on Phoenix. Although the honor of the sweetest, smartest boy in the Colony went to Luke. Luke, who was no longer in her life.

The only thing that kept Glass sane was the growing presence inside her. Placing her hand on her stomach, Glass whispered to the baby, telling him again—she felt certain, somehow, that it was a boy—how much she loved him.

There was a sudden knock at the door, and Glass hurried to stand up, to try to run into her bedroom and lock it shut. But the three guards had already burst inside.

"Glass Sorenson," one of them barked, his eyes traveling to her stomach, the bump glaringly obvious. "You are under arrest for violation of the Gaia Doctrine."

"Please just let me explain." She gasped as panic gushed through her. It felt like she was drowning. The room was spinning, and it was hard to tell which words were coming out of her mouth and which were dashing manically through her skull.

In a flash, one of the guards grabbed her arms and wrenched her wrists behind her back while another secured them with cuffs. "No," she whimpered. "Please. It was an accident." She pressed her feet into the floor, but there was no use. The guards were forcibly dragging her across the room.

And then some wild, frantic instinct took over, and Glass thrashed against the guard restraining her, kicking wildly against his shins and shoving her elbow into his throat. He tightened his grip on her shoulder as he dragged her out through the corridor and into the stairwell.

A sob wrenched up from inside her as Glass realized that she would never see Luke again, the knowledge hitting her with all the force of a hammer. Her legs suddenly gave out. The guard holding her staggered back as she slid, trying to keep her upright.

I could do it, Glass thought, taking advantage of his momentary imbalance to surge wildly forward. For a brief, shining moment, Glass felt the thrill of hope pushing through the panic. This was her chance. She would escape.

But then the guard snatched at her from behind and she lost her footing. Her shoulder smacked against the landing and, suddenly, she was falling down the sharp, narrow, dim staircase.

Everything went dark.

When Glass opened her eyes again, her whole body ached. Her knees, her shoulders, her stomach—

Her stomach. Glass tried to move her hands to feel it, but they were strapped down. No, *cuffed* down, she realized in growing horror. Of course; she was a criminal.

"Oh, sweetie, you're awake," a warm voice greeted her.

Through her blurry vision, she could just make out the shape of a figure approaching her bed. It was a nurse.

"Please," Glass croaked. "Is he okay? Can I hold him?"

The woman paused, and Glass knew even before she spoke what she would say. She could already sense it, the horrible, aching emptiness inside her.

"I'm sorry," the nurse said quietly. Glass could barely see her mouth, which gave the impression that the voice was coming from somewhere else entirely. "We couldn't save him."

Glass turned away, letting the cold metal of the handcuffs press angrily against her skin, not caring about the pain. Any feeling was better than this, this heartache that would never go away.

Finally, the two figures reappeared from underneath the skybridge. Glass exhaled loudly as she brought her hand to the window. How long had she been holding her breath?

"Are you okay?" a voice asked, and for a moment, Glass thought with horror that she was back in that hospital room with the nurse. But it was only Luke's guard friend Bekah, looking at her with concern.

Her face was wet, Glass realized. She'd been crying. She couldn't even bring herself to feel embarrassed, she was so relieved that Luke had made it back safely.

"Thanks," Glass managed, taking the handkerchief that Bekah offered, wiping away her tears. Outside, Luke was pulling himself back along the cord, placing one gloved hand over the other as he moved back toward the airlock chamber.

Around her, various onlookers started to clap and high-five one another, but Glass stayed at the window, her eyes fixed on the spot she'd last seen Luke. The thoughts that Glass had carried with her onto the skybridge seemed as distant as a long-forgotten dream. She couldn't sever their tie any more than she could cut the wire tethering him to the ship. Without Luke, life would be as empty and cold as space itself.

"Hey, you," his voice came from behind her, and Glass

spun around, throwing herself into his arms. His thermal shirt was soaked with sweat, his curls damp and dirty, but Glass didn't care.

"I was worried about you," she said, her voice muffled into his shirt.

He laughed and wrapped his arms tighter around her, planting a kiss on the top of her head. "This is a nice surprise."

Glass looked up at him, not caring that her eyes were puffy and that her nose was running. "It's fine," Luke said, exchanging an amused look with Ali before turning back to Glass. "It's all part of the job."

Her heart was still pumping too fast to speak, so she nodded, shooting an embarrassed smile at Bekah and Ali and the others. "Come on," Luke said, taking her hand and leading her down the skybridge.

As they crossed onto Walden, Glass's breathing finally returned to normal. "I can't believe you do that," she said quietly. "Aren't you terrified?"

"It's scary, but it's exhilarating, too. It's so . . . enormous out there. I know that sounds kind of stupid." He paused, but Glass shook her head. They both knew about enclosed spaces, how you could feel trapped in them, even one as vast as the ship.

"I'm just glad everything went okay," she said.

"Yeah, it did. Well, mostly." Luke's fingers loosened their grip around hers, and his voice grew slightly strained. "There was something weird going on with the airlock. Some valve must've come loose, because it was releasing oxygen out of the ship."

"But you guys fixed it, right?"

"Of course. That's what we're trained to do." He squeezed her hand.

Suddenly, Glass stopped short, turning to Luke and rising up on her toes to kiss him, right there in the middle of the crowded hallway. She didn't care anymore who saw them. No matter what happened, she thought, kissing him with an almost desperate need, she would never let anything keep them apart again.

CHAPTER 25

Bellamy

Bellamy stared into the flickering flames, the buzz of conversation around him mingling with the cracking of the logs. It had been a few hours since his confrontation with Octavia, and so far there'd been no sign of her. He hoped she'd return the medicine soon. He couldn't force her to hand it over, he knew, or their relationship would never recover. He had to show that he trusted her, and she had to do the right thing to win back that trust.

The rain had stopped, but the ground was still damp. A few scuffles had broken out over the handful of rocks that had become VIP seating around the campfire, but for the most part, everyone seemed willing to tolerate the soggy grass to sit close to the warmth of the flames. A few girls had sought out a third option and were now perched on the laps of smug-looking boys.

He scanned the circle, searching for Clarke. There was much more smoke than usual, probably because all the firewood was wet, and it took a few moments for his eyes to settle on the familiar glint of her reddish-gold hair. He squinted and realized, to his surprise, that she was sitting next to Wells. They weren't touching, or even speaking, but something had changed between them. The tension that wracked Clarke's body whenever Wells came near had disappeared, and instead of shooting wounded, furtive looks at Clarke when her head was turned, Wells was staring placidly into the fire, a content look on his face.

A shard of resentment worked its way into Bellamy's stomach. He should have known it would only be a matter of time before Clarke went running back to Wells. He should never have kissed her in the woods. He'd only ever really cared about one other girl before—and he'd gotten hurt that time too.

The clouds were thick enough to block out most of the stars, but Bellamy tilted his head back anyway, wondering how much warning they'd have before the next dropship arrived. Would they be able to see it tearing toward them—a warning flare in the sky?

But then his eyes fell on a figure moving through the darkness toward the fire: the shadowy outline of a tiny girl with her head held high. Bellamy rose to his feet as Octavia stepped into the pool of light cast by the dancing flames, sending a ripple of whispers around the circle.

"Oh, for the love of god." Bellamy heard Graham groan. "Who the hell was supposed to be watching her tonight?"

Wells shot Clarke a look, then stood to face Graham. "It's fine," he said. "She can join us."

Octavia paused, looking from Wells to Graham as the boys glared at each other. But before either of them had time to speak, she took a breath and stepped forward. "I have something to say," she said. She was trembling, but her voice was firm.

The excited whispers and confused murmurs trailed off as nearly a hundred heads turned to face Octavia. In the flickering firelight, Bellamy could see the panic creeping across her face, and felt a sudden urge to run over and hold her hand. But he forced his feet to stay rooted to the ground. He'd spent so long trying to take care of the little girl in his mind that he'd never gotten to know the person she'd become. And right now, this was something she had to do on her own.

"I did take the medicine," Octavia began. She paused to let her words sink in, then took a deep breath and continued as a rumble of *I knew its* and *I told you sos* began to build like thunder. Octavia told the group a similar version of the story she'd told Bellamy earlier that day—how hard it'd been growing up in the care center, how her dependence on pills had turned into an addiction.

The muttering ceased as Octavia's voice cracked. "Back on the Colony, I never thought I was hurting anyone. Stealing just seemed like a way to get what I deserved. I figured everyone deserved to be able to fall asleep at night. To wake up without feeling that your nightmares had left scars inside your head." She took a deep breath and closed her eyes. When she opened them, Bellamy could see the faint shimmer of tears. "I was so selfish, so scared. But I never meant to hurt Thalia, or anyone." She turned to Clarke and swallowed the sob that seemed to be forming in her throat. "I'm so sorry. I know I don't deserve your forgiveness, but all I can ask is that you give me a chance to start over." She raised her chin and looked around the circle until she saw Bellamy, and she gave him a small smile. "Just like everyone here wants to do. I know a lot of us have done things we're not proud of, but we've been given a chance for a new beginning. I know I almost ruined it for a lot of you, but I'd like to start over—to become a better person, to help make Earth the world we want it to be."

Bellamy's heart swelled with pride. Tears were beginning to blur his vision, although if anyone called him out on it, he'd blame it on the smoke. His sister's life had been full of suffering and hardship from the very beginning. She'd made mistakes—they both had—but she'd still managed to stay brave and strong.

For a moment, no one spoke. Even the crackling of the fire faded away, as if Earth itself were holding its breath. But then Graham's voice barreled through the silence. "That's bullshit."

Bellamy bristled as a spark of anger sizzled across his chest, but he gritted his teeth. Of course Graham was going to be a bastard about it—that didn't mean the others hadn't been touched by Octavia's speech. But instead of prompting scoffs or disapproving whispers, Graham's words unleashed a tide of murmured assent that swelled quickly into shouts. He looked around the circle as he continued. "Why should we bust our asses all day, chopping wood, hauling water, doing whatever it takes to keep everyone alive, just to let some delusional drug addict walk all over us? It's like being—"

"Okay, that's enough," Bellamy said, cutting him off. He glanced at Octavia. Her bottom lip had begun to quiver as her eyes darted around the fire. "You've made your point. But there are ninety-four other people here with opinions of their own, and they don't need you to tell them what to think."

"I agree with Graham," a girl's voice called out. Bellamy turned and saw a short-haired Waldenite glaring at Octavia. "We *all* had shitty lives back on the Colony, but you don't see anyone else stealing." She narrowed her eyes. "Who knows what she'll take next time."

"Everyone just relax." Clarke had risen to her feet. "She apologized. We have to give her a second chance." Bellamy stared at her in surprise, waiting for the surge of indignation. After all, she was the one who'd accused Octavia in the first place. But as he looked at Clarke, all he felt was gratitude.

"No." Graham's voice was hard and as he looked around the circle, his eyes flashed with something other than reflected firelight. He turned to Wells, who was still standing next to Clarke. "It's just like you said. There has to be some kind of order, or else there's no way in hell we'll make it."

"So what do you recommend?" Wells asked. Graham smiled, and Bellamy felt like someone had poured ice water down his back. Fixing Graham with a glare, he hurried over to Octavia and put his arm around her.

"It'll be okay," he whispered.

"I'm sorry," Graham said, turning to Bellamy and Octavia. "But we don't have a choice. She put Thalia's life at risk. We can't take any chances. Octavia needs to die."

"What?" Bellamy sputtered. "Are you *insane*?" He jerked his head from side to side, expecting to see a sea of similarly revolted faces. But while a few people were staring at Graham in shock, a number were nodding.

Bellamy stepped protectively in front of Octavia, who was

trembling violently. He'd burn the goddamn planet to a crisp before he let anyone near his sister.

"Should we put it to a vote?" Graham raised his chin and nodded at Wells. "You're the one who was so excited to bring *democracy* back to Earth. It seems only fair."

"This is *not* what I meant," Wells snapped. His face had lost its politician's reserve, his features twisted with anger. "We're not going to vote about whether to *kill* people."

"No?" Graham raised an eyebrow. "So it's okay for your father, but not for us."

Bellamy winced and closed his eyes as he heard sounds of agreement ripple through the crowd. It was exactly what he would've said in that situation, except that Bellamy would have only meant it as a jab at Wells. He'd never *actually* propose killing someone.

"The Council doesn't execute people for fun." Wells's voice shook with fury. "Keeping humanity alive in space required extraordinary measures. Sometimes *cruel* measures." Wells paused. "But we have a chance to do better."

"So what?" Graham growled. "You're just going to give her a slap on the wrist and then make everyone pinky swear not to break the rules?" A few snickers rose up from the crowd.

"No." Wells shook his head. "You're right. There needs to be consequences." He took a deep breath. "We'll banish them from camp." His voice was firm, but when he turned to Bellamy, his eyes seemed to contain a strange mixture of anguish and relief.

"Banish?" Graham repeated. "So they can sneak back whenever they want and steal more supplies? That's bullshit."

Bellamy opened his mouth to speak, but his voice was drowned out as the buzz of voices grew louder. Finally, a girl Bellamy vaguely recognized from Walden stood up. "That sounds fair," she called out, shouting to be heard over the crowd, which grew quiet as heads turned to look at her. "As long as they promise never to come back."

Bellamy tightened his arm around Octavia, who'd gone limp. He nodded. "We'll leave at sunrise." He turned to smile at Octavia—this is what he'd planned all along. So then why did he feel more apprehension than relief?

The fire died down, and darkness settled over the camp like a blanket, muffling footsteps and muting voices as shadowy figures disappeared into tents or carried blankets toward the edges of the clearing.

Bellamy set up a makeshift cot for Octavia at the short end, near the wreckage of the dropship. They hadn't said it aloud, but they both knew neither of them wanted to sleep in a tent tonight.

Octavia curled up on her blanket and closed her eyes, though it was clear she wasn't sleeping. The trip back into the woods with Clarke to retrieve the medicine had been a tense one. No one had spoken, though Bellamy could feel Clarke's eyes boring into his back as he led the way.

Now he sat next to Octavia, his back against a tree, staring into the darkness. It was hard to wrap his mind around the fact that tomorrow, they would leave forever.

A shape moved through the shadows toward them. Wells. He had Bellamy's bow slung over his shoulder.

"Hey," Wells said quietly as Bellamy rose to his feet. "I'm sorry about what happened back there. I know banishment sounds harsh, but I wasn't sure what else to do." He sighed. "I really thought Graham was going to convince them to . . ." He trailed off as his eyes fell on Octavia. "Not that I would've let that happen, but there's only two of us and a lot of them."

Bellamy felt a smartass retort rise in his throat but swallowed it back down. Wells had done the best thing he could under the circumstances. "Thank you."

They stared at each other for a moment, then Bellamy cleared his throat. "Listen, I should probably . . ." He paused. "I'm sorry about your father." Bellamy took a deep breath and forced himself to meet Wells's eyes. "I hope he's okay."

"Thank you," Wells said quietly. "I do too." He fell silent for a moment, but when he spoke again, his voice was firm. "I know you were just trying to protect your sister. I would've done the same thing." He smiled. "I suppose I sort of did."

Wells extended his hand. "I hope you and Octavia stay safe out there."

Bellamy shook his hand and smiled ruefully. "I can't imagine anything out there worse than Graham. Keep an eye on that kid."

"Will do." Wells nodded, then turned around and headed back into the darkness.

Bellamy lowered himself to the blanket and stared out into the clearing. He could just make out the shape of the infirmary tent where Clarke would be giving Thalia the long-awaited medicine. His stomach twisted strangely as he thought back to the scene by the fire, the flames flickering over Clarke's determined face. He'd never known a girl who was so beautiful and intense at once.

Bellamy leaned back with a sigh and closed his eyes, wondering how long it would take until she stopped being the last person he thought about before he fell asleep.

CHAPTER 26

Clarke

The antibiotics were working. Although it had been less than a few hours since Clarke burst into the tent, clutching the medicine under her arm, Thalia's fever had already gone down, and she was more alert than she'd been in days.

Clarke lowered herself to perch on the edge of Thalia's cot as her friend's eyes fluttered open. "Welcome back," Clarke said with a grin. "How are you feeling?"

Thalia's eyes darted around the empty tent, then looked up to meet Clarke's. "This isn't heaven, is it?"

Clarke shook her head. "God, I hope not."

"Good. Because I always assumed there'd be boys there. Boys who didn't use water rationing as an excuse not to bathe." Thalia managed a smile. "Did anyone build the first shower on Earth while I was passed out?"

"Nope. You didn't miss much."

"Somehow, I find that hard to believe." Thalia raised her shoulders in an attempt to sit up, but settled back down with a groan. Clarke gently placed a rolled-up blanket behind her. "Thanks," she muttered and surveyed Clarke for a moment before she spoke again. "Okay, what's wrong?"

Clarke gave her a bemused smile. "Nothing! I'm just so happy you're feeling better."

"Please. You can't hide anything from me. You know I always manage to get your secrets out of you," Thalia deadpanned. "You can start by telling me where you found the medicine."

"Octavia had it," Clarke explained and quickly filled Thalia in on what had happened. "She and Bellamy are leaving tomorrow," she finished. "That's part of the deal Wells made with everyone. I know it sounds crazy, but it really felt like they were close to attacking her." She shook her head. "If Wells hadn't stepped in, I'm not sure what would've happened."

Thalia was staring at Clarke with a curious expression on her face.

"What?" Clarke asked.

"Nothing, just—this is the first time I've ever heard you

say his name without looking like you want to punch a hole through a wall."

"True," Clarke admitted with a smile. She supposed her feelings had changed—or at least, were starting to.

"So?"

Clarke began to fiddle with the pill bottles. She hadn't wanted to tell Thalia about what happened in the woods in case it made Thalia feel guilty—after all, she'd gone out looking for plants to help her and had ended up almost getting killed. "There's something else I haven't told you. It didn't seem important before, when you were so sick, but . . ." She took a breath and gave Thalia a brief account of Wells rescuing her from the ruin.

"He followed you all the way there?"

Clarke nodded. "The weird thing is, while I was hanging on that ledge, convinced I was going to die, he was the one person I was thinking about. And when he showed up, I wasn't even angry that he'd followed me. I was just relieved that he'd cared enough to go after me, despite the terrible things I've said to him."

"He loves you. Nothing you do or say can ever change that."

"I know." Clarke closed her eyes, though she was afraid of the images that she knew would emerge from the shadows. "Even when we were in Confinement and I told you I wanted to see his organs explode in space, I think there was a part of me that still loved him. And that made the pain even worse."

Thalia was looking at her with a mixture of pity and understanding. "It's time to stop punishing yourself, Clarke."

"You mean punishing him."

"No. I mean it's time to stop punishing yourself for loving him. It's not a betrayal of your parents."

Clarke stiffened. "You didn't know them. You have no idea what they'd think."

"I know they wanted what was best for you. They were willing to do something they knew was wrong in order to keep you safe." She paused. "Just like Wells."

Clarke sighed and tucked her legs up underneath her, sitting on Thalia's bed just like she used to back in their cell. "Maybe you're right. I don't know if I can fight this anymore. Hating him is exhausting."

"You should talk to him."

Clarke nodded. "I will."

"No, I mean right now." Thalia's eyes were bright with excitement. "Go talk to him."

"What? It's late."

"I'm sure he's lying wide-awake, thinking about you. . . ."

Clarke unfolded her legs, then rose to her feet. "Fine," she said, "if that's what it takes to get you to be quiet and rest."

She walked across the tent, playfully rolling her eyes at

her friend as she pulled the flap aside. She stepped into the clearing and paused, wondering if she was making a mistake.

But it was too late to turn around. Her heart was beating so fast, it seemed to have a momentum of its own, pounding a frantic message to Wells through the darkness. *I'm coming.*

CHAPTER 27

Wells

Wells stared up at the sky. He'd never felt at ease in the over-crowded tents, and after what had happened tonight, the thought of being crammed next to people who'd been ready to tear Octavia apart was unbearable. Despite the cold, he liked falling asleep looking at the same stars he'd seen from his bed at home. He loved the moments when the moon disappeared behind a cloud and it became too dark to see the outlines of the trees. The sky would seem to stretch all the way down to the ground, creating the impression they weren't on Earth at all but back up among the stars. It always gave him a small pain to open his eyes in the morning and find them gone.

Yet even the sky wasn't enough to quiet Wells's mind

tonight. He pushed himself into a seated position, wincing as he pried his blanket off the scattered rocks and branches. A rustling in a nearby tree caught his attention and he rose to his feet, craning his neck for a better look.

Wells stared in wonder as the tree, which had never boasted a single blossom since they'd landed, burst into bloom. Glimmering pink petals unfurled from pods he hadn't noticed before, like fingertips reaching out in the dark. They were beautiful. Wells rose onto his toes, stretched his arms above his head, and wrapped his fingers around a stem.

"Wells?"

He spun around and saw Clarke standing a few meters away.

"What are you doing?"

He was about to ask her the same question, but instead he walked silently toward her and slipped the flower into her hand. She stared at it, and for a moment he thought she might shove it back at him. But to his surprise and relief, she looked up at him and smiled. "Thank you."

"You're welcome." They stared at each other for a moment. "You couldn't sleep either?" he asked, and she shook her head.

Wells sat down on an exposed tree root, which was just large enough for two, and gestured for her to sit beside him.

After a moment she sank down, keeping a sliver of empty space between them. "How's Thalia doing?" he asked.

"Much better. I'm so thankful Octavia came forward." She looked down and ran her finger along the blossom. "I just can't believe they're leaving tomorrow."

There was a note of regret in her voice that made Wells's stomach clench. "I thought you'd be happy to see her go, after what she put you through."

Clarke was quiet for a moment. "Good people can make mistakes," she said slowly. She looked up, and her eyes met Wells's. "It doesn't mean you stop caring about them."

For a long moment, all they could hear was the wind rustling the leaves, the silence filling with all the words that had been left unsaid. The apologies that could never begin to convey his sorrow.

The trial of Phoenix's two most famous scientists had turned into the event of the year. There were more people gathered in the Council chamber than had ever shown up for a lecture, or any event other than the Remembrance Ceremony.

But Wells was only vaguely aware of the audience. The disgust he'd felt at their morbid curiosity—like Romans waiting for bloodshed at the Colosseum—faded away the moment his eyes landed on the girl sitting alone in the front row. He hadn't seen Clarke since the night she'd confided in him about her parents' research. Wells had told his father, who weighed the information carefully. As Wells had expected, the Chancellor had known nothing about the experiments and had immediately launched an inquiry. Yet the investigation had taken a terrible turn Wells hadn't expected, and now Clarke's parents were going to face the Council on criminal charges. Guilty and terrified, Wells had spent the past week desperate to find Clarke, but his deluge of messages had gone unanswered, and when he went to her flat, he found it sealed off by guards.

Her expression was blank as she watched the Council members take their seats. But then she turned and saw Wells. Her eyes locked with his, her gaze filled with hatred so intense that it sent bile shooting up from his stomach.

Wells shrank back into his seat in the third row. He'd only wanted his father to stop her parents' research, to put an end to Clarke's misery. He never imagined they'd end up on trial for their lives.

Two guards escorted Clarke's mother to a bench in the front. She kept her chin high as she surveyed the Council, but then her eyes settled on her daughter, and her face fell.

Clarke jumped to her feet and said something Wells couldn't hear, but it didn't matter. The sad smile on her mother's face was enough to cleave Wells's heart in two.

Another pair of guards led her father in, and the trial began.

A female member of the Council opened the proceedings by giving an overview of the investigation. According to the Griffins, she reported, they had been ordered by Vice Chancellor Rhodes to conduct human radiation trials, which Rhodes vehemently denied.

A strange numbness spread over Wells as he watched the Vice Chancellor stand, his face grave as he explained that while he'd approved their request for a new lab, he never said a word about experimenting on children.

Everyone's voices seemed very far away—the fragments of the Council members' questions and the Griffins' replies that reached his ears distorted, like sound waves from a distant galaxy. Wells heard the crowd's gasps before his brain had time to process what they were reacting to.

Then, suddenly, the Council was voting.

The first *guilty* broke through the haze that had settled over Wells. He turned to look at Clarke, who was sitting still and rigid.

"Guilty."

No. Wells thought. *No, please*.

"Guilty." The word echoed down the table until it was his father's turn. He cleared his throat, and for a brief moment, Wells believed there was a chance. That his father would figure out a way to turn the tide.

"Guilty."

"*No!*" Clarke's anguished shriek rose above the din of shocked whispers and satisfied murmurs. She jumped to her feet. "You can't do this. It wasn't their fault." Her face twisted with rage as she pointed at the Vice Chancellor. "*You.* You forced them to do it, you evil, lying bastard." She took a step forward and was immediately surrounded by guards.

Vice Chancellor Rhodes gave a long sigh. "I'm afraid you're much better at experimenting on innocent children than you are at lying, Miss Griffin." He turned to Wells's father. "We know from the security log that she visited the lab on a regular basis. She *knew* about the atrocities her parents were committing and did nothing to stop it. She may have even helped."

Wells inhaled so sharply, he could feel his stomach scrape against his ribs. He waited for his father to give Rhodes one of his dismissive glares, but to Wells's horror, the Chancellor was staring gravely at Clarke. After a long moment, his jaw tightened, and he turned to face the other Council members.

"I hereby put forward a motion to try Clarke Griffin for the crime of accessory to treason."

No. His father's words sank into his skin like a paralytic, stopping his heart.

Wells could see the Council members' mouths moving, but he couldn't make out what they were saying. Every atom in his body was focused on praying to whatever forgotten god might be listening. *Let her go*, he pleaded. *I'll do anything*. It was true. He was ready to offer his life in exchange for hers.

Take me instead.

The Vice Chancellor leaned over to whisper something to Wells's father.

I don't care if it's painful.

The Chancellor's face grew even graver than it had been before.

Shove me through the release portal so my body implodes.

The person next to Wells shuddered at something the Chancellor said.

Just let her go.

He had the uncomfortable sensation of sound returning as gasps rose up from the audience. Two guards grabbed Clarke and began dragging her away.

The girl he'd do anything to protect would soon be sentenced to death. And she would have every right to die hating him.

It was all his fault.

"I'm sorry," Wells whispered, as if somehow, that could make it better.

"I know," she said, her voice soft.

Wells froze, and for a moment, he was too afraid to look at her, afraid to see the grief welling up from the wound he knew would never heal. But when he finally turned, he saw that while her eyes glistened with tears, she was smiling.

"I feel closer to them here," she said, glancing up at the trees. "They spent their lives trying to figure out how to get us home."

Wells didn't know what he could say without breaking

the spell, so instead, he leaned forward and kissed her, holding his breath until he saw her teardrop-tipped lashes flutter closed.

At first it was soft, his lips lightly brushing over her mouth, but then he felt her kiss him back, igniting every cell in his body. The familiarity of her touch, the taste of her kiss, released something in him, and he pulled her closer.

Clarke sank into Wells, her lips clinging to his lips, her skin melting into his skin, her breath mixing with his breath. The world around them faded away as Earth became nothing more than a swirl of pungent scents and damp air that made him press himself closer to her. The soft ground cradled them as they slid off the log. There was so much he needed to tell her, but his words were lost as his lips traveled across her skin, moving from her mouth to her neck.

In that moment, there was no one else. They were the only two people on Earth. Just like he'd always imagined they would be.

CHAPTER 28

Glass

Music played on Phoenix twice that year. The Council had approved the exception, and for the first time anyone could remember, the Earthmade instruments were taken from their preservation chambers and carried carefully to the observation deck for the comet viewing party.

It should have been one of the most magical nights of Glass's life. The entire population of Phoenix had flocked to the observation deck in their finery, and the elegantly dressed crowd buzzed with excitement. All around her, people were talking and laughing as they strode toward the enormous windows, clutching glasses of sparkling root wine.

Glass stood next to Huxley and Cora, who were talking

animatedly. But although Glass could see her friends' mouths moving, their words never reached her ears. Every cell in her body was focused on the musicians who were quietly taking their seats on the far side of the observation deck.

But as the musicians began to play, Glass shifted from one foot to another, growing restless, as she thought of Luke. Without him, the music that normally wrapped around her like an enchantment felt strangely empty. The melodies that once seemed to express the deepest secrets of her soul were no less beautiful now, but it made her chest ache to know that the only person she wanted to share them with was somewhere else.

Glass looked over and quickly found her mother, wearing a long gray dress and their family's gloves—kid leather, one of the only pairs left on the ship, stained with age but still infinitely precious. She was talking to someone in the Chancellor's uniform, but it wasn't the Chancellor. Glass realized with a start it was Vice Chancellor Rhodes. Though she'd only seen him a few times, she recognized his sharp nose and mocking smile.

Glass knew that she should go over, introduce herself, smile at the Vice Chancellor, and raise her glass to him in a toast. She should thank him for her freedom and look grateful and overjoyed as the crowd of well-dressed Phoenicians looked on and whispered. It's what her mother would have wanted; it's what she should have done, if she valued her life. But as Glass stared at his hateful dark eyes, she found she couldn't bring herself to move toward him.

"Here, take this. I need some air," Glass said, handing Cora her still-full glass of wine. Cora raised her eyebrows, but didn't argue—they were allotted only one glass each tonight. With a final glance to make sure that her mother wasn't watching, Glass wove her way through the crowd and back into the corridor. She didn't run into a single person as she made her way quickly to their flat, where she slipped out of her gown and into a pair of nondescript pants, piling her hair under a hat.

There was no designated observation deck on Walden, but there were a number of corridors with small windows on the starboard side, where the comet was expected to make its appearance. The Waldenites who didn't have shifts that day had begun gathering early in the morning to reserve the best seats. By the time Glass arrived, the hallways were flooded with crowds, talking in excited voices and clustering around the small windows. Some of the kids were already pressing their faces against the quartz glass or clambering onto parents' shoulders.

As she turned a corner, Glass's eyes settled on a group at the window a few meters down: three women and four children. She wondered whether the women were watching the fourth child for a neighbor, or if it was an orphan they'd taken in.

The youngest child toddled over to Glass and blinked up at her with a shy smile. "Hi there," Glass said, leaning forward so that she was level with the girl. "Are you excited for the comet?" The girl didn't say anything. Her large, dark eyes were fixated on Glass's head.

Glass brought her hand up self-consciously, grimacing slightly when she realized that her hair had fallen out of her hat. She began to tuck it back inside, but the little girl reached up and pulled at one of the loose strands.

"Posy, leave the lady alone." Glass looked up and saw one of the women walking toward them. "Sorry," she said to Glass, with a laugh. "She likes your hair."

Glass smiled but didn't say anything. She'd learned how to downplay her Phoenix accent, but the less she spoke, the better. "Come on, Pose," the woman said, placing her hand on the child's shoulder and guiding her away.

It was past 2100. The comet was due to appear any moment now. Up on Phoenix, the observation deck would be silent as everyone waited in quiet reverence. Here, children were laughing and jumping, and a couple of teenagers were yelling out a countdown.

Glass looked up and down the corridor, but there was no sign of him.

"Look!" a little girl called out. A white line was rising over the outline of the moon. Instead of fading away like most comets, it grew larger, the tail expanding as it blazed through space. It made even the stars look dim.

Glass stepped forward almost unconsciously, and a couple leaning up against the nearest window shuffled aside to give her space. It was so beautiful, Glass thought in wonder. And terrifying. It was growing larger and larger, filling up the entire viewing space in the porthole, as if it were coming straight for them.

Could there have been a miscalculation? Glass pressed her hands into the ledge so hard, she could feel it cutting into her palms. Around her, people started to step back, with a flurry of low murmurs and frightened cries.

Glass closed her eyes. She couldn't look.

An arm wrapped around her. She didn't even have to turn to know that it was Luke. She knew the scent of him, the feel of him, like a second skin.

"I was looking for you," she said, glancing back at him. Although the astronomical event of a lifetime was playing out right before his eyes, he was looking only at her.

"I hoped you would come," he whispered into her ear.

The crowd's anxious murmurs bubbled into exclamations of astonishment as the comet swept up and above the ship in a blaze of fire. Luke's arm tightened around her, and she leaned into his chest. "I couldn't imagine seeing this without you," she said.

"You didn't have any trouble getting away?"

"No, not really." Her stomach twisted at the thought of her mother standing next to the Vice Chancellor. "I just wish we didn't have to sneak around." She reached up and ran her fingers along his cheek.

Luke took her hand and brought it to his lips. "Maybe there's a way to change your mom's mind," he said earnestly. "Maybe I could talk to her. You know, prove that I'm not some barbarian. That I'm serious about my future—*our* future. That I'm serious about you."

Glass gave him a soft smile. "I wish it were that easy."

"No, I mean it." He took her hands in his. "She thinks I'm just some Walden jerk taking advantage of you. She needs to know that this isn't just a fling. It's real."

"I know," Glass said, squeezing his hand. "I know."

"No, I don't think you do," Luke said, pulling something out of his pocket. He turned to face her, his gaze unblinking.

"Glass," he began, his eyes glowing, "I don't want to spend another day without you. I want to go to sleep every night with you by my side and wake up next to you every morning. I want nothing else but you, for the rest of my life."

He held out his outstretched palm, with a small, golden object in it. It was her locket.

“I know it’s not exactly a ring, but—”

“Yes,” she said simply, because there was nothing else to say, nothing else to do but put on the locket and kiss the boy she loved so much it hurt, as behind them the comet streaked the sky with gold.

CHAPTER 29

Bellamy

Bellamy couldn't sleep. His mind was a jumble of thoughts all elbowing for his attention, making it impossible to tell where one stopped and the other began.

Staring up at the stars, he tried to imagine what was happening on the ship. It was strange to think of life going on as usual hundreds of kilometers away—the Waldenites and Arcadians toiling away while the Phoenicians complimented one another's outfits on the observation deck and ignored the stars. That was the only thing he'd miss about the Colony—the view. Before the launch, he'd heard of a comet passing, which would've been pretty spectacular to see from the ship.

He squinted into the darkness, trying to figure out how many days they'd been on Earth. If he'd counted correctly, then the comet was meant to appear tonight. There was going to be a fancy viewing party on Phoenix, and less-formal gatherings on Walden and Arcadia. Bellamy sat up and scanned the sky. He couldn't see anything from the clearing—the trees blocked too much of the sky—but he'd have a better view from the ridge.

Octavia was sleeping peacefully beside him, her glossy hair fanned out underneath her, her red hair ribbon tied to her wrist. "I'll be right back," he whispered, then took off at a jog across the clearing.

The thick canopy of leaves blocked most of the starlight, but after all his hunting expeditions, he knew this area of the forest well, anticipating every slope and turn and hidden log. When he finally reached the ridge, he paused to catch his breath. The cool night air had helped to clear his head, and the burning in his calves was a welcome distraction.

The star-filled sky looked just as it had every other night since they'd landed on Earth, and yet there was something different about it—the stars were pulsing, charged, as if waiting for something big to happen. And then, all at once, it did. The comet erupted across the sky, a streak of gold against the glittering silver, brightening everything around it, even the ground.

His skin sizzled as if some of the sparks had seeped into his own body, invigorating his cells with something beyond energy—with hope. Tomorrow he and Octavia would leave here for good. Tomorrow they would be free of the Colony forever, no one telling them what to do or how to be.

He closed his eyes and imagined how that would feel. Freedom from everyone and everything—even from his past. Even, perhaps, from the memories that had haunted him all his life.

Bellamy ran down the walkway, ignoring his neighbors' grumbles and the empty threats of the guards he knew were too lazy to chase a remarkably fast nine-year-old just to issue a reprimand. But as he got closer to his flat, his excitement slipped away. Ever since that terrible night when he caught his mom trying to hurt Octavia, he got nervous coming home.

He unlocked the door and burst inside. "Mom?" he called, carefully shutting the door behind him before he said anything else. "Octavia?" He waited, but there was only silence. "Mom?" he said again. He walked through the main room, his eyes widening at the overturned furniture. His mother must have been in another one of her bad moods. He crept toward the kitchen, his stomach wriggling like it was trying to escape through his belly button.

Someone groaned, and he rushed inside to find his mother

on the floor, lying in a sticky puddle of blood. A knife lay beside her.

He gasped and hurried over, shaking her shoulder frantically. "Mom," he shouted. "Wake up. *Mom.*" But all she did was flutter her eyelids and let out another faint groan. Bellamy leapt to his feet, gasping as he realized the knees of his pants were soaked with blood. He had to find someone. He had to get help.

He dashed back into the main room and was about to go run for a guard when a noise brought him skidding to a halt. His eyes fell on the closet, which was slightly open, a sliver of shadow creeping out of the gap between the door and the wall. He took a few steps toward it as a tiny tearstained face peeked out.

"Are you okay?" he whispered to his sister, reaching for her hand. "Come on." But she shrank back into the darkness, trembling. Bellamy's fear for his mother slid away as he stared at the little girl she'd made terrified to come into the light. "Come on, Octavia," he coaxed, and slowly, tentatively, she poked her head out again.

Finally, she toddled out of the closet, looking around the room with wide eyes. "Here," Bellamy said, picking up the red ribbon he'd given her from the floor of the closet. He tied it around her dark curls in his best approximation of a bow. "You look beautiful." He grabbed her hand, feeling his heart swell as her little fingers wrapped around his. He led her to their mother's bedroom, lifted her onto the bed, then curled up next to her, praying that he wouldn't hear any other noises from the kitchen.

They sat there together on the bed, waiting quietly, until finally their mother's moans stopped and there was only silence.

"It's okay, O," he said, holding his little sister tight to his chest. "It's okay. You'll never have to hide again."

As the comet's trail faded into blackness, Bellamy hurried back down the slope, eager to get back before Octavia woke up and realized he'd gone. But as he came around the bend, searching for the familiar collection of tents, all he could see were flames.

The entire camp was on fire.

Bellamy skidded to a stop, gasping as his lungs took their first breath of smoke-filled air. For a moment, his vision was filled with flames and shadows, but then shapes began to emerge. Figures were sprinting in every direction, some pouring out of the burning tents while others rushed toward the trees.

Only one thought consumed him as he jogged over to their blankets, his eyes searching the darkness for his sister's sleeping form. The knot of dread in his stomach told him what he already knew. Octavia wasn't there.

He called her name, jerking his head from side to side,

praying that she'd call to him from the edge of the clearing, from someplace safe.

"Octavia!" he yelled again, looking wildly in all directions, squinting to see through the smoke. *Don't panic*, he told himself, but it was no use. The flames tore through the darkness and Octavia was nowhere to be found.

Bellamy had come down from scanning the heavens only to find himself in the depths of hell.

CHAPTER 30

Clarke

For some period of time—minutes, hours, Clarke wasn't sure—all she could hear was the sound of their hearts, the whisper of their mingled breaths. But then a scream clawed its way out from the clearing, dragging them apart. Clarke and Wells jumped to their feet, Clarke holding on to Wells's arm for balance as the world slid back into terrifying focus.

He grabbed her hand and they ran back into the clearing. She heard more screams, but none were as frightening as the roar and crackle that made every nerve in her body stand at attention.

Flames rose up from the tents, some of which had already collapsed into smoldering heaps, like corpses on an ancient battlefield. Shadowy figures sprinted for the safety of the forest, pursued by tendrils of hungry flames.

Thalia, Clarke thought in horror, and started to run. She was too weak to make it out of the infirmary tent on her own.

"*No!*" Wells shouted, forcing his voice over the chaos of screams. "Clarke, it's not safe!"

But his words slid off her like a spray of ash. She made a beeline for the tent, smoke filling her lungs, blinking to see in the smoldering air.

His arm wrapped around her waist like a steel band, pulling her forcibly into the shelter of the trees. "Let me go," she shrieked, thrashing with all her might. But Wells held her tight, forcing her to watch helplessly as fire engulfed the infirmary fewer than a hundred meters away. The entire side of the tent was up in flames. The plastic tarp on top was melting, and smoke filtered out of the gap between the front flaps.

"Get *off*." She sobbed, twisting again as she tried to wrestle free.

He slid his arm under her and began dragging her backward. "*No*," she shrieked, feeling the sound tear her throat, pounding at him helplessly with her fists. "I need to get her out." She dug her heels into the grass, but Wells was stronger, and she couldn't hold her ground. "*Thalia!*"

"Clarke, I'm so sorry," Wells whispered in her ear. She

could tell he was crying, but she didn't care. "You'll die if you go in there. I can't let you."

The word *die* ignited a reserve of power that exploded through her. Clarke gritted her teeth and lunged forward, momentarily escaping Wells's hold. Her entire being had reduced to a single, desperate thought—saving the only friend she had left in the universe.

She screamed as her arm was wrenched behind her back. "Let me *go*." This time, it was more of a plea than an order. "I'm begging you. Let me go."

"I can't," he said, wrapping his arms around her again. His voice was shaking. "I can't."

The clearing was empty now. Everyone had made it into the woods, taking whatever supplies they could carry. But no one had thought to grab the frail girl who was now being burned alive just a few meters away.

"Help," Clarke cried. "Someone, *please* help." But there was no answer except for the roar and crackle of the fire.

The flames on the top of the infirmary tent rose higher, the sides collapsing toward each other, as if the fire were inhaling the tent and everything inside of it. "*No*."

There was a crack, and the flames shot up even higher. Clarke shrieked with horror as the entire tent collapsed into a storm of fire, then slowly crumbled into ash.

It was over.

As she walked away from the medical center, Clarke could almost feel the vial pulsing in her pocket, like the heart in the old story Wells had discovered at the library the other day. He'd offered to read it to her, but she'd flatly refused. The last thing she needed right now was to hear creepy pre-Cataclysm literature. She had enough scenes of horror playing out in her real life.

The vial Clarke carried in her pocket could never have a heartbeat, she knew; just the opposite. The toxic cocktail of drugs inside was designed to stop a heart for good.

When Clarke got home, her parents weren't there. Although they both spent most of the day in their lab, over the past few weeks, they'd conveniently found excuses to leave right before Clarke returned from her training and rarely came back until just before she went to sleep. It was probably for the best. As Lilly grew sicker, Clarke could barely look at her parents without feeling a surge of rage. She knew she wasn't being fair—the moment anyone protested, the Vice Chancellor would have her parents executed and Clarke Confined within days. But that didn't make it any easier for her to meet their eyes.

The lab was quiet. As Clarke wound her way through the maze of empty beds, all she could hear was the drone of the ventilation system. The soft buzz of conversation had faded as more and more bodies were secreted away.

Lilly seemed even thinner than she'd been the day before.

Clarke crept toward her bed and ran her hand gently down her friend's arm, shuddering as bits of her skin fell away. She slipped her other hand into her pocket and wrapped her fingers around the vial. It would be so easy. No one would ever know.

But then Lilly's pale lashes fluttered open, and Clarke froze. As she stared into Lilly's eyes, a cold wave of terror and revulsion crashed over her. What was she thinking? An overpowering urge to destroy the vial tore through her body, and she had to take a deep breath to keep herself from hurling it against the wall.

Lilly's lips were moving, but no sound was coming out. Clarke leaned forward and gave her a small smile. "Sorry, didn't catch that, Lil." She lowered her head so her ear was closer to Lilly's mouth. "What did you say?"

At first, Clarke could only feel the soundless wisp of air on her skin, as if there wasn't enough breath in Lilly's lungs to push the words out of her mouth. But then a faint moan escaped from her chapped lips. "Did you bring it?"

Clarke raised her head to look into her friend's panic-filled brown eyes. She nodded slowly.

"Now." The word was barely audible.

"No," Clarke protested, her voice shaking. "It's too soon." She blinked back the tears that had begun to fill her eyes. "You could still get better," she said, but the lie sounded hollow, even to her.

Lilly's face contorted in pain, and Clarke reached for her hand. "Please." Lilly's voice was ragged.

"I'm sorry." Clarke gave Lilly's fragile hand a gentle squeeze as tears began to trickle down her cheeks. "I can't."

Lilly's eyes grew wide, and Clarke inhaled sharply. "Lil?" But Lilly remained silent, staring at something only she could see. Something that filled her eyes with terror. The physical pain racking Lilly's body was terrible, Clarke knew, but the hallucinations, the demons who were with her every moment, hovering at her bedside, were worse.

"No more."

Clarke closed her eyes. The guilt and remorse she'd feel could never compare to Lilly's pain. It'd be selfish to let her own fear prevent her from bringing her friend the peace she wanted—the respite from pain she deserved.

Her whole body was trembling so hard, she could barely remove the vial from her pocket, let alone fill the syringe. She stood next to the bed and clasped Lilly's hand with one arm, using the other to position the needle over Lilly's vein. "Sleep well, Lil," she whispered.

Lilly nodded and gave Clarke a smile that she knew would be burned into her brain for the rest of her life. "Thank you."

Clarke held Lilly's hand for the few minutes it took for her friend to slip away. Then she rose and placed her fingers against Lilly's still-warm neck, searching for a pulse.

She was gone.

Clarke sank to the damp ground, gasping as her lungs reached desperately for the cool air, then rolled onto her side. Through the tears blurring her vision, she could make out the shapes of people standing all around her, their dark, featureless silhouettes still and quiet.

Her best friend, the only person who truly knew Clarke, who knew what she had done to Lilly and still loved her. Thalia had told her to make things right with Wells tonight—and then Wells had held Clarke back while they watched Thalia die.

"I'm so sorry, Clarke," Wells was saying, reaching for her. She pushed his hand away.

"I can't believe you," she said, her voice cold and quiet. Rage billowed in her chest, as if there were flames inside her that needed only fury and grief to blaze into an inferno.

"There was no way you'd make it," Wells stammered. "I just—I couldn't let you go. You would've been killed."

"So you let Thalia die instead. Because you get to decide who lives and who dies." He started to protest, but she kept going, shaking with rage. "Tonight was a mistake. You destroy everything you touch."

"Clarke, please, I—"

But she just stood up, shaking the bits of cinder from her clothes, and walked into the forest without looking back.

They all had ash in their lungs and tears in their eyes. But Wells had blood on his hands.

CHAPTER 31

Glass

"I'll get a ring as soon as I find one at the Exchange," Luke said to Glass, his hand on her lower back as he guided her through the crowded corridors back toward Phoenix. Most of the people who'd assembled to watch the comet were heading back to their residential units on the lower decks, making it difficult to move toward the skybridge. But Glass was hardly aware of which direction they were heading. Her heart was still thumping with joy, and she was shaking, holding tight to Luke's hand.

"I don't need a ring." She reached up to touch the locket, which seemed to be radiating warmth through her chest. Nothing could happen immediately, she knew. Although she turned eighteen in a few weeks, they couldn't risk getting married until the Chancellor woke up and confirmed her pardon—or never woke up at all. Her mother would understand eventually, once she saw how much Luke loved Glass. They'd get married and apply for permission to start a family, someday. But for now, just the promise of a future together was enough. "This is perfect."

They turned out of the stairwell and into the corridor that led to the skybridge. Luke stopped short and pulled Glass to him as a dozen guards jogged by, so close a few of their sleeves brushed against Glass's arm, although their eyes trained straight ahead. She shivered and leaned into Luke, who was watching them with a strange expression on his face. "Do you know what's going on?" she asked.

"I'm sure it's nothing," Luke said too quickly, his words at odds with the tension in his jaw. But then he raised their interlocked fingers to his lips and kissed her hand. "Let's go."

Glass smiled as they continued walking. The thud of the guards' boots had faded away, and they had the whole hallway to themselves. Suddenly, Luke stopped and raised her arm into the air. Before Glass had time to ask what he was doing, he'd spun her around and lowered her into a dip.

Glass laughed as Luke wrapped one arm around her waist and swept her across the empty hallway. "What's gotten into you?"

He paused and pulled her even closer to him, then leaned in and murmured into her ear. "I hear music when I'm with you." Glass just smiled and, in the middle of the hallway, closed her eyes as they swayed from side to side.

Finally, Luke stepped back, gesturing in the direction of the skybridge. "It's almost curfew," he said.

"Okay," she agreed, sighing. They walked hand in hand across the skybridge, exchanging knowing smiles that made every cell in Glass's body buzz with excitement. At the entrance to Phoenix, they stopped, reluctant to say good-bye. Luke ran his finger along the locket chain.

"I love you," he said, squeezing her hand before giving her a little shove. "Let me know once you get home. I'll come by tomorrow to talk to your mom."

"Okay," she agreed. "Tomorrow."

Finally, Glass turned and began walking across the skybridge. She'd made it halfway across when a shrill beep echoed through the empty space. She looked around, startled. The cluster of guards at the Phoenix end of the bridge broke apart, and she could hear someone barking orders. Glass froze as the sound grew louder and more urgent. She turned to look at Luke, who'd started taking a few hesitant steps forward.

"The bridge is closing," a disembodied woman's voice announced over the speakers. "Please clear the area." There was a brief pause, then the message repeated. "The bridge is closing. Please clear the area." Glass gasped as a barrier began to descend at the Phoenix checkpoint. She lunged forward and could see Luke running as well, but they were both too far away.

Glass reached the clear partition just as it locked into the floor, slamming her hands against it. Luke slid to a stop on the other side. He was saying something, but although she could see his mouth moving, no sound reached her ears.

Tears filled her eyes as she watched him bang his fists against the wall in frustration. She didn't understand. The skybridge hadn't been closed since the plague outbreak in the first century. She knew if it was closing now, it might not open again.

"Luke!" she cried, the word falling uselessly from her lips. She pressed her hand against the clear partition and held it there. Their eyes locked.

"I love you," Glass said.

Luke pressed his own hand to the wall, and for a moment, Glass could almost feel the warmth of his skin. *I love you too*, he mouthed. He gave her a sad smile and motioned for her to start walking. She paused, not wanting to leave without knowing what was going on, when she'd see him again. The alarm was still sounding overhead, ringing in her ears.

Go, Luke mouthed, his face serious.

Glass nodded and turned, forcing herself to keep her eyes straight ahead. But before she turned onto the hallway that led away from the skybridge, she glanced over her shoulder one last time. Luke hadn't moved. He was still standing there, his hand pressed against the wall.

Glass ran home, weaving through crowds of panicked civilians and stone-faced guards.

"Oh, thank god," Sonja said as Glass rushed into the flat. "I was so worried." She shoved a water pitcher into Glass's arms. "Go fill this up in the bathroom. I'm not sure how much longer the water will last."

"What's going on?" Glass asked. "They closed the skybridge."

"What were you doing near the bridge?" her mother asked, then blinked, taking in the clothes Glass had changed into after the comet viewing party. "Oh," she said flatly, a wearied understanding overtaking her features. "That's where you were."

"What's happening?" Glass repeated, ignoring her mother's look of disapproval.

"I'm not sure, but I have a feeling . . ." She trailed off, then pressed her lips together. "I think this is it. The day we all knew was coming."

"What are you talking about?"

Her mother took the pitcher back from Glass and turned to the sink. "The ship wasn't built to last this long. It was just a matter of time before things started to break down."

The water had reached the top of the pitcher and was now overflowing into the sink, but Sonja just stood there. "Mom?"

Finally, her mother shut off the water and turned around to face Glass. "It's the airlock," she said quietly. "There's been a breach." A shout rang out from the corridor, and her mother shot a quick glance at the door before she forced a smile and continued. "But don't worry. There's a reserve of oxygen on Phoenix. We'll be okay until they figure out what to do. I promise, Glass, we'll get through this."

Glass felt the realization dawning in her mind, twisting her stomach with dread. "What does that have to do with the bridge?" she asked, her voice so quiet it was almost a whisper.

"They're already running out of oxygen on Arcadia and Walden. We had to take security precautions to make sure . . ."

"No," Glass breathed. "The Council is going to let them all *die*?"

Sonja stepped forward and squeezed Glass's arm. "They had to do something, or else no one would survive," she was saying, but Glass barely registered her words. "It's the only way to protect the Colony."

"I have to find him," Glass said, trembling. She took a

shaky step back. Her head was a frenzy of words and images that bounced off one another, creating more panic than sense.

"Glass," her mother said, with something that sounded like pity. "I'm so sorry, but you can't. There's no way. All the exits are sealed." She stepped forward and pulled her daughter into a hug. Glass tried to wriggle free, but her mother tightened her hold. "There's nothing we can do."

"I love him," Glass sobbed, her body shaking.

"I know." Sonja reached out and took Glass's hand. "And I'm sure he loves you too. But maybe this is for the best." She gave a sad smile that sent chills down Glass's spine. "At least this way, you don't have to say a terrible good-bye."

CHAPTER 32

Wells

Wells watched Clarke stride off into the woods, feeling as if she'd punched through his sternum and torn away a chunk of his heart. He was only vaguely aware of the gleeful roar of the flames as they swallowed the supplies, the tents . . . and anyone who'd been unfortunate enough to be left inside. Around him, a few people had fallen to the ground, gasping for breath or shaking with horror. But most were standing shoulder to shoulder, facing the inferno, their figures still and quiet.

"Is everyone okay?" Wells asked hoarsely. "Who's missing?" The numbness at Clarke's words was burning away, replaced by a frantic energy. He stepped forward to the edge of the tree cover, shielding his eyes as he tried to peer through the wall of flames. When no one answered, he took a breath and shouted, "Did everyone make it out?" There was a ripple of vague nods.

"Do we need to go farther?" a small Walden girl asked, her voice trembling as she took a step deeper into the woods.

"It doesn't look like it's spreading to the trees," an Arcadian boy said hoarsely. He was standing next to a few battered water jugs and blackened containers he'd carried out of the camp.

The boy was right. The ring of bare dirt that bordered the clearing was wide enough that the flames engulfing the tents flickered just out of reach of the lowest branches.

Wells turned, searching through the darkness for a sign of Clarke. But she'd disappeared into the shadows. He could almost feel her grief pulsing through the darkness. Every cell in his body was screaming at him to go to her, but he knew it was hopeless.

Clarke was right. He destroyed everything he touched.

"You look tired," the Chancellor said, surveying Wells from across the dinner table.

Wells looked up from the plate he'd been staring at, then nodded curtly. "I'm fine." The truth was, he hadn't slept in days. The look of fury Clarke had given him was branded into his brain, and every time he closed his eyes, he could see the terror on her face as the guards dragged her away. Her anguished scream filled the silence between his heartbeats.

After the trial, Wells had begged his father to lift the charges. He swore Clarke had nothing to do with the research, and that the guilt she'd been carrying around had nearly killed her. But the Chancellor had simply claimed that it was out of his hands.

Wells shifted uncomfortably in his chair. He could barely stand to be on the same ship as his father, let alone sit across from him at dinner, but he had to maintain some semblance of civility. If he allowed his rage to break free, his father would simply accuse Wells of being too irrational, too immature to understand the law.

"I know you're angry with me," the Chancellor said before taking a sip of water. "But I can't overrule the vote. That's why we have the Council, to keep one person from becoming too powerful." He glanced down at the chip flashing in his watch, then looked back at Wells. "The Gaia Doctrine is harsh enough as it is. We have to hold on to whatever shred of freedom we have left."

"So you're saying that even if Clarke is innocent, it'd be worth it to let her die in order to keep *democracy* alive?"

The Chancellor fixed Wells with a stare that, a few days ago, would've made him sink into his chair. "I believe *innocent* is a relative term here. There's no denying she knew about the experiments."

"Rhodes *forced* them to conduct those experiments. He's the one who should be punished!"

"That's enough," the Chancellor said in a voice so cold, it almost extinguished Wells's rage. "I refuse to listen to this heresy in my own home."

Wells was about to launch an angry retort, but he was interrupted by the sound of the doorbell. His father silenced him with a final look as he opened the door and ushered in the Vice Chancellor himself.

Wells could barely contain his hatred as Rhodes gave him a curt nod in greeting. The Vice Chancellor wore his usual self-satisfied look as he followed the Chancellor into his study. After they closed the door firmly behind them, Wells stood up from the table. He knew he should go to his room and shut the door, like he always did when his father took meetings in their home.

A few days ago, he might have. A few days ago, he wouldn't have dared to eavesdrop on a private conversation. But now he didn't care. He crept toward the door and pressed himself against the wall.

"The dropships are ready," Rhodes began. "There's no reason to wait."

"There are plenty of reasons to wait." There was a note of irritation in his father's voice, as if they'd already had this discussion many times. "We're still not sure if the radiation levels are safe."

Wells inhaled sharply, then froze to keep his breath from disturbing the silence outside the study door.

"That's why we're emptying the detention center. Why not put the convicts to good use?"

"Even Confined children deserve a chance at life, Rhodes. That's why they're given a retrial on their eighteenth birthday."

The Vice Chancellor scoffed. "You know none of them are going to be pardoned. We can't afford to waste the resources. We're running out of time as it is."

What does he mean, running out of time? Wells wondered, but before he had a chance to think it through, his father broke in.

"Those reports are grossly exaggerated. We have enough oxygen for another few years at least."

"And then what? You'll order the entire Colony onto the dropships and just hope for the best?"

"We'll send the Confined juveniles in the detention center, like you suggested. But not yet. Not until it's our last resort. Unless the breach in sector C14 worsens, we've got a little time left still. The first prisoners will be sent in a year."

"If that's what you think is best."

Wells heard the Vice Chancellor rise from his chair, and in a flash, he ran silently into his room and collapsed onto the bed. He stared up at the ceiling, trying to make sense of what he'd heard. The Colony was on its last breath. They had only a few years left up in space.

It all clicked into place, why everyone was being found guilty: There weren't enough resources on the ship to support its population. It was a horrifying thought, but an even more terrible realization was making its way to the front of his brain. Clarke's birthday was in six months. Wells knew he'd never convince his father to pardon her. Being sent to Earth would give her a second chance. But they weren't going to start the mission for another year. Unless he did something, Clarke was going to die.

His only chance was to speed up the mission, to have the first group sent right away.

A terrifying plan began to take shape, and his chest tightened in fear as he realized what he would have to do. But Wells knew there was no other way. To save the girl he loved, he'd have to endanger the entire human race.

CHAPTER 33

Bellamy

Bellamy slid down the trunk of the tree and sank to the ground, feeling as hollow as the burned-out shell of the dropship. He'd been searching for Octavia for hours, tearing through the forest and screaming her name until his throat was raw, but the woods had answered him with nothing but maddening silence.

"Hey." A weary voice interrupted his thoughts. Bellamy turned to see Wells walking slowly toward him. Soot was smeared across his face, and the skin on his left forearm was badly scratched. "Any luck?"

Bellamy shook his head. "I'm so sorry." Wells pressed his lips together and stared at a spot on the ground just beyond

Bellamy for a long moment. "If it's any consolation, I really don't think she was here. We just searched the clearing pretty thoroughly. Everyone made it out in time except . . ." His voice trailed off.

"I know," Bellamy said quietly. "I'm really sorry, man. I'm sure you did your best."

Wells winced. "I don't even know what that means anymore." Bellamy looked at him in confusion, but before he had time to say anything, Wells gave him a small smile. "Octavia will turn up soon. Don't worry." Then he turned and trudged back into the clearing, where a few people were sifting through the ashes, looking for anything that had survived the blaze.

In the rosy dawn light, Bellamy could almost make himself believe that the horrors of the last few hours were nothing but a nightmare. The flames had long since died out, and while much of the grass had been burned away, the soil underfoot was damp. The fire hadn't reached the trees, whose flowers stretched out to greet the light, blissfully unaware of—or unconcerned with—the tragedy below. But that was the thing about grief, Bellamy knew. You couldn't expect anyone else to share your suffering. You had to carry your pain alone.

He heard a few of the kids arguing over what they thought had started the fire: whether the wind had carried a spark from their campfire to scorch the tents, or if someone had done something stupid.

But Bellamy didn't give a shit what had caused it. All he cared about was Octavia. Had she gotten lost while running for safety, or had she left camp before the fire even started? And if so, why?

He rose shakily to his feet, holding on to the tree trunk for balance. He couldn't stop to rest, not now, when every hour meant Octavia might be in danger. Now that it was light, he could search again. Farther this time. It didn't matter how long it took. He wouldn't stop moving until he found her.

As Bellamy moved deeper into the shade, he exhaled, relieved to be away from the insultingly bright sunlight. Relieved to be alone. But then his eyes landed on a figure winding its way toward him. He paused and squinted through the green-shadowed gloom. It was Clarke.

"Hey," he asked hoarsely, his stomach twisting uneasily at the sight of her pale, drawn face. "Are you okay?"

"Thalia's dead?" She said it more like a question, as though hoping he would assure her that it wasn't true.

Bellamy nodded slowly. "I'm sorry." She started to tremble, and he instinctively pulled her into his arms. For a long moment they just stood there, Bellamy holding Clarke's shaking form tight against him. "I'm so sorry," he whispered into her hair.

Finally, Clarke straightened up and stepped back with a sigh. Although tears were running down her face, the brightness had returned to her eyes, and a hint of color had snuck back into her cheeks. "Where's your sister?" she asked, wiping her nose with the back of her hand.

"She's not here. I've been searching for hours, but it's been too dark. I'm going out to look for her again."

"Wait." Clarke reached into her pocket. "I found this in the woods. Out past the stream, toward that giant rock formation." She placed something in Bellamy's hand. He inhaled audibly as his fingers closed around the familiar strip of satin. It was Octavia's red ribbon.

"Was it tied to a tree?" he asked faintly, unsure what he hoped the answer would be.

"No." Clarke's dirt-streaked face softened. "I saw it on the ground. It must've fallen out of her hair at some point. She was wearing it last night, wasn't she?"

"I think so," Bellamy replied, his brain frantically racing for snippets of memory. "Yes. She had it when she went to sleep."

"Okay," Clarke said with sudden firmness. "So that means she left the camp before the fire started. Look," she added, in answer to Bellamy's questioning look, "there's no ash on it. No sign that it was anywhere near the flames."

"You may be right," Bellamy said softly, rubbing the

ribbon between his fingers. "I just don't understand why she would have left before the fire started." He glanced back up at Clarke. "Weren't you outside the infirmary last night? Did you notice anything?"

Clarke shook her head, her expression suddenly unreadable. "I stepped away for a while," she said, her voice tense. "I'm sorry."

"Never mind," Bellamy said. He slipped the ribbon into his pocket. "I never got to apologize. You were right about O all along. I'm sorry." Clarke just nodded in acknowledgment. "Thanks for telling me about the ribbon. I'm going out to look for her."

He started to turn away, but Clarke reached out to lay a hand on his wrist. "I'll come with you."

"That's nice of you, but I have no idea how long I'll be gone. This isn't like when we went out to find the medicine. It might be a while."

"I'm coming with you," she repeated. Her voice was firm, and there was a fire in her eyes that made him hesitate to contradict her.

"Are you sure?" Bellamy raised an eyebrow. "I doubt Wells will be happy to hear that."

"He's not going to hear it from me. We're done."

Bellamy's brain buzzed with questions that never made it to his lips. "Okay, then." He took a step forward and gestured for her to follow. "But I should warn you . . . I'll probably take off my shirt at some point." He glanced over his shoulder and saw a smile flicker across her face, so small it might have been a trick of the light filtering through the heavy leaves.

CHAPTER 34

Glass

The Colony was eerily quiet, even for one in the morning. Glass didn't see anyone else as she dashed through the dark hallways, lit only by the dim glow of the blue emergency lights along the floor.

She'd slipped out after her mother had finally gone to bed, and now she tried to banish the image of her mother waking up and finding Glass gone. The hurt and horror that would contort her delicate features, just as they'd done countless times over the past two years. Glass would never forgive herself for the pain she'd caused her mother, but she didn't have a choice.

She had to get to Walden, and to Luke.

She paused on the landing to F deck, straining her ears for footsteps, but she heard nothing except the sound of her own ragged breath. Either the guards were on patrol in some other part of Phoenix, or they'd all been banished back to Walden and Arcadia, where they wouldn't steal any more of the air that had been reserved for Phoenician lungs.

Glass darted down the unfamiliar corridor, straining her eyes for the telltale silver gleam of an air vent. Nearly at the bottom of the ship, F deck was mostly devoted to storage. The air vent she'd crawled through after she'd escaped the dropship had led to the F deck on Walden. She just hoped that the same applied on Phoenix. Slowing to a walk, she scanned the walls for an opening, feeling dread seep into her with each step. What if she'd been wrong about the layout? Or perhaps the vent had once connected Walden and Phoenix, but it had been filled long ago?

Then a glint of metal caught her eye, and the tension building in her chest was swept away by excitement and relief. She quickly rose onto her toes, reaching for the edge of the grate, but it was too high up. She let out a frustrated sigh and turned to survey the hallway. None of the doors were marked, but they didn't seem to be protected by retina scanners. She grabbed the nearest handle and yanked. It groaned open, revealing a dark supply closet.

Glass's eyes settled on a small barrel, which she rolled out into the hallway. She stepped on top, removed the grate, and pulled herself up into the shadowy space.

Glass thought briefly of her last crawl through an air shaft, how the metal walls had seemed to press in on her from all sides, and shivered, reaching for her back pocket. At least this time she'd brought a flashbeam. She directed the feeble beam of light forward, but there was nothing in sight except the air shaft, stretching endlessly ahead.

It would end eventually, Glass knew. She just hoped she wouldn't run out of air before she got there. If she had to die, she wanted it to be in Luke's arms.

The scene on Walden was different than she'd expected. The lights seemed to be functioning normally, and as she hurried toward Luke's flat, Glass didn't see any guards. For a moment, she felt a brief surge of hope. Perhaps her mother had been wrong. The panic on Phoenix was all a misunderstanding. But as she climbed the stairs, she felt a strange tightness in her chest that only got worse when she paused to catch her breath. Her eagerness to see Luke might account for her racing pulse, but Glass knew she couldn't ignore the truth. Oxygen was already running low on Walden.

She forced herself to move slowly as she turned onto Luke's floor, breathing careful, shallow breaths to keep her heart rate steady. The corridor was full of adults speaking in low voices, shooting worried looks at the children scampering up and down the hall, so excited to be out of bed at such a late hour that they hardly noticed their labored breaths. Glass wanted to tell the parents to keep the children calm and still to conserve oxygen, but that would only create more panic, and there was nothing they could do, anyway.

Glass had barely started to knock on Luke's door before he'd pulled her inside and into his arms. For a moment, all she was aware of was the warmth of his body and the weight of his embrace. But then he broke away, and she could see shock and concern warring with the joy in his eyes. "What are you doing here?" he asked, running his hand along her cheek as if needing more proof that she wasn't an illusion. He glanced toward the closed door and lowered his voice before continuing. "It's not safe."

"I know," Glass said quietly, slipping her hand into his.

"I don't know how you even got here, but you need to go back," Luke said, shaking his head. "You have a better chance of surviving on Phoenix."

"I'm not going back without you."

He led her over to the couch with a sigh and pulled her onto his lap. "Listen," he said, as he wrapped a strand of her hair around his finger, "if the guards catch us sneaking onto Phoenix, they'll shoot me, and then they'll probably shoot you." He closed his eyes, wincing. "This is what they've been training us for, Glass. It was never said overtly, but . . . we all had a sense something big was coming, and we've been drilled on what to do." When he opened his eyes again, they were full of a cold fury she'd never seen in them. He must've noticed the worry on her face, because his expression softened. "But that's not any of your concern. You'll be fine. And that's all I care about."

"*No*," Glass said, startled by her own vehemence. "I *won't* be fine." Luke frowned and opened his mouth to speak, but Glass cut him off. "It'll kill me, knowing you're down here alone. It'll *kill* me," she repeated, suddenly frantic, gasping as she fought for air. "And if I have to die, I want it to be down here with you."

"*Shhh*," Luke murmured, running his hand down the back of her head. "Okay, okay." He smiled sadly. "The worst thing we can do is run out of oxygen arguing."

"Are you afraid?" Glass asked after a long moment of silence.

Luke turned back to her and shook his head. "No." He placed his finger under her chin and tilted it up, so that she was looking straight into his eyes. "I'm never afraid when I'm with you." He leaned forward and kissed her softly. She shivered, his breath making her skin tingle.

Glass pulled away with a smile. "Isn't this a waste of oxygen?"

"Just the opposite," Luke whispered, drawing her back. "We're conserving it." His mouth found hers again, and she parted her lips as his kiss grew deeper.

Glass ran her hand up his arm, smiling as he shivered. Without breaking away, she began to unbutton his shirt, telling herself that his unusually rapid heartbeat was a response to her touch. Her lips moved to his jaw, then trailed down his neck. She paused at his chest. There were numbers tattooed on his ribs. Two sets of dates that made Glass's stomach churn.

"What's wrong?" Luke asked, sitting up.

She lowered her finger toward the tattoo, then snatched it away, afraid to touch the ink. "What's that?"

"Oh." Luke frowned as he glanced down. "I thought I told you. I wanted something to honor Carter." His voice grew distant. "It's his birthday and the day he was executed."

Glass barely managed to suppress a shudder as she looked back at the second set of numbers. Glass didn't need a tattoo to remind herself of the day Carter had died. The date was branded as clearly in her mind as it was on Luke's skin.

Glass groaned as she brought her knees up to her chest. The sheets on her cot were twisted and damp with sweat. She was desperate for a drink, but it'd be hours before they brought her dinner tray and her evening water allotment. She thought longingly of all the years she'd spent blissfully unaware that water was rationed elsewhere on the Colony.

There was a low beep, followed by footsteps. Glass winced as she lifted her throbbing head from the pillow and saw a figure in the door. It wasn't a guard. It was the Chancellor.

Glass drew herself into a seated position and pushed a strand of damp hair away from her face. She braced for a flare of fury as she locked eyes with the man who'd ordered her arrest, but through the haze of pain and exhaustion, she didn't see the head of the Council. All she saw was the concerned face of her best friend's father.

"Hello, Glass." He gestured toward the other side of the cot. "May I?"

She nodded weakly.

The Chancellor sighed as he sat down. "I'm sorry about what happened." He looked more haggard than she'd ever seen him, worse even than when his wife was dying. "I never wanted to see you get hurt."

Without thinking, Glass brought her hand to her stomach. "I'm not the one who was hurt."

The Chancellor closed his eyes for a moment while he rubbed his temples. He never showed frustration or fatigue in public, but Glass recognized the expression from the few times she'd seen him working in his study at home. "I hope you understand that I didn't have a choice." His voice grew firm. "I swore an oath to uphold the laws of this Colony. I don't have the luxury of turning a blind eye just because the criminal in question happens to be my son's best friend."

"I understand that you need to believe that," Glass said, her voice hollow.

His face hardened. "Are you ready to tell me the name of the father?"

"Why should I do that? So you can lock him up in here with me?"

"Because it's the *law*." The Chancellor rose to his feet and took a few steps toward her. "Because it's not fair that the father not be punished equally. And because it won't take my investigators long to go through the retina scanner records and figure out where you've been spending your time. We're going to find him either way. But if you help us, you'll have a much better chance of being pardoned at your retrial."

Their eyes met, and Glass turned away from him, wincing as she imagined Luke being dragged away in the middle of the night, the terror on his face as he begged the guards to tell him what was going on. Would they tell him the truth, allowing just enough time for the pain to register before they plunged the needle into his chest? Or would he die believing he'd been the victim of a terrible mistake?

She couldn't let that happen.

But the Chancellor was right. The Council wouldn't stop until they'd found the accessory to her crime. Eventually, one of the guards would trace Glass's movements to Walden, to Luke's floor—maybe even to his flat.

Slowly, she turned back to the Chancellor, knowing what she had to do. When she finally spoke, her voice was as cold as a death sentence.

"The father was Carter Jace."

There was a loud creaking noise in the hallway. She sat up, straining her ears in the darkness. She felt a coil of panic tighten around her chest. It sounded almost like the ship was moaning.

"Oh my god," Luke whispered, rising quickly to his feet. The sound came again, followed by a rumbling that shook the walls. "Let's go."

The corridor was still full of people, although now even the children had fallen silent. The lights began to flicker. Luke held Glass's hand tightly as he wove through the crowd toward his neighbor. Her face was grave as she whispered something to Luke that Glass couldn't hear, though Glass could tell from her expression that it was nothing good. Then another figure materialized next to them, and Glass inhaled sharply.

It was Camille. Her eyes narrowed as they settled on Glass.

Glass turned away, unable to look at Camille right now. She couldn't help feeling guilty about how things had turned out. She wouldn't blame the other girl for hating her.

A group of children was huddled on the floor next to their parents, who talked in low, worried tones. One of the little girl's lips had a bluish cast, and the boy whose hand she was clutching was struggling for breath.

The lights sputtered one more time, then went out. A series of gasps rose up in the thick, sudden darkness. Unlike Phoenix, Walden didn't have any emergency lights.

Luke wrapped his arm around Glass's waist and drew her closer to him. "We're going to be okay," he whispered in her ear.

But then another voice reached through the shadows. Camille had snuck over and was now standing on Glass's other side. "Are you going to tell him, or should I?" she said, too quietly for Luke to hear.

Glass turned to her, startled, but she couldn't make out the expression on Camille's face. "What are you talking about?"

"He deserves to know the truth. That his friend *died* because of you."

Glass shuddered, and even though she couldn't see Camille smile, she could hear it in her voice.

"I know your secret. I know what you did to Carter."

CHAPTER 35

Clarke

They had been walking for hours, making widening concentric circles through the woods, trying to cover every inch of terrain. The backs of Clarke's legs were burning, but she relished the sensation; the physical pain was a welcome distraction from her thoughts. The flames engulfing the sides of the infirmary tent . . . Wells's arms like handcuffs around her . . . the sickening crack as the walls collapsed.

"Hey, look over here." Clarke turned to see Bellamy kneeling on the ground near the spot where she'd discovered Octavia's ribbon, staring intently at what appeared to be footprints in the dirt. She was no tracker, but the marks of struggle were easy to read. Whoever had left the prints hadn't been on a pleasant stroll through the woods.

"It looks like someone was running, or in a fight," Clarke said softly. She refrained from finishing the sentence: *almost like someone had been dragged away.* They'd assumed Octavia had run away . . . but what if she'd been taken?

She could read the same terrible line of questioning on Bellamy's furrowed brow, and knelt down beside him. "She can't be far," Clarke said, meaning it. "We'll find her."

"Thank you." Bellamy nodded as he rose, and they continued walking. "I'm . . . I'm glad you're here with me."

They trudged on for what felt like hours, the sun rising and then sinking in the sky. As their circles grew wider, Clarke could tell they were approaching the edge of the forest. Through the outlines of the trees she saw a clearing and paused. There were more trees, but these looked different from the ones in the woods. They had massive, gnarled trunks and thick limbs covered with a canopy of green leaves. The branches sagged with round, red fruit. Apples.

Clarke approached the apple trees, Bellamy close behind her. "That's strange," she said slowly. "The trees are spaced so evenly. It almost looks like an orchard." She walked over to the closest one. "But could it really have survived all these years?"

Although the tree loomed over her, the lowest branch was fairly close to the ground. Standing on her toes, it was easy for

Clarke to stretch up and pluck an apple. She twisted around and tossed it to Bellamy before reaching for another one.

Clarke held the apple up to her face. They grew fruit in the solar fields on the ship, but those apples looked nothing like these. The skin wasn't just red; it had threads of pink and white running through it, and it gave off a scent unlike anything she had smelled before. She took a bite and gasped as juice began running down her chin. How could something taste sweet and tart at the same time? For just a moment, Clarke allowed herself to forget everything that had happened on Earth and let the sensation overtake her.

"Are you thinking what I'm thinking?" Bellamy asked, and Clarke looked over. While she'd been busy eating, he'd begun using fallen branches to measure the distance between the trees.

"To be honest, I wasn't thinking anything beyond how good this tastes," Clarke admitted, feeling the hint of a smile curl her lips. But Bellamy didn't laugh or tease her. He just kept staring at the perfectly spaced trees.

"These didn't survive the Cataclysm, and they didn't just grow like this," he said slowly, his voice filled with wonder and dread. Before he'd even finished, Clarke knew what he was going to say. Her chest tightened with fear. "Someone planted them."

CHAPTER 36

Wells

"Is this better?"

Wells turned and saw Asher, the Arcadian boy, pointing to the log he'd been chopping. The grass was covered with wood shavings and pieces that had been discarded after false starts—but this one actually looked promising.

"Definitely." Wells nodded and crouched down next to the log, running his fingers over the grooves Asher had carved into the wood. "Just make sure they're all approximately the same depth, or else the logs won't lock into place." As Wells stood up, Graham walked by, carrying a shred of melted tarp toward the growing mound of salvaged supplies in the middle of the clearing. Wells stood a little taller, bracing for a scoff or snide remark, but Graham kept his eyes forward and continued on without a word.

The fire had destroyed their tents, but most of the tools had been spared, and the medicine, too. It had been Wells's idea to try to build permanent wood structures. It was a thousand times more difficult than it sounded in books, but they were slowly figuring it out.

"Wells!" A girl from Walden ran over. "How are we going to hang the hammocks? Eliza says they're going to hang from the roof beams, but those aren't going to be ready for days, right? Also, I was thinking—"

"I'll come over in a few minutes, okay?" Wells said, cutting her off. A look of hurt flitted across her round face. "I'm sure you and Eliza are doing a great job," he added, giving her a small smile. "I'll be right there."

She nodded and dashed away, darting around a pile of melted tent rods that still looked too hot to touch.

Wells glanced over his shoulder, then started walking toward the tree line. He needed a moment to himself, to think. He moved slowly, the heaviness in his chest seeming to seep into his limbs, making every step laborious and painful. At the edge of the forest, he paused, breathing the cooler air deep into his lungs, and closed his eyes. This was where he'd kissed Clarke for the very first time on Earth—and for what was surely the last time in his life.

He thought he'd already experienced the most terrible kind of pain possible—knowing that Clarke hated him, that she couldn't stand the sight of him. But he'd been wrong. Watching her leave with Bellamy had nearly killed him. She hadn't even looked his way when she'd come to collect what was left of her gear. She'd just nodded silently at the rest of the group before following Bellamy into the forest.

If only she knew what he'd really done to be with her on Earth. He'd risked everything. And it was all for nothing.

None of the guards gave Wells more than a cursory glance as he raised his eyes to the retina scanner, then strode through the doors. Entry to sector C14 was highly restricted, but his officer's uniform, purposeful walk, and well-known face guaranteed access to pretty much any part of the Colony. He'd never taken advantage of his status, until now. After he'd heard his father's conversation with the Vice Chancellor, something inside of Wells had snapped.

His plan was reckless and stupid and incredibiy selfish, but he didn't care. He had to make sure Clarke was sent to Earth instead of the execution chamber.

Wells jogged down the empty, narrow staircase, lit only by faint emergency lights. There was no reason for anyone to visit the airlock except for routine checks, and Wells had already hacked into the maintenance files to check the schedule. He would be totally alone.

The airlock in C14 was original to the ship. And despite the engineers' efforts to keep it in top condition, after three hundred years of facing the extreme temperatures and UV rays of space, it had started to deteriorate. There were tiny cracks along the edge and shiny squares where newer material had obviously been patched over the airlock.

Wells reached behind him for the pliers he'd tucked into the waistband of his pants. It would be fine, he told himself, his arms shaking. They were all going to be evacuated soon, anyway. He was just speeding up the process. Yet in the back of his mind, he knew that there weren't enough dropships for everyone. And he had no idea what would happen when it came time to use them.

But that was his father's concern, not his.

He reached out and began to pry up the flimsy edge of the airlock, wincing when he heard the faint hiss. Then he turned and raced back toward the stairs, trying to ignore the horror welling up in his stomach. He could barely stand to think of what he'd done, but as he hurried down the stairs, he told himself he'd done what he had to do.

Wells rose wearily to his feet. It was getting dark, and there was still a lot of work to do on the new cabins. They needed to finish at least some of the shelters before the next storm. As he approached camp, wondering if Clarke had taken enough blankets with her, if she would be warm when the temperature dropped, Asher came up beside him and launched into another line of questioning. He held one of the trimmed logs and seemed to want Wells's opinion on the size and cut.

Wells was too absorbed in his own thoughts to hear what Asher was saying. As they walked side by side toward the tents, he could see the boy's mouth moving, but the words never made it to Wells's ears.

"Listen," Wells began, ready to tell Asher it could wait until morning. Just then, something streaked past his face. There was a sickening thwack, and Asher flew backward. Blood bubbled out of his mouth as he fell to the ground.

Wells dropped to his knees. "*Asher*," he screamed as his eyes struggled to make sense of the image in front of him. There was an arrow sticking out of the boy's neck.

His first, mad thought was Bellamy. He was the only one who could shoot like that.

Wells spun around with a yell, but it wasn't Bellamy behind him. A line of shadowy figures stood at the bottom of the hill, the setting sun behind them. He gasped as shock and horror raced through his veins. Suddenly, it became clear who had set fire to the camp—and who had taken Octavia. It wasn't anyone from the Colony.

The hundred might have been the first humans to set foot on the planet in three centuries, but they weren't alone.

Some people had never left.

ACKNOWLEDGMENTS

I owe an immeasurable debt of gratitude to Joelle Hobeika, who not only dreamed up the premise for *The 100*, but whose imagination, editorial acumen, and tenacity were essential in bringing it to life. The same applies to Katie McGee, Elizabeth Bewley, and Farrin Jacobs, whose incisive questions and intelligent suggestions shaped the book at every level. I'm also grateful to the intimidatingly clever people at Alloy, specifically Sara Shandler, Josh Bank, and Lanie Davis, and the dedicated teams at Little, Brown and Hodder & Stoughton.

Thank you to my remarkable friends on both sides of the East River, the Gowanus Canal, the Mississippi, and the Atlantic for your support and encouragement. A special "shout"-out to my confidants and coconspirators at both ends of 557 Broadway, to the Crossroads crew, who first introduced me to science fiction, and to Rachel Griffiths for going light-years beyond the call of duty to help me grow as a writer and editor.

Most of all, I am grateful to my family—my father, Sam Henry Kass, whose writing overflows with unmatched wit and unparalleled heart; my mother, Marcia Bloom, whose art shimmers with the wisdom of a philosopher and the soul of an aesthete; my brilliant brother, Petey Kass, who makes me laugh until I can't breathe; my inspiring grandparents, Nance, Peter, Nicky, and David; and the Kass/Bloom/Greenfield clans, who make so many places feel like home.

Michael Bisberg

KASS MORGAN

received a bachelor's degree from Brown University and a master's from Oxford University. She currently works as an editor and lives in Brooklyn, New York.